ADVANCED THEORY OF TABLA

THE COMPLETE REFERENCE FOR TABLA
VOLUME 2

ADVANCED THEORY OF TABLA
Fifth Edition

by
David R. Courtney

Sur Sangeet Services
Houston

Fifth Edition

© 2000, 2022 David R. Courtney
All rights reserved.

Perfect binding
ISBN 978-1-893644-16-8

The author can be reached at:
(713) 665 4665 (tel)
david@chandrakantha.com (E-Mail)
http://chandrakantha.com (Personal web page)

TABLE OF CONTENTS

PREFACE — vii

1. INTRODUCTION — 1
2. TIMBRE — 9
3. TIMEKEEPING — 35
4. LAY (TEMPO) — 49
5. DYNAMICS — 57
6. LAYAKARI AND COUNTER-RHYTHMS — 63
7. ANCIENT AND OBSOLETE THEORY — 71
8. INTRODUCTION TO COMPOSITIONAL THEORY — 81
9. COMPOSITIONAL THEORY (CYCLIC FORMS) — 87
10. COMPOSITIONAL THEORY (CADENTIAL FORMS) — 127
11. IMPROVISATION — 153
12. PHYSICS OF THE TABLA — 161
13. ACOUSTIC FIELDS AND MICROPHONES — 177
14. SOUND REINFORCEMENT — 191
15. RECORDING — 209
16. LIGHTING — 223
17. STAGECRAFT — 231
18. CONCLUSION — 247

APPENDIX 1. - LAHARA — 251
APPENDIX 2. - THE STROKES — 277
APPENDIX 3. - MITRA'S LAHARA PETI — 285
APPENDIX 4. - COURTNEY SYSTEM — 289

INDEX — 293

OTHER BOOKS — 299

PREFACE

I will start this preface with an explanation concerning the edition of this book. This is the latest edition of *Advanced Theory of Tabla*, therefore we are calling this the 5th edition. However, there is no 2nd, 3rd, or 4th edition. I figure that if Microsoft can just skip Windows 9 and jump from Windows-8 to Windows-10, I should be able to do the same. I hope that by bring the numbering in line with the first volume, that it will avoid confusion. (But it is entirely possible that this effort will fail.)

It is difficult to say how long it has taken to put this book together. The fieldwork goes back as far as 1971, and the actual writing started in 1990. Since the fieldwork must be taken for granted, it is reasonable to say that it took 10 years for the first edition to come out in 2000. But this edition is coming out at the end of 2022. Therefore, it has taken about 22 years of off-and-on work to bring it to this point.

But the first edition was only on the market for about four years before it fell out of publication. It was out of print for about 18 years. It was a victim of instability in the mechanics of the printing industry coupled with the fact that the source was all in an obsolete digital format (MacWrite files on floppy disks.) It is only due to resolve on my part, that it is now available.

There are a few things to keep in mind if one is to make the most use of this work. These deal with the totality of the set, the style of writing, the inclusion of material, and other points.

The first thing to note is that this a multi-volume set. One should understand the relationship between the various volumes. I strongly recommend that you become familiar with the first volume, *Fundamentals of Tabla*. The third volume (*Manufacture and Repair of Tabla*) and fourth volume (*Focus on the Kaidas of Tabla*) are optional.

The next thing to keep in mind is that I am trying to make a book which is readable. I strongly believe that it should be understandable by anyone with a high school education (matriculate.) Occasionally we will be dealing with technical subjects such as resonance modes, Fourier transforms, inverse domains, and similar material. These are subjects that one would not expect the average musician to be comfortable with. But we will approach this material in the simplest way possible. There will be a lot of "hand holding" as we move from basic material up through more complicated material. The essentials can be grasped by anyone, as long as one takes the time to go through them properly. If this material is still inaccessible, I apologise, because it is entirely my fault as a writer.

But writing a readable book of this nature poses some challenges. There is certain material which resists being simplified. But a complete understanding of the arcane minutia of specialised scientific or engineering fields should not be necessary for the book to flow. In such situations, the more complicated material is either relegated to footnotes or the appendices.

Another point to keep in mind concerns my use of English musical terms. My desire to come up with a book which is readable occasionally forced me to take liberties with the definitions of words. The English lexicon did not develop to encompass Indian music. Therefore, there are cases where I was forced to make a decision as to whether to use a Hindustani term or adapt an existing English word. In situations where I adapt English words, the fit is sometimes uncomfortable. Two words that I have taken liberties with are "cadenza" and "cadence". The strict definitions of these words are at odds with the way that I use them. With these, or any of the other terms which raise your eyebrow in disapproval, I humbly beg your forgiveness, and hope that you will understand my situation.

Related to the treatment of English musical terms is the treatment of certain academic terms. You may notice references in this book to "functionalism", "structuralism", and other terms that are significant to the social sciences. You may also notice upon reading these sections that they have nothing to do with the linguistic, anthropological, or social definitions, except in the broadest of terms. I know that there are many academics who enjoy making a strict and formal applications of theories such as transformational-generative theory, post-Blumfieldian structuralism, etc. But such endeavours contribute little of value to musical studies. Quite the contrary, they obscure musical discussions with irrelevant jargon.

A major point to keep in mind concerns the treatment of conflicts between theory and practice. There are sometimes major conflicts between the way contemporary musicians treat things and the way that a few Indian music scholars say they should be. In many areas, I have found that accepted musical theory has nothing to do with contemporary practice. The reason for the acceptance is often determined by social, rather than musical criteria. My job is to explore tabla as it is today, and not get bogged down with irrelevant social issues.

I would just like to say one final thing concerning conflicting views. I have written this book to be *gharana* agnostic, that is to say that I am not pushing any particular *gharana's* viewpoint. Consequently, if you are a student of tabla, you will run across conflicts between what your teacher is telling you and some of the material in this book. This is inevitable. The reason stems from the nature of the *gharana* system. The *gharana* system instils a sectarian approach to the subject of tabla. Just as the Protestant, the Catholic, the Muslim, and the Jew all "know" with certainty the nature of the relationship between God and man, so too musicians from every *gharana* "know" with certainty how musical forms are to be used. Yet just as one's certainty in the religious field becomes softened once one transcends the pettiness of sectarianism; in the same way we must tolerate a certain ambiguity once we begin to transcend the pettiness of the *gharana* the mentality. I do not expect all of my readers to be able to do this. If you are inclined to take a more ecumenical approach to tabla, then I think that you will find this to be a very useful book. If you are not so inclined, then I leave it to you to pick and choose what elements you wish to accept.

Still another point for your consideration is the situation of gender and writing. This book sometimes refers to the tabla players in the masculine gender. I assure you that no sexism is implied. Over the years some of my best students have been female. I have made some attempts to deal with the topic in a non-gendered way, but the awkwardness of the writing style is sometimes too much.

Another point to keep in mind concerns my approach to the inclusion of material. I think that a large portion of the material may seem daunting when first encountered. At least it should be. Hopefully it will be well understood after some discussion. But there is other material that may seem laughably obvious to the reader. I would like to remind the reader of the intended audience of this book.

Preface

My approach is to include virtually everything. The intended audience is so varied that I am unable to make basic presumptions as to what is "obvious". Many readers are Indian while many readers are Western, therefore one may be unaware of even the most basic cultural conditions of the other. Some will have strong technical and scientific backgrounds, while others may be scientifically illiterate. My approach to this situation is to go ahead and give these topics a reasonable treatment, no matter how trivial. What is obvious to one person, may not be to another.

This edition has numerous changes from the first edition. Chapter 12- *Physics of the Tabla,* has been shifted from Volume Three- *Manufacture and Repair of Tabla* into this volume. Chapter 13 - *Acoustic Fields and Microphones*, and Chapter 15 - *Recording*, are a totally new. Chapters 14, 16, 17, and 17 are based up the chapter on stagecraft in the last edition, but have been re-written.

This series could not have been written without the assistance of many good people. The first and foremost are my teachers, the late Ustad Shaik Dawood Khan and Ustad Zakir Hussain. I would also like to thank K. S. Kalsi, and Jayant Kirtane for getting me started down this long path.

I am also indebted to the many musicians who have helped supply the material for this work. I would particularly like to thank Jashwant Bhavsar, Dr. Shankar Bhattacharyya, Pratap Pawar, Mukunda Datta, Anju Babu, Dr. Rohini Prasad, Shabbir Nisar Khan, and Rathna Kumar. This is really their work as much as it is mine.

Finally, I would like to thank several people for their assistance in proof-reading the manuscripts. Susan Alcorn, the late Jo Anne Courtney, the late Robert Goldman, Siraj Parmar, Ms Bobbie Parr, Dr. Victor Parr, Dr. Ashutosh Patwardhan, Masood Raoofi, Dr. Ananth Reddy, Udai Kiran Vadali, and Kiran Kulkarni, were especially helpful.

Finally, I must thank my wife for all her patience. It is not easy to look at the back of a person while he is typing at a word processor. This volume has taken four years to write the first edition, and a few months to update to the latest edition. Her understanding is especially appreciated.

Finally (yes - I know that there have already been two previous "finallies"), we should never take ourselves too seriously. To this end, I am not above including a bit of levity. I hope that this will make wading through 300 pages of tome a bit less daunting.

David Courtney,
August 25th, 2022

CHAPTER 1

INTRODUCTION

This book deals with the theoretical aspects of tabla (तबला). Many may not be aware that tabla even has any advanced theory. It certainly does. The relationship between theory and practice is central to almost every human endeavour, including Indian music. Lord Chesterfield once said:

> The world can doubtless never be well known by theory: practice is absolutely necessary; but surely it is of great use to a young man, before he sets out for that country, full of mazes, windings, and turnings, to have at least a general map of it, made by some experienced traveller. (Chesterfield 1774)

This theory is very important. The student of tabla, especially a Western student, often finds the entire field to be *terra incognito*. This series of books is written to be our "map". This map makes it easier to understand this complex, yet exciting subject of tabla.

The theory may also be compared to the grammar of a language. Just as knowledge of grammar separates a literate speaker from the masses, likewise an understanding of the theory of Indian rhythm and compositional form separates a master from one who is merely functional. With these few points in mind let us begin our study.

BACKGROUND (REVIEW)

There is a large body of material that must be well understood before we can proceed with our discussion of the advanced theory. All of this material was covered in the first volume of this series, *Fundamentals of Tabla*. Let us take a quick review.

Tabla is the most important drum in the field of North Indian music. The word tabla is Arabic for drum, but the tabla as we think of it is purely of North Indian origin. It is not a very old instrument, only about 300 years. It is commonly believed to have been derived from a barrel shaped drum known as *pakhawaj* (पखावज). This may be the common view, but it is more likely that while the wooden drum may have been derived from *pakhawaj*, the metal drum was derived from Turkish military drums.

The tabla is composed of two drums. Strictly speaking, only the smaller wooden drum is the tabla. However, it has become such a common practice to refer to them collectively as the tabla, that we may bow to common usage. Therefore, if we wish to indicate one drum over the other, we can call the wooden drum the *dayan* (दायां), and the metal drum the *bayan* (बायां). *Dayan* and *bayan* mean right and left respectively.

The parts of the tabla are shown in Figure 1.1. There is the lacing known as *tasma* (तस्मा), also called *dori* (डोरी), *vadi* (वादि), or *baddhi* (बद्धी). There is also the wooden shell called *lakadi* (लकड़ी) or *kath* (काठ). There is the drumhead, which is known as *pudi* (पुड़ि), also called the *chamada* (चमड़ा). There is also the metallic shell called *pital* (पीतल) or *kudi* (कुड़ी). There are wooden dowels used to tighten the drums, called *gatta* (गट्ठा). There is a ring at the bottom which may be made of either rawhide, iron, or tightly woven metal wires, called *kundal* (कुण्डल).

The parts of the *pudi* are shown in Figure 1.2. There is the outer weaving which is called *gajara* (गजरा). There is a skin with a hole cut in it; this is called the *chat* (चाट), *kinar* (किनारा), *chati* (चाटी), *chanti* (चांटी), or *got* (गोट). There is the main membrane that covers the entire opening, called the *maidan* (मैदान), the *lab* (लब), *sur* (सुर) or *lav* (लव). The most distinctive portion of the *pudi* is called the *syahi* (स्याही), or *gab* (गाब). The above nomenclature is but a small sampling of the variations in terms. India is a land of extreme linguistic diversity, and it is beyond the scope of this book to attempt to give every possible variation.

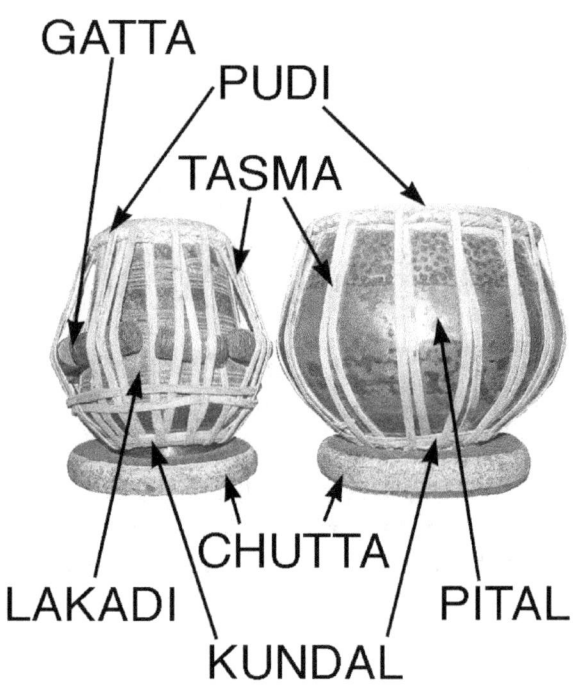

Figure 1.1. The parts of the tabla

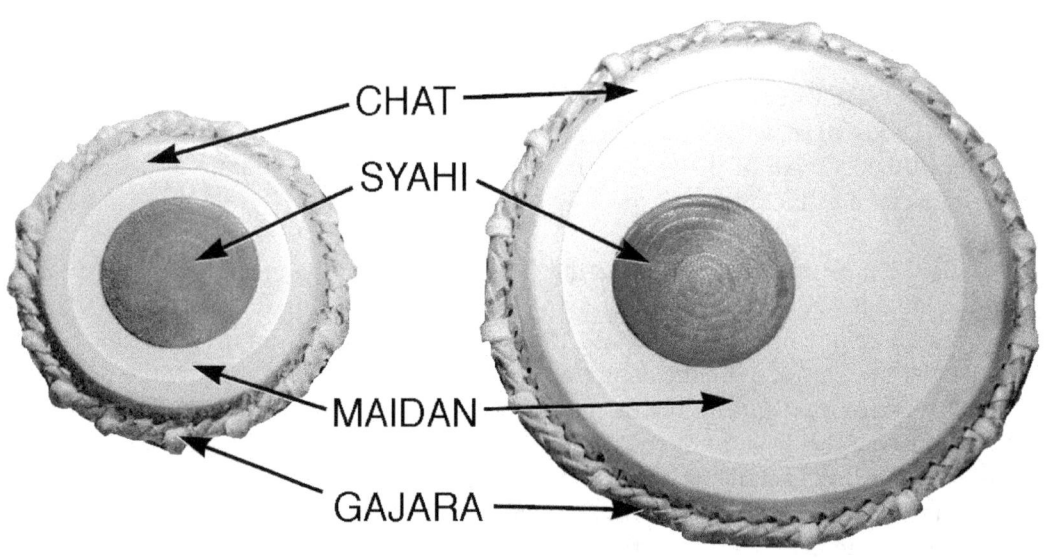

Figure 1.2. Parts of the pudi

Ch.1. Introduction

PEDAGOGIC TRADITION

The tabla and its pedagogic tradition are profound. This is very important to understand, because it influences the conceptualisation of the instrument. Improper conceptualisation will inevitably be reflected in improper performance. For centuries the tabla has been taught by a system of apprenticeship; this is known as *Guru Shishya Parampara* (गुरु शिष्य परम्परा). This makes a profound statement as to the fundamental Indian view of knowledge.

The Indian concept of knowledge is reflected in the Sanskrit term *"vidya"* (विद्य). Although this word may be translated into the English word "knowledge", it is clear that there are numerous different kinds of knowledge. One of the highest is called *"Gurumukhavidya"* (गुरुमुखविद्य), which implies knowledge which must be attained by years of discipleship under the teacher *(guru)*.

The result of this strongly vertical flow of knowledge was that over the years different stylistic schools of tabla developed. These schools are called *gharana* (घराना). There are six major *gharanas* of tabla: *Dilli, Punjabi, Ajrada, Benares, Lucknow,* and *Farukhabad*; which are shown in Figure 1.3. Each of these schools had a slightly different approach to technique and compositional structure. (Today these technical differences are greatly reduced.) The names of the *gharanas* represent the city or region of northern India where they developed.

There were profound social effects of the *gharana* system. Although the original purpose of the system was to create an environment which promoted a certain standard of musicianship among the students, it soon became corrupted. The *gharanas* became the centre of musical politics (Neuman 1980). Patronage and musical opportunities were often influenced by one's particular *gharana* rather than one's musical abilities.

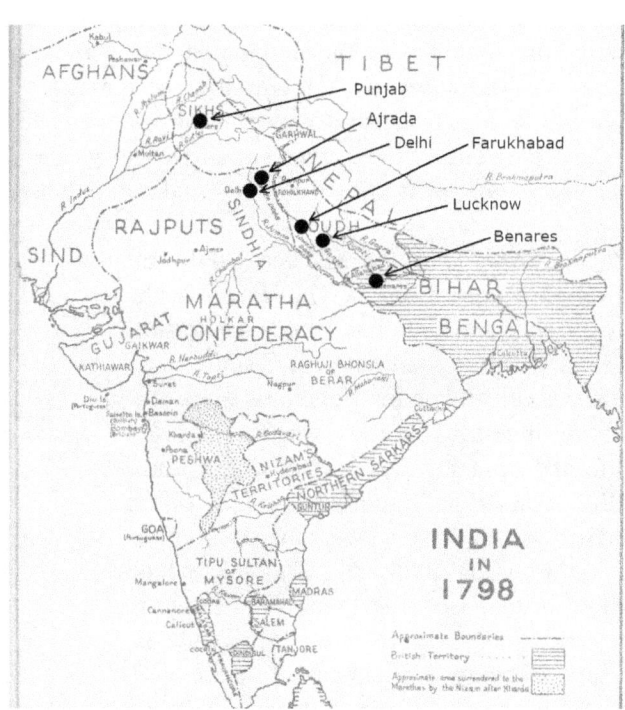

Location of tabla gharanas set against political map of northern India at end of 18th Century. (Davies 1959)

Figure 1.3. Gharanas of tabla

There was also a great degree of secretiveness in the *gharana* system. This was exhibited both in teacher / disciple relationships as well as relations between the *gharanas*. It was common for a teacher to reserve certain material for his immediate kin. Musical material was even used as dowry. The greatest degree of secrecy was shown in keeping people from other *gharanas* from getting certain material.

It must be admitted that secretiveness was not the only hindrance to the flow of information. Undoubtedly the greatest hindrances were from poor systems of communication and transportation. Although a hundred miles may not seem like a long distance today, 150 years ago it was a major journey, fraught with much hardship and danger.

MUSICAL STYLES AND TECHNIQUE
Over the years, each *gharana* developed its own approach to the tabla. Although many of these differences were merely stylistic, there developed fundamentally different technical approaches. Today, there are two basic approaches, *Dilli baj* (a.k.a. *Paschami Baj*), and *Purbi baj*. The term "*baj*" (बाज) literally means "a technique of playing". *Dilli baj* gets its name from the city which today is called Delhi (part of the New Delhi metropolitan area.) The term *"purbi baj"* (पूरबी बाज) literally means "Eastern style of playing", and is so called because they originated in areas east of Delhi.

We must not forget that these two styles of playing represent a mere slice in time. 100 years ago it seems that every *gharana* had its own *baj*. 100 years from now the techniques will probably merge into one single style. Therefore, the division of technique into two *bajs* must be viewed as merely a simple model in which to place today's performance practice, and not something which is fundamental to the science of tabla. With this caveat in mind, we may take a brief overview of the two *bajs*.

Dilli Baj - The *Dilli baj* has a number of interesting characteristics. For this style, we may think of the hand as consisting of three independent parts as shown in Figure 1.4. These three parts are the index finger, the middle finger and the ring / little finger together. Note that the ring and little finger move as a single unit. We can discount the thumb because the thumb is almost never used to play the *dayan*. Additionally the majority of the playing in the *Dilli* style is on the rim. Therefore, it is sometimes referred to as *"kinara baj"* or "the rim style of playing". This style is generally considered the "pure" tabla style of playing, because it is devoid of *pakhawaj* technique. This approach has traditionally been used in the *Dilli*, and *Ajrada gharanas*. However the *Punjab gharana* uses a large amount of this technique. The *Dilli baj* is known for its speed and delicacy.

Purbi Baj - The *Purbi baj* (Eastern style of playing) is also interesting. The *Purbi* style generally looks at the right hand as consisting of two major elements as depicted in Figure 1.5. We see that there is the index finger and there are the last three fingers. These last fingers (middle, ring, and little finger), move as a single unit. Again the thumb is ignored. One other characteristic is that there is much less of a tendency to play on the rim. This style has historically been used by the *Farukhabad, Lucknow,* and *Benares gharanas*. This style is known for a heavy influence of *pakhawaj* technique. The *Punjab gharana* also uses a large amount of this technique. The *Purbi baj* is known for its power and majesty.

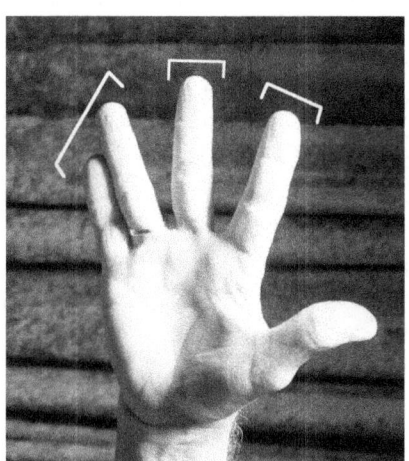

Figure 1.4. Dilli approach to the hand

Today, there is a tendency for musicians to mix the *bajs* together. This is an absolute necessity. Although the *Dilli* style is known for its speed and delicacy, at times this delicacy amounts to weakness and insipidness. Also, though the *Purbi baj* is known for its power and majesty, it is also at times sluggish, awkward, and limited as to what *bols* may be executed. Only when a musician is comfortable with both techniques is he (or she) able to really do justice to the instrument.

The last few observations are of course mere generalisations. With these two *bajs* there previously were significant variations due to the different *gharanas*. Today, a large portion of the variations are a reflection of the artistic idiosyncrasies of the individual musicians.

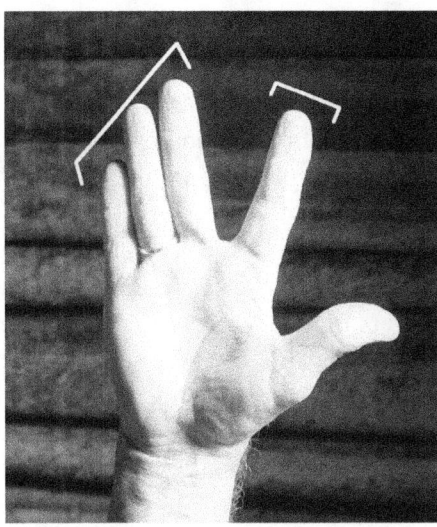

Figure 1.5. Purbi approach to the hand

Although there are numerous techniques to playing tabla, we may make a few basic observations. The first is that there are a tremendous variety of sounds that may be produced. This large variation in tone is produced by selectively accentuating or muting the various vibrational modes. In its most general terms, the sounds of the tabla may fall into one of two categories. Sounds may either be resonant or nonresonant. Resonant sounds are pitched and have long sustains. In traditional terminology such sounds are said to be *"khula"* (खुला). The word *khula* literally means, "open". Sounds may also be muted and nonresonant; such sounds are traditionally referred to as *"bandh"* (बंध). The term *bandh* literally means, "closed". *Bandh* sounds are unpitched and have shorter sustains. These acoustical properties will be examined in greater detail in Chapter 2 of this work.

BOL

The mnemonic syllables are central to the classical system of tabla. We have already alluded to the secretive nature of the teachers in the old *gharana* system. With such secretiveness it is obvious that the old musicians would have hesitated to write anything down. This would have made it too easy for other people to steal their material. Therefore, a complex system of mnemonics developed that allowed a musician to keep the composition in memory for years, and when necessary, transmit it to the disciple. This system uses a series of syllables that correspond to the particular strokes. This system is called *bol* (बोल) and is derived from the Hindi word *"bolna"* (बोलना) which means, "to speak".

Here are a few major *bols* of tabla. There are pictures of the common techniques for these *bols* in Appendix 2 of this book. Nevertheless one should really turn to Volume One - *Fundamentals of Tabla* for a better discussion of technique. Videos of these strokes may be found and discussed online at:

https://chandrakantha.com/music-and-dance/instrumental-music/indian-instruments/tabla-basic-strokes-bols/

<u>Ka</u> (क) - This is a simple slap of the left hand against the drum (Appendix AP2.1). It is nonresonant.

<u>Ga</u> (ग) - This is a resonant stroke of the left hand, which may be executed in any number of ways. The most common way is to strike the *maidan* of the *bayan* with the extended fingers of the left hand (Appendix AP2.3). A common alternative is to use the index finger (Appendix AP2.15).

Naa (ना) - This is a rim stroke of the *dayan*. It is made by placing the last two fingers of the right hand lightly against the *syahi*, and striking with the index finger against the *chat (kinar)* (Appendix AP2.2).

Na (न) - This is a nonresonant stroke of the right hand. For this, one simply brings down the last two fingers sharply against the edge of the *syahi* (Appendix AP2.9). In some cases it uses the last three fingers.

Tin (तिं) - This stroke may be executed several ways. The traditional *Dilli* style is to place the last two fingers lightly against the *syahi* while lightly strike the *maidan* with the index finger in a resonant fashion (Appendix AP2.5). Although this is the traditional technique, it is very difficult to effectively play in this manner. Such a technique shows a clear ignorance of the physics of the *dayan*. An easier way is to slightly move the striking position to the margin between the *syahi* and the *maidan*. For reasons that are not possible to go into here, this produces a cleaner sound and is much easier to execute. Another way to produce this stroke is to substitute the *Toon* (तूं) (Appendix AP2.10) for *Tin* (तिं).

Taa (ता) - There are a number of ways to produce this *bol*. The two most common are the *Dilli Taa* and the *Purbi Taa*. In the *Dilli* style, it is the same as *Naa* (ना) (Appendix AP2.2). In the *Purbi* style it is played in the *maidan* in a fashion very much like the *Tin* (तिं) (Appendix AP2.5), but significantly louder. The *Purbi Taa* is also sometimes called a "*Sur Taa*".

Dhaa (धा) - This is a simultaneous execution of *Taa* (ता) and *Ga* (ग). Any version of *Ga* (ग) may be used with any version of *Taa* (ता).

Dhin (धिं) - This is a simultaneous execution of *Tin* (तिं) and *Ga* (ग). Any form of each may be used.

Tun (तूं) - *Tun* is played by lifting the whole right hand off of the drum and lightly striking the centre of the *syahi* with the index finger (Appendix AP2.10).

TiTa (ति ट) - There are at least five ways to execute this stroke. Refer to *Fundamentals of Tabla* for a more detailed discussion.

TiRaKiTa (ति र कि ट) - Estimates run from 4 to 15 different techniques for executing this *bol*. Refer to *Fundamentals of Tabla* for a more detailed discussion.

TeTeKataGaDeeGeNa (ते टे क त ग दी गे न) (a.k.a. TiTaKataGaDeeGeNa ति ट क त ग दी गे न) - This *bol* is of *pakhawaj* origins. There are several techniques for its execution. Refer to *Fundamentals of Tabla* for a more detailed discussion.

These basic *bols* may be assembled into longer and more complex structures. Such structures and their manipulation form the basis for our entire compositional theory (Chapters 8-10).

TAL

Strokes and *bols* themselves have no meaning without a conceptual framework. This conceptual framework is called *tal*. *Tal* is derived from the Sanskrit word which means "clapping". There are three levels of structure in the traditional concept of *tal*. These three levels are the cycle (*avartan*), the measure (*vibhag*), and the beat (*matra*). An example of these three levels is shown for *Tintal* in the following illustration:

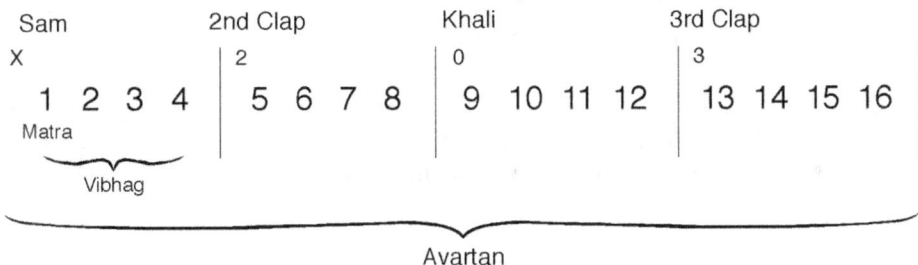

This conceptual framework is important but not complete. At one time the basic structure of *avartan*, *vibhag*, and *matra*, was sufficient to define a particular *tal*. However, in contemporary north Indian music another element has been added. This is called *theka*.

THEKA

Theka is a conventionally accepted series of *bols,* which along with their arrangement of claps and waves, defines a particular *tal*. A few common *thekas* are:

Tintal

ˣधा	धिं	धिं	धा	²धा	धिं	धिं	धा	⁰धा	तिं	तिं	ना	³ना	धिं	धिं	धा
Dhaa	Dhin	Dhin	Dhaa	Dhaa	Dhin	Dhin	Dhaa	Dhaa	Tin	Tin	Naa	Naa	Dhin	Dhin	Dhaa

Rupak Tal

⁰तिं	तिं	ना	¹धिं	ना	²धिं	ना
Tin	Tin	Naa	Dhin	Naa	Dhin	Naa

Dadra

ˣधा	धिं	ना	⁰धा	तिं	ना
Dhaa	Dhin	Naa	Dhaa	Tin	Naa

Kaherava

ˣधा	गे	ना	ती	⁰ना	क	धिं	ना
Dhaa	Ge	Naa	Tee	Naa	Ka	Dhin	Naa

Jhaptal

ˣधिं	ना	²धिं	धिं	ना	⁰तिं	ना	³धिं	धिं	ना
Dhin	Naa	Dhin	Dhin	Naa	Tin	Naa	Dhin	Dhin	Naa

Ektal Theka

ˣधिं	धिं	⁰धा गे	तिरकिट	²तूं	ना	⁰कत्	ता	³धा गे	तिरकिट	⁴धिं	ना
Dhin	Dhin	DhaGe	TiRaKiTa	Tun	Naa	Kat	Taa	DhaGe	TiRaKiTa	Dhin	Naa

These are but a few of the common ones.

It is useful to note that there are numerous variations upon these common *thekas*. These variations are known as *prakar*. The *raison d'etre* for these variations may be technical or artistic. Either way, they do not detract from the theoretical importance of the conventionally accepted *theka*.

This sums up the basic material that a student must know in order to make use of this book. If any of this is not fully understood, I strongly advise you to return to *Fundamentals of Tabla* and review. Only then will you be able to derive benefit from the following chapters.

WORKS CITED

Lord Chesterfield
1774,   1901 Letter, 30 Aug. 1749 repr. in "The Letters of the Earl of Chesterfield to His Son", vol. 1, no. 190, *The Columbia Dictionary of Quotations*. Columbia University Press. Copyright (c) 1993 by Columbia University Press.

Courtney, David
1998   *Fundamentals of Tabla*, 3rd edition, revised and expanded, Sur Sangeet Services, Houston, TX

Davies, C. Collin
1959   *An Historical Atlas of the Indian Peninsula*. Second edition. Delhi, Oxford University Press.

Neuman, Daniel M.
1980   *The Life of Music in North India: The Organization of an Artistic Tradition*. Wayne State University Press. Detroit

CHAPTER 2

TIMBRE

The sound of tabla is one of its most alluring characteristics; therefore we cannot write a book on this unless we pay attention to this sound. One would be mistaken to think that writing about the quality of sound is an impossible task, for we have some very useful tools to help us. But these tools force us to pay attention to the physical foundation of sound. The most important tool is a process called spectrum analysis. Unfortunately, the average musician may have only a slight familiarity with the subject. For the unscientific, this will require a bit of science. Therefore, before we discuss the timbre of tabla, we will briefly look at the field of acoustics and psychoacoustics.

BASICS OF PSYCHOACOUSTICS
Psychoacoustics is the field of study which deals with the relationship between perceived sound and the physical vibrations. Psychoacoustics has had tremendous practical impact in the development of telephones, CDs, radios, and a host of other devices which we take for granted.

Let us review what we learned about sound in our school days. Although this view is oversimplistic, it is still a convenient place to begin.

Any source of sound vibrates. It doesn't matter whether we are talking about a tuning fork, a transistor radio, or a tabla, there must be some vibration. These vibrations are then transferred to the air in the form of sound waves. These waves are alternations between compressions and expansions of air.

The rate or frequency at which the sound waves change is very important. This rate is measured in cycles-per-second, or as it is more commonly called "Hertz". One Hertz, abbreviated as Hz, is equal to one cycle-per-second. Since the unit of Hertz is very slow for sound, we sometimes use a unit called a kilohertz which is abbreviated kHz. One kilohertz is equal to one thousand Hertz. The range of hearing is generally considered to extend from 20Hz up to 20kHz.

Many things happen when sound strikes the ear. The eardrum, otherwise known as the tympanic membrane, converts the vibrations of air into mechanical vibrations. These mechanical vibrations travel along a series of bones, and are transferred to the inner ear, where they are converted into neural impulses, which are then fed to the brain.

There are many different types of sounds in the world. Generally there are musical sounds and nonmusical sounds. Musical sounds have a regularity about them, while nonmusical sounds are more random.

The simplest musical sound is the sine wave (Figure 2.1). A sine waves has only a single frequency. If you were to take a tuning fork and attach a pin to one of the forks, then slide a smoked glass under the vibrating tuning fork, you would get something extremely close to a sine wave.

Period - The period is a concept that we will refer to frequently. Musical sounds tend to revolve around repeating patterns. When they are recorded, they are referred to as "periodic waveforms". With any repeating pattern, if we take some arbitrary point within the cycle, and follow it to its corresponding point in the next cycle, this span is called a period.

Musical Sounds - Musical sounds are not as simple as single sine wave. There are many more complexities.

A musical sound has three qualities: volume, pitch and timbre. Volume or loudness is the amplitude of the sound wave. More simply put, this is the degree of difference between the compressions and expansions of air. The pitch is the frequency at which these waves hit the ear. A higher pitch corresponds to compressions hitting the ear more rapidly while a lower pitch corresponds to fewer compressions. Timbre, or the quality of the sound corresponds to the shape of the wave. These qualities are shown in Figure 2.2.

This is the model of sound and hearing that each of us received in our early schooling. This is the view that was given to us in the 19th century by the founder of modern psychoacoustics, Hermann von Helmholtz. Is this view correct? We do not wish to say that it is incorrect, but it is a gross oversimplification. Let us now look at some of the twists and turns which make the subject much more complicated.

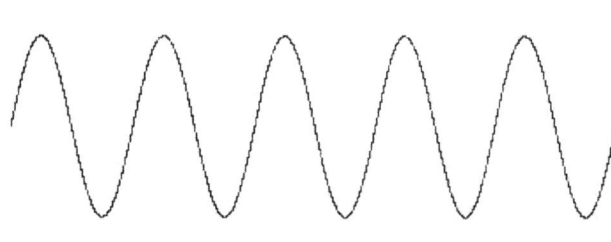

Figure 2.1. Simple Sine Wave

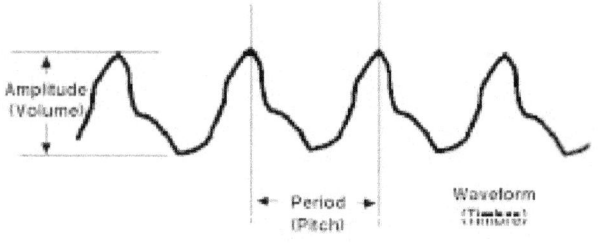

Figure 2.2. Volume, pitch and timbre

Volume - The simple relationship of amplitude and volume (loudness) is an oversimplification. There are many factors which influence our perception of volume. Frequency, ambient noise, even previous sounds all have an influence.

Frequency is one factor in determining loudness. This was demonstrated in the 1930's by the work of Fletcher and Munson at Bell Laboratories. The result of their work is the famous Fletcher-Munson Equal Loudness Curves (Fletcher and Munson 1933). This is shown in Figure 2.3. For those of you who do not like graphs the bottom line is simple. If you take a sound at some middle frequency and increase the frequency, the perceived volume will decrease gradually. At some point it will be inaudible, like a dog whistle. This is called ultrasound and is commonly heard by small animals. Conversely, you can take some middle frequency sound and start to decrease the frequency. Again at some point, its perceived volume starts to go down until it is no longer audible to humans. This type of sound is commonly heard by large animals. Elephants for example, use these sounds to communicate over great distances. These examples show us that the volume of a sound is partly a function of frequency.

Ambient noise conditions can also influence loudness; this phenomenon is known as the "masking effect" (Egan and Hank 1950). It is easily demonstrated by a dripping faucet on nights when you cannot sleep. A quiet environment makes the drips seem loud. However if you turn on the TV or radio, you will not be able to hear the same dripping no matter how hard you try. The amplitude of the sound waves was not reduced by turning on the TV, but the perceived loudness was. This phenomenon is what made things like Dolby or DBX noise reduction systems work in old analogue audio systems.

The effects of masking may be reduced by altering the harmonic structure. If we have a sound which is being partially masked by background sound, we can make the foreground sound appear louder by the addition of harmonics, especially even harmonics. This is the principle behind the aural exciter, or the aural enhancer. This demonstrates that an alteration of the harmonic structure can affect perceived volume.

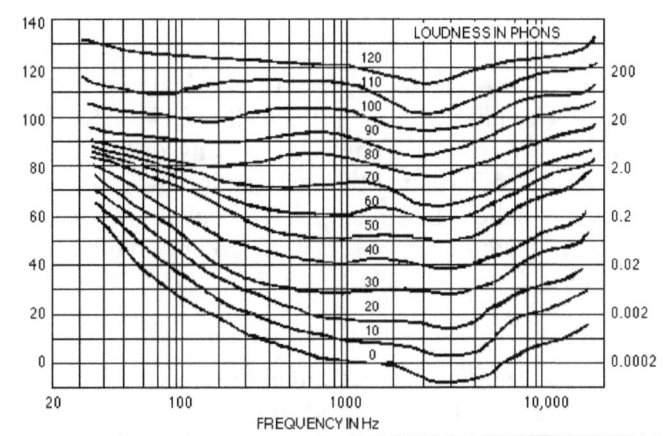

Figure 2.3. Fletcher - Munson equal loudness curves

Loudness is also influenced by preceding aural events. This is easily demonstrated. Go to a courtyard and stand five feet from a wall and clap your hands. You will easily hear your hands clapping, but no matter how hard you try, you will not be able to hear an echo from the wall. Now begin to walk further from the wall. At some point the echoes of your clapping hands will start to become audible. The amplitude of the echoes did not suddenly start to increase, but were actually decreasing. What changed were the preceding aural events. The brain is constantly sifting through the sounds we hear. Anytime a sound is encountered that resembles another sound which was just heard, only the first sound will register, the second sound will be blocked by the brain. This is known as the Haas effect and is discussed in Chapter 13.

Loudness curves, masking, echoes, what do all of these things mean? Loudness is not just a simple question of the amplitude of the vibration. Rather than being a simple physical parameter it is actually an unfathomable mixture of physical and psychophysical factors. Therefore, our simplistic high school model of loudness as a function of amplitude is not exactly correct.

Pitch - Let us return to our simple model of pitch. The simple view of pitch equated it with the frequency of the vibrations. This is a convenient model which is generally true, but there are other factors which must be considered.

Amplitude can influence our perception of pitch. It has been shown that you can take a very low frequency sound, increase the amplitude, and the perceived pitch goes down (Walliser 1969). It has also been shown that if you take a high frequency sound and raise the amplitude, the perceived pitch also rises.

The shape of the waves (i.e., timbre) can also influence the perception of pitch. There are certain "shapes" of waves that produce perceived pitches for which there are no vibrations. This was empirically discovered by European organists many centuries ago. Organists used to routinely imply a bass notes by playing various combinations which would relate harmonically to the note being simulated (Roederer 1975:42). This concept is also very important to tabla because we routinely tune to a pitch for which there is no corresponding vibration. (There is a lot of important stuff going on in this paragraph, but don't worry if this doesn't make sense now. We will come back to this later.)

Timbre - This brings us to the topic of timbre. Previously we said that the timbre was the shape of the waveform, strictly speaking this is not correct. It is possible to take a sound and change the shape without affecting the sound[1]. Clearly the concept of timbre is more complicated than merely the shape of the wave.

There are two major aspects of musical timbre. The most important aspect is the harmonic structure. Harmonic structure reflects the fact that most sounds are not composed of only a single frequency, but are instead composed of many different frequencies. This is similar to the way that the flavour of food is determined by the quantity and makeup of the ingredients. There is another aspect of timbre which is called the envelope. The envelope is the characteristic manner in which the sound rises and dies away. Both of these aspects are so important that we will delve into them at great length.

ENVELOPE

The envelope is the overall pattern that the sound of a musical instrument makes. This is really a simple concept; it is the way that the sound rises and falls away.

Anyone who is involved in crafting sounds for synthesisers or similar applications realises how important the envelope can be in determining the timbre. In these applications, the envelope has a shape that is divided into four parts, referred to as Attack, Decay, Sustain, Release, (ADSR)(Figure 2.4). A typical ADSR is shown in Figure 2.4.a.

We can clarify our understanding of envelope with a couple of examples. Imagine the sound of a clarinet. When the clarinet is blown, it goes from an amplitude of zero to its full amplitude very quickly. The sound will continue until the blowing stops; then the sound dies down very quickly. This is shown in Figure 2.4.f. Now imagine a guitar. When it is struck the sound rises nearly instantaneously; however the moment it reaches its highest point the sound starts to decay. This is shown in Figure 2.4.d. For most instruments, the envelope is relatively consistent. Figure 2.4 shows the envelopes of a number of common instruments.

The envelope of tabla *dayans* is not constant but has many variations. Each stroke has its own attack and decay characteristics. Figure 2.5. shows the envelopes of the common strokes. We see that the more resonant strokes *(khula)* have a very long decay, while the nonresonant stroke *(bandh)* have a relatively short decay. There are also variations according to the size of the drum. *Dayans* that have large heads (e.g., over 6 inches in diameter), tend to have very long decays, while *dayans* that are small (e.g., 5 inches or less) have very short decays.

These variations in the rate of decay are of tremendous practical importance. For instance, a large *dayan* produces a delightful effect when played slowly because of its long sustain. But if it is played very fast the sound becomes muddy and indistinct. This is because the attack of the next stroke comes before the previous stroke has died away. Conversely, a small *dayan* sounds empty when played at very slow tempos, but very crisp and distinct at high speeds. This is due to the very quick decay of the smaller *dayans*. This is one reason why tabla players have more than one *dayan*.

---

[1] This is possible because altering the phase relationship of the harmonics will alter the shape of the waveform without substantially changing the timbre. However, this is a topic which is beyond the scope of this book.

We have spoken of the envelope in very general terms; but it is helpful if we can quantify these characteristics. For our purposes, the envelope of the tabla sounds can be defined using two parameters; the attack time and the decay time.

The attack time is conceptually simple; it is the time it takes for the sound to rise to its maximum value. For the *dayan*, this usually is on the order of 5-15msec.

The decay time is not so simple. Intuition says that the decay time is the time it takes for the sound to completely die away. Unfortunately, even a brief glance at the envelopes in Figure 2.5 show that they all tend to have an exponential decay. Therefore the sound does not actually go away, but approaches the baseline asymptotically. They functionally disappear only when they become lost in background noise. An easier way to express this concept is called

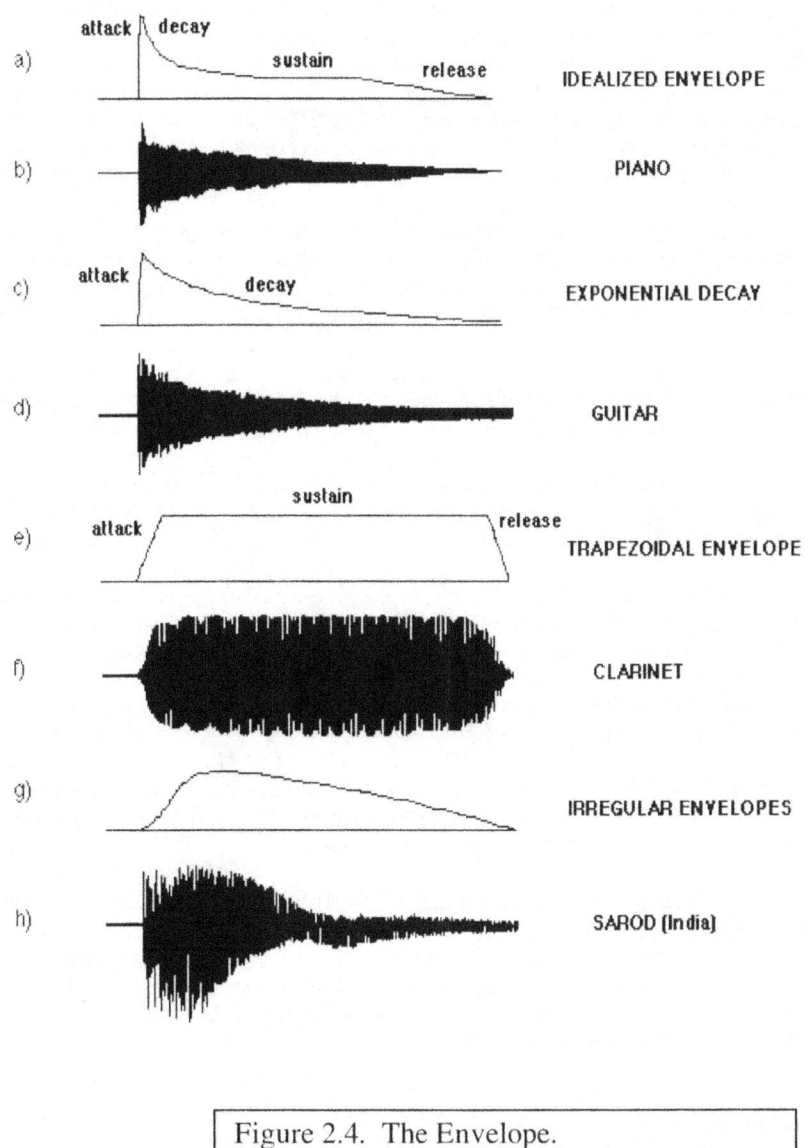

Figure 2.4. The Envelope.

"decay half-time". Decay half-time is the interval in which the signal decays to half of its maximum value. Let us say that an ideal exponential decay has a decay half-time of 100msec. After 100msec the amplitude will be 50% of the maximum. After 200msec it will again decrease by 50%, so that it will be 25% of the original value. After 300msec the value will be 12.5%. This process of taking a value and cutting it into successive halves continues indefinitely. An illustration of attack and decay half-times are shown in Figure 2.6.

It is good to be familiar with the envelope of tabla and its parameters for several reasons. When one is editing or mastering music with a computer, the information will be displayed in this form. It is also useful in computer-aided transcription.

Let us quickly review what we learned about the tabla and its envelope. We saw in this section that the manner in which a sound rises and falls is called the envelope. For this chapter, we will only look at two parameters, the attack time and the decay half-time.

Although the envelope makes a significant contribution to the timbre, it is relatively minor compared to the harmonic content. This concept deserves further attention.

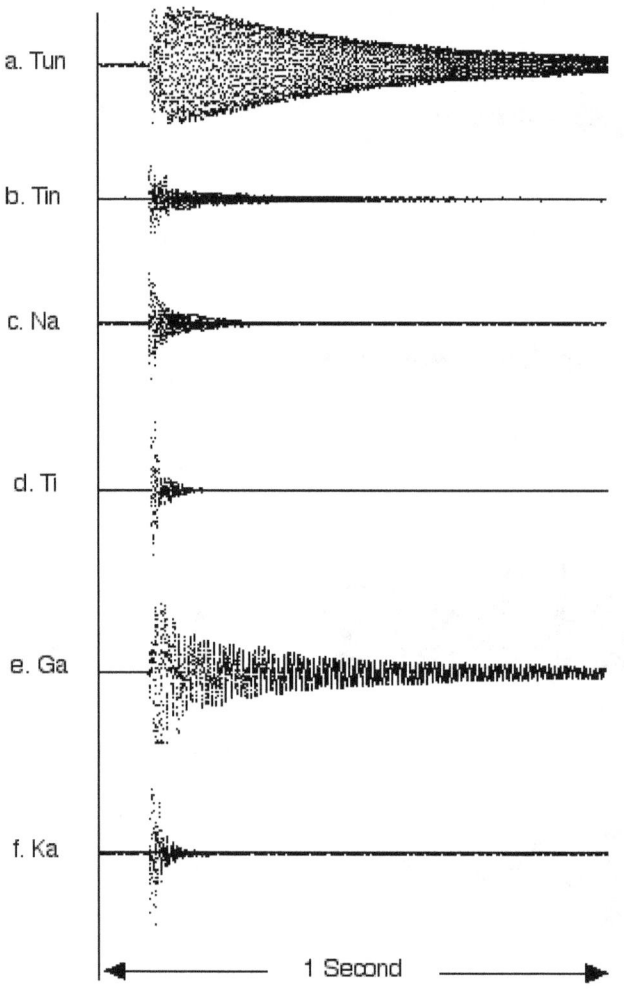

Figure 2.5. Envelopes of common tabla strokes

HARMONIC CONTENT AND SPECTRUM ANALYSIS

Harmonic content is the most important factor in determining the timbre of musical instruments. It is extremely rare to find a sound that is only a single frequency; one normally finds sounds as a complex mixture of different frequencies. The proportion of these various frequencies is referred to as the harmonic content or spectrum. In this section we will discuss the nature of spectra as well as graphically representing them in spectrograms.

The relationship between the shape of the sound wave and its harmonic content is important. Previously we alluded to the waveform as being the cause of timbre; now we talk about harmonic content. You may be asking yourself, "What is happening? What's the connection?" The connection between the two can be illustrated with a simple example. Let us take two sine waves, one twice the frequency of the other, and add them together. This is shown in Figure 2.7. The addition of sine wave "a" with sine wave "b" will produce the non-sinusoidal wave "c". Remember that the frequency of "b" is twice the frequency of "a"; this is called a harmonic relationship. This little illustration leads us to an important concept. Any waveform may be produced by the simple addition of harmonics!

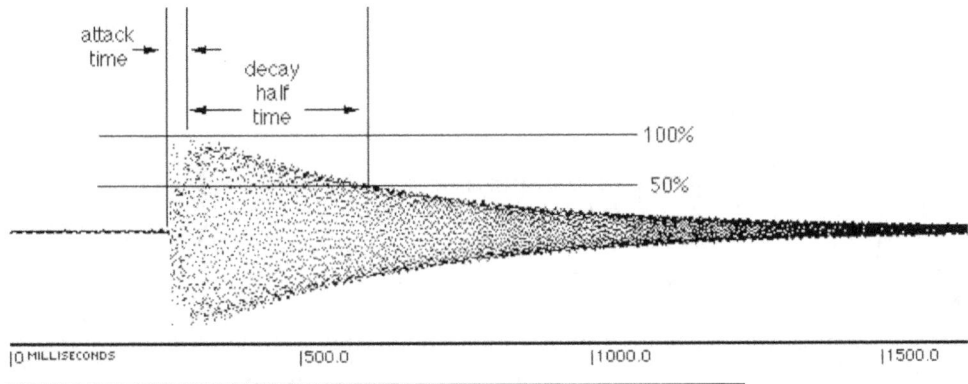

Figure 2.6. Attack-times and decay-half-times of tabla strokes

If we wish to understand spectrum analysis, there is one thing which we must remember. Just as the addition of sine waves of different frequencies produces nonsinusoidal waveforms, the reverse of this is also true. We can take any complex waveform and break it down into a series of sine waves. Some of the amplitudes may be zero, and the series may stretch into infinity, but it is still possible. This is the foundation of spectrum analysis.

Spectrum analysis is very useful. It is roughly like having a magic box. If we go into a restaurant and taste some food that we like, we may wish to find out what is in it. Imagine if we could just drop a sample of the food into our magic box and automatically get a printout of the ingredients. Such a magic box would be marvellous indeed. Yet this is exactly what spectrum analysis is to sound; it is our magic box.

There is good news and bad news about spectrum analysis. The bad news is that it involves some complicated mathematics. It also has some tricky practical considerations. The good news is that modern computers and software packages can take most of the pain and drudgery out of the entire process. Nevertheless, there are still some basic mathematical concepts that we have to learn; one of which is the concept of inverse domains.

<u>Inverse Domains and Spectra</u> - Inverse domains are two mathematical domains which have a reciprocal relationship with each other. No - don't close this book! It is not nearly as difficult as you may fear!

We can illustrate the concept of inverse domains with a simple illustration. Let us imagine a simple sine wave, 60Hz wall current for example. This sine wave may be graphically displayed in two ways as shown in Figure. 2.8. In the first view (2.8.a) we see the familiar depiction of a sine wave. It is shown as amplitude (vertical axis) as a function of time (horizontal axis). Since everything in this graph is a function of time, we call this the time domain. But we could show it in a different form. In Figure 2.8.b it is displayed as a single spectral line with amplitude as function of frequency. Since everything in this graph is a function of frequency, we call this the frequency domain.

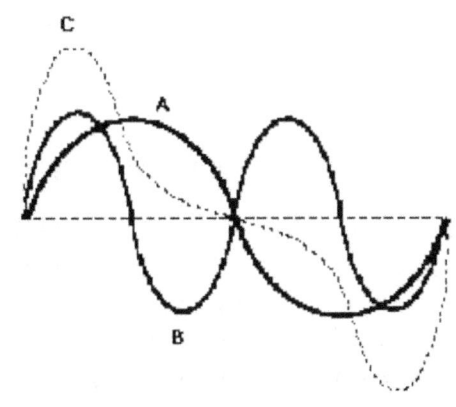

Figure 2.7. Addition of sine waves

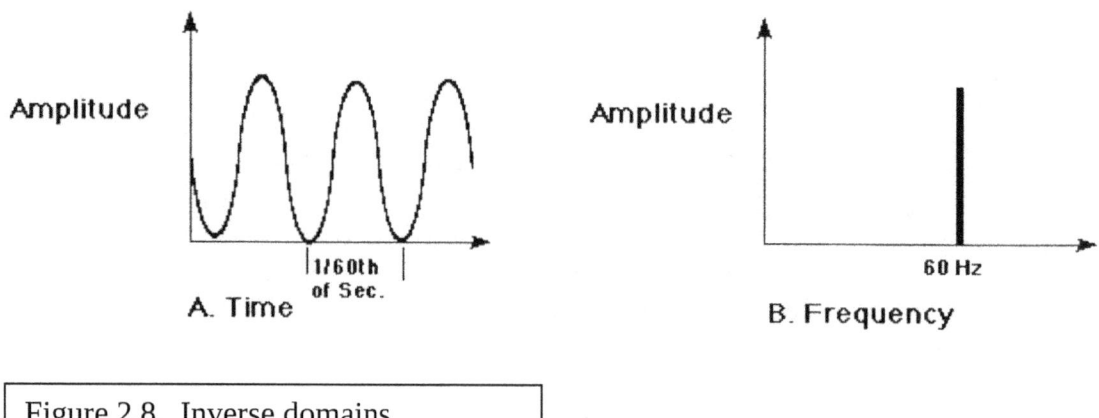

Figure 2.8. Inverse domains

The origin of the term "inverse domain" is very simple. If we have the frequency (frequency domain), but wish to know how long one cycle is (referred to as the "period" in technical jargon), all we have to do is take the inverse of it. Therefore:

$$\frac{1}{\text{Frequency}} = \text{Period}$$

By the same token, if we have the period (time domain), and wish to find the frequency, then all that we have to do is take the inverse of it. Therefore:

$$\frac{1}{\text{Period}} = \text{Frequency}$$

This simple relationship is why we call them inverse domains.

Unfortunately in the real world, the mathematics is seldom this simple. The complexities of real world sound, mean that we must resort to a complicated mathematical process, which is called a Fourier transform. Fortunately, modern computers are so powerful that we do not need to understand the nuts and bolts of the Fourier transform. To us it is a mere black box in which we put a waveform (time domain) and get out a spectrum (frequency domain).[2] This is shown diagrammatically in Figure 2.9.

---

[2] The Fourier transform does not just yield the frequency information. It also yields information concerning the phase relationships. However, since this information is not normally necessary to the music student, we will not approach the topic

Ch. 2. Timbre

Figure 2.9. Spectrum analysis with a Fourier transform

The Fourier transform is to sound what a glass prism is to light. Just as a prism separates light into the visible spectrum, so too our Fourier transform separates the sound into an audio spectrum. Just as the visual spectrum covers a range which extends between red to deep violet, so too the audio spectrum covers a range which extends between deep bass (20 - 30 cycles per second) and the highest treble (15 - 20 thousand cycles per second). Component frequencies determine the timbre in the same way that the mixture of colours determine the shade of an object.

The breakdown of the various frequencies is called a spectrum. We generally say that there are two classes of spectra; harmonic and inharmonic. A harmonic spectrum has an even relationship between the component frequencies while the inharmonic spectrum has an uneven relationship. We shall look into this in greater detail.

The harmonic spectrum is particularly interesting. An example is shown in Figure 2.10a. There is a base frequency, referred to as the "fundamental", and an indefinite number of overtones. The fundamental is important because it determines what the numeric values of the overtones will be. These overtones will have an integral relationship to the fundamental. Stated simply, the overtones will be 2X, 3X, 4X etc. of the fundamental. Therefore, if the fundamental frequency should be 100Hz, then it would likely have overtones at 200Hz, 300Hz, 400Hz, etc. Most musical instruments have harmonic spectra. The fundamental is generally what determines the pitch. There are of course some interesting twists. For instance, even if the amplitude of the fundamental is zero, we will still hear a pitch which corresponds to the nonexistent frequency.

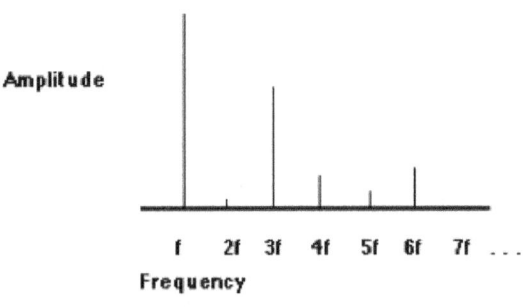

a. Harmonic Spectrum

The inharmonic spectrum is very different from a harmonic spectrum. An inharmonic spectrum has frequency components which do not have a simple mathematical relationship. Most of the nonmusical sounds that we hear each day are inharmonic. Wind in the trees, screeching breaks, and breaking concrete are just a few examples. A graphic illustration is shown in Figure 2.10b.

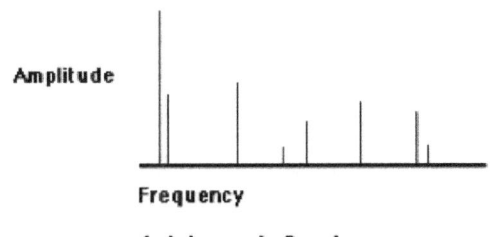

b. Inharmonic Spectrum

Figure 2.10. Harmonic and inharmonic spectra

page 17

There is a problem with our discussion of spectra; it is all so static. We indicated earlier that the sound of the tabla is continually changing throughout its envelope. Just as the amplitude is continually changing. so too the spectrum changes. We need a tool that will allow us to visualise continually changing harmonic structures.

The 2D Spectrogram - A 2D spectrogram is one way to view continually changing spectra. A simple spectrogram is too simple and static, like a snapshot. But if we take a number of snapshots, each separated by a small unit of time and flash them before our eyes, then we get a moving picture. In this same way if we take a number of samples of spectra, we can then visualise the entire sonic event. We could film these spectra and flash it back on a monitor but this is not really a practical solution. This is a book, and we are only interested in ways of representing this information on the printed page. Since a piece of paper is inherently a two-dimensional medium, then a technique called a 2-D spectrogram is a reasonable choice.

A 2D spectrogram is shown in Figure 2.11. In this example, we see that the vertical axis represents frequency; the horizontal axis represents time; and the amplitude is indicated by the degree of blackness on the chart. This particular example is a sample of music.

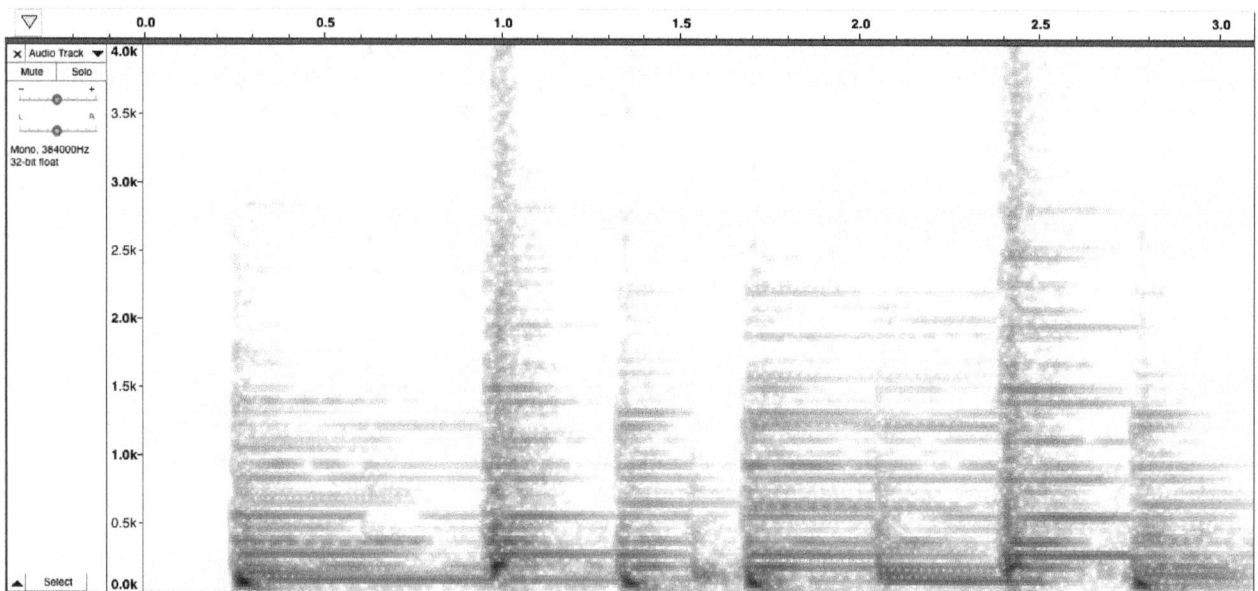

Figure 2.11. 2D Spectrogram

One problem of the 2D spectrogram is that it does not show the envelope very clearly. Therefore it is common to find the time domain tracing displayed simultaneously with the spectra. An example is shown in Figure 2.12.

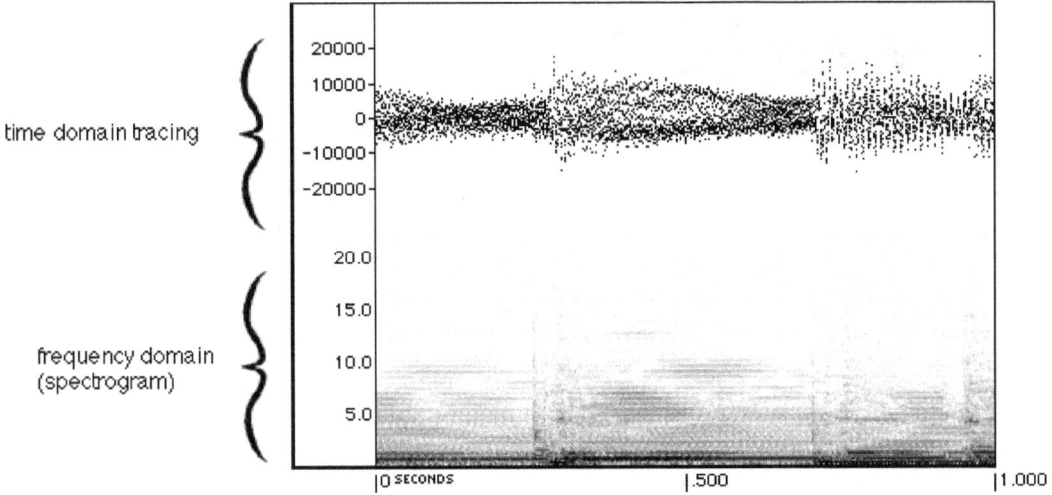

Figure 2.12. 2D Spectrogram and time domain tracing

Let us review what we learned about spectra and the spectrogram. If we look at an event as a waveform, it is said to be in the time domain. If we look at the component frequencies, then it is said to be frequency domain. The frequency domain and the time domain are called inverse domains because of the nature of the math which converts from one to the other. The mathematical process for making the conversion is known as a Fourier transform. Our ears do not work well in the time domain, therefore the frequency domain is much closer to the way that we hear. The proportions of the different frequencies is called a spectrum. Musical instruments usually do not have static spectra but have spectra which are continually changing. These changing spectra are easily shown using a 2D spectrogram. A 2D spectrogram, coupled with a time domain tracing, is a very powerful tool for visualising sound. Figure 2.11 and Figure 2.12 showed 2D spectrograms. Did these spectrograms make any sense to you? If you are an average reader, you probably looked at the two examples and could make no sense of them, don't worry because we will take care of that.

MINI-TUTORIAL ON READING SPECTROGRAMS
We will return repeatedly to 2D spectrograms throughout this series. Therefore it is useful to embark upon a mini-tutorial to teach you how to read them. Let us first look at some extremely simple examples.

Figure 2.13 shows the spectrogram of a 1kHz signal with a triangular envelope. Notice that the envelope is shown two ways. The clearest representation is the time domain tracing at the top portion of the Figure. But it is also indicated by the dark band which runs across the middle of the spectrogram. Notice that it is grey at both ends where the signal is the weakest and it is darkest at the centre where the signal is strongest. This band is located at the one kilohertz position (i.e., 1000 cycles per second). The time scale at the bottom shows that this entire event lasted 500 milliseconds (i.e. half a second). Notice that there are calibrations on the right hand side of the time domain tracing. In all our examples, these numbers tell us nothing other than the scale is linear.

When reading a spectrogram one should not be mislead by artefacts. Look at the light grey band running across the bottom of the spectrogram; this is an example of a sampling artefact. There is no actual signal at this frequency. Although artefacts are certainly important, it is not possible to go into them in detail in a music book. If one is interested, there are many good books on the subject which discuss them in greater detail.

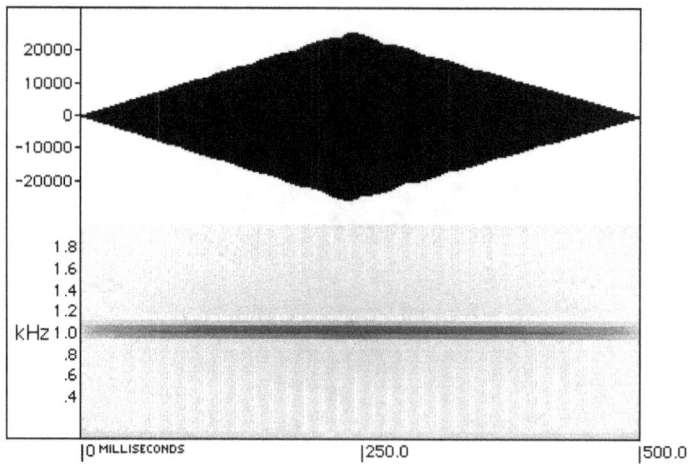

Figure 2.13. 1 kHz sine-wave with triangular envelope

Let's look at another spectrogram. Figure 2.14 is a little more complex. In the upper part of this example (time domain tracing) we see that throughout this 500msec period, there is no activity except for a 100msec triangle wave burst in the middle. The time domain tracing shows that this burst has a smooth and well rounded envelope. The spectrogram (lower section) shows a fundamental at 200Hz with harmonics at 600Hz, 1kHz, 1.4kHz and 1.8kHz. This corresponds to 3 times, 5 times, 7 times, and 9 times the fundamental frequency.

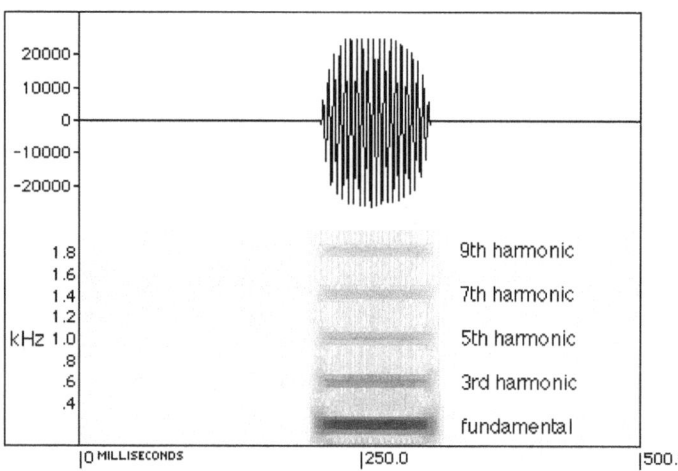

Figure 2.14. 100mSec burst of 200 Hz triangle-wave

Let us move on to another example. Figure 2.15 shows an example of "white noise". Just as white light is a mixture of all of the wavelengths of light, white noise contain all of the frequencies. Therefore in the accompanying spectrogram, we will not see any recognisable harmonic structure. Instead there is a relatively constant band of dark extending over the entire test range (0 - 2kHz). This type of white noise is very common in the real world. It is important for tabla because a certain amount of white noise is a ubiquitous component of tabla sounds.

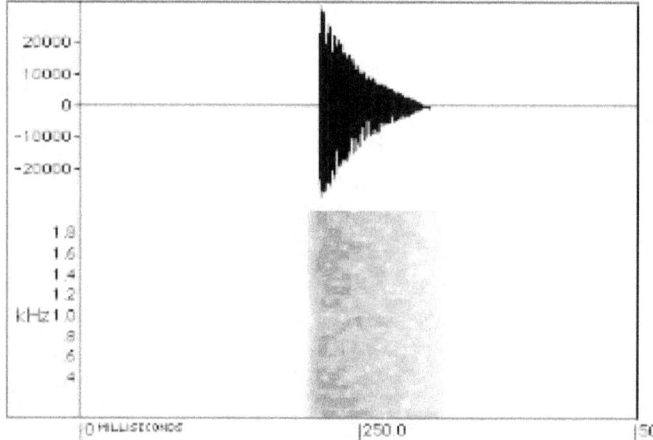

Figure 2.15. White-noise with decay

We have covered a lot of information in only a few pages. The essential information is shown in Table 2.1. Make certain that these points are thoroughly understood before progressing further.

We embarked upon a mini-tutorial on the reading of two-dimensional spectrograms. Several simple examples, much simpler than we would find in the real world, were shown. This is an uncomfortably large amount of new material for the typical musician. However, we tried to make it as simple and painless as possible. Although this has not been very detailed, it will allow us to read the spectrograms which appear elsewhere in this book.

THE SPECTRA OF THE DAYAN
Armed with these new conceptual tools, we will now look at the sounds of tabla, specifically the right hand drum (*dayan*). We will see how the character of each stroke of the *dayan* is marked by certain distinctive qualities. Some of these qualities relate to the envelope, and others relate to the harmonic content.

General Characteristics of the Dayan The sounds of most drums are characterised by strongly inharmonic spectra; however tabla, especially the *dayan,* is an exception. This was pointed out by the famous C.V. Raman as early as 1920 (Raman & Kumar 1920). This was further refined in a later paper (Raman 1935). From that time, it has been a simple question of further refinement.

Table 2.1 - Important Information for Reading Spectrograms

----

1) The characteristic pattern that the sound makes as it rises then falls away is called the envelope.

2) Tabla envelopes may be described in terms of attack and decay.

3) The attack time is the length of time that it takes for the sound to rise to its maximum amplitude. We will measure it in milliseconds.

4) Rather than measure a decay time we instead measure a decay half-time. This is the time it takes for the signal to decay to half its starting amplitude. This is measured in milliseconds.

5) A spectrogram is a graphical breakdown of the component frequencies of any particular sound.

6) Frequency is measured in either Hz (Hertz = 1 cycle-per-second) or kHz (Kilohertz = 1,000 cycles per second.)

7) The strength of the signal is shown by the degree of darkness.

8) 1 msec (one-millisecond) equals .001 second, or one thousandth of a second.

9) A harmonic spectrum is one where the component frequencies are all 1X, 2X, 3X, 4X, etc. a base frequency.

10) The base frequency is called the fundamental.

11) Every harmonic except the fundamental is called an overtone.

12) Sometimes a spectrum has component frequencies which do not have a simple relationship with each other. This is called an inharmonic spectrum.

The model is very neat. It represents the sound of Indian drums, like the *tabla-dayan*, as having a spectrum consisting of five harmonics; these are the fundamental with four overtones. An example of this harmonic structure is shown in Figure 2.16. We see that Raman's five harmonics are quite clear. Additionally we see some other overtones which were not mentioned in Raman's early work. Raman was dealing with very primitive equipment, so it is not surprising that he missed these other components. Yet, even with our modern equipment, the musical significance of many of these remains unclear.

There are a few general comments that we can make concerning these harmonics. They are the building blocks of the tone of the *tabla-dayan*. Each harmonic represents at least one vibrational mode. The act of playing is based upon selectively accentuating or suppressing these various vibrational modes. Another observation concerns their numerical value. A close examination shows that they do not all have an integral relationship to each other (i.e., their relationship is not always 1X, 2X, 3X, etc.).

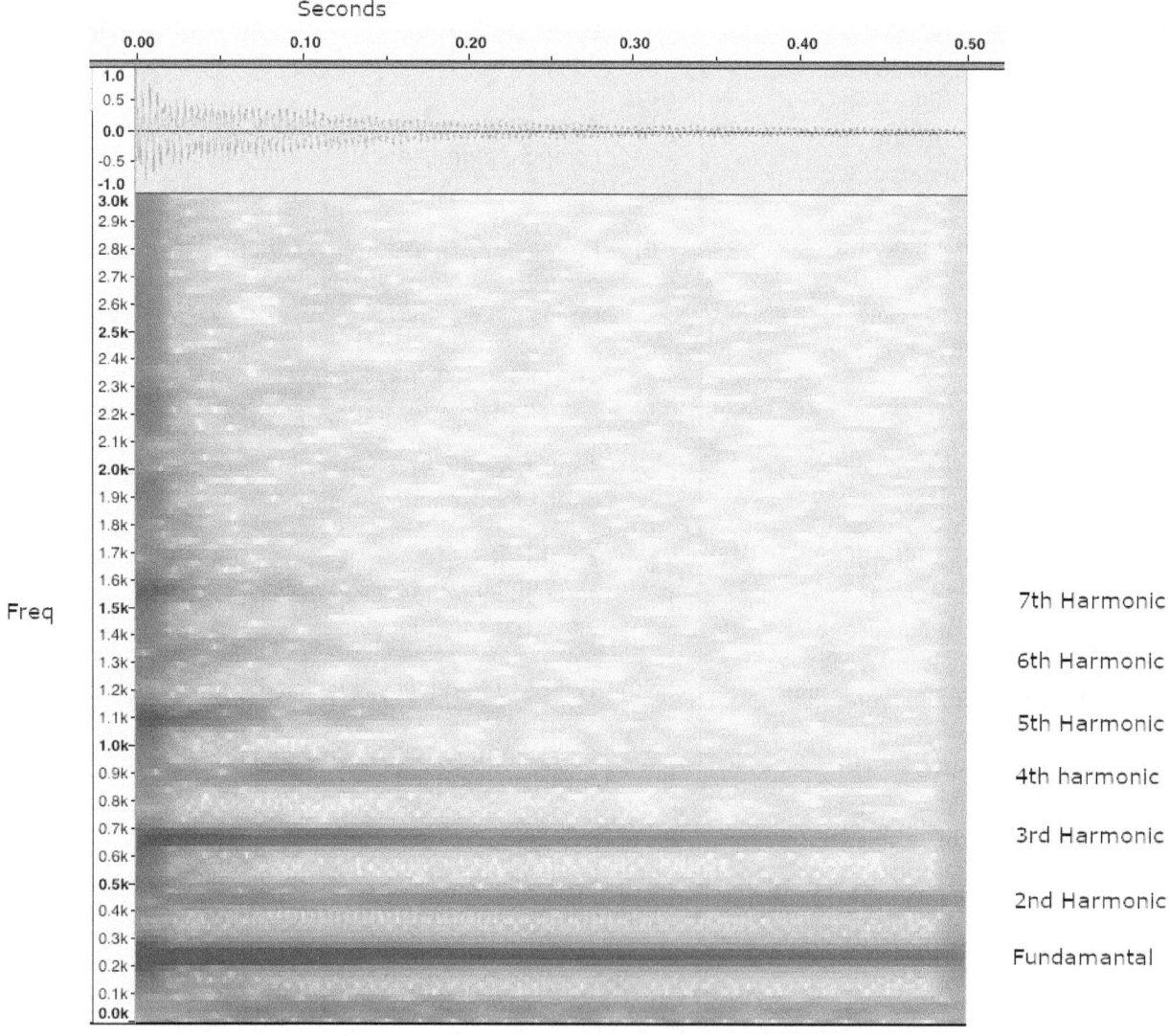

Figure 2.16. Harmonics of dayan

Naa - *Naa* (ना) is a good place to begin our discussion of the spectra. This is shown in Appendix 2, Figure AP2.2. *Naa* (ना) is played by striking the edge of the *dayan* with the index finger. The vibrations are controlled by placing the last two fingers of the right hand lightly against the *syahi* (refer to volume one, *Fundamentals of Tabla* of this series for a better description). This stroke shows a reasonable balance of the various harmonics. But *Naa* (ना) comes in several "flavours". Just as each *Naa* (ना) has a different sound, there will also be differences in the spectra.

A 2D spectrogram for a closed *Naa* (ना) is shown in Figure 2.17. In this example, the finger does not bounce off the drum but stays in contact at all times. This type of *Naa* (ना) is most common in the *Dilli* style of playing. The upper portion of the 2D spectrogram shows a time domain representation. We see that it has a fairly sharp decay half-time of 20msec.

There are two things to note about this stroke. To begin with, there is a marked suppression of the fundamental. This is to be expected because we are muting this vibration by placing the last two fingers against the skin. There is a strong showing of the second and third harmonics. The third harmonic is especially important, because it is more pronounced in *Naa* (ना) than in any other stroke. This is denoted by the particularly black portion of the third harmonic.[3]

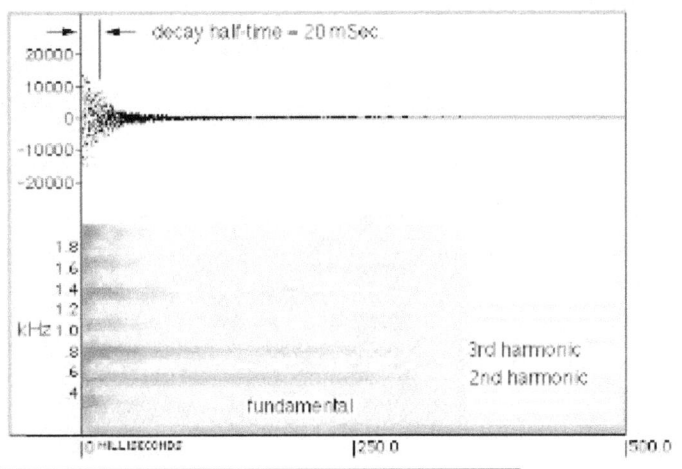

Figure 2.17. Spectrogram of Naa (ना) (closed)

An open *Naa* (ना) is shown in Figure 2.18. In this variation the index finger is allowed to bounce after the drum has been struck. This difference is most pronounced in the time domain. Notice that the sustain (indicated in the upper half of the record) is 50% longer than in the previous closed *Naa* (ना). The spectrum of this stroke shows the very prominent third harmonic, which is the defining quality of *Naa* (ना). This stroke shows an even longer sustain of the third harmonic.

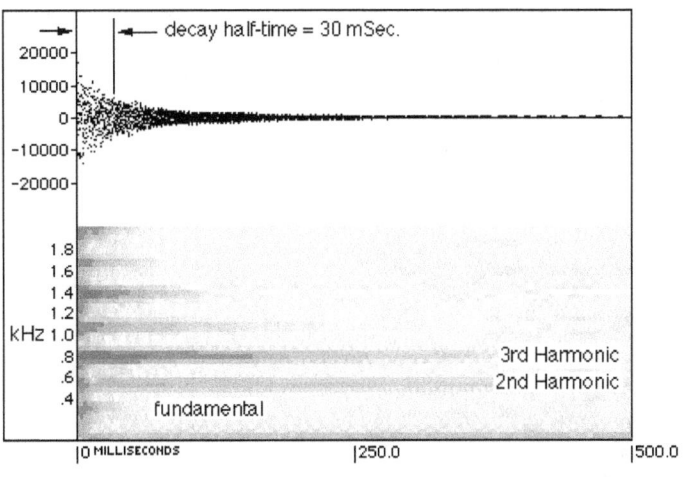

Figure 2.18. Spectrogram of Naa (ना) (open)

---

[3] When reading 2D spectrograms, do not be confused by the length of the line; length indicates the sustain. The strength of the harmonic is shown by how dark it is. In the case of this *Naa* (ना) the strength of the 3rd harmonic is considerably greater than that of the 2nd harmonic.

Tak (तक्) or "sticky" Taa (ता) (Appendix 2. Figure AP12) - This stroke is not very common, but it has a very distinctive sound. It is played by placing the first three fingers against the skin to mute the vibrations and striking sharply against the *chat* with the index finger. The spectrogram for this stroke is shown in Figure 2.19. One of its most distinctive characteristic is the extremely sharp decay. This is shown in the upper half of the Figure. We see that it has a decay half-time of only around 8msec. The spectrum shows the second and third harmonics are very strong, but are of short duration. It is this short duration, coupled with a clear harmonic structure, which is the defining quality of this stroke.

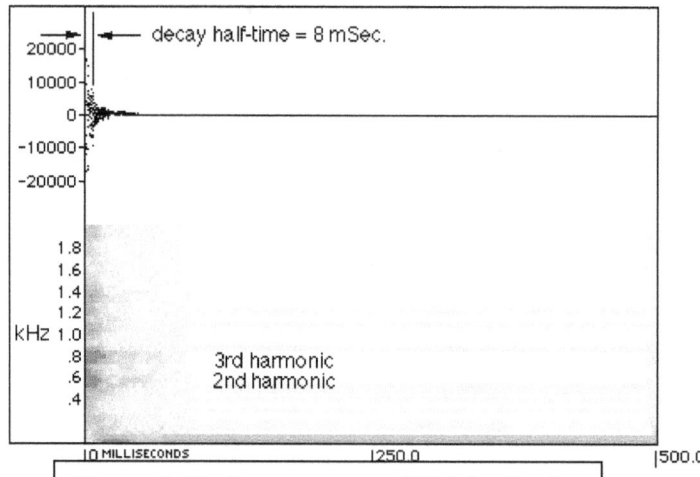

Figure 2.19. Spectrogram of "Sticky Taa"

Toon (तूं) (Appendix 2. Figure AP10) - The sound of *Toon* (तूं) is a simple resonant stroke, where the index finger strikes the centre of the *syahi*. The skin is allowed to rebound, so that the drum can resonate without any dampening from the fingers. This unhampered vibration is readily seen in the time domain. This stroke has the longest decay of all. Figure 2.20 shows an example with a decay half-time of approximately 200msec. The strongest component is the fundamental. This is fully to be expected since there is no muting action of the last two fingers and the drum is struck in the centre. All of the other harmonics may also be heard, but in a weak form.

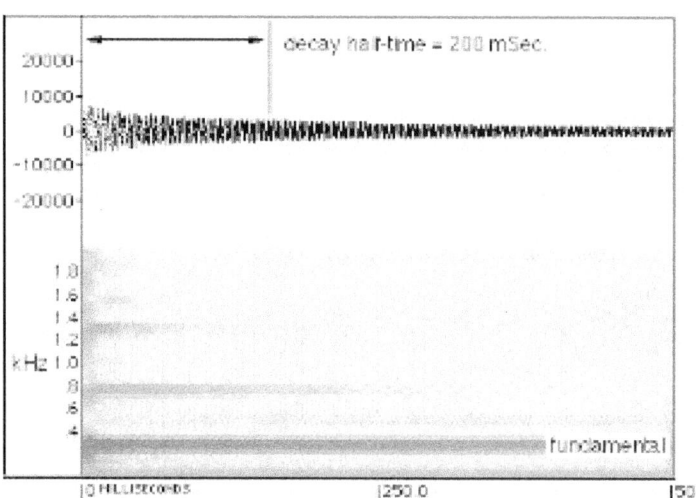

Figure 2.20. Spectrogram of Toon (तूं)

Tin (तिं) (Appendix 2. Figure AP5) - *Tin* (तिं) is played by lightly holding the last two fingers of the right hand against the skin, and striking softly against the *syahi*. Its 2D spectrogram is shown in Figure 2.21. The time domain tracing shows a moderate decay half-time of about 15msec. If we turn our attention to the frequency domain, we see a suppression of the fundamental. This is again due to the muting action of the last two fingers. This stroke has a very prominent second harmonic.

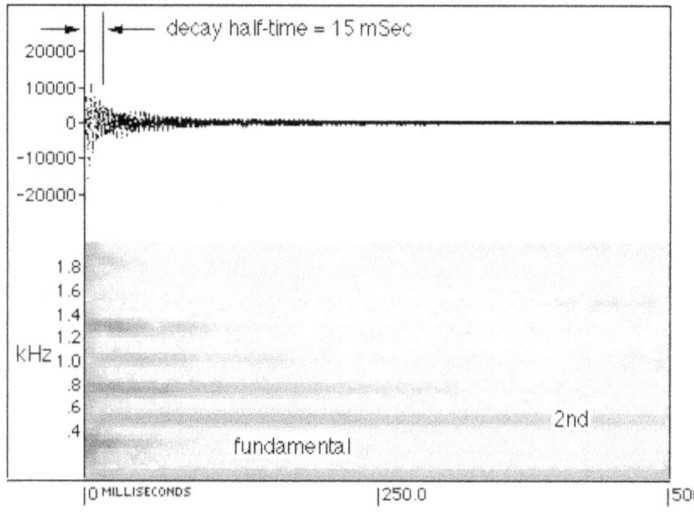

Figure 2.21. Spectrogram of Tin (तिं)

Da (ड) or Na (न) (Appendix 2. Figure AP9) - This stroke is played by striking the edge of the *syahi* with the last two fingers. This stroke is generally considered to be *bandh*, or nonresonant. However, both the time domain tracing and the spectrogram do not entirely bear this out. It has both resonant and nonresonant characteristics. Its spectrogram is shown in Figure 2.22. We see that it has a moderate decay half-time of about 15msec. Unfortunately this parameter must be called into question on this stroke. The concept of half-time is relevant for anything which approximates an exponential decay. This example clearly is not an exponential decay. Therefore the measured half-time in this example is misleading because it implies that it has a longer sustain than it really has. In this example we find that none of the harmonics have a significant showing after 150msec. Contrast this with other strokes with comparable decay half-times. Although there are several harmonics clearly shown, the overall feel of this stroke is unpitched. This involves some interesting psychoacoustics; however, we should postpone a discussion about the pitch of *dayans* until later in this chapter.

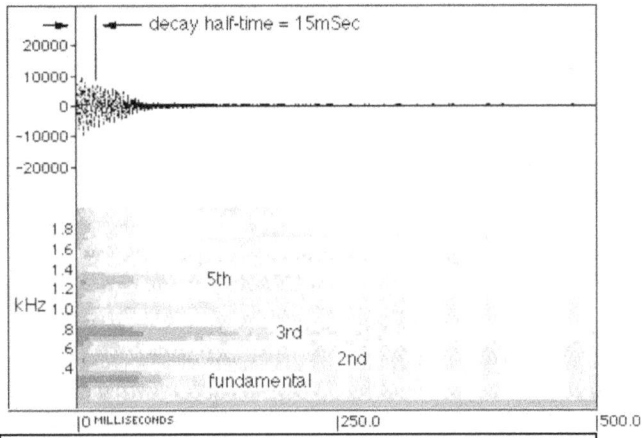

Figure 2.22. Spectrogram of Da (ड) or Na (न)

Ti (ति), Tee (ती) or Ta (ट) (Appendix 2. Figures AP7, AP8, AP22) - The flat sounds of the *dayan* are very distinctive. They are made by striking the inside of the skin with any combination of fingers. A typical 2D spectrogram is shown in Figure 2.23. The most interesting thing is that it shows a large degree of randomness or white noise. Needless to say, it does not have a clear pitch.

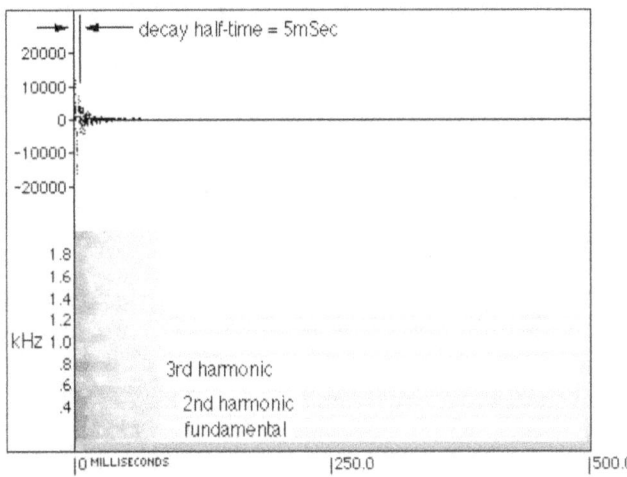

Figure 2.23. Spectrogram of Ti (ति), Ti (ती) or Ta (ट) etc.

Raa (रा or ड़ा) (Appendix 2. Figure AP33) - This is a relatively rare stroke. It is played by striking the very edge of the *chat* with the index finger. We find it in *bol* expressions such as Gin - Ta Raa - Na (गिं - ता रा - न). It is similar to Naa (ना) (Appendix 2. Figure AP2) except that there is no muting action of the last two fingers. Since there is no muting we have a relatively long decay half-time (Figure 2.24). In this case, it is around 50msec. This stroke shows quite clearly all of the harmonics.

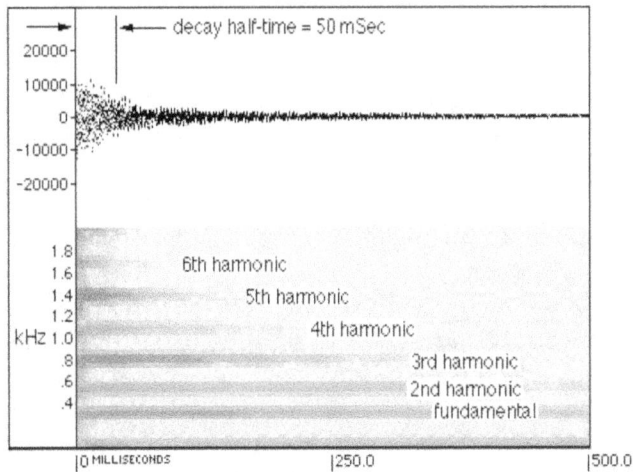

Figure 2.24. Raa (रा or ड़ा)

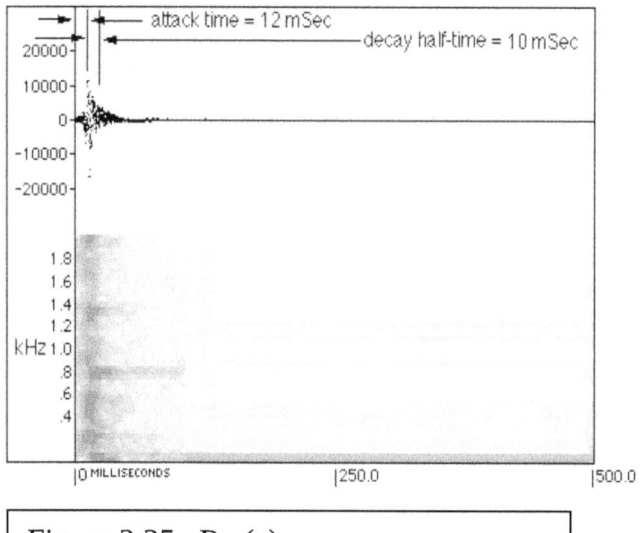

Figure 2.25. Ra (र)

Ra (र) (Appendix 2. Figure AP35) - This is a very expressive stroke of the right hand. It is played by striking with the part of the palm near the thumb. It is unusual in that it has a very sluggish attack time. The example in Figure 2.25 has an attack time of about 12msec. It also has a fairly sharp decay; the decay half-time in this example is around 10msec. The substantial attack time coupled with a relatively sharp decay makes this stroke almost sound as though it were recorded and played backwards. The spectral content is mixed. The spectrum is very close to white noise.

General Observations About the Spectra of the Dayan - There are a number of ways to look at the physical characteristics of the *dayan* sounds. It is especially interesting when we try to correlate these physics characteristics to the timbre and pitch of the drum.

The harmonics from the fourth up are of less importance to the musician. They merely establish the overall timbre of the instrument. To a great extent, they are determined at the time of manufacture. But to a certain extent, when someone is said to have a "sweet hand", these harmonics may play a role in this. Still, they play no importance in the definition of the *bols*.

The first three harmonics are the most important. All of the strokes may be differentiated by simply looking in this range. It is the way that these three behave, that provides the musical cues which keep the performers in step.

The fundamental is the least emphasised harmonic of the entire spectrum. It is the defining characteristic of the *bol Toon* (तूं), but *Toon* (तूं) occurs relatively infrequently. The reasons for this relate to pitch; therefore we will postpone this discussion until later.

The second harmonic is very important. It is the defining quality of *Tin* (तिं). It is also very important for tuning the instrument. Again, we shall defer this discussion until later.

The third harmonic is also very important. This is the defining quality for *Naa* (ना). It is also very important for tuning the instrument. Once again, we shall defer this discussion.

Toon (तूं), *Naa* (ना), and *Tin* (तिं), are easily defined by our lower three harmonics; however, the other strokes are not so easily defined. They are defined by more complex mixtures of time and frequency domain information.

We have repeatedly shied away from discussing the pitch of the *dayan*. This is because there are difficulties in describing pitch using the simple psychoacoustic models that we have been using.

Ch. 2. Timbre

<u>Difficulties Associated with the Perception of Pitch</u> - The perception of pitch in the *dayan* does not follow our simple conceptual model as neatly as we would like. It would be very convenient if we could simply close the chapter here and leave everything nice and tidy; unfortunately, we cannot do that. As we have gone over the 2D spectrograms in this chapter, there were major inconsistencies that we did not discuss. The most notable are the problems associated with the spectral content and the perception of pitch.

We adopted the classical model in looking at the spectrum of *dayan*; but this is not necessarily correct. Although this model has been invoked from the time of Raman, a closer inspection shows the numbers to be incorrect. Let us examine the harmonics of a tabla tuned to B in international, pitch (i.e., A=440Hz). This is shown in Figure 2.26. If we calculate where the harmonics should be, we find small discrepancies. Only two of the harmonics correspond to the predicted frequencies. Everything else is way off the mark.

There are several approaches we can take when viewing the physical foundation of the pitch of the *dayan*; unfortunately they are not all acceptable.

One traditional approach would be to declare that the spectrum is inharmonic; therefore, the sound must be unpitched. This is clearly false, because the tabla is very much a pitched instrument. Entire melodies are commonly played with numerous *dayans* tuned to different pitches (i.e., *tabla tarang*).

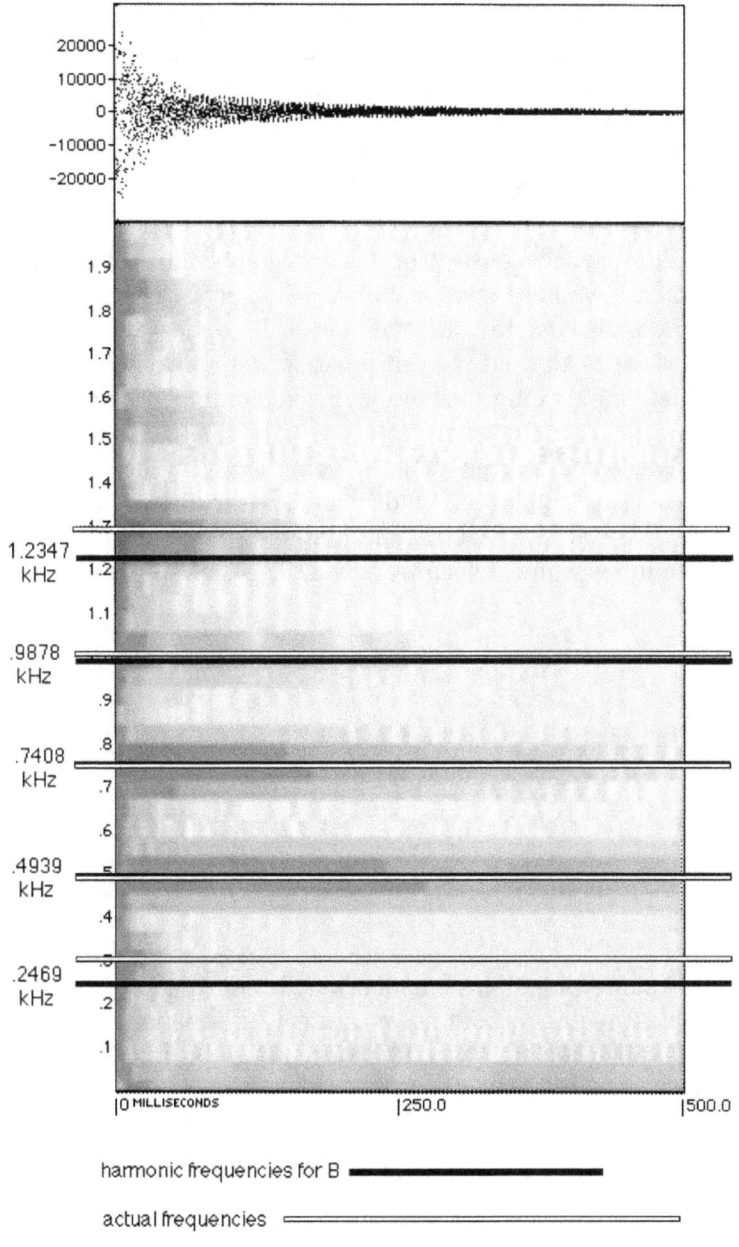

Figure 2.26. Actual vs. predicted frequencies for the pitch of tabla.

Another traditional approach is to say that the fundamental frequency determines the pitch. If we consider the lowest resonant frequency to be the fundamental, then it is out of pitch with the upper harmonics. If you listen to the pitch of *Toon* (तूं) you will clearly hear that it is about one step higher than the rest of the drum.

We are forced to accept a rather non-classical (i.e., non-Helmholtzian) explanation for the pitch of tabla. At least it is not in conformity with our simple high school model of pitch. For this, it is the second and third harmonics which determine the pitch. Therefore, the perceived pitch corresponds to a nonexistent harmonic. The frequency of this nonexistent harmonic is approximately one step below the one that we have been calling the fundamental. From a musical and psychoacoustic standpoint it is perhaps more correct to refer to the lowest measurable frequency as the pseudo-fundamental rather than a fundamental (Courtney 1991).

The psychoacoustics of what is happening may best be illustrated with a visual analogy. In Figure 2.27 we have some patterns which anyone would recognise as the alphabet. But if you tried to scan the images and read it with an OCR (optical character recognition) software, it will probably fail. The reason is that critical information which defines the characters are lacking. Instead, secondary information regarding shadows is invoked to imply the forms of the letters.

The same is true with the brain's ability to hear the pitch of the tabla-*dayan*. Information concerning the pitch (i.e., fundamental) is lacking or conflicting; but the second and third harmonics are present. Because of which, the brain is still able to hear the implied pitch. The brain is a pattern recognition machine, which works on the gestalt of patterns.

Figure 2.27. The brain's ability to fill in missing information

An interesting phenomenon was demonstrated by both the visual analogy, as well as in the sound of the tabla-*dayan*. In both cases, critical information was missing. However, since the overall patterns were familiar, the brain was able to step in and fill in the missing information.

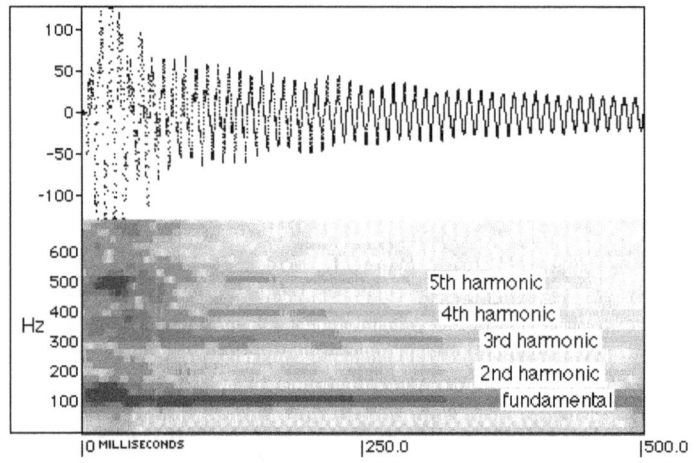

Figure 2.28. Spectrogram of Ga (ग)

THE SPECTRA OF THE BAYAN

The relationship between the spectra of the *bayan* and the perceived sound is much easier to understand. We do not have to delve into obscure areas of psychoacoustics in order to understand why it sounds the way it does.

Ga (ग) (Appendix 2. Figure AP3, AP14, AP15, & AP16) - The spectrogram of Ga (ग) is shown in Figure 2.28. It is not surprising that we find five harmonics. These five harmonics have been clear for many years (Raman & Kumar 1920). However, for the *bayan*, the overtones are mere tonal coloration. Unlike the *dayan,* these overtones do not play a part in the definition of the strokes. We see that the fundamental is so prominent and so stable that we need not look further than this to find the source of our musical information.

Modulation of the *bayan* is fairly straight forward. Figure 2.29 shows what happens to the fundamental when we slide the hand forward. There is a marked rise in the frequency of this harmonic. Yet there is an interesting event in the time domain. Notice that the envelope actually rises in amplitude after the *bayan* has been struck.

Figure 2.30 shows a *Ga* (ग) that uses a backwards slide. Notice the drop in the frequency of the fundamental.

Figure 2.31 shows a *Ga* (ग) with a compound slide. In this stroke, the *bayan* is struck, the wrist moves backwards, but before the sound dies away the hand is again brought forward. Therefore the pitch goes down, then turns back up. One of the characteristics of this style of modulation, is the rise in amplitude towards the end of the stroke. This is shown in the time domain tracing.

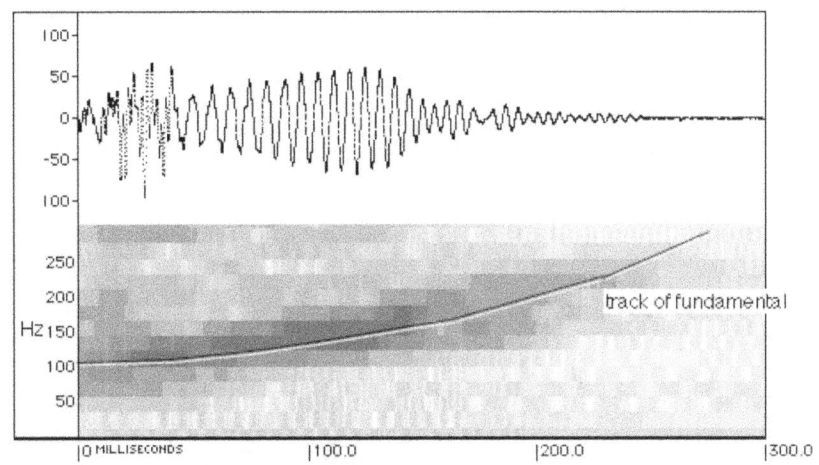

Figure 2.29. Forward-slide modulation

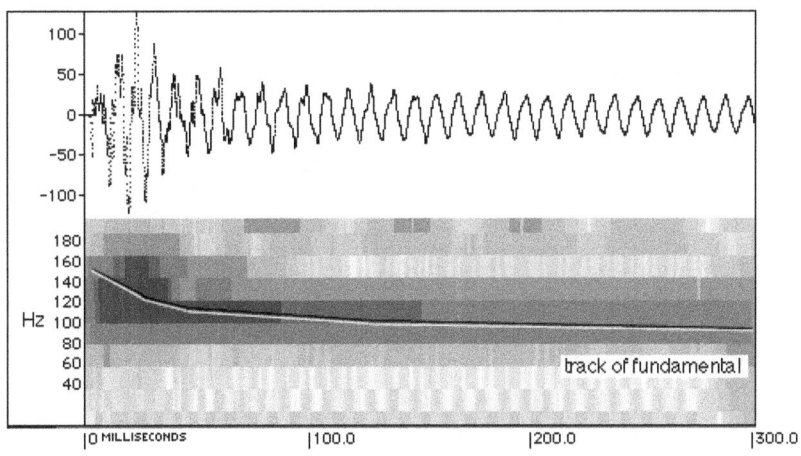

Figure 2.30. Reverse-slide modulation

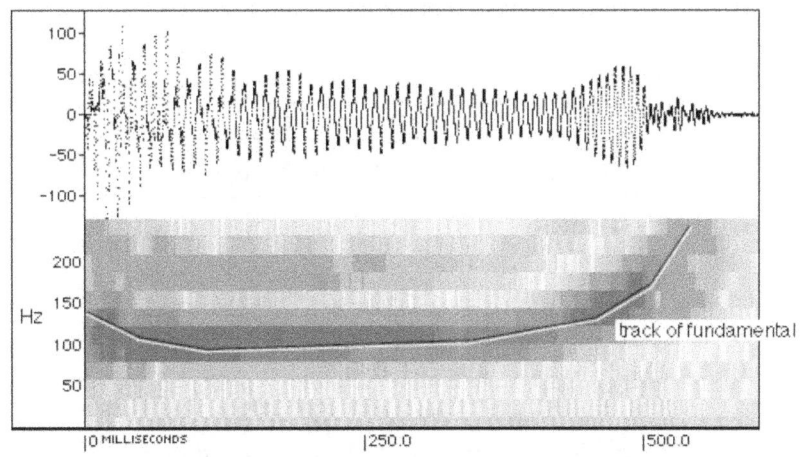

Figure 2.31. Compound-slide modulation

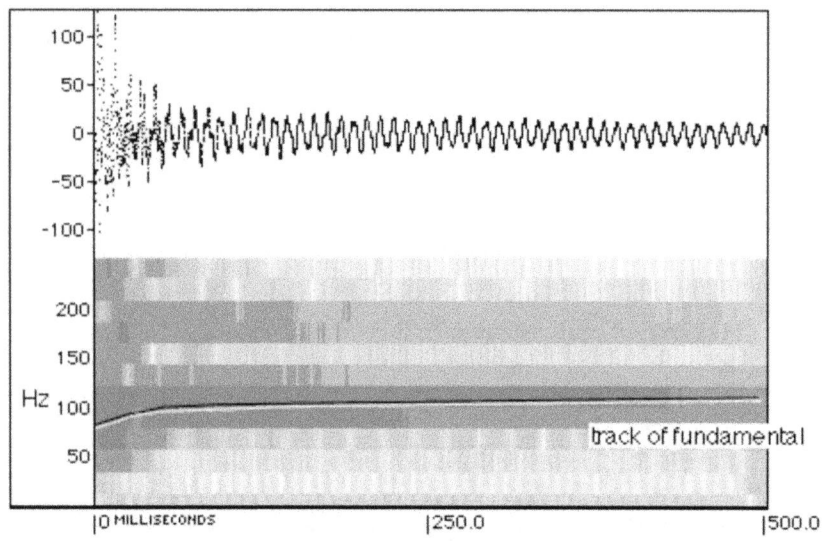

Figure 2.32. Pakhawaj style Ga (ग)

A very interesting variation of *Ga* (ग) is shown in Figure 2.32; this is a *pakhawaj* style *Ga* (ग) (Appendix 2. Figure AP17). In this style, the fundamental sometimes rises in frequency (but sometimes not). Remember, the hand is not in contact with the skin, so there is no obvious mechanism to explain this. This phenomenon has been observed by other investigators (Rossing 1992:42).

Ka (क) (Appendix 2. Figures AP1, AP18, AP19, AP20, AP21.) The stroke *Ka* (क) is very common. There are several forms; yet in each case the spectral information is uninteresting. For all practical purposes the spectra of the *Ka* (क) is white noise.

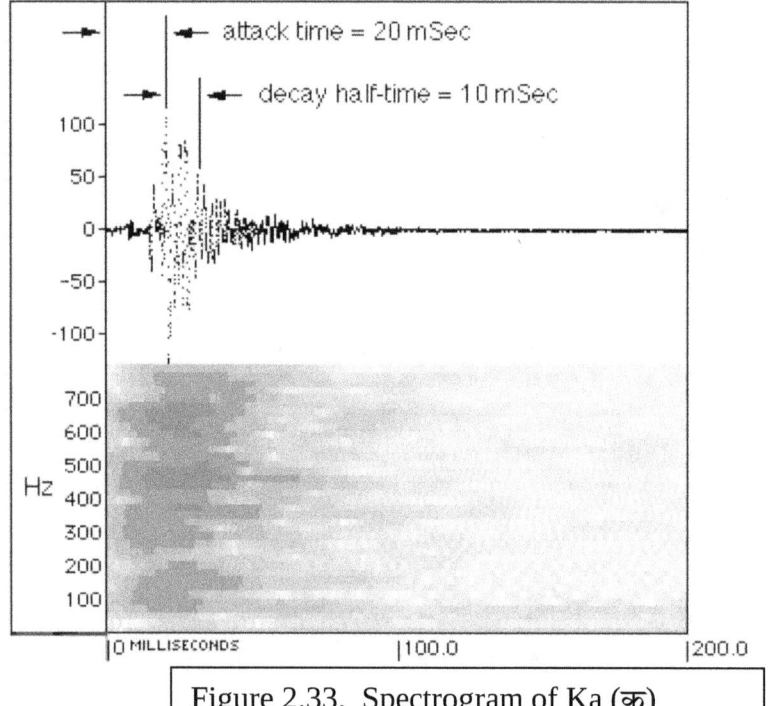

Figure 2.33. Spectrogram of Ka (क)

The standard *Ka* (क) is shown in Figure 2.33 (Appendix 2. Figure AP1). It has a very significant attack time. This is probably due to the finite time that it takes for the hand to make full contact with the drum. The decay half-time for this stroke is merely moderate.

A different type of *Ka* (क) is shown in Figure 2.34. This style is played by striking with the extended fingers at the back portion of the *bayan* (Appendix 2. Figure AP21). This is sometimes called "*top*". Its important characteristic is its loud volume. All of the records that we have been looking at; have been normalised for the purpose of showing the spectra and envelope. Therefore the loudness of this stroke is not evident in this record. Still the envelope does show interesting features. Notice that it has a very small attack time. This contributes to the strong percussive quality of "*top*".

There is another type of *Ka* (क) which is sometimes called a "snap" (Appendix 2. Figure AP38). It is shown in Figure 2.35. This type of *Ka* (क) is executed by pressing the index finger of the left hand against the thumb. The thumb is then withdrawn and the nail of the index finger strikes the *chat* of the *bayan*. We see in this illustration that it has a totally insignificant attack time.

We may summarise our discussion of the sounds of the *bayan* quite simply. A simple acoustic model works quite well in describing the timbre. In every case, a glance at the spectra tells us what the particular stroke sounds like. The resonant strokes which are basic variations of *Ga* (ग) are characterised by long decay times and a prominent fundamental. The non-resonant *Kas* (क) are characterised by white noise and short decay times.

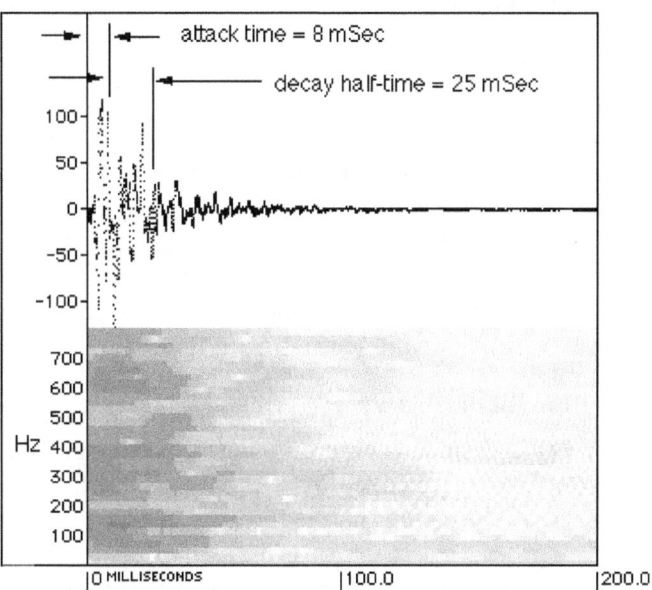

Figure 2.34. Spectrogram of Ka (क) (back position)

CONCLUSION
We have covered quite a bit of ground in psychoacoustics. At this point, we may do some reflection.

"If a tree falls in the forest and no one is around to hear it, does it make a sound?" As a child, I used to laugh at the ridiculousness of such debates. I have stopped laughing. It has become clear that sound is a group of subjective phenomena which exists only in the mind of the listener. Physical vibrations, conversely are quantifiable. There is a loose relationship between the physical vibration and the perceived sound, but only a loose one. Sound and physical vibrations remain totally different entities. Investigating and describing the physical phenomena will never have value unless we keep the relationship between the two fields in mind.

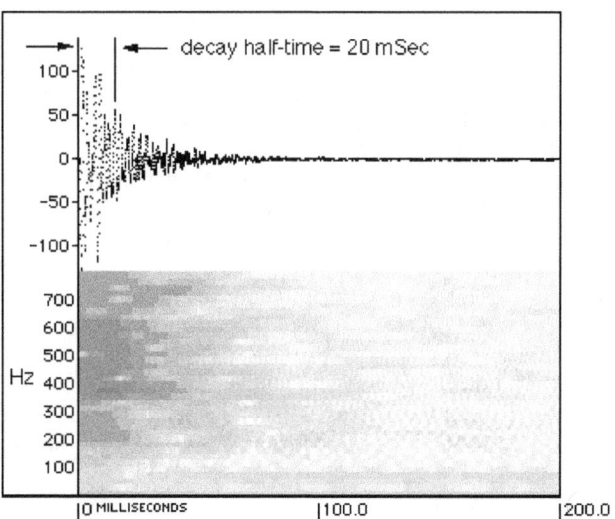

Figure 2.35. Spectrogram of Ka (क) (snap)

This chapter has given us a conceptual model which allows us to deal with timbre. We can view the sound of tabla in terms of a harmonic spectrum. This model works moderately well but is not exactly correct. Do not forget that most drums are so inharmonic that the tabla seems very harmonic in comparison. It is like the dancing bears in the circus. It is not a question that they dance badly; it is impressive that they can dance at all. In the same manner it is not a question that the numbers do not exactly create a clean harmonic spectrum; it is impressive that they can come as close as they do. The close approximation of the spectra of *dayan* to a harmonic spectrum allows it to be tuned for a performance. However, the inharmonic quality shows up in interesting places. For instance, the relatively rare use of the open *Toon* (तूं), is probably due to the fact that this stroke emphasises a harmonic which is about a full step higher than where it should be. Although the harmonic model is not strictly correct, we shall continue using it.

All of the strokes may be differentiated by characteristics that lie within the first three harmonics. *Toon* (तूं) is defined by a prominent fundamental. *Tin* (तिं) is defined by a prominent second harmonic. *Naa* (ना) is characterised by a prominent third harmonic. The other strokes are defined by complex mixtures of the various harmonics.

Another powerful tool we have in describing the timbre is the envelope. Traditional approaches to acoustics tend to downgrade the importance of the envelope as a means of describing timbre. Yet anyone who has been involved in crafting sounds for synthesisers, realises how important the envelope is. It is especially important given the short attack/decay characteristics which characterise the tabla.

We see that there are tremendous variations in the attack and decay characteristics of both drums. Attack times of the *dayan* vary from essentially nonexistent to about 12msec. The attack times for the *bayan* vary from negligible to about 20msec. For the decay times, we are forced to express it as decay half-time. The decay half-time is the length of time that it take the signal to decay to half of its peak value. The decay half-times of the *dayan* may vary from 8msec to over 200msec. For the *bayan* the range is even greater. Unfortunately, the *bayan* can produce highly irregular and unusual envelopes. These unusual forms are a result of the constant interaction of the hands and fingers with the skin of the drums.

WORKS CITED

Banerjee, B.M. & Dipali Nag
1989   "A Comparison of Acoustic Characters of Sounds from Indian Drums", *Journal of the Acoustical Society of India*. Vol. 17, No. 3&4, Pg. 295-298.

Banerjee, B.M.
1989   "Research on Musical Acoustics in Sangeet Research Academy", *Journal of the Acoustical Society of India*. Vol. 17, No. 3&4, Pg. 25-30.

Courtney, David R.
1991   "Tuning the Tabla: A Psychoacoustic Perspective", *Percussive Notes*. Vol 29, No 3, pg 59-61.
1992   "Introduction to Spectrum Analysis", *Experimental Musical Instruments*. Vol VIII, No. 1, pg.18-22.

Egan, J.P. and H.W. Hank
1950   "On the masking pattern of a simple auditory stimulus." *Journal of the Acoustic Society of America*. Vol.22:pp622.

Fletcher, H. and W. A. Munson.
1933   "Loudness, Its Definition, Measurement and Calculation." *Journal of the Acoustic Society of America*. Vol. 5. pp82.

Raman, C.V.
1934   "The Indian Musical Drums", *Proc. Indian Acad. of Science*. Vol 1A, pg. 179-188

Raman, C.V. and S. Kumar
1920 "Musical Drum with Harmonic Overtones", *Nature*. Vol 500, pg. 104.

Roederer, Juan G.
1975 *Introduction to the Physics and Psychophysics of Music*. New York: Springer-Verlag.

Rossing, Thomas D.
1992 "Acoustics of Drums", *Physics Today*. Woodbury, NY: American Institute of Physics. March 1992.

Runstein, Robert E.
1974 *Modern Recording Techniques*. Indianapolis: Howard W. Sams & Co.

Walliser, K.
1969 "Über die Abhängigkeiten der Tonhöhenempfindung von Sinustönen von Schallpegel, von überlagertem drosselnden Störscall und von der Darbietungsdauer." *Acoustica*. Vol 21. pg.211.

CHAPTER 3
TIMEKEEPING

This chapter deals with timekeeping; this is of great practical importance for any performance. One may ask, "What do we mean by timekeeping?" The Oxford Universal English Dictionary gives one of the definitions of timekeeper as "one who beats time in music". (Oxford University Press 1937:vol.9:pp.2194). This definition is correct, but we should elaborate on it.

Timekeeping revolves around a very practical consideration; in order for music to flow, there must be somebody who determines the beat. In contemporary popular music it is the drummer who keeps the beat. Every member of the band consciously or unconsciously follows the rhythmic lead of the drummer. Yet timekeeping is not an inherent function of the drum. Let us take the percussionist in a classical symphony for example. Although he too may be playing a drum, he is not keeping time. The timekeeper in a symphony is always the conductor. Sometimes the timekeeper is not even human; for instance a session musician in a studio may be playing against a click-track or drum machine.

Imagine playing music without a timekeeper. What would a symphony sound like if there was no conductor? The inevitable cacophony defies the imagination. But how does this relate to Indian music?

Indian *tals* can be quite complex, and there are a lot of things happening simultaneously on stage. Add to this the requirement of improvisation, and you have a very challenging situation. It is easy to imagine the performers getting totally lost. Fortunately this is quite rare because there is an elaborate system of timekeeping whereby somebody on stage is always keeping track. Usually, it is a simple process of "trading off", which allows the musicians to keep track of the time.

Not all Indian timekeeping is relevant to stage performances; a lot of it is directed toward the pedagogic process. Many of these are simple vocal techniques or hand gestures; but some are elaborate mechanical and electronic timekeepers. In this chapter we will discuss the various approaches that are used in both performance and pedagogic situations.

USING THE HANDS IN TIMEKEEPING
The use of the hands in timekeeping. is the most ancient and fundamental approach. The word *tal* itself implies the clapping of the hands. In Hindi, the expression that is used for clapping is *tali bhajana*, which literally translates into "to play the hands". The various uses of the hand has a hoary past. It appears that this present practice is derived from the ancient Indian method know as *kriya*. This extensive and complex system of timekeeping using the hands is documented all the way back to the *Natya Shastra* (circa 200BCE). This is explained in greater detail under the discussion of the *Dasa Pran* in Chapter 7.

There are many ways that we can use the hands to keep time. In northern India, there are basically four approaches: The clap/wave, simple clapping, finger counting, and finally snapping the fingers.

<u>Clap/Wave Timekeeping</u> - This approach to timekeeping has been referred to throughout this series. It is inextricably linked to the concept of the *vibhag* or measure. The *vibhag* is actually defined by being either clapped or waved. The clap is shown in Figure 3.1 while the wave is shown in Figure 3.2. For example, *Tintal* would be denoted by: clap, clap, wave, clap.

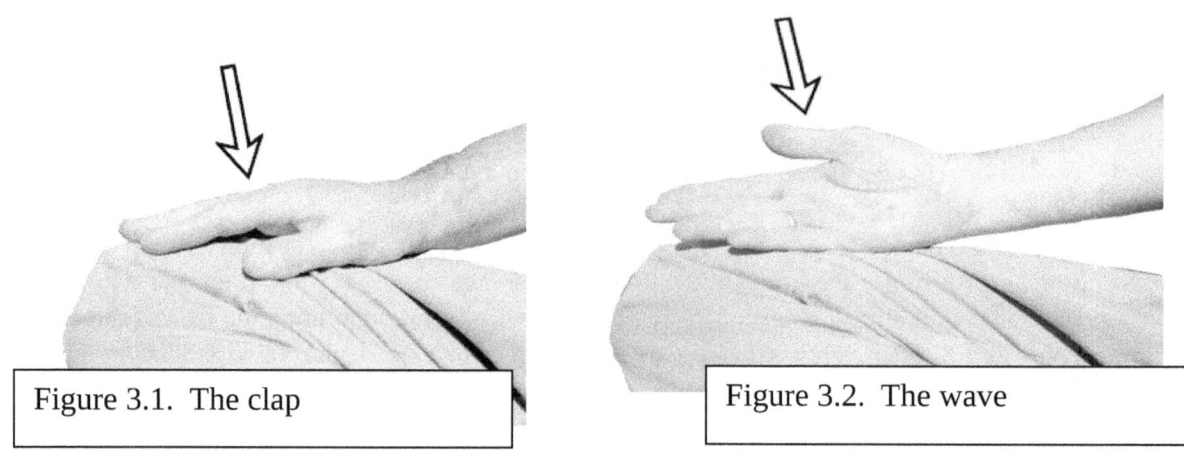

Figure 3.1. The clap   Figure 3.2. The wave

It is sometimes helpful to denote the individual beats. Obviously, we cannot use either a clap or a wave to denote the individual beats, or else there will be confusion; we get around this confusion by using the fingers. Therefore, *Tintal* can be denoted as in Figure 3.3. Notice that in this approach the second *matra* of each *vibhag* is denoted by the little finger; the third *matra* of each *vibhag* is denote by the ring finger; and finally the fourth *matra* is denoted by the middle finger. The particular use of fingers is not fixed and numerous variations may be seen; this is just one example. The clap, wave, finger approach to timekeeping is very common in the south, but it is not so common in the north. Even the *Hindustani* musicians who do use this approach, generally confine it to the slow tempos.

<u>Simple Clapping</u> - There is another common way to use the clapping of hands to keep the time. This is exactly like the Western approach, where the simple beat is kept. This is common with the lighter forms of music. We must remember that not every musician in India is classically trained, therefore folk, *filmi* and other light musicians often do not know the science of music. It would be unreasonable to expect them to denote structures and concepts, such as *vibhag* and *sam,* which are unknown to them.

Ch.3. Timekeeping

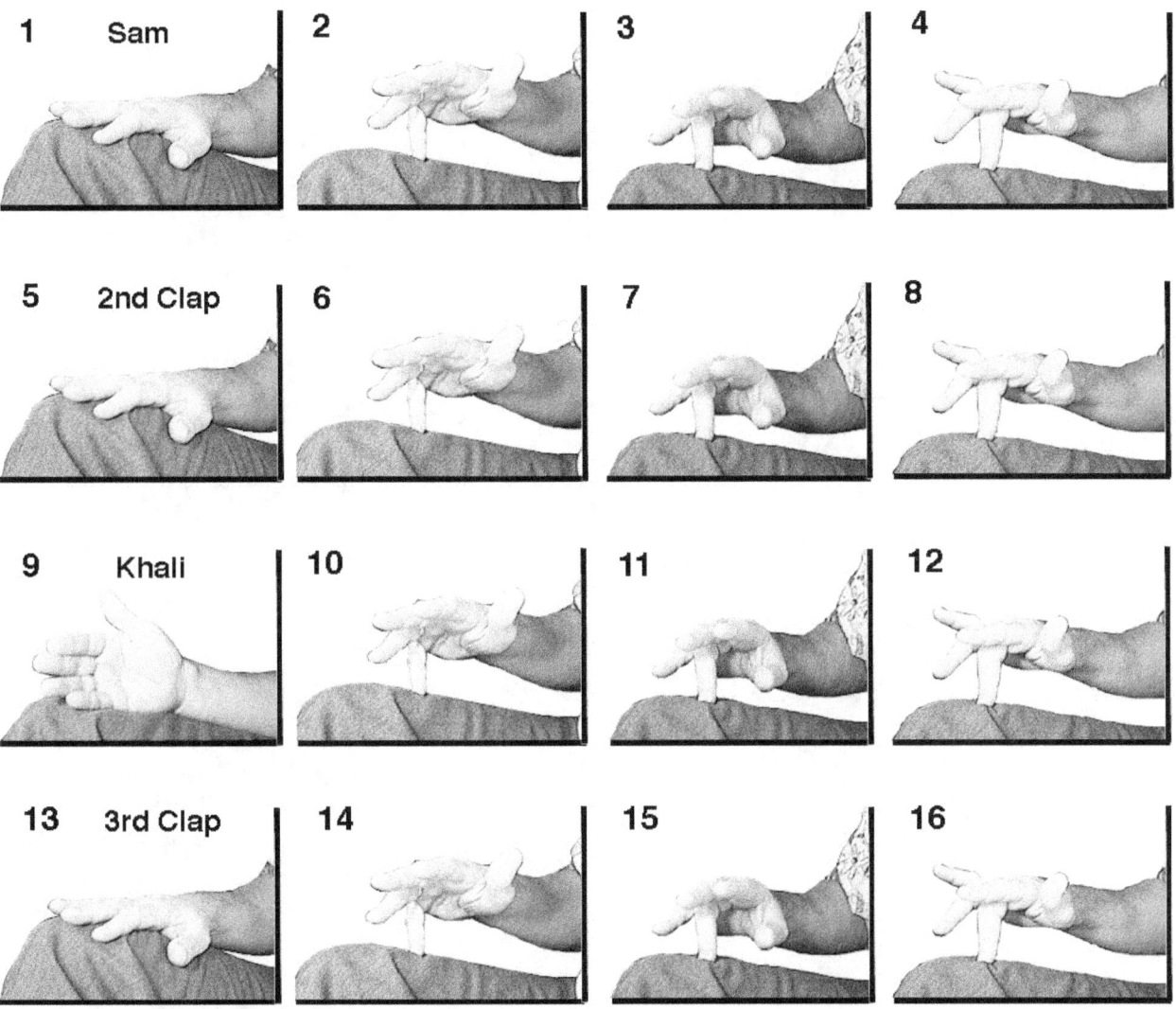

Figure 3.3. Clap, wave, finger counting

<u>Finger Counting</u> - Counting on the fingers is a very common way that north Indian musicians keep track of the *tal*. This approach uses only parts of the fingers to represent the *tal*. There are several variations for this. Some people count the bumps of the fingers while some count the cracks. Figure 3.4 shows *Tintal* as it would be illustrated on the hand by counting the bumps. Each "bump" corresponds to an individual *matra*; each finger corresponds to one *vibhag*; finally the entire hand is equivalent to a single *avartan*. This is a very convenient model. Figure 3.5 shows *Tintal* by counting the cracks. Notice that the tips of the fingers are used for the 4th, 8th, 12th and 16th *matras*. One may count out the beats of a composition by taking the thumb and moving it along the various positions described in Figure 3.6. This convenient model may be applied to virtually any *tal,* and is an extremely useful tool for working out compositions on tabla.

page 37

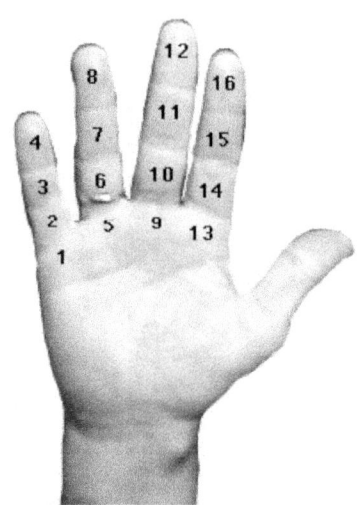

Figure 3.4. Finger counting (bump method)

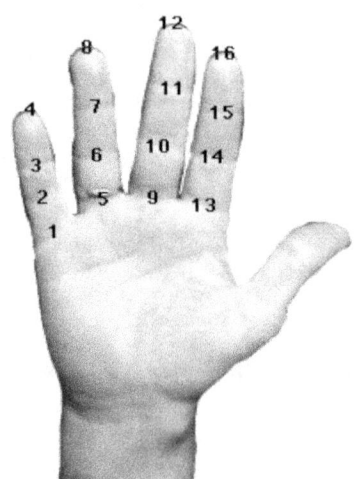

Figure 3.5. Finger counting (crack method)

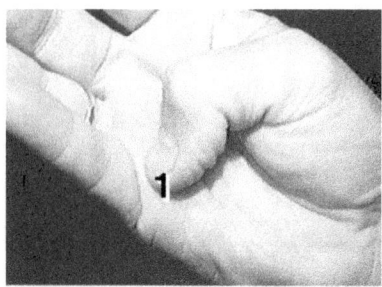

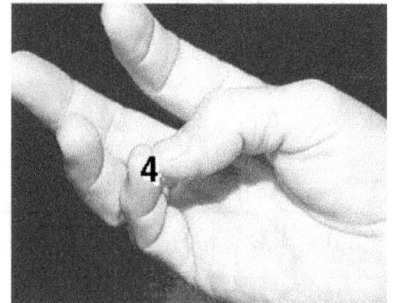

5, 6, 7, 8, 9, 10, 11, 12, 13, 14, 15

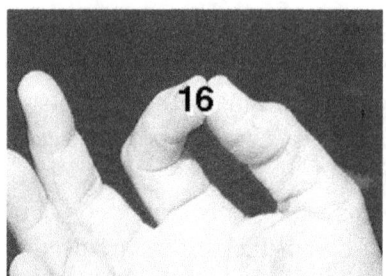

Figure 3.6. Counting the matras

Another source of variation, is the way in which *tals* that do not use *vibhags* of four beats are handled. One approach is to simply start at the first position and progress until the proper number of *matras* have been executed. This approach has been documented elsewhere (Leake 1993:50). Another method is to maintain the *vibhag* structure. Both of these approaches are shown in Figures 3.7 - 3.9.

Snapping the Fingers - There is one more very minor technique for timekeeping with the fingers; this is a simple snapping of the fingers. It has no place within the present classical system: it is used only in the lightest forms. The only reason that we mention it is because one form of snapping is particularly interesting; it uses both hands. This style is largely unknown in the West. Snapping fingers are shown in Figure 3.10.

USING THE VOICE AS TIMEKEEPER

It is no surprise that the voice is also used in timekeeping. The exact processes varies considerably depending upon the circumstances.

For pedagogical purposes, it is common to count out the number of beats. Naturally the tendency is to count in whatever the common language may be. The numbers 1-16 are shown for a number of Indian languages in Table 3.1.

Sometimes the numbers are actually part of the *bol*. There is a compositional form which is much used in *kathak* dance known as *ginti tihai, ginti tukada, or ginti paran*. In this form the dancer makes a large number of revolutions before resolving on the *sam*. Each revolution is denoted with the number, usually in Hindi or Urdu. Therefore the numbers actually become the *bol*. An example of a *ginti tukada* is shown toward the end of Chapter 10 - *Compositional Theory (Cadential Forms)*.

It is very common for *filmi* and light musicians to count off before starting a song. The form of "1, 2, 3, 4 (music)", which is so common in the West is, also to be found in India. This however, is confined to the lighter genre, and is possibly of European origin.

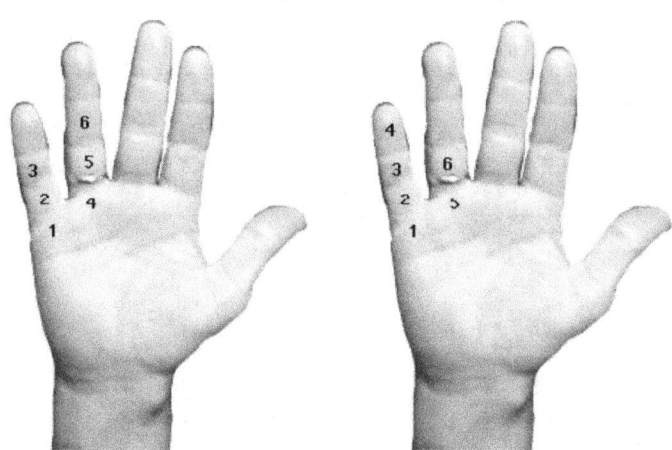

Figure 3.7. Two approaches for dadra

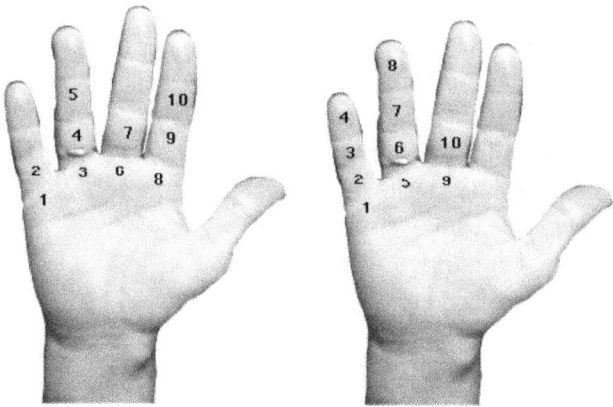

Figure 3.8. Two approaches for jhaptal

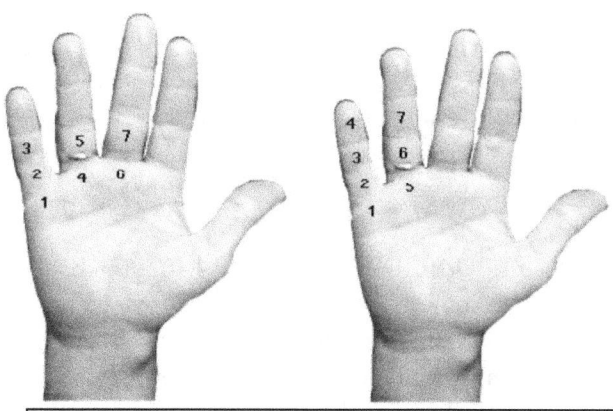

Figure 3.9. Two approaches to rupak tal

Table 3.1 - The numbers between 1-16 in a Variety of Indian languages.

English	Hindi	Oriya	Telugu	Tamil	Marathi	Malayalam	Punjabi	Bengali	Gujarati
one	ek	ek	okati	onrru	ek	onnu	ikk	ek	ek
two	do	dui	remdu	eranndum	don	rantu	do	duee	be
three	teen	tini	mudu	moonrru	teen	munnu	tinn	tin	tra
four	chaar	chaari	naalugu	naanku	chaar	naalu	chaar	chaar	char
five	paanch	paanchi	aidu	iynthu	paanch	anchu	panj	paanch	paanch
six	chhe	chaa	aaru	aarru	sahaa	aaru	chhe	chhay	cha
seven	saat	saat	edu	aezhu	saat	elu	satt	saat	sat
eight	aath	aath	enimidi	addu	aath	ettu	atth	aat	ath
nine	no	naa	tommidi	onpathu	nau	onpatu	naun	nay	nav
ten	das	dash	padi	paththu	dahaa	pattu	dass	dash	das
eleven	giyaarah	egaar	padunokamdu	pathenonrru	akraa	patinonnu	giyaaraan	egaara	agiyar
twelve	baarah	baar	pamdremdu	panneranndu	baaraa	pantrantu	baaraan	baara	bar
thirteen	terah	ter	padamudu	pathemoonrru	teraa	patimunnu	teraan	tera	ter
fourteen	choudha	chaud	padunalugu	pathenaanku	chaudaa	patinaalu	chowdaan	choudda	chaud
fifteen	pandrah	pandar	padunaidu	pathenainthu	pandhraa	patinaanchu	pandaraan	panera	pamdar
sixteen	solah	sol	padunaru	pathenaarru	solaa	patinaaru	solaan	sola	sol

A much more subtle form of timekeeping with the voice is found in every classical vocal performance. There is a type of "trading off" between the vocalist and the tabla player. Most of the time the tabla player is keeping time, while the vocalist is free to improvise. However there are times when the vocalist pulls back and allows the tabla player to improvise. For such cases, the vocalist simply repeats the primary theme, which is known as *sthai* or *asthai*. This may be interpreted by the uninitiated as a mere refrain, but it actually

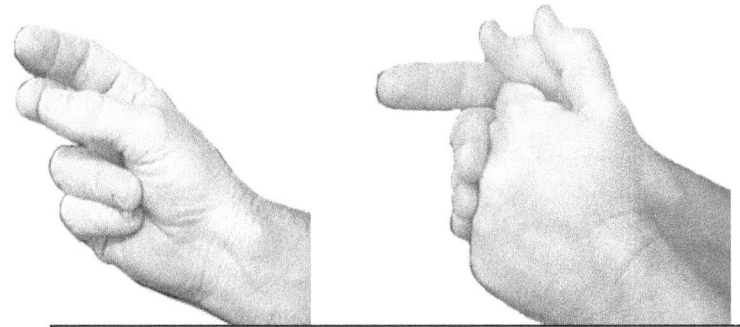

Figure 3.10. Snapping fingers (one hand technique and two hand technique)

represent a shifting of artistic duties within the performance. When the tabla player has finished improvising, he (or she) resumes the duties of timekeeping, and the vocalist is again free to resume their improvisations. Generally, classical vocalists give the tabla player very little opportunity to "show their stuff"; so this trading off is not nearly as common as it is in the instrumental styles.

USING MELODIC INSTRUMENTS IN TIMEKEEPING

It is very common to use melodic instruments as timekeepers. There are two basic approaches to doing this. One way is to do this in the normal process of "trading off"; this was mentioned in the previous section. This trading off is a very important part of a typical classical instrumental performance. Another way is when the melodic instrument never assumes the dominant position. That is to say, the melodic instrument is consistently the timekeeper from beginning to end. This is called *lahara*.

Ch.3. Timekeeping

<u>Lahara</u> - *Lahara* is a simple melody which is repeated indefinitely. It is used in tabla solos as well as in *kathak* recitals. It is interesting that it represents a complete reversal of the responsibilities of the musicians. It is usually the responsibility of the tabla player to keep time while the main instrumentalist (or vocalist) decides the tempo and performs the improvisations. However in this capacity, it becomes the responsibility of the melodic instrument to keep time, while the tabla player determines the tempo and performs improvisations.

Sitar, sarod, flute, harmonium, virtually any melodic instrument may be used; however the preferred instrument has traditionally been the *sarangi,* with harmonium a close second. Vocal is not normally a *lahara* for tabla solos, but may be used in *kathak* recitals.

The simplicity of the *lahara* belies the difficulty of its execution. Few musicians have a sense of rhythm required for its proper performance. This is because the tabla solo involves numerous complex cadences, many of which are located off the beat. This may confuse many musicians. Furthermore, the complex manipulations of tempo (*layakari*) must not be confused with intentional changes in tempo. This makes its performance very challenging.

Although the performance of *lahara* is difficult, their creation is simple. The most common approach is to take any song or *gat* and use only a small portion. The portion is usually the *sthai*; however, on occasion other sections such as the *antara,* may be used. It is usually a single cycle; however, occasionally it is two, three, or even more cycles in duration; this however is generally found only in the very short *tals* (e.g., *Dadra, Rupak)*. There are many *laharas* in use. A large number are shown in Appendix-1 of this book.

Here is one very common *lahara* in *Tintal*:

Chandrakauns (Shepherd 1976:122)

MISCELLANEOUS NON-MELODIC INSTRUMENTS IN TIMEKEEPING
Drums such as tabla and *dholak* are an obvious choice for timekeeping. Yet we must not forget that there are other, less obvious nonmelodic instruments in use.

<u>Cymbals</u> - The use of cymbals is moderately common today; yet it appears to be one of the most ancient timekeeping instruments in India (Figure 3.11). Although they are conspicuously absent in north Indian classical performances, this class makes up a large percentage of the instruments depicted on the walls of ancient temples. The cymbal appears to be nothing more than a metallic model of the hand. They are struck in the same way that hands are clapped. Cymbals may be called many things; *thalam* and *manjira* are two common terms. Cymbals may not be used much in classical music but they are still very popular with Hindu devotional music. These musical forms may be called *dhun* or *bhajan,* and are a part of the worship in any Hindu temple. The most common pattern for playing the cymbals is: strike, rest, strike, strike.

Kartal, Chimptas, Ghungharu - These instruments have been described in the first volume. They are found mainly in the lighter *genres*, such as folk music and *bhajan*. The *ghungharu* are noteworthy in that they are often played with the dancer's feet.

Ektar, Dotar, etc. - The *ektar* and *dotar* are seldom more than a gourd which has been penetrated with a piece of bamboo. One or two strings are then stretched over them to make a simple lute. (The *ektar* is defined by one string and the *dotar* is defined by two strings.) Sometimes the bridge rests over some taught skin covering an opening in the gourd. These instruments are interesting because they perform two functions. They provide a tonic base for the music, but they also are a means of timekeeping.

It is impractical to name all of the instruments which perform this same function. Generally, these instruments are limited to folk music, for which every different region has its own variety.

Figure 3.11. Cymbals as timekeepers

USING DRUMS AS TIMEKEEPERS
Drums are the most obvious choice for timekeeping. But the approaches to timekeeping may vary considerably from drum to drum.

Folk drums such as *dholak, nal, daf,* etc. are very common timekeepers. Their use is simple because folk rhythms do not have complicated *vibhag* structures. One simply establishes a "groove" and holds it. These grooves are usually in *Kaherava* or *Dadra*.

The tabla too, is primarily a timekeeper. In the lighter styles of music the use of tabla is very similar to that of *dhol* or any similar folk drum. However, in the classical styles there are complex *vibhag* structures which must be delineated. Therefore, unlike the folk patterns where a simple groove is sufficient, classical tabla players are constantly having to feed certain musical cues to the main performers. This point is vital for any student to keep in mind!

One way to cue the main artist is by the strokes that are played. Not all strokes have the same value in timekeeping. The newcomer to tabla hears a bewildering assortment of strokes in the typical *theka*, yet most of theses strokes are mere ornamentation. The majority of the timekeeping cues are stored in only a few strokes. These are *Naa* (ना), *Taa* (ता), *Tin* (तिं), *Ga* (ग), *Dhaa* (धा) and *Dhin* (धिं). Most of the common *thekas* can be played using only these strokes. Therefore, when one is assuming the duties of timekeeping, one must play these strokes very clearly. This is not to imply that liberties can never be taken, for they can. It is up to the performer to decide when elaborate improvisations may be made, and when one must retrench to basic *theka*. This point is taken up in Chapter 11.

Another set of cues is handled by the left hand. The main artist is going to spend a considerable amount of time listening for the presence or absence of open left handed stroke (e.g., *Ge* गे, *Ghe* घे, *Dhaa* धा, *Dhin* धिं, etc.). If one is improvising, one should avoid making substitutions that might compromise the overall character.

These previous points are mere recommendations. As an accompanist one must be sensitive to the main performer to know when and how liberties may be taken.

Not all percussionists are timekeepers. *Mridangam* players in south India do not have this duty. There is always somebody "keeping *tal*", so the *mridangam* player can simply play along without having to be bothered with this chore. Traditionally, *pakhawaj* players were in a similar situation.

MECHANICAL & ELECTRONIC AIDS TO TIMEKEEPING
Mechanical and electronic timekeepers may be used to keep time while one is practicing. Today, they tend to be apps that one downloads to one's smartphone or computer. Historically they were mechanical devices. In recent history they were stand-alone electronic devices that produced either a melodic *lahara* or a *theka*. Even today such devices are available.

Theses aids have strong points and weak points. One very great advantage is that the rhythm is absolutely even. This is a convenient benchmark against which the student can gauge their progress. However, these mechanical devices have one great disadvantage; the rhythm is absolutely even.

It may seem paradoxical that an even rhythm can be both an advantage and disadvantage. Although the advantages of an even rhythm are self-evident, the disadvantages are not so obvious. The disadvantages stem from the fact that Indian performances are never in one even rhythm. There are numerous subtle changes in the tempo. These subtle changes in timing must be felt. But it is difficult for students to learn to feel them if they are constantly bombarded with a mechanically perfect beat. (The nature of these rhythmic variations will be discussed in Chapter 4 and Chapter 6.)

HISTORY OF AUTOMATED LAHARA/THEKA GENERATION
The present smartphone/app approach is convenient; but obviously things were not always like this. It is useful to look at their history so that we can see how we came to our present situation.

<u>Metronome</u> – The metronome is undoubtedly the oldest form of mechanical timekeeper (Figure 3.12). It is said that the first metronome was invented in the 9th century by Abu al-Qasim Abbas ibn Firnas ibn Wirdas al-Takurini, more simply known as Abbas ibn Firnas. However, the first metronome in the modern sense was invented by Johann Mälzel, and patented in 1815.

For many decades this was the only aid that was available to the music student in India. It was portable and could keep track of a variety of rhythms. The metronome had one limitation, it merely kept track of the rhythm. This was addressed in the late 1960s and early 1970s by the cassette tape.

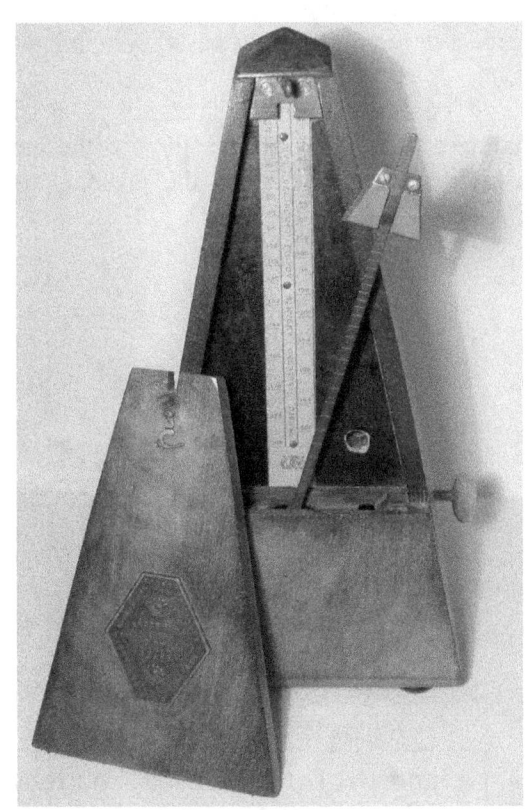

Figure 3.12. Metronome
Courtesy of Wikimedia Commons

Cassettes - A very old and common form of automatic *lahara* and *theka* generation was simply a prerecorded cassette. This was a cheap and accessible technology that required nothing more than an inexpensive cassette recorder and a friend who was willing to sit down and play.

Although the cassette was an accessible technology, it was inflexible.

The disadvantage of this approach may easily be demonstrated with a little arithmetic. Let us say that there are five tempos (i.e, *ati drut, drut, madhya, vilambit,* and *ati vilambit;*) 12 keys (C, C#, D, D#, E, F, F#, G, G#, A, A#, B;) and six common *tal (Tintal, Rupak, Dadra, Ektal, Jhaptal,* and *Kaherava)*. To be practical, the *lahara* should be at least one side of the cassette. Therefore, 12 x 6 x 6 = 432 sides or 216 cassettes would have been required! This is clearly impractical. It was this problem which forced people to explore other methods.

Mitra's System - The first electronic approach to *lahara* generation is traceable to the mid 1970s. It was a hybrid approach in that it used an ingenious mixing of analogue and digital components. It was limited to a single *lahara* in *Tintal*. But it did allow for a considerable variation as to key and tempo. A detailed discussion is to be found in Appendix 3.

Courtney System - The first major effort at a software package for *lahara* generation was in the mid 1980s. This was the "Courtney System" based upon the old C=64 computer. (Indian Express 1987). This was the first all digital approach to *lahara* generation and is the forerunner of all modern systems (Figure 3.13).

Later Computer Systems and the Swar Shala - The C=64 based Courtney System was doomed to obsolescence along with the C=64. But the concept of using computers continued, A decade after the demise of the C=64, a PC based system known as the Swar Shala was introduced.

Swar Shala was, and still is, a software package that did not require anything other than a standard PC. The software allowed the input and performance of both *laharas* as well as *thekas*. This software has continued to the present, and is now in its third decade. A screen shot is shown in Figure 3.14.

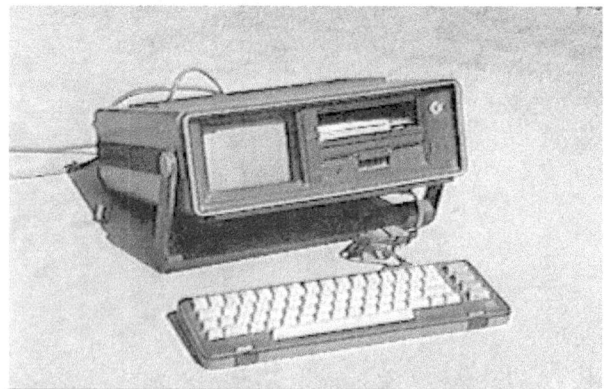

Figure 3.13. C=64 based Courtney system on SX64 (circa 1986)

Stand-Alone Lahara Petis - The turn of the 21st century saw a number of dedicated hardware devices come onto the market to address the needs of students. In the area of automatic *lahara* generation, the *Sunadamala* is particularly noteworthy (Figure 3.15). This dominated the field of *lahara* generation until the last few years when it was displaced by smartphone apps. It was manufactured by Sunaada Associates. They contained well over a hundred different *laharas* in all of the common *tals*. At the turn of the 21st century, their prices were around Rs2500 ($75). By Indian standards this was considered quite expensive, but it was still within the reach of most middle class Indians.

Automatic Theka Generation - Automated *theka* generation is the process of timekeeping whereby a machine creates the *theka* (characteristic *bol* patterns of the various *tals*). This is very popular in pedagogy because it allows a vocalist, instrumentalist, or dancer to practice without having to bear the expense and inconvenience of having a real person. There were a number of ways that this was done.

In the latter portion of the 20th century, *theka* generation had challenges that *lahara* generation did not have. Where any musically well defined pitch was sufficient to produce a *lahara*, the *thekas* required a level of control over the timber that was not within the reach of the equipment at the time. As previously mentioned, cassettes tended to be used because their sound was much more natural than other systems on the market. Sampling as a means of *theka* generation required much more sophisticated hardware than was commonly available.

Taalmala - The *Taalmala* was the preferred form of automatic *theka* generation (Figure 3.16) for many years. This device was manufactured by Radel Systems of Bangalore. It contained all of the popular *thekas*. There were several models with varying prices, but in 2000CE, their price was about Rs3500. This device was very interactive with an intuitive user interface (Figure 3.17). The *tals* were entered with a well-marked keypad. Volume, tempo, and the balance between the *bayan* and *dayan*, were all entered with convenient controls.

The *taalmala* had good points and bad points. One obvious advantage was convenience. Unfortunately the sound quality was terrible. The poor sound quality was a consequence of the additive/subtractive approach used to synthesise the tabla sounds.

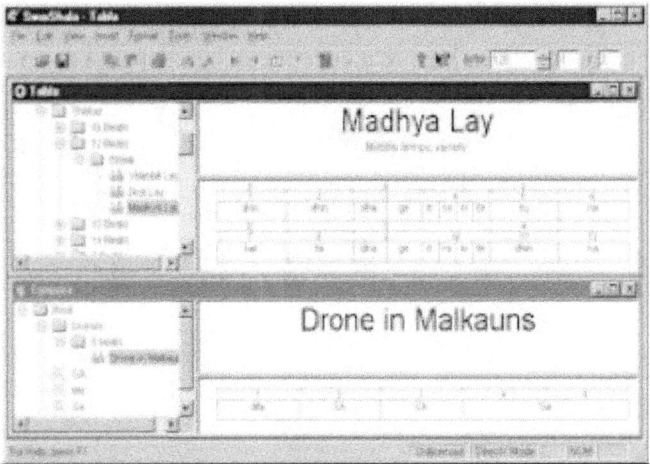

Figure 3.14. Screen shot of Swar Shala (circa 2000)

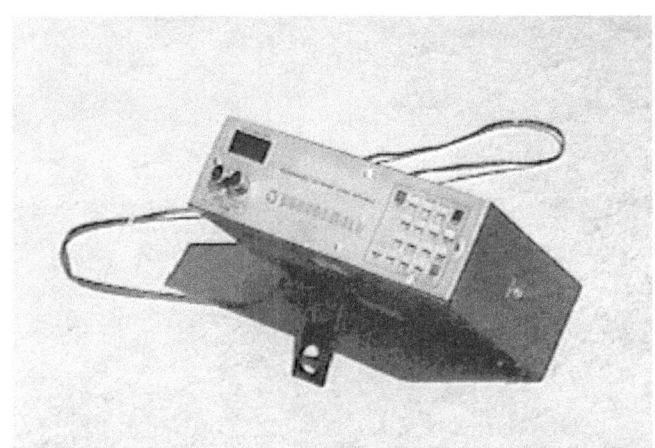

Figure 3.15. Sunaadmala (lahara machine)

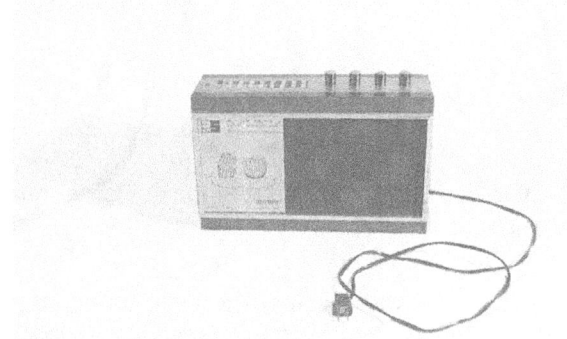

Figure 3.16. Taalmala

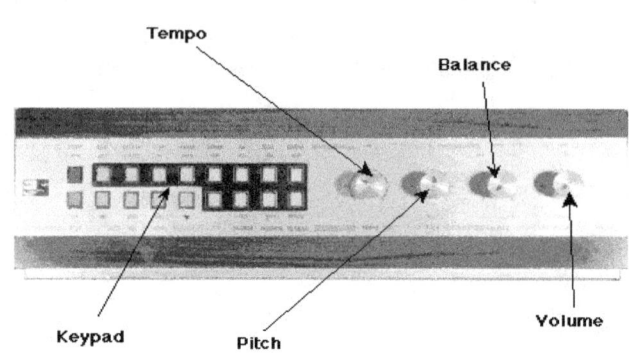

Figure 3.17. Taalmala's user interface

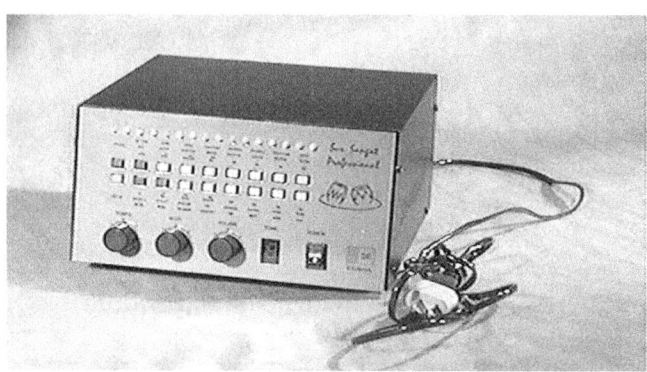

Figure 3.18. Sur Sangat Pro.

Sur Sangat Professional - Another device was introduced which posed stiff competition for the *Taalmala;* this device was called "Sur Sangat Professional" (Figure 3.18). It was manufactured by a small company called Shivmaal, which was located in Ahmedabad, Gujarat. Although it was extremely costly for the average Indian (approximately Rs6500 or US $200), it had a very realistic sound.

Unlike the *Taalmala*, the *Sur Sangat* was based upon the manipulation of digitised samples, rather than synthesised sounds. This yielded a high quality sound that the *Taalmala* was not capable of.

MODERN APPROACHES

Today, sophisticated digital technology is at hand for everyone. Smartphones are everywhere; computers are everywhere, even the old stand-alone hardware is more accessible. Consequently, there are a variety of approaches to accommodate every preference. Apps and software perform the function of metronomes, *lahara*, and *theka* generation with an economy, accuracy, and capability that were unimaginable a generation ago. A complete survey of everything that is available is impractical. But we will make some general observations. Please look into Appendix 7 of Volume 1, *Fundamentals of Tabla* for a list of smartphone apps.

There are still many stand-alone devices on the market, but let us confine our discussion to software for a moment.

Swar Systems - Swar systems is a Swiss based company that produces a variety of software products for the student or producer of Indian music. These include VST plugins for existing Digital Audio Workstations (DAW), stand-alone DAWs, and smartphone applications. They have tools which offer both *laharas* and *thekas* for the student, as well as systems which allow you to compose your own. A screen shot of one of their products, iShala, is shown in Figure 3.19.

Prasad Upasani - Prasad Upasani is another producer of a line of timekeeping apps for the iOS, the most popular being iLehra and iTabla Pro. These perform the function of *lahara* and *theka* respectively.

Stand-Alone Systems - The smartphone app may be the most popular approach for music students today, but "old-school" stand-alone hardware is still available, and is of a high quality that was unapproachable years ago. The Sunadamala Plus, Sangat, Swarangini, Nagma (Figure 3.20), and the Taal Tarang are just a few examples.

The topic of *lahara/theka* generation is simply too vast to do justice here. A generation ago the options that were available could be counted on one's fingers. Today there are so many apps and hardware options that it is pointless to go into any real depth. Furthermore, the flux of available software and hardware is so rapid that it makes no sense to attempt it in something static such as a book. Interested readers are urged to check the internet for availability, prices, etc.

CONCLUSION

This chapter dealt at great length with the topic of timekeeping as it pertains to Indian music. In any practice or performance situation it is always helpful to have someone or something to keep time. This is especially important on the stage. We have seen that the voice, drums, virtually any instrument, and even a surprising array of electronic and mechanical devices can be used.

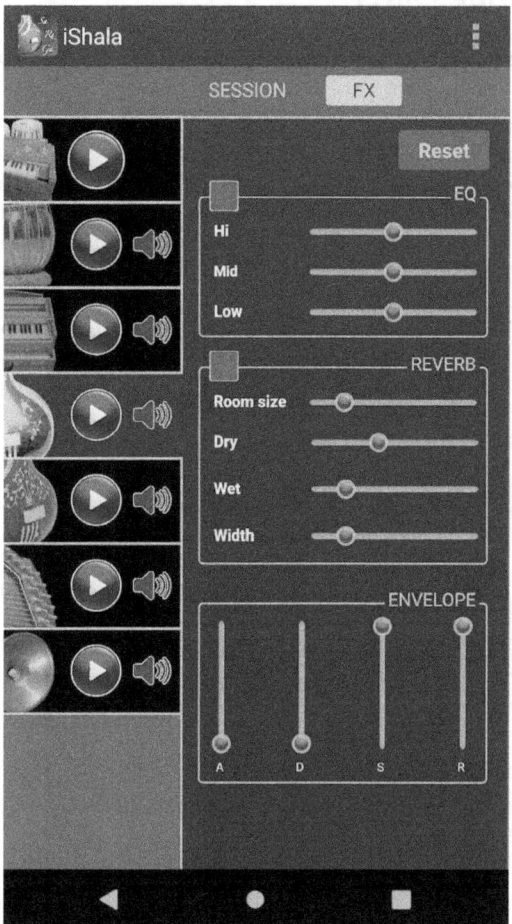

Figure 3.19. iShala – smartphone app

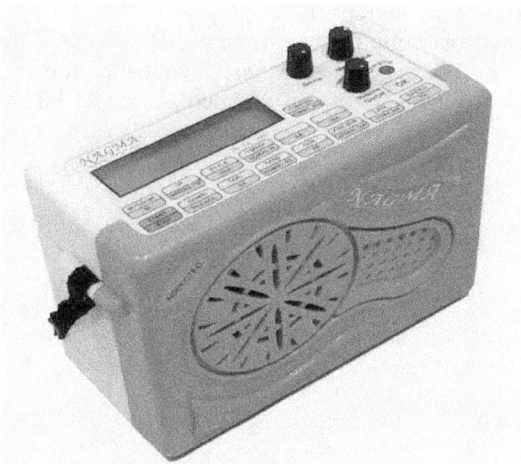

Figure 3.20. Nagma

WORKS CITED

Amma, C.L.Meenakshi
1993   *Learn Malayalam in 30 Days*. Madras:Balaji Publications

Ganathe, N.S.R.
undated *Learn Urdu in 30 Days*. Madras:Balaji Publications.
1990   *Learn Punjabi in 30 Days*. Madras:Balaji Publications.
1991   *Learn Bengali in 30 Days*. Madras:Balaji Publications.
1992   *Learn Oriya in 30 Days*. Madras:Balaji Publications.

Gottlieb, R. S.
1977a   *The Major Traditions of North Indian Tabla Drumming*. Munchen, Germany: Musikverlag Emil Katzbichler.
1977b   *The Major Traditions of North Indian Tabla Drumming. Transcriptions* :Munchen, Germany: Musikverlag Emil Katzbichler.

Indian Express
1987   "Raga Recording on Computer", *Indian Express*. India November 18, 1987.

Jegtheesh, N.
1993   *Learn Tamil in 30 Days*. Madras: Balaji Publications.

Leake, Jerry
1993   *Indian Influence (Tabla Perspective), Series A.I.M. Percussion Text* (Second Edition). Boston: Rhombus Publishing.

Oxford University Press
1937   *Oxford Universal English Dictionary on Historical Principals*, Vol 9. Oxford University Press / Doubleday, Doran and Co.

Sanjay
1989   *Learn Marathi in 30 Days*. Madras: Balaji Publications.

Shepherd, Frances Ann
1976   *Tabla and the Benares Gharana*. Doctoral Dissertation, Wesleyan University. (Available through University Microfilms International. Ann Arbor Michigan.)

Srinivasachari, K.
1993   *Learn Telugu in 30 Days*. Madras:Balaji Publications.

Unknown photographer
undated photograph of metronome, CC BY-SA 3.0 <https://creativecommons.org/licenses/by-sa/3.0>, via Wikimedia Commons, downloaded July 4, 2022 from
https://commons.wikimedia.org/wiki/File:Metronome_M%C3%A4lzel_1.jpg

CHAPTER 4
LAY (TEMPO)

This chapter deals with the concept of tempo. Tempo is simply the frequency or rate in which the beats (*matra*) come. The Hindi term for tempo is *lay* (लय) and is derived from the Sanskrit term *laya* (लय). It is a very simple concept, but its application to the tabla is sometimes involved.

GENERAL QUALITIES OF LAY

As we progress through this chapter, it is helpful to remember the relationship between the interval and the tempo. An interval is the period of time between two events; specifically it is how much time there is between two beats. If we are performing very fast, the interval will be very short. Conversely, if the tempo is very slow, then the interval will be very long. This is intuitively obvious. What may not be so obvious is the clean mathematical relationship that exists. This relationship may be expressed as:

$$\text{tempo (in beats per minute)} = \frac{1}{\text{Interval (expressed in minutes)}}$$

There has to be some practical limit to usable tempos. I am reminded of a line in a song by the "Incredible String Band" where the singer refers to trees as those "who dance to slower time". This is a very good reference to the difference between the general concept of tempo and the practical music application. For instance, one beat every ten minutes would be so slow as to be musically useless. At the other end of the spectrum, we find that 100 beats-per-second would be so fast that it would be perceived as a tone, and not as a rhythm.

When we extend this concept, we encounter some interesting things. We see similar relationships between musical tempo, musical harmony, progression of the years and aeons, nuclear magnetic resonance, and a host of other phenomena. These relationships were certainly known to the ancients. Let us take the metaphor of the dancing Shiva whose rhythmic movements dictate the birth and death of the entire universe. Although the cosmic nature of rhythm is certainly fascinating and well worth our consideration, it is beyond the scope of this book to delve into abstract points of Hindu philosophy. We must stick with mundane musical concerns.

A breakdown of useful tempos and their nomenclature is shown in Table 4.1. This table is an idealised breakdown of *lay*, because the real world is considerably more complex. For example the designations of *ati drut, ati vilambit*, etc. are seldom heard among practising musicians. This tends to stretch the previous table so that there is no longer a 2-1 relationship between the various designations. To make matters even more complex, it has been observed that vocalists use a slower definition of time than do instrumentalists (Gottlieb 1977a:41). Furthermore, the rhythmic concepts of the light and film musicians run at a higher tempo but show a peculiar compression of scale. A table which is more consistent with the real world is shown in Table 4.2

Table 4.1 - Approximate Tempos for Lay

Tempo = Beats-per-min.

ati-ati-drut	640
ati-drut	320
drut	160
madhya	80
vilambit	40
ati-vilambit	20
ati-ati-vilambit	10

Table 4.2 - Approximate Tempos for Different Musical Styles

	Kheyal	Classical Instrumentalists	Light / Filmi singers
Vilambit	20 beats per min	50 beats per min.	100 beats per min.
Madhya	90 beats per min	125 beats per min.	150 beats per min.
Drut	200 beats per min	>300 beats per min.	250 beats per min.

PROGRESSION OF LAY IN THE PERFORMANCE

The *lay* or tempo, may change throughout the performance. These changes in tempo are inextricably linked to the various musical styles. In general we can say that only very short pieces will maintain a fairly steady pace. Most styles will start at one tempo, and then increase in speed. Since this is dependent on the style, we should look at this in greater detail.

INSTRUMENTAL FORMS

The progression of tempo for a typical classical instrumental performance is shown in Figure 4.1. This particular example is *Rag Sree* (Imrat Hussain Khan, 1974). This example flows in a manner very typical of other *sitar, santur, sarod* instrumental performances. One of the first things to notice is that there is a progression from slow to fast. For the typical Indian this progression seems like such a natural flow that it hardly seems mentioning. Yet from a global standpoint, a progression in tempo is not universal.

Let us look at exactly how the tempo progresses. Notice the first section; this is called *alap* and it has no tempo at all. The *alap* is an important opening for any classical performance. This rhythmless elaboration allows the full character of the *rag* to be expressed. The *alap* is then followed with a slow *gat*. This slow *gat* is often called *Masitkhani gat* and is so named after a famous musician, *Masit Khan*. Notice that the slow *gat* is not performed entirely in one tempo, but shows a steady progression. This particular example shows a progression from about 60 bpm to nearly 150 bpm.

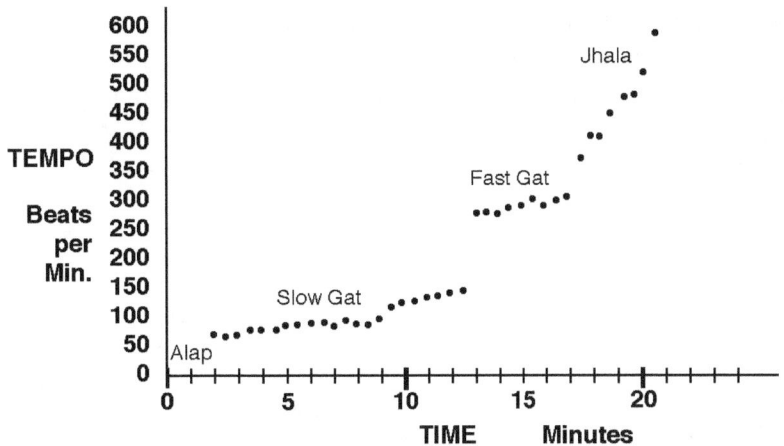

Figure 4.1. Progression of lay in an instrumental piece.

We then shift to the fast *gat*, or *drut gat*. Notice that there is an abrupt discontinuity as slow *gat* changes to fast. My students often ask how one knows when the shift will come. One simply has to listen, and one's own experience will tell you when the change is coming. The fast *gat* also shows the distinctive steady increase in tempo.

At some point the fast *gat* is abandoned, and the piece shifts to a purely instrumental style called *jhala*. *Jhala* is an improvised section that is based upon the alternation between the melody string and the drone strings. It is very fast and lends itself to intricate rhythmic patterns. Notice too, that in this piece the *jhala* steadily increases to about twice the tempo from which it started.

Alternate Ending - We should point out that there are exceptional instances where the tempo actually slows down at the end. There are recordings of the late Nikhil Banerjee that display this form. However, I must reiterate that this is most unusual and is very uncharacteristic of the modern Indian instrumental forms.

Continuous Tempo - Occasionally one finds instrumental pieces where the tempo is fairly constant. This is most often found in short light pieces such as *dhun*.[1]

VOCAL STYLES

Vocal styles give many more approaches to tempo than the instrumental styles. One finds extreme variations between the slow and fast pieces. Additionally, there are many more ways that the tempo may progress.

---

[1] The word "*dhun*" does not have a consistent meaning. To the instrumentalist it means a "song" which is played as an instrumental piece. The song is often known to the audience. However, to the vocalist it is a simple call-and-response religious chant. These two totally different meanings should not create any confusion.

Continuous Tempo - As in the instrumental counterparts, it is rare to maintain the same rhythm throughout a piece. The use of the continuous tempo is restricted to the lighter forms. Undoubtedly, the most common usage for the tabla in light songs is the film song. It is not unusual to find film songs which are no longer than about 3 minutes. With such a short pieces it is not practical to introduce major changes in tempo.

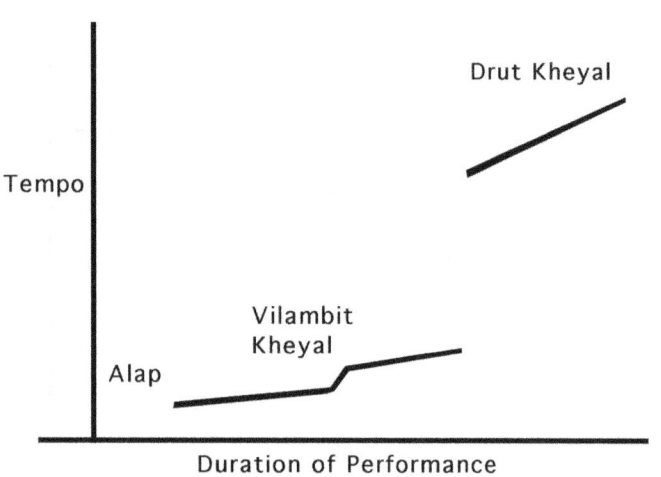

Figure 4.2. Progression of lay (tempo) in kheyal

Increasing Tempo - As in the instrumental forms, the most common approach is to start at a slow tempo, and gradually increase the tempo. This is found in classical, *bhajan*, and other light or semiclassical forms. One of the most interesting examples is seen in the *kheyal* (Figure 4.2). One will note certain similarities between the *kheyal* and the instrumental *gats*. There are two distinct movements, a very slow section and a fast section. The initial slow movement is called the *bada kheyal* or the *vilambit kheyal*. At some point, it shifts to the second movement; this movement may be called the *chotta kheyal* or the *drut kheyal*. This strong discontinuity between the two forms is very similar to the transition between the slow and fast *gats* in the instrumental styles.

The similarity between the vocal and instrumental forms is no accident. The instrumental styles in India have always followed the vocal forms. The only purely instrumental style is the *jhala,* and that too may be argued to be the equivalent of the *tarana*.[2]

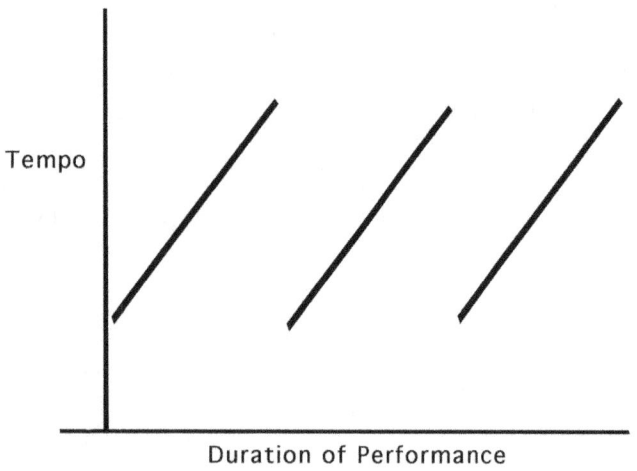

Figure 4.3. Progression of lay (tempo) in the vocal dhun

The "Sawtooth" Progression - This is a manner of progression of the tempo that has no parallel in the instrumental forms. In this form the tempo starts off in a slow pattern and gradually begins to increase in tempo. At some point when it is at a relatively high tempo, it suddenly drops down to a lower value. Thereupon, the entire process repeats itself for an indefinite number of times (Figure 4.3).

---

[2] It has also been suggested that the *tarana* could actually be a vocal imitation of the *jhala* instrumental style.

Ch. 4. Lay (Tempo)

This sawtooth pattern may take two forms. One form is exhibited in the performance of a vocal *dhun* in the Hindu temples; and the other form is found in music from Afghanistan.

The *dhun* form is the most common example of the sawtooth progression in India. The vocal *dhun* is a type of call-and-response singing that is found in the temples. Although it is extremely common in temples, it is extremely rare in recordings. In this style, one starts off in a modest tempo; then as the mood strikes, the tempo is gradually increased. The tempo continues increasing until a feeling of religious frenzy grips the participants (*josh*). When the speed is so high that the structure of the call/response is on the verge of breaking down, the tempo is suddenly dropped. Typically the drop is an even half or one-quarter of the fast speed. Having this relationship produces fewer problems in making the transition with participants of mixed musical abilities. The speed then gradually increases so that the process may be continued through an indefinite number cycles.

Another fascinating form of sawtooth progression is found in Afghanistan[3]. This is only vaguely reminiscent of the Indian *dhun*. One starts off with the theme in a modest tempo. One then moves into the various stanzas at approximately the same speed. One then returns to the theme and begins to speed up. Then the theme is replaced with a musical interlude and the increase in speed progress to a remarkable rate. One then concludes with a *tihai*-like cadence and suddenly returns to the original slow tempo. This process continues for as many times as there are poetic stanzas. It is very beautiful, but very rare in Indian musical forms.

DANCE STYLES

There are numerous styles of dance in India, but the tabla is found only in *kathak*. It is sufficient to note that there are no new twists on the progression of tempo. Whatever we discussed in our vocal and instrumental forms also holds true with the *kathak*. Therefore, further elaboration is unnecessary.

SUMMARY OF LAY

We have discussed the overall patterns in which the tempo progresses in a performance. We have seen that the general form is to start at a slow tempo, and increase to a faster speed. One of the most notable observations is that decreasing the tempo as the performance progresses is almost nonexistent. These overall changes of tempo must be intuitively felt so that the performance can go on in a comfortable manner consistent with the style of Indian music.

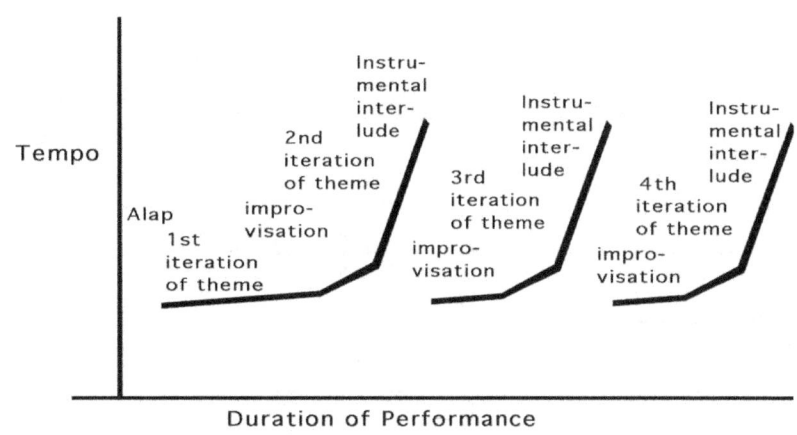

Figure 4.4. Progression of lay (tempo) in Afghan song.

---

[3] Now many of you may be questioning why we deal with Afghan music here. I must remind you that this is first and foremost a book on tabla, and only secondly a book on Indian music. The tabla is commonly used in traditional Afghan music. Therefore we must at least touch upon this usage.

RUBATO

The *rubato* is small change in tempo which is effected for a very short period of time. Typically, it is an increase in tempo for one or more beats, followed by a decrease in tempo for one or more beats. These are very much a part of Indian music. The *rubato* is easily heard and easily quantified with modern computers; however it is very difficult for some musicians to accept. It is generally an unconscious part of a performance and not taught as part of the traditional *taleem*, or body of pedagogic material. Nevertheless it is absolutely imperative for the student to grasp these concepts or the music will sound flat, clunky, and lacking in fluidity. Since many of the readers of this book reside outside of India, we cannot expect everyone to grasp these points intuitively; therefore, we should discuss them in very unambiguous terms.

One of the most distinctive *rubatos* occurs as a part of the cadence. When one is approaching the *sam* (the first beat of the cycle) in this manner, there is a characteristic increase in tempo. When the *sam* is hit, it is elongated (retard). This produces a characteristic tension and relaxation.

It is interesting to note that this type of *rubato* is not acknowledged in traditional Indian pedagogy or theory. However it is so ubiquitous, that its absence is often times considered the mark of an amateur and produces a somewhat "clunky" feel.

There is another type of *rubato* which is found in the folk styles of *Kaherava* or *Dadra*; specifically *Kaherava*. This type is restricted to only single beats. Most often it shows itself in the form of a characteristic, "swing". Again, this type of *rubato* should be felt in order to be executed correctly.

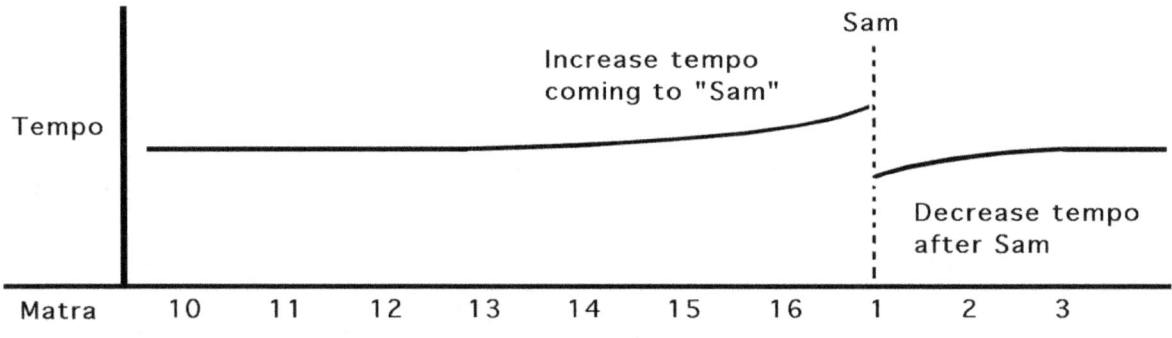

Figure 4.5. Tempo change around sam

CONCLUSION

We have covered a lot of material concerning the *lay*, or tempo of Indian music. The key point that should be grasped is that there is a fluidity that must be felt. The concept of "metronome time" is totally counter to north Indian performance practice.

Ch. 4. Lay (Tempo)

WORKS CITED

Apte, Vasudeo Govind
1987 *The Concise Sanskrit English Dictionary*. Delhi: Motilal Banarsidas.

Gottlieb, R. S.
1977a *The Major Traditions of North Indian Tabla Drumming*. Munchen, Germany: Musikverlag Emil Katzbichler.
1977b *The Major Traditions of North Indian Tabla Drumming. Transcriptions* :Munchen, Germany: Musikverlag Emil Katzbichler.

Kapoor, R.K.
no date *Kamal's Advanced Illustrated Oxford Dictionary of Hindi- English*. Delhi, India: Verma Book Depot.

Khan, Imrat Hussain
1974 *Surbahar / Sitar- Raga Shree*. Dum Dum, India: Odeon/Gramophone Company of India, Ltd.

Leake, Jerry
1993 *Indian Influence (Tabla Perspective), Series A.I.M. Percussion Text* (Second Edition). Boston: Rhombus Publishing.

CHAPTER 5
DYNAMICS

This chapter deals with the topic of dynamics. *The Harvard Concise Dictionary of Music* (Randel 1978) defines dynamics as "that aspect of music relating to degrees of loudness". It stands to reason that any music must have a loudness, otherwise it will not be able to be heard. However, the loudness or dynamics of the tabla, is one of the defining aspects of an individual's style, one which separates a master from a beginner.

We will see in this section that dynamics influences the performance in a number of ways. It presents an overall emotional statement. It affects the timbre of the strokes. It aids in coordinating the tabla and the main musician (Clayton, et al. 2019). Furthermore, it may be used to define the basic rhythmic feel.

EMOTIONAL EFFECT OF OVERALL DYNAMICS

Changes in dynamics are important for creating a sense of emotion. Just as a public speaker creates a sense of movement and emotion by alternately raising and lowering their voice; so too a musician is able to control the emotional flow by appropriate changes in dynamics (Singh 2022). It has received considerable attention in its numerous aspects (e.g., Srinivasan 2004).

When to play forcefully and when to pull back, are very important considerations. The correct decision greatly affects how the audience will react to one's performance.

Playing loudly is forcing one's presence. When done correctly, it infuses the performance with a feeling of excitement. Unfortunately the downside of playing too loudly for too long is that one's strokes tend to be muddy, and unclear. It also becomes tiresome to the audience; it is somewhat like shouting at an audience non-stop for extended periods of time. One additional drawback of playing too loudly is that it reduces one's stamina as a performer. This is very important because Indian performances may go on for many hours.

Playing softly has the effect of an artistic understatement. Remember that one of the main jobs of the tabla player is as an accompanist. One of the best ways to fulfil this duty is to drop into a basic "groove", pull back and play softly. This is an excellent way to support the main performer. However, the down side of playing too softly for too long is that one's performance tends to be lacklustre and unimpressive.

The bottom line is that there should be an ebb and flow in the dynamics. There should be times when one pulls back and plays softly. There should also be times when one should burst forth with loud and aggressive playing. The juxtaposition of loud and soft playing is very important to moving the performance along.

EFFECT OF DYNAMICS ON THE TIMBRE

Playing loudly or softly has a tremendous affect on the timbre of the drum. This may not be intuitively obvious, so we may resort to a simple analogy to clarify things. If one takes a small portable radio (the old style with the built in speaker) and turns the volume all the way up, it produces a characteristic distortion. This distortion is the introduction of upper frequency harmonics which were not present in the original music. This is very similar to what happens when you play the tabla loudly. For example, some strokes stress the lower harmonics (e.g. *Tin* तिं). However, if you play it very loudly, it will have a different sound due to the increase in upper harmonics. This is how the *purbi Taa* (i.e., *sur Taa* ता) can have the same fingering as *Tin* (तिं). *Tin* (तिं) is not alone in this phenomena. Virtually every stroke of the tabla may have its colour changed in this manner.

PROPER BALANCE OF THE STROKES

There are several issues that need to be addressed when determining the correct weight that the strokes should receive. One issue is the artistic responsibility at the particular moment; another is the balance between the left and right hands. Finally, there is the weight that certain strokes have within a *bol* expression.

<u>Right Hand and Theka</u> - You will be playing *theka* and its *prakars* more often than anything else. It therefore make sense to spend a lot of effort to be sure that the dynamics is acceptable. Probably the right hand is the first issue that the typical student needs to address. Let us look at it through a very common example; *Tintal*.

Therefore we are playing:

Tintal

ˣधा धिं धिं धा | ²धा धिं धिं धा | ⁰धा तिं तिं ना | ³ना धिं धिं धा |
Dhaa Dhin Dhin Dhaa Dhaa Dhin Dhin Dhaa Dhaa Tin Tin Naa Naa Dhin Dhin Dhaa

If we are a rank beginner, there is a tendency to play our right hand with equal dynamics. This essentially amounts to over-emphasising the *Tin* (तिं) and *Dhin* (धिं). Therefore, what we are actually playing is something like this[1]:

Tintal

ˣधा **धिं** **धिं** धा | ²धा **धिं** **धिं** धा | ⁰धा **तिं** **तिं** ना | ³ना **धिं** **धिं** धा |
Dhaa **Dhin** **Dhin** Dhaa Dhaa **Dhin** **Dhin** Dhaa Dhaa **Tin** **Tin** Naa Naa **Dhin** **Dhin** Dhaa

From the standpoint of effective accompaniment, this is the worst thing that we can do. This approach to dynamics is ineffective because the main artist is going to be listening for the strong *Dhaa* (धा) to feel the *vibhag* structure. When everything is coming out in equal dynamics, it makes it more difficult for the main artist to get the right musical cues. Furthermore when playing *Tin* (तिं) too loudly, it actually begins to sound like a *Taa* (ता) due to an enhancement of the upper harmonics. The combination of these effects is to make a *theka* which is unintelligible.

---

[1] In this chapter we will be using bold text to indicate a more forceful stroke. One should not presume that this is a standard in Indian musical notation. The notation of musical dynamics is very well developed in Western traditions (e.g., Read 1999), but is virtually nonexistent in Indian music. Traditionally one learned the particulars of dynamics through the apprenticeship that music students immersed themselves.

Ch. 5. Dynamics

The easiest way to make a clear and easy-to-follow *theka*, is to emphasise the *Naa* (ना) and *Dhaa* (धा), while de-emphasising *Tin* (तिं) and *Dhin* (धिं). Therefore, a more correct performance would be something like this:

Tintal

^xधा धिं धिं धा | ²धा धिं धिं धा | ⁰धा तिं तिं ना | ³ना धिं धिं धा |
Dhaa Dhin Dhin **Dhaa** **Dhaa** Dhin Dhin **Dhaa** **Dhaa** Tin Tin **Naa** **Naa** Dhin Dhin **Dhaa**

This is an example of good dynamics for basic accompaniment. It is easy for any main artist to follow. Although this example is very nice, we may wish to vary things for artistic effect. Just as we may vary the *bols* (refer to the *prakar* in *Fundamentals of Tabla*), we may also wish to vary the dynamics. Here are some nice ones to experiment with:

Tintal

^xधा धिं **धिं** धा | ²**धा** धिं **धिं** धा | ⁰**धा** तिं **तिं** ना | ³ना धिं **धिं** धा |
Dhaa Dhin **Dhin** Dhaa **Dhaa** Dhin **Dhin** Dhaa **Dhaa** Tin **Tin** Naa Naa Dhin **Dhin** Dhaa

This last example alters the basic feel of *Tintal*. However, it does give a basic driving rhythm which may be very pleasant when properly used. Let us look at another example:

Tintal

^xधा धिं **धिं** **धा** | ²**धा** धिं **धिं** **धा** | ⁰**धा** तिं **तिं** **ना** | ³**ना** धिं **धिं** **धा** |
Dhaa Dhin **Dhin** **Dhaa** **Dhaa** Dhin **Dhin** **Dhaa** **Dhaa** Tin **Tin** **Naa** **Naa** Dhin **Dhin** **Dhaa**

This last one has a *laggi* feel when played at moderate to high speed. It is very attractive.

Bol Density - There is another very good rule of thumb to help you control your dynamics; pay very close attention to the *bol* density. As the *bol* density increases, play more loudly. As the *bol* density decreases, play softly. For example if one is playing the expression:

धा   धा   तिर   किट
Dhaa Dhaa **TiRa** **KiTa**

In this example, the *Dhaa Dhaa* (धा धा) has half the *bol* density of *TiRaKiTa* (ति र कि ट). Therefore, you should make an effort to play the *TiRaKiTa* (ति र कि ट) with greater volume while you pull back and play *Dhaa Dhaa* (धा धा) at a lower volume.

Here is another common example. Let us look at the following *swatantra rela*. This *rela* is played in triple time, and works well in any 4, 8, or 16 beat structure:

Example 1

धा - तिर किट त क तिर किट त क तिर किट
Dhaa - Ti Ra Ki Ta Ta Ka Ti Ra Ki Ta Ta Ka Ti Ra Ki Ta

धा	-	ति	र	कि	ट	त	क	ति	र	कि	ट	त	क	ति	र	कि	ट
Dhaa	-	Ti	Ra	Ki	Ta	Ta	Ka	Ti	Ra	Ki	Ta	Ta	Ka	Ti	Ra	Ki	Ta

धा	-	ति	र	कि	ट	त	क	ति	र	कि	ट
Dhaa	-	Ti	Ra	Ki	Ta	Ta	Ka	Ti	Ra	Ki	Ta

This last example followed the rule of thumb. You see that we have increased the weight of our *TiRaKiTaTaKas* (ति र कि ट त क). This is a very common example which may be played with a beautiful effect.

This last material brings up one importance of the correct balance between the left and right hands. It is very difficult to get all of the *TiRaKiTaTaKas* (ति र कि ट त क) to be well balanced. Failure to do so will compromise one's performance. So it is very important to spend much time practising them.

I have one word of warning. You can practice for ten years and get these strokes perfectly balanced at home, and then go on stage and fail to attain the right weight. We must not forget that the balance that the audience hears is not just how well you balance the playing, but also how the microphone hears things. A small change in the microphone's position may have a tremendous impact on what the audience actually hears. This topic will be taken up in greater detail in Chapter 13 where we discuss microphones and acoustic fields.

Let us return to the topic of weighting the higher density *bols*. I must stress that this rule of thumb is merely a good place to begin. If one plays it exclusively without paying attention to the artistic requirements, then one's playing will sound flat and mechanical. Let us look at some different directions that we may take the previous example by using alternative emphasis.

Example 2

धा	-	ति	र	कि	ट	त	क	ति	र	कि	ट	त	क	ति	र	कि	ट
Dhaa	-	Ti	Ra	Ki	Ta	Ta	Ka	Ti	Ra	Ki	Ta	Ta	Ka	Ti	Ra	Ki	Ta

धा	-	ति	र	कि	ट	त	क	ति	र	कि	ट	त	क	ति	र	कि	ट
Dhaa	-	Ti	Ra	Ki	Ta	Ta	Ka	Ti	Ra	Ki	Ta	Ta	Ka	Ti	Ra	Ki	Ta

धा	-	ति	र	कि	ट	त	क	ति	र	कि	ट
Dhaa	-	Ti	Ra	Ki	Ta	Ta	Ka	Ti	Ra	Ki	Ta

This last example did exactly the opposite of our rule of thumb. In most cases, it will sound shallow and amateurish. However, there are situations where this could be used to good effect. For instance if one is following a vocalist or an instrumentalist who is playing something in exactly the same structure. This note-per-note execution could work nicely.

Let us look at another example:

Example 3

धा	-	ति	र	कि	ट	त	क	ति	र	कि	ट	त	क	ति	र	कि	ट
Dhaa	-	Ti	Ra	Ki	Ta	**Ta**	Ka	Ti	Ra	Ki	Ta	**Ta**	Ka	Ti	Ra	Ki	Ta

धा	-	ति	र	कि	ट	त	क	ति	र	कि	ट	त	क	ति	र	कि	ट
Dhaa	-	Ti	Ra	Ki	Ta	**Ta**	Ka	Ti	Ra	Ki	Ta	**Ta**	Ka	Ti	Ra	Ki	Ta

धा	-	ति	र	कि	ट	त	क	ति	र	कि	ट
Dhaa	-	Ti	Ra	Ki	Ta	**Ta**	Ka	Ti	Ra	Ki	Ta

Ch. 5. Dynamics

This last example has a nice driving feel (in triple time) to it. Certainly it could get boring if overused; but if used in moderation it may produce a nice effect.

This last example brings us to an interesting topic. We can construct entire rhythmic patterns which are produced almost entirely by the manipulation of dynamics. Let us take a simple repetition of a *purbi TiTa* (ति ट) for example:

Example 4
ति ट ति ट ति ट ति ट ति ट ति ट ति ट ति ट
Ti Ta Ti **Ta** Ti Ta **Ti** Ta **Ti** Ta Ti **Ta** Ti Ta **Ti** Ta

Example 5
ति ट ति ट ति ट ति ट ति ट ति ट ति ट ति ट
Ti Ta Ti **Ta** Ti Ta **Ti** Ta **Ti** Ta Ti Ta **Ti** Ta Ti Ta

Example 6
ति ट ति ट ति ट ति ट ति ट ति ट ति ट ति ट
Ti Ta Ti **Ta** Ti Ta **Ti** Ta Ti **Ta** Ti Ta **Ti** Ta **Ti** Ta

These are not merely exercises, but useful tools for both accompaniment and solo. At the time of writing, the acknowledged master of this approach is Zakir Hussain.

<u>Dynamics and the Bayan</u> - The *bayan* has received very little attention so far in this chapter. Much of our discussion of has centred around the *dayan*. There are good reasons for this. One of the reasons is psychoacoustic. The spectral content of the *dayan* lies much closer to the centre of our range of hearing than the *bayan*. Our brain has a much better ability to discriminate and analyse acoustic events in this range. Therefore, acoustic events in the lower ranges that the *bayan* occupies, are going to be less noticed.

This does not mean that we cannot make a few general observations regarding the dynamics of the *bayan*. One of the most important concerns our modulation. We know that if we initiate a *Ga* (ग) sound with the wrist at the back (i.e. close to the body) it will produce a very loud sound. Conversely, we also know that if we initiate a *Ga* (ग) with the wrist placed toward the front (i.e., toward the audience) it will tend to be more quiet. It is very important that one's modulations be somewhat balanced. Therefore, special efforts should be made to emphasise and play strong *Ga* (ग) which initiate in the forward position while one should resist the temptation to play loudly the strokes which originate in the back position.

This too, is merely a rule of thumb. There is a style called *"top"* which actually makes use of extremely loud *bayan* sounds. This topic though, will be put off until a later chapter.

ELECTRONIC MEDIUM AND DYNAMICS

Working on your dynamics without paying attention to your electronic medium is pointless. Practising at home and working on your dynamics without paying attention to the electro-acoustic chain is very much like paddling a boat in a swiftly moving stream without paying attention to the movement of the water. Just as it is impossible for a person to paddle against a strong stream; in the same manner, it is absolutely impossible to work against your sound reinforcement / recording system. If you do not pay attention to the intricacies of microphone placement and other matters, the quality of your performance will suffer. You will loose the balance between the left and right hand, you will suffer from thin and unimpressive sounds, and a host of other problems. Just as it is the duty of a mechanic is to truly understand his tools, so too it is your duty to understand the nature of microphones and the sound reinforcement/ recording process. This will be taken up in greater detail in later chapters.

CONCLUSION

Dynamics is very important to the performing artist. It is one of the areas that separates the amateur from the professional. It is important from several standpoints. Dynamics is a way to make artistic statements. Dynamics also is inextricably linked to the quality of the sound. The dynamics also allows us to alter the basic feel of the rhythm.

There are a few basic rules of thumb that help us to establish correct dynamics. When playing *theka*, always keep the right hand of the *Tin* (तिं) and the *Dhin* (धिं) quiet, while the *Naa* (ना) and the *Dhaa* (धा) should be strong. When playing anything with varying *bol* densities, play the higher *bol* densities loudly and play the lower *bol* densities softly. Whenever playing *bols* revolving around *TiRiKiTa* (ति र कि ट) or its variants, try keeping the dynamics equal. Above all, remember that these are merely rules of thumb. After these points have been mastered, experiment with shifting the emphasis to see how the colour of the material may be changed.

Your dynamics is at the mercy of your electro-acoustic chain (i.e., microphones, amplifiers etc.). It is up to you to understand the issues surrounding microphone placement, compressor operation, etc. Failure to do so will cost you dearly!

WORKS CITED

Clayton, Martin, Kelly Jakubowski, and Tuomas Eerola
2019 "Interpersonal Entrainment in Indian Instrumental Music Performance: Synchronization and Movement Coordination Relate to Tempo, Dynamics, Metrical and Cadential Structure", *Musicae Scientiae*. Durham University, UK:SAGE.

Randel, Don Michael
1978. *Harvard Concise Dictionary of Music*. The Belknap Press of Harvard University P. Cambridge (MA).

Read, Gardner
1999 *Music Notation*. Crescendo Book. Taplinger Pub Co

Singh, Manjit
2022 *Towards A Model Of Indian Music Studies For New Zealand Classrooms: A Skill-Based, Multicultural Approach*. Master of Music Thesis, University of Auckland.

Srinivasan, S.H.
2004 "Characterizing Music Dynamics for Improvisation", *2004 IEEE International Conference on Multimedia and Expo (ICME) (IEEE Cat. No.04TH8763)* pp. 1339-1342 Vol.2, doi: 10.1109/ICME.2004.1394476.

CHAPTER 6
LAYAKARI AND COUNTER-RHYTHMS

We must always remember that the beat is not something that we play; the beat is a mental concept which is suggested by what we play. Therefore a performance of Indian music must be looked at in terms of two separate rhythms, one which is conceptual and stored in our mind, and another which is actually being performed. This opens up an area of study into the relationship between the conceived rhythm and the performed rhythm. This dual-rhythm concept has profound implication for the Indian musical performance. At times, the performed beats reinforce the conceived rhythm. At other times it will suddenly cut across and play against the conceptual rhythm in a nearly unfathomable fashion. This is what makes Indian musical performances so exciting.

There are two classes of counter rhythms. One type maintains the integrity of the *matra* yet alters the points of emphasis; this is essentially the Western concept of syncopation. Another type of counter rhythm takes liberties with the *matra* itself. This approach is more closely allied to the Western concept of the polyrhythm. This chapter will look at both approaches in greater detail.

SYNCOPATION

Syncopation is the process of shifting the emphasis of the beats to unexpected positions. It is a very difficult proposition to talk about Indian syncopation because, in Western terms, all of Indian percussion is syncopated. This varied emphasis is so ubiquitous and taken for granted to the extent that there is not even a Hindi word for it. I am reminded of the saying that if you wish to understand water, you do not ask the fish!

Syncopation may be analysed from two standpoints. In one case we will look at the manipulation of structures and in another case we will look at the change of emphasis within existing structures. From a Western standpoint, the distinction between the two positions is merely academic. However, as we progress through our study of Indian music we will see that they are fundamentally different.

Let us first look at the alteration of a structure. This is in a rhythmic pattern known as *Kaherava tal*:

Clap				Wave				
1	2	3	**1**	2	3	**1**	2	PERFORMED RHYTHMIC PATTERN
1	2	3	4	**1**	2	3	4	BASIC RHYTHMIC CONCEPT

In this example, we see that *Kaherava* revolves around a 4+4 beat structure. However, we are actually performing a more complex 3+3+2 pattern. This simple example shows that we have deviated from the four beat pattern; therefore the pulse of the music is inconsistent with the structure of the *tal*.

We illustrated this with an abstract model. Perhaps it is better to give some concrete examples which adhere to this model.

^xधा गे ना ती | ^oना क धिं ना | ^xधा तिर किट धा | ^oतिर किट धा ती | ^xधा
Dhaa Ge Naa Tee   Naa Ka Dhin Naa   Dhaa TiRa KiTa Dhaa   TiRa KiTa Dhaa Tee Dhaa

In the previous example we showed two cycles. The first cycle is part of a continuing process of musical accompaniment (i.e., the basic *theka* or "groove"). This "groove" established the basic 4+4 pattern of *Kaherava*. At a point which is musically appropriate, we cut across this 4+4 pattern with a 3+3+2 pattern. This sudden shift in phrasing is immediately apparent and is very much like the Western concept of syncopation.

We must not think that this is the only way that we can cut across a 4+4 pattern. We could rearrange it in a 3+2+3, or 2+3+3, just to name a few. Furthermore we are not confined to our 8-beat cycle; we are free to span multiple cycles with patterns such as 3+3+3+3+4, 3+2+3+3+3+2, etc.

These examples illustrated a very important process in Indian music. It is so common, and so widely used, that it is probably better to discuss this in Chapters 8, 9, and 10, where we deal with compositional theory. There, we will develop this process even further.

Folk musicians have another approach to syncopation. They do not normally think in terms of *bol*, because it is a classical concept; and folk musicians seldom have classical training. Therefore, specifying the left and right hand as separate patterns is much closer to the way that folk musicians conceptualise their music.

The folk musician's conceptual separation of the left and right hands opens up a different approach to syncopation. One can have a left hand pattern which is stressed one way, but a right hand which is stressed differently. Below is a very common example of *Kaherava tal* which is found in film music, *ghazals*, and a variety of lighter forms:

Kaherava Prakar

^xति	ट	ना	ना	^oति	ट	ना	ना	Dayan
Ti	Ta	Naa	Naa	Ti	Ta	Naa	Naa	
ग	-	-	कत्	-	ग	ग	-	Bayan
Ga			Kat		Ga	Ga		

It is fascinating to analyse the previous example. We see that it may be considered syncopation from several angles. The theoretical form of *Kaherava* is 4+4, however the stress from the right hand is on beats 3, 4, 7 and 8. To further complicate things, the stress on the left hand is on beats 1, 4 and 7, (Note that the *Ga* ग on the sixth beat is considered a foreshadow to the *Ga* ग on the 7th beat, and is not considered a stress.)

The previous examples of syncopation are fairly straightforward. They are easily described by Western theoretical concepts. However, there is another style which is problematic. This style is inextricably linked to the nature of the strokes of the tabla.

Ch. 6 Layakari and Counter-Rhythms

Let us look at the basic *Jhaptal theka* as an example.

Jhaptal

^Xधिं ना | ²धिं धिं ना | ⁰तिं ना | ³धिं धिं ना |
Dhin Naa Dhin Dhin Naa Tin Naa Dhin Dhin Naa

A Western musician or musicologist will listen to this and immediately pronounce that it is syncopated. The reason for the pronouncement is the presence of the sharp, and by Western ears, emphasised 2nd, 5th, 7th, and 10th beats. This apparent emphasis is in stark contrast to the internal structure which is based upon the 1st, 3rd, 6th, and 8th beats. This may sound syncopated and peculiar to the Western ear, but very balanced and natural to the Indian.

This problem forces the Westerner to be introspective. It begs the question, "What is not syncopated?" A close examination of Western music reveals that virtually anything other than a simple, "one two, three four", with the emphasis solidly on the "one," technically is syncopated. This brings us to the uncomfortable conclusion that the term "syncopation" is ethnocentric and applies a standard of normality to a rhythm that would appear absolutely childish to most of the world's musicians. It especially seems childish compared to the rhythmically rich traditions of Africa, India, and the Caribbean.

It is very clear that the Western term "syncopation" has very limited applicability to Indian music. All of Indian music is "syncopated", therefore the term loses its ability to convey anything meaningful. It is for this reason that we will rarely use the term in this work.

Yet there is an interesting observation that we may make about both of these forms of syncopation. In both cases, there is a change in the basic pulse of the piece, but the actual *matra* remains unchanged. They are merely changing which *matras* will be emphasised. We will see that there is another form of counter rhythm that actually affects the beats. This is much closer to the Western concept of the "polyrhythm".

LAYAKARI (POLYRHYTHM)

The word polyrhythm literally implies two rhythms being performed simultaneously. In practice, it may be expressed two ways. In one form, both rhythms are being performed; this is close to the Western concept of the polyrhythm. However in another of these forms, one of the rhythms is not actually played, but merely implied. This is to say that there is a performed rhythm which is different from the pattern that was built up in the listener's mind. This approach is called *layakari* (लयकारी)

<u>Polyrhythm with an Implied Beat *(layakari)*</u> - There are many examples of polyrhythms with implied beats. This is called *layakari*. An example for *Kaherava* is shown below:

```
Clap                     Wave                          Clap
1    2    3    4    1    2    3    4    5    6    1  PERFORMED RHYTHMIC PATTERN
1    2    3    4    1    2    3    4         1       BASIC RHYTHMIC PATTERN
```

In the previous example, only the last *vibhag* increase the *bol* density; in this case a factor of six-over-four. Since this is such a short period of change, psychologically, the initial rhythm is maintained with the altered rhythm being laid over it[1].

---

[1] I am sure that there are a number of people who are dissatisfied with the use of the term polyrhythm in situations where only one rhythm is actually played. I am less than satisfied myself. I request the reader to indulge me in these matters, because it is difficult to find Western terms for many aspects of Indian music.

The term *"layakari"* is usually reserved for the more exotic rhythmic relationships. However if we look closely, we see that this actually points to a more general process. This is a general relationship between the performed beat and the implied theoretical *matra*. Let us look more closely at these fundamental relationships.

TERMINOLOGY FOR LAYAKARI

The fundamental rhythmic relationships are reflected in a variety of musical terms. Yet we find a great degree of non-standardisation in the terminology of *layakari* (we should be used to that by now). This non-standardisation results partly from the multilingual character of India, and partly because of the weak academic tradition in the field of music. Here we shall acquaint you with the more common terminology.

Barabar / One-to-One - The simple one-to-one relationship is the most fundamental relationship between our performed and our conceptual rhythm. It is sometimes called *barabar* (बराबर), *thah* (ठाह), *thahdun* (ठाह दून), *thay* (ठाय) or *ekgun* (एकगुन). This is shown below:

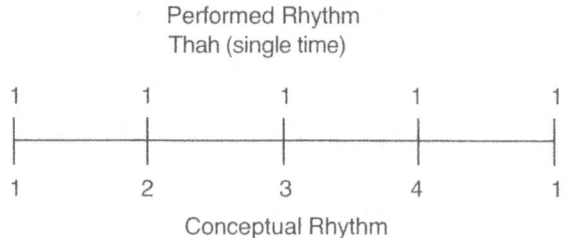

Dugun / Two-to-One - This is also a basic rhythmic relationship. It is so closely allied with our one-to-one that the expression *barabar* (बराबर) is sometimes applied to this as well. The two-to-one relationship is usually referred to as *dugun* (दुगुन). This is shown below:

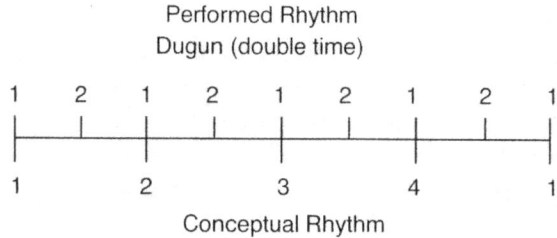

Tigun / Three-to-One - This is a simple triplet. For each *matra*, there are three equally spaced strokes. This is usually referred to as *tigun* (तिगुन), but it is sometimes referred to as *mahaadi* (महाआड़ी). This is shown below:

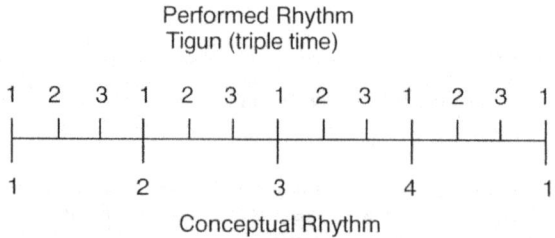

Ch. 6 Layakari and Counter-Rhythms

<u>Adi / Three-over-Two</u> - This is a very common relationship whenever one is wishing to show a little musical tension. In the West this is commonly referred to as a "hemiola". It is where one plays three strokes for every two beats. It may be referred to as *dedh* (डेढ), *adilay* (आड़ी लया) or simply as *adi* (आड़ी). This is shown below:

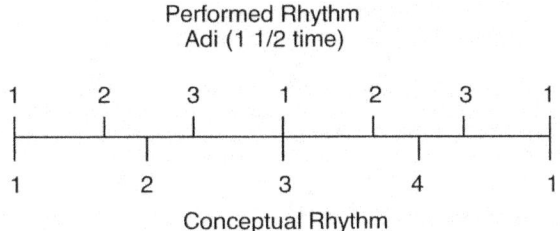

<u>Kuadi / Five over Four</u> - This style of syncopation is somewhat less common. Like *adi (dedh)*, it is used to show a musical tension. It is usually referred to as *kuadi* (कुआड़ी) or *savai* (सवाइ). This is shown below:

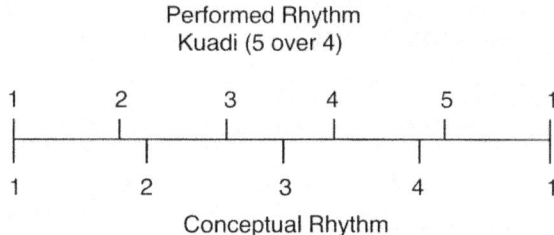

<u>Mahakuadi / Five-over-Two</u> - This is simply five-over-four played double-time. This is called *mahakuadi* (महाकुआड़ी). It is shown below:

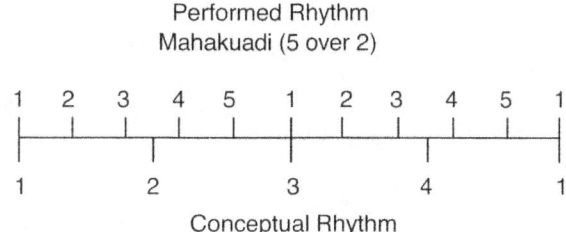

<u>Biadi / Seven-over-Four</u> - This too is a relatively uncommon form. In the space of four *matras*, one plays seven strokes. It is sometimes called *biadi* (बिआड़ी) or *Paune Dugun* (पौने दुगुन). This is shown below:

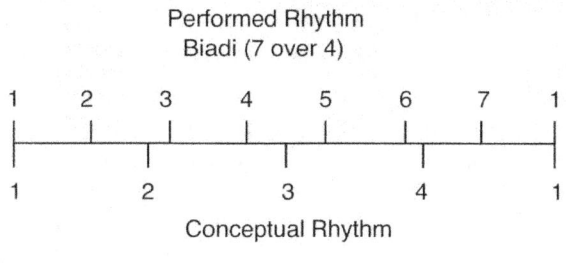

page 67

Mahabiadi / Seven-over-Two - When one plays seven strokes over two *matras*, it is called *mahabiadi* (महाबिआड़ी). This is nothing more than *biadi* (seven-over-four) played double-time. *Mahabiadi* is shown below:

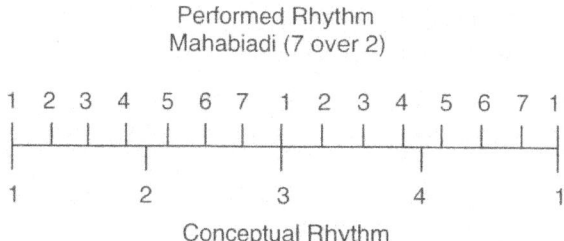

Other-Relationships - There are many other relationships whose terminology and concepts are very simple. For instance, there is quadruple time (*chaugun* चौगुन), octuple time (*aathgun* आठगुन), etc. It is not necessary to diagram all of these relationships because once the general principle is understood, the rest is easy. An extensive list of relationships is shown in Table 6.1.

Table 6.1. The Common Relationships.

English	Hindi	Urdu
single time	barabar lay	ekgun
five beats over four matras	kuadi lay	savai
six beats over four matras	adi lay	derdh
seven beats over four matras	biadi lay	paune dugun
double time	dogun or dugun	dugan
five beats over two matras	mahakuadi	
six beats over two matras	mahaadi or tigun	tigun
seven beats over two matras	mahabiadi	
quadruple time	chaugun	chogun
five beats per matra	panchgun	panchgun
six beats per matra	chegun	chegun
seven beats per matra	satgun	satgun
eight beats per matra	athgun	athgun

There are several points which should be kept in mind about the previous table. To begin with, there is a tremendous overlap between Hindi and Urdu in northern India. Also, one tends to find broad definitions for the word *lay* which often overlap the strict definition of *layakari*.

In this section we discussed the relationships that exist between the performed and the conceptual rhythms. Still there are cases where two rhythms are performed simultaneously. We will discuss this in the next section.

Ch. 6 Layakari and Counter-Rhythms

<u>Both Rhythms are Expressed</u> - There are many situations where one finds polyrhythms. This is most evident in the folk styles. This is a bit different from the previous examples where one rhythm lies in the mind and another is performed. In this case, both rhythms are performed simultaneously.

Hinch is a very popular rhythm in Gujarat. It is a very interesting polyrhythm based upon six beats placed over four. The four-beat component is the dominant characteristic in most interpretations. However, there are interpretations which stress the six-beat aspect. Here are two notations. The first is noted as a six-beat *tal* with a *vibhag* arrangement of $1\frac{1}{2} + 1\frac{1}{2} + 1 + \frac{1}{2} + 1$. The second is noted as a four *matra tal* divided as $1+1+1+\frac{1}{3} + \frac{2}{3}$. It is important to remember that both of these interpretations are correct, even though they are very different.

Hinch (noted as 6 matras)

धिं	ना	तिं	ना	तिं	ना	धिं	धा
Dhin	Naa	Tin	Naa	Tin	Naa	Dhin	Dhaa

Hinch (noted as 4 matras)

धिं - ना	तीना -	तिं - ना	धी	धा ना
Dhin - Naa	TeeNaa -	Tin - Naa	Dhee	DhaaNaa

<u>Folk Dadra</u> - Below is a folk version of *Dadra tal*. This version has two pulses which continue simultaneously.

धिं	तिं	ना	धिं	धिं	ना	धिं	Bol
Dhin	Tin	Naa	Dhin	Dhin	Naa	Dhin	
1			2			1	Accent #1
1		2		3		1	Accent #2

In the previous illustration, we may accent it in two ways. If we accent the first beat of the *vibhag* (accent #1), it feels like two measures of three beats. Although this method is more closely associated with the theoretical structure, a fast folk *Dadra* is more likely to be accented as in accent #2.

One cannot help but notice that this folk form of *Dadra* produces a feel very similar to that of *Hinch*. Whether this represents a fundamental quality of north Indian folk music or a mere coincidence is difficult to say.

CONCLUSION

We have described the basic system of counter rhythms use by the tabla to perform Indian music. We saw that there was a considerable amount of traditional terminology to describe these counter rhythms. When counter rhythms are used effectively they produce much of the varied and interesting texture which is a characteristic of Indian music.

WORKS CITED

Apte, Vasudeo Govind
1987 *The Concise Sanskrit English Dictionary*. Delhi: Motilal Banarsidas.

Gottlieb, R. S.
1977a *The Major Traditions of North Indian Tabla Drumming*. Munchen, Germany: Musikverlag Emil Katzbichler.
1977b *The Major Traditions of North Indian Tabla Drumming. Transcriptions*: Munchen, Germany: Musikverlag Emil Katzbichler.

Kapoor, R.K.
no date *Kamal's Advanced Illustrated Oxford Dictionary of Hindi- English*. Delhi, India: Verma Book Depot.

Khan, Imrat Hussain
1974 *Surbahar / Sitar- Raga Shree*. Dum Dum, India: Odeon/Gramophone Company of India, Ltd.

Leake, Jerry
1993 *Indian Influence (Tabla Perspective), Series A.I.M. Percussion Text* (Second Edition). Boston: Rhombus Publishing.

CHAPTER 7

ANCIENT AND OBSOLETE THEORY

This chapter deals with the large amount of obsolete theoretical material which one may encounter. Although it is obsolete, I still have an obligation to put this it in front of you; otherwise this would not be a complete work. Remember the term "obsolete" does not mean that this it is useless; for it is very good at illustrating the development of Indian music. It also provides a fascinating insight into Indian worldviews. Yet its applicability to the present music is dubious or nil.

WHAT IS ANCIENT AND OBSOLETE THEORY
Ancient and obsolete theory is a body of musical theory which is passed down from antiquity. It is generally accepted without question because it is old. Relevance to contemporary practice is seldom considered. There are numerous sources for such theory, but some of the most notable material comes from the *Natya Shastra*.

WHAT ARE THE PROBLEMS WITH THE THEORY
This body of material poses major problems for the student of contemporary music. When the student is fumbling to absorb the vast amount of information, it does them great disservice to introduce out-of-date concepts and terminology. It is very much like intentionally feeding an infant by giving them a random assortment of edible and inedible objects. A young infant does not have the experience to know what is edible and what is not, and will place anything into its mouth, sometimes with disastrous results.

A random assault of irrelevant material upon the music student is a great disservice. They will attempt to absorb any musical theory which is placed before them. If the theory is relevant, it makes it easier for the student to gain a mastery over the subject. Conversely, if the material is out-of-date and irrelevant, it becomes a stumbling block to the advancement of the student.

The presence of this obsolete theory is a special problem with the literature available in Hindi. These books present a confusing hodgepodge of material ranging from the useful to the irrelevant and misleading. It is for this reason that we have segregated this material into this chapter. We presume that by the time a reader is into the second volume of this series, that one has a sufficiently firm background not to be misled and confused.

TIME, ANTIQUITY, & HERMENEUTICS
This whole section can be summarised very simply. According to traditional Hindu concepts, if something is old, it is automatically of great esteem. Similarly, if something is of great esteem it must be of great antiquity. This world view is never questioned, and is the source of a large body of spurious scholarship (e.g., Subhash Kak). When translated to tabla, this means that since it is of great social and musical value, tabla must be very old, or at least have deep unbroken roots in antiquity.

The History of The Rise in Irrelevant Theory - The rise of irrelevant musical theory is directly attributable to the change in world views that occurred during India's independence movement. The failed uprising of 1857 made it very clear that an independent India could only come if there was a concerted effort to create a national identity.

It was vitally important that a system of world views be developed that supported the concept of a nation. But Hindus and Muslims were failing to come to an agreement as to what this should be. Whereas Muslims were looking back to the *Moghal* period to provide their spiritual, political, and psychological *desiderata*, India's Hindus were going back to the Vedic period.

The position of music within the emerging Hindu self-image was very different from that of the Muslims. Where Islam's injunction against music placed musicians in the same category as drunkards and prostitutes, Hindus valued music as a means of spiritual upliftment.

It was clear that music would be important in establishing this sense Indian/Hindu self-identity. But there was a small problem. The traditional hereditary musicians were by and large Muslim. Between 1890 and 1950, classical music began to shift from Muslim hereditary musicians to middle and upper-class Hindus. This appropriation was accompanied by a major shift in the social significance of music.

It would be impossible to name all of the musicians and scholars who were involved in this process. Two notable figures were V. N. Bhatkhande and V. D. Paluskar. Paluskar was responsible for the establishment of India's first Western style music college at the beginning of the 20th century. Bhatkhande was responsible for the monumental task of collecting and organising countless compositions and *rags*. But these were but two people involved in a larger social movement.

The work of spreading classical music to the masses democratised the music, but with unintended cultural consequences. The majority of the Indian population was Hindu. Therefore, the appropriation of classical music by the Hindu middle class began to change its entire colour. This was especially evident in the creation of an historical narrative for music.

Hindu Concepts of Time and Antiquity - There are fundamental differences between the Hindu and Occidental mind regarding time. In general, we may say that the Occidental concept of time is linear and progressive while the Indian concept of time is cyclical and degenerative. Of these qualities it is the teleology of progression vs. degeneration which is most pertinent to our study.

In traditional Hindu world views, the passage of time is equated with decay. The world starts off perfect, but with the passage of time decay sets in. This process is divided into four aeons, each with a successively greater degree of evil, decay, and chaos. These aeons, known as *yuga*, are called, *Krita (Satya), Treta, Dvapara*, and *Kali* (Klostermaier 1994). At the end of *Kali-yuga* the world is in such an abysmal state that it must be destroyed and a new perfect world created. Thus the cycle continues *ad infinitum*. This process of creation, decay, recreation, etc., is why we refer to the Indian concept of time as being degenerative and cyclical.

Conversely in the West, the passage of time is equated with improvement. The Western concept of the world portrays man starting out in a state of barbarity; from this barbarity he gradually ascends to civilisation. This civilisation is seen as a never ending improvement of his moral, technological, and scientific state of being. (The sexist tone of this statement is not an oversight.) Even the English words, "forward", "progress", and "advance", all mean a "direction of motion" as well as "improvement". Even in the study of evolution, terms such as "higher organism" reflect this teleology.

Ch. 7. Ancient and Obsolete Theory

Teleology may be a part of the human mind-set, but it has no basis in reality. The negative teleology of the Indian mind (i.e., old=good, new=bad), is just as fallacious as the positive teleology of the West (e.g., new=good, old=bad). Just as Western scholarship has on numerous occasions been compromised by an unjustified attachment to a positive teleology. (e.g., Marx's approach to historical materialism), Indian musical scholarship is continually compromised by an unjustified attachment to negative teleology (e.g., Aban Mistry's otherwise laudable work on the history of tabla and *pakhawaj*.) (Mistry 1999).

In passing we should mention that the South Asian, Islamic concept of time is completely different. Among India's Islam population, history is divided into two periods. There is the time that occurs before the prophet Muhammad (p.b.u.h), and there is the period after. Each has substantial qualitative differences. But since post-independence India has a limited influence of this world view, we will not go into the matter further.

Establishing the link with Antiquity - Negative teleology was a guiding influence in Indian historical scholarship. Music was of great social value, so it had to be very old, this point was beyond question. Therefore, it was simply a question of finding the link.

The *Samaveda* provided one means to establish music's credentials. This work is probably one of the oldest song books in the world. However, Vedic verse intended to be chanted or sung, does not in itself make it a work on music; therefore, another attachment had to be found.

The next link with antiquity was to be found in the *Natya Shastra*. At one time, this treatise on stagecraft had been thought lost, but under the British rule, portions of it began to be found. By the 20th century, virtually all the pieces had been found, and it was possible to reconstruct this work. Today, it stands as the oldest surviving work on stagecraft in the world.

It is a difficult job to establish a date at which the *Natya Shastra* was written. Reasonable estimates run from the 3rd century BCE to the 3rd century CE. The matter is complicated by the piecemeal fashion in which the sections were found and reconstructed. It is obvious that the *Natya Shastra* was written and rewritten over several centuries. Since different pieces belong to different dates, it is hard to establish the date of the original.

It is also difficult to say exactly who wrote it. It is commonly attributed to the sage Bharata; however, it seems likely that Bharata was a title rather than a name (Saletore 1982). There may have been numerous authors. This view is substantiated by the differing styles in which the various pieces were written.

Ultimately, questions concerning authorship or the exact time of writing were irrelevant. Its antiquity was unassailable, and the detail of its discussion of stagecraft was amazing. Here was the link with antiquity that the new scholars needed to establish the *bona fides*.

An Uncomfortable Fit - The new system of music was nearly complete; virtually all of the pieces were in place. There was an extremely sophisticated artform; there was a tradition of scholarship extending back comfortably close to the Vedic period. There was a system of apprenticeship which nicely echoed the *guru-shishya-paramapara* of the Vedic tradition. Everything was intellectually neat and tidy - or was it?

Unfortunately, the system set forth in the *Natya Shastra* clearly had no relationship to the contemporary practice of music. The *Natya Shastra* spoke of many things that did not exist anymore. Furthermore, the *Natya Shastra* was uncomfortably silent about concepts that were fundamental to contemporary practice. So now what was to be done?

It is human nature that when things do not go according to planned, one looks for a scapegoat. Conveniently, a scapegoat was already in front of them. Several centuries of Muslim musicians were the "problem". They were obviously uneducated and had corrupted the music through their ignorance. All that one had to do was educate the new generations of music students with the correct *shastric* approach to music, and everything would be all right.

But blaming hereditary Muslim musicians, and foisting an irrelevant theoretical system upon students, did not make things right. There was no amount of hermeneutics that could bridge the gap between the *Natya Shastra,* and contemporary musical practice. We are already three quarters of a century into Independence, and this effort has failed miserably[1].

We should not be too hard on these musicologists of the last century. They did a remarkably good job of lifting the music out of its intellectual quagmire and giving it a good academic base. Any theoretical changes that we need to make in the 21st century are merely minor adjustments, rather than major revamps. This is the real testament to their fine work.

THE THEORY

We will now go into our discussion of the ancient, yet often irrelevant theory behind the tabla. However, before we go into it, there are a few things that we need to keep in mind. The most important is the distinction between the various interpretations of time.

The study of tabla is dependent on the study and understanding of rhythm; by the same token, the study of rhythm is inextricably tied to concepts of time. Therefore, it is proper that we devote this section to understanding the nature of musical time.

The traditional term for "time" is *"samay"* (समय); it means "time" in a very broad sense. This chapter deals with time from two different standpoints; one is in absolute terms and the other is in relative terms. Absolute time is quantifiable in terms of years, seconds, centuries, nanoseconds or any other suitable unit. This is the time that we normally think of. However, there is a musical time which is measured in beats. A beat has no fixed value in absolute terms. It is merely defined in regards to itself; therefore, we can call this relative time.

Relative Time - Relative time is any unit of time which has no fixed value. We deal with these units every day. One common example is the "round". A round of poker is a very different length of time from a "round" of golf. Another example is the school semester. No one can say exactly how long a semester is, because it varies from school to school. All of these examples may seem very trivial but this concept, when applied to music, is far from trivial.

The most fundamental example of relative time is the beat. The beat does not have any intrinsic value. In a slow tempo the beat will be very long while in a fast performance the beat will be very short. To make matters even more confusing, we find situations where the *matra* has different values depending upon where it is within the cycle (e.g., the first beat tends to be longer than the 16th beat in *Tintal*).

Absolute Time - Absolute time is that which may objectively be measured in fixed units. The units may be centuries, or nanoseconds. Although the units may vary, the basic philosophy is the same.

The difference between relative-time and absolute time is crucial to our understanding of many of the old concepts. Where modern musical practice concentrates on relative time (e.g., the beat), much of the ancient theory deals with absolute concepts of time.

---

[1] It is very easy to sit here in the early part of the 21st century and criticise the academically questionable manner in which ancient theory was applied to contemporary Indian music. Before we criticise, we should keep several things in mind. Western scholarship is not immune to such folly either. The misapplication of ancient musical theories to contemporary music echoes the folly of Western academics in their futile efforts to foist Latin grammar on the Germanic English language.

DASA PRANA

Much of the ancient theory behind *tal* is dominated by the concept of *Dasa Prana*, or "ten vital breaths" of rhythm. Although most of the individual terms were in existence during the time of the *Natya Shastra*, the term *Dasa Prana* is hard to trace back further than the 11th century. (Shepherd 1976). The *Dasa Prana* (ten airs) is presented in Table 7.1.

Let us start our discussion with a definition of *tal* (Hindi ताल) or *tala* (Sanskrit ताल). The word *tal* is said to be a combination of *"Ta"* and *"La"*. *"Ta"* is derived from *Tandava* which represents the masculine principle embodied in *Shiva*. The *"La"* on the other hand, is derived from *Lasya* with represents *Paravati* or the feminine aspect of *Shiva*. Therefore *Ta-La*, or "*tala*", is emblematic of the union of the universal masculine and feminine principles (Mani undated).

Table 7.1 The Ten Vital Airs of Rhythm (Dasa Prana)

1. Kal - The time
2. Marg - The pause
3. Kriya - The action of timekeeping
4. Ang - The sections
5. Graha - The process of starting
6. Jati - The classes of rhythmic patterns
7. Kala - The sections
8. Lay - The tempo
9. Yati - The Arrangement
10. Prastar - The permutations.

The preceding story is amusing but has no relationship to reality. The etymology of the word is extremely simple, and requires no metaphysical interpretations. The word "*tal*" in Hindi is derived from the Sanskrit "*tala*" (ताल). The word literally means the "palm of the hand", but it also means "clapping". Therefore, *tala* as representing "rhythm" is merely a generalisation of the Sanskrit word for "clap".

We will now proceed with a typical interpretation of the *dasa prana* as derived from contemporary sources (e.g., Vinjamuri 1986). It must be reiterated that the concept of *"Dasa Prana"* is of questionable relevance to contemporary practice. We are presenting it here so the student can get a sense of perspective.

1ST ASPECT OF DASA PRANA (KAL)

The word *kal* (काल) literally means "time". Conceptually, it is an absolute framework for denoting the duration of a beat.

The Hindi word *kal* is derived from the Sanskrit *kala* (काल), and has a number of uses and precise meanings. *The Concise Sanskrit-English Dictionary* (Apte 1987) gives the definitions of *"Kala"* as "black, time; proper time; God of death; destiny; the planet Saturn; poison and iron". From the list of meanings it is clear that there are two root concepts: one being time and the other being the concept of blackness. Perhaps these represents two Proto-Indo-European homonyms; perhaps there is a deeper philosophic connection between the words "black" and "time". I do not know, and it is beyond the scope of this work to look further into this. This is a series on tabla and Indian music, therefore we shall concern ourselves with the definition of the word which represents time.

Kshan (क्षण) or *kan* (कन) is the shortest interval acknowledged. According to ancient scriptures, it is the interval required to quickly pierce one hundred lotus leaves with a needle. *Kshan, lav, kasth, nimish, kala, chaturbhag,* are referred to as *"sukshma kal"*, which means "micro-time", while *anudrut, drut, laghu, guru, plut,* and *kakapad* are called *"sthul kal"*, which means "macro-time" (Sharma 1973). The relationship is shown in Table 7.2.

Table 7.2 Relationship Between the Various Times

8 kshan	= 1 lav
8 lav	= 1 kashth
8 kashth	= 1 nimish
8 nimish	= 1 kala
2 kala	= 1 chaturbhag
2 chaturbhag	= 1 anudrut
2 anudrut	= 1 drut
2 drut	= 1 laghu
2 laghu	= 1 guru
3 laghu	= 1 plut
4 laghu	= 1 kakapad

Figure 7.3. Simplified Interpretation

1 syllable = anudrut	=	1 akshar-kal
drut	=	2 akshar-kal
laghu	=	4 akshar-kal
guru	=	8 akshar-kal
plut	=	12 akshar-kal
kakapad	=	16 akshar-kal

This approach to *kshan* (क्षण) is interesting, but sometimes hard to work with; therefore it is usually interpreted slightly differently. In the contemporary interpretation, the system is defined according to the *anudrut*. In this approach, the smallest practical unit is defined as the length of time it takes to utter one short syllable *(akshar-kal)*. The relationship of the other units then falls into place as follows (Table 7.3).

2ND ASPECT OF DASA PRANA (MARG)

Marg appears to define that which lies between the beats. To some, this implies an interval. To others it implies a way of playing things between the beats. It is therefore very difficult to make any statement concerning *marg* which is either relevant or broadly accepted.[2]

3ND ASPECT OF DASA PRANA (KRIYA)

The term *kriya* literally means activity, and refers to the act of timekeeping. In the most general terms the movement of the conductor's baton, or the clapping and waving of the hands to denote the *tal*, is *kriya*. There are two factors; 1) does the timekeeping make sound and 2) is the process consistent with the *margi* system of music. When the two factors are combined, this gives us four classes of timekeeping (*kriya*). Let us look at these factors in greater detail.

<u>Margi vs. Deshi Tal</u> - In ancient times, a *tal* was categorised as being *deshi* or *margi*. The concept of a *margi tal* as opposed to a *deshi tal*, was a natural outgrowth of the concept of *margi sangeet* as opposed to *deshi sangeet*. The literal meaning of *marg* means "path", while *deshi* means "indigenous".

Margi tals are supposedly those attached to the *margi* class of music. It is supposedly music whose function is a path towards spiritual improvement.

Deshi tals are derived from the "worldly" music. In contrast to *margi sangeet*, *deshi sangeet* is music which is for the sensual enjoyment of mortals. Some opine that all of the music, including the classical music, is *deshi*. This is in contrast to others who are of the opinion that only the more vulgar genre represents the *deshi* variety (e.g., *filmi sangeet*). The *tals* of *deshi sangeet* are defined as *deshi tals*

---

[2] The topic of *marg* has always amazed me. I am not surprised that there are numerous interpretations of what *marg* means. What is completely surprising is that the various interpretations often have absolutely nothing to do with each other. It is as though people were coming up with a meanings in a totally random fashion.

Ch. 7. Ancient and Obsolete Theory

There have been historical and anthropological interpretations of these terms. It has been proposed that at some dim period in history a ruling class, possibly of foreign extraction, looked upon their traditional music as being superior to the music of the indigenous populations. The terms *margi* became applied to the ruling class's music, while the indigenous population's music was referred to as *deshi*.

Today, the distinction between *margi* and *deshi* music is difficult to make. Many people consider the classical music to be *margi*, and by extension, the classical *tals* to be *margi tals*. Conversely, the lighter, folk, film etc. genre are considered be *deshi*. This is an extremely simplistic view which is held by some practising musicians, but is generally rejected by Indian scholars. Most Indian scholars believe that classical music is derived from the *deshi* styles, and that the *margi sangeet* disappeared ages ago. Regardless of the interpretation, the concepts of *margi / deshi* are totally irrelevant to contemporary music.

Sashabd vs. Nishabd Kriya - In its most general sense, any act of timekeeping is referred to as *kriya*. The concept of *nishabd* as opposed to *sashabd* simply reflects whether this timekeeping makes a sound or not. *Sashabd kriya* is any form of timekeeping that makes a sound. Conversely, *nishabd kriya* is any form of timekeeping that is silent.

Marg/ Sashabd Kriya - This is timekeeping with sound in the *marg* tradition. a) *Dhruva* - Snap fingers. b) *Samyak* - Hold right hand stationary and beat with the left hand c) *Tal* - Hold left hand stationary and clap with the right. d) *Sanipat* - Clap by moving both hand together.

Marg / Nishabd Kriya - This is timekeeping without sounds in the *marg* tradition. a) *Avapap* - Count the time with the fingers of the hand turned upwards. b) *Nishkram* - Count time with the fingers of the hand turned downwards c) *Vikshep* - Move hand to right side. d) *Pravesh* - Move fingers to left.

Deshi / Sashabd Kriya - Any variety of clapping or snapping of fingers in the *deshi* tradition.

Deshi / Nishabd Kriya - This is timekeeping without sounds in the *deshi* tradition a) *Sarpini* - Move your hand to the right. b) *Krshya* - Move your hand to left. c) *Padmini* - Throw down the hand with the palm turned upwards. d) *Visarjit* - Move the hand upwards with the open hand up. e) *Vikshipt* - To indicate time by closing the fingers. f) *Patak* - Raise the open hand. g) *Patit* - Bring the hands downward.

The preceding discussion, although clearly irrelevant to contemporary practice, is nonetheless fascinating. We see that the system of clapping and waving of hands to keep the *tal*, is of extreme antiquity. Although the particulars have ebbed and flowed with the passage of time, the general theme has been remarkably consistent.

4TH ASPECT OF DASA PRANA (ANG)

The word *ang* literally means "limb" or "organ"; this implies a section of the *tal*. Each *ang* is defined by the clap. The *ang* may be specified according to one of six durations as shown in Table 7.4. This system has been expanded to include a number of combinant forms as shown in Table 7.5.

It has been applied to contemporary practice in an interesting manner (Sharma 1977). The division of *angs* in *Tintal* is said to go as follows:

    1 2 3 4   5 6 7 8 9 10 11 12   13 14 15 16

Table 7.4. The Ang

anudrut	U	1
drut	0	2
laghu	|	4
guru	8	8
plut	8	12
kakapad	+	16

Table 7.5. Durations of the Angs

Name	Duration
drut viram	3
laghu viram	5
laghu drut	6
laghu drut viram	7
guru viram	9
guru drut	10
guru drut viram	11
plut viram	13
plut drut	14
plut drut viram	15

We see that the *ang* is roughly comparable to the modern concept of *vibhag*. But there seems to be one fundamental difference. The *khali* is unable to define an *ang*, where it is able to define a *vibhag*. It should be brought out that the distinction between *ang* and *vibhag* may be purely academic. It appears that in past, there often was no *khali* as we think of it today. Therefore, with such a conceptual model, one would not be able to make any distinction between *vibhag* and *ang*. It is also possible that this distinction between *vibhag* and *ang* is purely idiosyncratic to this author (Bhagavat Sharma).

There is a more fundamental problem with modern interpretations of *ang*. *Ang* is based upon an absolute concept of time. The durations are clearly specified in terms of *aksharkal*. One *aksharkal* is defined as the length of time it takes to utter one syllable. Contemporary practice is based upon the *matra*. *Matra* is not defined according to any particular duration. In fast pieces the duration is short, in slow piece the duration is long. Therefore, these fundamental philosophic incompatibilities make the entire concept of questionable relevance to contemporary practice.

5TH ASPECT OF DASA PRANA (GRAHA)

Graha is the method of starting the percussion. If the percussion starts at the same time as the rest of the music, it is referred to as *samagraha*. If the percussion and the rest of the music start at different times, it is said to be *visham*.

Within *visham graha,* there are two varieties; *atit* and *anagat*. *Atit* is the process of starting after the *sam* while *anagat* is the process of starting before the *sam*. One should keep in mind that while the ancient interpretation of *graha* concerns the starting of the piece, contemporary interpretations concern the resolution of the piece. Therefore today, *atit graha* refers to a composition which ends after the *sam,* while *anagat* is a composition which ends before the *sam*.

The discrepancy between the ancient approach to *graha* and contemporary may not be as much of a contradiction as it might appear. We should keep in mind that the importance here is cadential rather than structural. This is to say that today the point of emphasis comes at the end of an expression, while there is much evidence that in centuries past, the point of emphasis was at the beginning of a structure. Take for an example South Indian music, where it is normal to start the composition on the first beat. This is very different from north Indian music where the tendency is to start at some point midway in the cycle, and lead up to *sam*. When we view the *graha* from the standpoint of the cadence rather than merely a starting point, we see that it has remained surprisingly consistent over the centuries.

6TH ASPECT OF DASA PRANA (JATI)

The word *jati* literally mean a "caste", "collection", or class. There are five *jatis: tryastra (tisra), chaturstra, khand, mishra, sankirna. Tryastra* is made of three beats, *chaturstra* is made of four beats, *khand* is made of five beats, *mishra* is made of seven beats, and *sankirna* is made of nine. It refers to the pulse of the piece. Therefore anything which has a strong triplet feel is *tryastra*, quadruple feel is *chatustra*, etc. This definition may be at times a little confusing, because *jati* may sometimes be applied to the entire *tal* (e.g., *dadra=triyastra, kaherava=chatustra*, etc.), while at other times it is applied to the *layakari* (e.g., *chogun=chutustra, adi or tigun=triyastra* etc.). Generally it is a question of *feel* rather than any theoretical structure.

The definition according to *feel* may be quite significant. It has been mention by other authors (Vinjamuri 1986) that the *jati* is defined according to the *laghu*. Therefore, it is defined in terms of absolute time, rather than relative time. The *laghu* appears to be approximately 1/80th of a minute. This is quite significant because this is an inborn rhythm. It is easily seen that the rhythm which is easiest to feel is one which is close to the human heartbeat. Although the *matra* may have any value, it is most perceptible when it is approximately 80 beats-per-min. Very fast or very slow must be perceived in terms of fractions or multiples in order to be easily felt. Therefore, defining the *jati* in terms of "feel" (i.e., *laghu*) is a vestigial concept from an era when the theory of rhythm was based upon an absolute reference of time (i.e., *anudrut, drut, laghu*, etc.), rather than the present relative reference of time (i.e., *matra*).

7TH ASPECT OF DASA PRANA (KALA)

This is a particularly difficult term to define. It is clear that it relates to some type of section or division, but the exact musical significance seems to be lost. According to some authors, it relates to the *vibhag*, or measure (Vinjamuri 1986). However, such a definition impinges uncomfortably on the concept of *ang*. According to other authors, it is relates to the size of a structure in each *matra* (Sharma 1973). Therefore if musical notes were used to express it; "1 kala" = SaReGaMa, "2 kala" = SaSaReReGaGaMaMa, "4 kala" = SaSaSaSaReReReReGaGaGaGaMaMaMaMa" etc. Unfortunately, this definition impinges on the concept of *jati*.

Most authors simply make some inscrutable remarks and move on. Since nobody seems to have any idea as to exactly what either the ancient or contemporary significance of *kala* is, we too shall just move on (after leaving you with these inscrutable remarks).

8TH ASPECT OF DASA PRANA (LAYA)

This is the tempo. This concept was explained in great length in Chapter 4.

9TH ASPECT OF DASA PRANA (YATI)

Yati has been described as the structure and arrangement of the various *ang*. That is to say that it is the way in which structures are put together within a composition. Although different authors have given slightly differently numbers of possible *yati* the common ones are: *sama, srotagata, mridanga, gopuchcha, damaru*.

10TH ASPECT OF DASA PRANA (PRASTAR)

Prastar is the process of mathematical permutation. There have been numerous discussions, interpretations, and reinterpretations over the centuries. We will illustrate a common contemporary interpretation. This contemporary interpretation is very relevant to the subject of theme-and-variation as found in *kaida* and *rela*. We will start with a four beat structure. It may then be broken up and recombined in the following manner:

4   2+2   1+3   3+1   1+1+2   1+2+1   2+1+1   1+1+1+1

We have given an extensive description of the *dasa prana* of *tal*; however, a few comments are in order. Although there is a tendency for many educated musicians to try and apply this to contemporary practice, there are fundamental difficulties.

The most fundamental problem is in the basic musical concept of time. It is clear that the *dasa prana* is based upon an absolute concept of time (e.g., seconds, milliseconds, etc), while the present north Indian system is based upon the relative concept of time (e.g. beats). This is indicated by the fact that the fundamental unit is the *anudrut,* which is defined as the length of time it takes to utter one syllable *(akshar kal)*. There is a general tendency equate the *laghu* with the *matra,* but the two are philosophically incompatible. In contemporary practice the *matra* is clearly a relative reference point while the *laghu* is fixed in absolute time. Since the entire system of *dasa prana* is based upon an absolute concept of time it renders much of this system irrelevant to contemporary practice.

CONCLUSION

If you have gone though this chapter you are probably baffled. I know that I was baffled the first time that I ran across it. For many years, I would be baffled every time I ran across this material. It took me a long time to realise that it was baffling because it has nothing to do with contemporary North Indian music. I am giving this material to you because this material is considered by many Indians to be important from a pedagogic standpoint. The major difference between my approach, and that found in most other books, is that I am telling you right off that it is irrelevant and not to worry about it.

WORKS CITED

Apte, Vasudeo Govind
1987   *The Concise Sanskrit English Dictionary*. Delhi: Motilal Banarsidas.

Klostermaier, Klaus
1994   *A Survey of Hinduism*. New York, NY:State University of New York Press.

Mani, T.A.S.
no date   *Sogasuga Mridanga Taalamu* K.C.P. Publications, Bangalore

Mistry, Aban E.
1999   *Pakhawaj & Tabla: History Schools and Traditions*. Mumbai: Pt. Keki S. Jijina, Swar Sadhna Samiti.

Saletore, R.N
1982   *Encyclopaedia of Indian Culture*, Bangalore, Sterling Publishers Pvt Ltd

Sharma, Bhagavat Sharan
1973   *Tal Prakash*. Hathras, India: Sangeet Karyalaya.
1977   *Tal Shastra*. Alighar, India: B. A. Electric Press.

Shepherd, F. A.
1976   *Tabla and the Benares Gharana*. Ann Arbor: University Microfilms International. (Ph.D. Dissertation).

Vinjamuri, Vara Narasimhacharya
1986   *Tal Lakshanam*. Kakinada, India: Padmini Printers

CHAPTER 8
INTRODUCTION TO COMPOSITIONAL THEORY

This chapter provides a general introduction to compositional theory. We will look at nomenclature and a brief overview of the compositional forms. These individual forms will be examined in greater detail in the next few chapters.

I have one word of warning when going through the material in the next few chapters. There are number of cases where contemporary usage is at odds with things that certain pandits deem acceptable. This is somewhat analogous to the constant conflict between grammatically correct English, as opposed to common day-to-day speech. Whenever I run across a conflict between contemporary usage and "grammatically correct" tabla forms, I must consider contemporary usage. I do this to develop a series which reflects the tabla as it is actually used, and not as a few pandits would wish it to be. However, I do make an effort to point out such conflicts when they occur.

NOMENCLATURE
An important part of our study of compositional forms must involve nomenclature; unfortunately this nomenclature is often confusing. Much of this confusion stems from the fact that the present system is derived from many different *gharanas*. This creates a situation where the same composition may be called different things. Fortunately the confusion can be minimised when we realise that the nomenclature may be based upon totally unrelated criteria.

This situation may be easily visualised with a simple analogy. Imagine a spaceman suddenly trying to make sense of the various classifications of human beings. Moving within human society, a particular individual may be classed as male, Democrat, Presbyterian, Freemason, or any of a number of labels. The overlapping nature of these classes will be very confusing to our spaceman until he realises that these labels are based upon totally different criteria.

This is the situation we find in the study Indian tabla. Traditional Indian nomenclature is based upon four separate criteria to define our composition: function, structure, *bol* and, in rare cases, technique. Furthermore, we have overwhelming reason to include a fifth criterion, overall philosophy, to the picture. One typically finds one or two criteria used for a definition, but rarely one will find more. Therefore, it is common to find the same composition called different things.

Differing criteria is critical for the proper definition of compositional forms, yet it is surprising that it has not been discussed in earlier work. Previous Western field investigators have largely failed to grasp this point, and it has never been an issue for the practising Indian musician. The various criteria are shown in Table 8.1.

> **Table 8.1. Defining Criteria for Tabla Compositions**
>
> **Overall Philosophy** - All material in North Indian music is ether cyclic or cadential.
>
> **Structure** - The structure of compositions are usually based upon 1, 2, 3, etc. well defined structures. There may be a symmetry to these structures or they may be asymmetric.
>
> **Bol Type** - Bols are derived from either Pakhawaj, "pure" tabla, dance, or standard speech.
>
> **Function (Style)** - This represents the usage of a composition. It varies tremendously between cyclic and cadential forms. It usually reflects stylistic conventions.
>
> **Technique** - Many compositions are characterized by an unusual technique. Common examples are one handed techniques (i.e., ekhatthu), or two handed techniques (i.e., dohatthu), etc.

<u>Structure</u> - Structure is the criterion based upon the anatomy of the composition. One piece may be based upon a phrase repeated three, four, or nine times. One piece may be evenly split in two. One may exhibit a symmetry, while another may be asymmetric. Some may cover several cycles, while others may be restricted to but a few beats. These are the structural considerations of a piece. *Tihai* and *kaida* are common forms which are defined by structure.

<u>Function or Style</u> - Function concerns how and when, a musician uses a composition. One composition may be used to start or end a section; one may be reserved for encores, or tabla solos. There are some pieces which are reserved for specific styles, such as light, classical, folk or dance music. Function may be thought of as a gestalt of artistic, and stylistic factors. The word "style" comes very close to describing function.

Two forms may be said to be functionally identical if they may be interchanged. For instance, although *tukada*, and *paran* are totally separate cadential forms, one may substitute a one-cycle *paran* for a one-cycle *tukada* without any break in the flow of a piece. Therefore, at the level of function, the two are identical, (However, they may be differentiated at another level.) This may not be intuitively obvious at this point; but it should become clearer as this work progresses.

<u>Bol</u> - The *bol* is an important criterion for defining some compositional forms. Some compositions may be based upon resonant strokes such as *Dhaa* (धा), *Ge* (गे), *Tun* (तुं), etc.; while some may be restricted to flat, non-resonant *bols*. Some may be based upon *bols* which are derived from the *pakhawaj*; while some may be based upon purely tabla *bols*. Some may be based upon dance *bols*, and some may even be based upon Hindi or Sanskrit poetry.

<u>Technique</u> - The technique is involved in the nomenclature in rare instances. One common example is known as *Ekhatthu*. *Ekhatthu* is a composition which is played only with one hand. Other examples will be shown later.

<u>Overall Philosophy</u> - We briefly mentioned that a fifth criterion has been added in recent years; this is the "overall philosophy". It is truly remarkable that this concept was never expressed earlier by Indian musicians/musicologists, because it is so clearly present in the music.

It is interesting how the concept of the overall philosophy developed. The seeds were sewn in the doctoral dissertation of Rebecca Marie Stewart. This dissertation was submitted in UCLA in 1974. It was a consistent theme throughout her work that all of the compositions and improvisations fall into two clear, distinct forms. One form shows process of tension /relaxation by driving forward to resolve on the *sam*. She referred to these as cadential forms. This was in contrast to the cyclic form. Cyclic forms simply roll along and are characterised by a sense of balance and repose. She referred to these compositions a being a "*gat*" form. Subsequent scholars, most notably Frances Shepherd (*Tabla and the Benares Gharana*) reflect this same observation, but with a slightly different terminology. Shepherd preferred the terms "symmetrical" and "climactic" (Shepherd 1976:251).

It is appropriate that we say a few words about these terms. As a sign of respect to Stewart's early work, I prefer to keep the term "cadential"; but I feel that there are serious problems with both the terms "symmetrical" and "*gat*". For example, *thekas,* which are considered a prime example of "symmetrical" forms by both Shepherd and Stewart, are often asymmetric (e.g., *Rupak tal*). The term *gat* is equally bad because it is so poorly defined. There are many *gats* which are actually cadential forms (e.g., *tipalli*). It is for this reason that I prefer the term "cyclic". All of this is of course mere academic quibbling over terms; the concepts elucidated by these early scholars are beyond question, and to them we owe a great debt.

The distinction between the cyclic and cadential forms is determined by the inclusion or exclusion of the *sam*. This has profound mathematical implications. The cyclic forms of tabla are those which do not include the *sam* as a termination. (e.g., *theka, kaida* and *rela*). Conversely the cadential material (e.g., *chakradar, tihai*) are defined by their inclusion.

Let us first look at the math behind the cyclic form. If we have a composition in *Tintal* of 16 beats, then these will consist of some multiple of 16 (i.e., 16, 32, 48, 64 etc.). Regardless of what multiplier is used, the terminal *sam* will never be included.

The math behind this forms is described in a simple example. If an article of clothing requires two meters of cloth, then two articles will require four metres, three will require six metres, etc. This form is so simple that it needs no discussion.

The simplicity of the math behind the cyclic form lies in stark contrast to the complexity of the cadential form. Since the *sam* of the final cycle is an inherent part of the cadential form, typical numbers of *matras* (beats) are always one more than one might expect. Therefore, for a *Tintal* cadential form, one would find them to be 17, 33, 49, 65 etc.

This may not be intuitive, so let us look at a simple analogy. Let us visualise a picket fence as shown in Figure 8.1 below. If we wish to have a picket fence that is 5 feet wide with pickets spaced evenly at 1 picket-per-foot, it will require 6 pickets. In a similar manner, if we wish this fence to be 10 feet wide, it would require 11 pickets; if we wished it to be 15 feet wide, it would require 16 pickets, etc. If this is difficult to understand, remember that a one foot picket fence still requires two pickets.

Figure 8.1. A 10 foot picket fence requires 11 pickets

COMPOSITIONAL FORMS

We will take an overview of the various compositional forms in tabla. This is just a very brief survey; a more in-depth look will come in the next two chapters.

Theka - *Theka* is the basic accompaniment pattern. In the last century or so, it has emerged to become the defining quality of a *tal*.

Prakar - *Prakars* are the variations upon the *theka*. Some of these variations are for technical reasons while others are artistic. Functionally, they are equivalent to the *thekas*.

Kaida - *Kaida* is a formal approach to theme-and-variation. The word *kaida* means "a system of rules" and implies a body of formulae by which one may mechanically generate such forms.

Gat - The word *gat* implies any of a variety of fixed compositions within the *purbi* traditions (Lucknow, Farukhabad, or Benares *gharanas*). The term is not very well defined and may be applied to a variety of forms.

Peshkar - The word *peshkar* literally means an "introduction". As such, the word is applied to several different forms. Nowadays, it is often used to refer to the loose improvisation performed by the tabla at the beginning of an instrumental piece. However, a more correct and formal definition refers to a style of theme-and-variation which is traditionally used to start tabla solos. It is especially common in the Punjab and Dilli *gharanas*.

Rela - *Rela* is a high speed improvisation. It is based upon simple *bols* which lend themselves to the high speeds required for *rela*.

Laggi - *Laggi* is a popular form of improvisation which is used in lighter forms such as *Dadra* and *Kaherava*. It is a ubiquitous part of the accompaniment of vocal styles, such as the *gazal*, *qawwali*, or *thumri*.

Mukhada - *Mukhada* is a small flourish culminating on *sam*. It is a small cadence that gives a little punch to one's musical accompaniment.

Tihai - The *tihai* is a small phrase repeated three times. Normally, it is executed in such a way that it culminates on *sam*.

Mohara - This is an ill defined term. According to many, the *mohara* is a small form which is similar in structure to the *tukada*. It has a body and a *tihai*. It is a small cadential piece that finishes on the *sam*. According to many this impinges upon the *paran*. The *mohara* is generally characterised by an unconventional structure, one who's culmination on *sam* is often surprising. However others opine that the *mohara* is very similar to the *mukhada*. For this series we will take the first approach.

Chakradar - Chakradar may be thought of as three *tihais* together. There are several variations depending on the structure. This will be discussed in greater detail later.

Paran - The *paran* is a form which is very much associated with the *pakhawaj* styles of playing. They are forceful and impressive. They may, or may not contain a *tihai*.

Uthan - *Uthan* may be thought of as a *tukhada* or *mohara* used in the Benares style to open a tabla solo.

Tukada - *Tukadas* are small cadential forms. They are found in musical accompaniment, solos, and dance accompaniment. According to some, they must be based upon closed *bols,* while other interpretations allow virtually any *bol* to be used.

Tipalli - *Tipalli* is a type of *gat* with three sections. Unlike the *tihai,* which is also of three sections, the *tipalli* has each section in a different *layakari*, usually ascending in speed.

Amad - The *amad* is an opening composition used by *Kathak* dancers. Although associated with the *kathak* dance, they may be found in tabla solos as well.

RELATIONSHIP BETWEEN THE CADENTIAL AND THE CYCLIC FORM
The way that the cadential and the cyclic forms interact is fundamental to the Indian performance. From an artistic standpoint, the cadential forms are our transitions, and the cyclic forms are our "grooves". Each has its own, and clearly delineated role.

The cyclic forms are used to provide the base for the music. In its simplest, it is merely *theka* for accompaniment. Even when we are being more aggressive with *laggis, relas,* or whatever, it is the cyclic form that drives everything on. Unfortunately another name for a "groove" is a "rut". Cyclic material has the disadvantage of turning into stagnation. At some point, we have to effect a transition, to "get out of the rut", so to speak.

This is where the cadential material comes in. Its nature is such that it breaks our basic groove, and introduces a distinct musical tension. This tension demands resolution, which it ultimately does on the *sam*. At which point, the artist is free to work with a new cyclic form. It maybe different, or faster. But even if it is the same material, it will have a different significance simply by being punctuated with a cadential form.

Therefore, we may recap the basic relationship between the two forms quite simply. An Indian musical performance is a constant process of cadence, cyclic, cadence, cyclic, cadence, etc. It is in this manner that the performance progresses

CONCLUSION
This is a very brief overview of the various compositional forms in tabla. We have seen that all compositions may be broken down into one of two mutually exclusive forms. One form is the cyclic; this is characterised by a sense of balance and repose. There is another form which is called cadential; this is characterised by sense of imbalance and musical tension. All performance of tabla may be seen as an interplay between these two forms.

WORKS CITED
Courtney, D.R
1998   *Fundamentals of Tabla*, Houston, TX Sur Sangeet Services.

Shepherd, Francis Ann
1976   *Tabla and the Benares Gharana*. Ann Arbor: University Microfilms International. Ph.D. Dissertation, Wesleyan University, Middletown, CT.

Stewart, R. M.
1974   *The Tabla in Perspective*. Ann Arbor: University Microfilms International. (Ph.D. Dissertation).

CHAPTER 9
COMPOSITIONAL THEORY (CYCLIC FORMS)

The cyclic form is a fundamental concept in Indian rhythm. It may even be the most fundamental form for any rhythmic system in the world. The cyclic form may be thought of as a "groove" in common musical parlance. It is a repetitive, flowing style which is characterised by a sense of musical balance and repose. Although variations are common, a basic repetitive quality is the norm.

MATHEMATICS OF THE CYCLIC FORM
The cyclic composition has a very specific mathematical form. The cyclic forms are structured around this simple formula:

$$\text{number of cycles} = \frac{\text{number of units in composition}}{(\text{number of matras in tal}) \cdot (\text{layakari})}$$

Let us look closely to see how this formula is applicable. Let us take a portion of the *kaida* that appeared in *Fundamentals of Tabla* (Courtney 1998):

Kaida #1 (theme) from *Fundamentals of Tabla*

धा	धा	ति	ट	धा	धा	तू	ना
Dhaa	Dhaa	Ti	Ta	Dhaa	Dhaa	Too	Na

ता	ता	ति	ट	धा	धा	धिं	ना
Taa	Taa	Ti	Ta	Dhaa	Dhaa	Dhin	Naa

The mathematics of this piece is extremely simple. In this piece, we see that the number of units is 16. This piece is performed in *Tintal*, so the number of *matras* is 16, the *layakari* is *barabar* (single time), therefore it has a value of 1.

Therefore, this piece takes one cycle or:

$$1 = \frac{16}{16 \bullet 1}$$

Let us look at a more complex piece and see how the numbers work:

<u>Variation #3 from Kaida #2 in *Fundamentals of Tabla*</u>

धा	तिर किट	धा	तिर किट	धा	ती
Dhaa	Ti Ra Ki Ta	Dhaa	Ti Ra Ki Ta	Dhaa	Tee

धा	धा	तिर किट	धा	धा	तू	ना
Dhaa	Dhaa	Ti Ra Ki Ta	Dhaa	Dhaa	Too	Naa

ता	तिर किट	ता	तिर किट	धा	ती
Taa	Ti Ra Ki Ta	Taa	Ti Ra Ki Ta	Dhaa	Tee

धा	धा	तिर किट	धा	धा	धिं	ना
Dhaa	Dhaa	Ti Ra Ki Ta	Dhaa	Dhaa	Dhin	Naa

As it is written his piece would have the following form. The number of units is 32, the number of beats in *Tintal* is 16, the *layakari* is *barabar*, therefore it has a value of 1, so the whole thing would come to 2 cycles or:

$$2 = \frac{32}{16 \bullet 1}$$

Now an astute reader will realise that there are other ways that this piece may be performed. Although the numbers may differ, the mathematics remain the same. For example let us say that we were to play the last piece in *dugan* (double time). Placing this new value into the formula now gives us 1, reflecting the fact that the whole piece will now come in a single cycle, or:

$$1 = \frac{32}{16 \bullet 2}$$

There is another thing that needs to be discussed; we mentioned the number of "units" without really defining what they were. We can say that a "unit" is basically a stroke, such that the entire piece has been normalised into equal values (huh?).

This is not really as difficult as it may at first appear. In the last example, we see that the four strokes of *TiRaKiTa* (तिर किट) have been normalised into two units. (Notice that unit is similar to *matra* but it need not be equivalent.) We could for example, have normalised in the other direction; therefore, the last piece could have been written as:

Variation #3 from Kaida #2 in *Fundamentals of Tabla*

धा -	ति	र	कि	ट	धा -	ति	र	कि	ट	धा -	ती -
Dhaa-	Ti	Ra	Ki	Ta	Dhaa-	Ti	Ra	Ki	Ta	Dhaa-	Tee -

धा -	धा -	ति	र	कि	ट	धा -	धा -	तू -	ना -
Dhaa-	Dhaa-	Ti	Ra	Ki	Ta	Dhaa-	Dhaa-	Too -	Naa -

ता -	ति	र	कि	ट	ता -	ति	र	कि	ट	धा -	ती -
Taa -	Ti	Ra	Ki	Ta	Taa -	Ti	Ra	Ki	Ta	Dhaa-	Tee -

धा -	धा -	ति	र	कि	ट	धा -	धा -	धिं -	ना -
Dhaa-	Dhaa-	Ti	Ra	Ki	Ta	Dhaa-	Dhaa-	Dhin -	Naa -

In this last example, we have normalised everything to the *TiRaKiTa* (ति र कि ट). Therefore we have had to pad the piece with a large number of pauses to maintain the same rhythmic balance. This is somewhat analogous to taking a piece originally scored in 2/2 time signature and rewriting it in 4/4 time signature. The process of re-normalising the piece to the *TiRaKiTa* (ति र कि ट) gives us a new set of numbers. We now find that the number of units has jumped to 64. The *layakari* automatically has jumped to *chaugan* (i.e., 4, remember we are now playing twice as many units in a *matra* as we were before). The number of *matras* in Tintal remains the same at 16; therefore, we now find that the formula is:

$$1 = \frac{64}{16 \bullet 4}$$

This is the basic mathematical characteristic of all of the cyclic material. Let us look now into the individual forms.

THEKA

The word "*theka*" literally means "support" (Pathak 1976). This term is indicative of the supporting nature that *theka* plays in a performance. *Theka* is perhaps the most fundamental example of a cyclic form. We saw in the last volume that *theka* is so fundamental to tabla that it has emerged as THE signature for any north Indian *tal*. Therefore, function is the important criterion for defining *theka* (Table 9.1.).

It is difficult to assess the importance of *bol* in defining *theka*. *Dhaa* (धा), *Dhin* (धिं), *Taa* (ता), *Naa* (ना), and *Tin* (तिं) are used to the extent that the majority of common *thekas* may be played using them.

Table 9.1. Defining Criteria of Theka

Overall philosophy	Cyclic
Structure	-
Bol Type	-
Function	"Signature" of tal and basic accompaniment
Technique	-

A very common example is *Tintal*:

Tintal

^xधा धिं धिं धा | ²धा धिं धिं धा |
Dhaa Dhin Dhin Dhaa Dhaa Dhin Dhin Dhaa

⁰धा तिं तिं ना | ³ना धिं धिं धा |
Dhaa Tin Tin Naa Naa Dhin Dhin Dhaa

Although our first response would be to say that *bol* is an important criterion for defining the *theka*; there is just one thing holding us back, the *pakhawaj tals*. They create a problem for us, because when *pakhawaj* material is played upon tabla, there is a tendency to conceptualise them in a modern fashion. Therefore we find "Chautal theka", "Dhammar theka", etc. They are problematic because they do not use the typical tabla *bols* that we have come to associate with *theka*. We could always perform some academic juggling and declare that they are not really *thekas* at all. We would be on easily defensible ground by doing this because, historically, the modern concept of *theka* is foreign to the old *pakhawaj* tradition. But this is a book about tabla as it is played today. As unhappy as we may be at the syncretism of old *pakhawaj* material with contemporary concepts, we must acknowledge and accommodate this situation. The presence of the "*pakhawaj thekas*" expands the number of usable *bols* to the extent that virtually any *bol* may be found. Since any *bol* may be used, it makes it difficult to say that *bol* is a defining criterion.

Structure is not a defining criterion for *theka;* but we may make a few observations. To begin with, there is a tendency for *theka* to be based upon two symmetrical structures. In *Jhaptal*, the structure *Dhin Naa Dhin Dhin Naa* (धिं ना धिं धिं ना) is opposed by *Tin Naa Dhin Dhin Naa* (तिं ना धिं धिं ना), or in *Dadra tal,* the phrase *Dhaa Dhin Naa* (धा धिं ना) is reflected in the structure *Dhaa Tin Naa* (धा तिं ना). It must be stressed that there are numerous *thekas* which do not exhibit this symmetry, *Rupak tal* for instance. Therefore, this must be considered a tendency rather than a rule.

Another structural observation is that there is a tendency for the *bols* to follow the structure of the *vibhag*. For instance the 2,3,2,3, clapping arrangement of *Jhaptal* is reflected in the *bols Dhin Naa | Dhin Dhin Naa | Tin Naa | Dhin Dhin Naa* (धिं ना | धिं धिं ना | तिं ना | धिं धिं ना |). Again, the numerous exceptions show that this is merely a tendency rather than a rule.

The topic of *theka* could take the better part of a book (It did take the better part of volume 1.) Since it has already been given adequate treatment, we will not delve further in this book.

PRAKAR

The word *"prakar"* literally means "kind", "type", or "method" (Kapoor no date)(Table 9.2). This implies that there are different types or methods by which a *theka* can be played. *Prakar* is so close to *theka* that in common parlance the two are synonymous. Because the *prakar* is derived from *theka,* it should be no surprise that it is functionally identical to *theka*. Yet, there is a very important and fundamental distinction between the two. *Theka* has become the defining pattern or signature for a *tal*, while *prakar* is merely an artistic or technical modification. *Prakar* is also known as *kisme*.

Bols are definitely not a defining criterion for *prakar*. Any *bol* may be present. However, there is a tendency to find the *bols* of the *theka* buried within the *prakar*. *Prakar* was dealt with in great length in the last volume, so we will not go into any great detail here.

Ch. 9. Compositional Theory - Cyclic Forms

Let us review a few important points about *prakar*. One point to remember is that there are a number of types of *prakar*. Each *prakar* is developed to satisfy a particular artistic or technical need.

One situation that requires a *prakar* is that of fast tempos. For example, it is common to play at speeds that make it impossible to play a standard *theka*. Therefore, a totally different technique is used. There is a strong effort to maintain the basic feel of the original, even though the *bols* may be different.

Table 9.2. Criteria for Prakar

Overall philosophy	Cyclic
Structure	-
Bol Type	-
Function	Basic accompaniment
Technique	-

Conversely, it is often necessary to play at extremely slow speeds. At such slow speeds, the use of the standard *theka* is inadvisable from both a technical and artistic standpoint. In such cases a different arrangement of *bols* is used which aids in the conceptualisation, and makes the performance feel more full.

There are also cases where there are alternative *bols*; often for no apparent reason. This is very evident in the lighter *tals* such as *Kaherava*. If one looks closely one often times finds processes at work such as the convergence of once different *tals*, or the differentiation of the same *tal*. These processes are merely academic and do not affect the performance.

The most common *prakars* are those which are mere artistic embellishments. This usually involves the substitution or addition of *bols*.

The various processes involved in the generation and performance of *prakars* are very involved. They were discussed in great length in Chapter 5 of *Fundamentals of Tabla*. Please refer back to this chapter in our first volume for further information.

KAIDA

Kaida is a prime example of a cyclic form (Table 9.3), especially one which is defined by its structure. Traditionally, the *kaida* has been the cornerstone for both performance of tabla solos as well as tabla instruction. The word *kaida* literally means "jurisprudence", or a "system of rules". *Kaida* is essentially a structural framework for theme-and-variation.

Today, the *kaida* is played throughout northern India; but this was not always the case. *Kaida* is said to have been invented by Nattu Khan of the *Dilli gharana*. Therefore, it has been most used by the musicians from this *gharana*. It has also been strong in the *Punjab* and *Ajrada gharanas*. In recent years, *kaida* has also been adapted to the *purbi* styles where it is sometimes referred to as *bant* or *banti*.

Table 9.3. Criteria for Kaida

Overall philosophy	Cyclic
Structure	Organized process of theme and variation
Bol Type	-
Function	-
Technique	-

It has already been mentioned that the word *kaida* means a system of rules. Here are the rules of *kaida*:

1. The overall structure is: *theka*, introduction (i.e. half tempo), theme (full tempo), variations, *tihai*, return to *theka*.
2. No *bols* should be introduced that are not in our theme.
3. The variations should proceed in a logical, mathematical process.
4. Every pattern should be played twice. The first section should be characterized by the use of resonant left hand strokes; this is often called *bhari*. The second section should be characterized by the absence of resonant left hand strokes; this is often called *khali*.

We will now look at the rules in greater detail.

<u>Kaida Rule #1 (Overall Form)</u> - The first rule of *kaida*, governs the overall form. We will use for our illustration a very famous *kaida* which has been attributed to the famous Nattu Khan[1]. Here we are giving it in its usual abbreviated notation. (The overall form will be discussed after going through this example.)

Theme

धा	ति	ट	धा	ति	ट	धा	धा	ति	ट	धा	गे	ति	ना	किं	ना
Dhaa	Ti	Ta	Dhaa	Ti	Ta	Dhaa	Dhaa	Ti	Ta	Dhaa	Ge	Tin	Naa	Kin	Naa
ता	ति	ट	ता	ति	ट	ता	ता	ति	ट	धा	गे	धिं	ना	गिं	ना
Taa	Ti	Ta	Taa	Ti	Ta	Taa	Taa	Ti	Ta	Dhaa	Ge	Dhin	Naa	Gin	Naa

Variation #1

धा	ति	ट	धा	ति	ट	धा	धा	धा	ति	ट	धा	ति	ट	धा	धा
Dhaa	Ti	Ta	Dhaa	Ti	Ta	Dhaa	Dhaa	Dhaa	Ti	Ta	Dhaa	Ti	Ta	Dhaa	Dhaa
धा	ति	ट	धा	ति	ट	धा	धा	ति	ट	धा	गे	ति	ना	किं	ना
Dhaa	Ti	Ta	Dhaa	Ti	Ta	Dhaa	Dhaa	Ti	Ta	Dhaa	Ge	Tin	Naa	Kin	Naa
ता	ति	ट	ता	ति	ट	ता	ता	ता	ति	ट	ता	ति	ट	धा	धा
Taa	Ti	Ta	Taa	Ti	Ta	Taa	Taa	Taa	Ti	Ta	Taa	Ti	Ta	Dhaa	Dhaa
धा	ति	ट	धा	ति	ट	धा	धा	ति	ट	धा	गे	धिं	ना	गिं	ना
Dhaa	Ti	Ta	Dhaa	Ti	Ta	Dhaa	Dhaa	Ti	Ta	Dhaa	Ge	Dhin	Naa	Gin	Naa

Variation #2

धा	ति	ट	धा	ति	ट	धा	धा	ति	ट	धा	गे	ति	ना	किं	ना
Dhaa	Ti	Ta	Dhaa	Ti	Ta	Dhaa	Dhaa	Ti	Ta	Dhaa	Ge	Tin	Naa	Kin	Naa
ति	ट	धा	गे	धिं	ना	गिं	ना	ति	ट	धा	गे	ति	ना	किं	ना
Ti	Ta	Dhaa	Ge	Dhin	Naa	Gin	Naa	Ti	Ta	Dhaa	Ge	Tin	Naa	Kin	Naa
ता	ति	ट	ता	ति	ट	ता	ता	ति	ट	धा	गे	धिं	ना	गिं	ना
Taa	Ti	Ta	Taa	Ti	Ta	Taa	Taa	Ti	Ta	Dhaa	Ge	Dhin	Naa	Gin	Naa
ति	ट	धा	गे	तिं	ना	किं	ना	ति	ट	धा	गे	धिं	ना	गिं	ना
Ti	Ta	Dhaa	Ge	Tin	Naa	Kin	Naa	Ti	Ta	Dhaa	Ge	Dhin	Naa	Gin	Naa

---

[1] If you are a student of tabla, it is very likely that you have been given this *kaida*; but it is likely that there are differences. For instance, it is usual for the variations to be different. There are differences from musician to musician and teacher to teacher. It is also possible that there will be differences in pronunciation (e.g., *Te Te* ते टे, or *Te Ta* ते ट instead of *Ti Ta* ति ट). We must not forget that India is a multilingual society; it is only natural that this will be reflected in the pronunciation of the *bols*.

Ch. 9. Compositional Theory - Cyclic Forms

Variation #3

धा	ति	ट	धा	ति	ट	धा	धा	ति	ट	धा	ति	ट	धा	ति	ट
Dhaa	Ti	Ta	Dhaa	Ti	Ta	Dhaa	Dhaa	Ti	Ta	Dhaa	Ti	Ta	Dhaa	Ti	Ta

धा	ति	ट	धा	ति	ट	धा	धा	ति	ट	धा	गे	तिं	ना	किं	ना
Dhaa	Ti	Ta	Dhaa	Ti	Ta	Dhaa	Dhaa	Ti	Ta	Dhaa	Ge	Tin	Naa	Kin	Naa

ता	ति	ट	ता	ति	ट	ता	ता	ति	ट	धा	ति	ट	धा	ति	ट
Taa	Ti	Ta	Taa	Ti	Ta	Taa	Taa	Ti	Ta	Dhaa	Ti	Ta	Dhaa	Ti	Ta

धा	ति	ट	धा	ति	ट	धा	धा	ति	ट	धा	गे	धिं	ना	गिं	ना
Dhaa	Ti	Ta	Dhaa	Ti	Ta	Dhaa	Dhaa	Ti	Ta	Dhaa	Ge	Dhin	Naa	Gin	Naa

Variation #4

धा	ति	ट	धा	ति	ट	धा	धा	ति	ट	-	धा	ति	ट	धा	धा
Dhaa	Ti	Ta	Dhaa	Ti	Ta	Dhaa	Dhaa	Ti	Ta	-	Dhaa	Ti	Ta	Dhaa	Dhaa

ति	ट	-	धा	ति	ट	धा	धा	ति	ट	धा	गे	तिं	ना	किं	ना
Ti	Ta	-	Dhaa	Ti	Ta	Dhaa	Dhaa	Ti	Ta	Dhaa	Ge	Tin	Naa	Kin	Naa

ता	ति	ट	ता	ति	ट	ता	ता	ति	ट	-	धा	ति	ट	धा	धा
Taa	Ti	Ta	Taa	Ti	Ta	Taa	Taa	Ti	Ta	-	Dhaa	Ti	Ta	Dhaa	Dhaa

ति	ट	-	धा	ति	ट	धा	धा	ति	ट	धा	गे	धिं	ना	गिं	ना
Ti	Ta	-	Dhaa	Ti	Ta	Dhaa	Dhaa	Ti	Ta	Dhaa	Ge	Dhin	Naa	Gin	Naa

Bharan

धा	ति	ट	धा	ति	ट	धा	धा	ति	ट	धा	गे	तिं	ना	किं	ना
Dhaa	Ti	Ta	Dhaa	Ti	Ta	Dhaa	Dhaa	Ti	Ta	Dhaa	Ge	Tin	Naa	Kin	Naa

ता	ति	ट	ता	ति	ट	ता	ता	ति	ट	धा	गे	धिं	ना	गिं	ना
Taa	Ti	Ta	Taa	Ti	Ta	Taa	Taa	Ti	Ta	Dhaa	Ge	Dhin	Naa	Gin	Naa

Tihai

[ति ट धा गे तिं ना किं ना धा] 3x   [- गिं ना] pause
  Ti Ta Dhaa Ge Tin Naa Kin Naa Dhaa   - Gin Naa

Let us go back and re-examine the performance of this *kaida* and see how it conforms to the first rule. In particular, we will not just give the abbreviated version, but will discuss how it is actually presented.

If we were to play this piece, the first thing that we will play is:

^xधा धिं धिं धा | ²धा धिं धिं धा | ⁰धा तिं तिं ना | ³ना धिं धिं धा |
Dhaa Dhin Dhin Dhaa Dhaa Dhin Dhin Dhaa Dhaa Tin Tin Naa Naa Dhin Dhin Dhaa

One will notice that this is basic *Tintal theka*. Although this is almost never specified in books of compositions, it is simply understood that *kaidas* must begin with *theka*. This goes back to our first rule.

Next, we play the basic theme in half of our desired tempo. This is our introduction.

Theme

धा	ति	ट	धा	ति	ट	धा	धा	ति	ट	धा	गे	तिं	ना	किं	ना
Dhaa	Ti	Ta	Dhaa	Ti	Ta	Dhaa	Dhaa	Ti	Ta	Dhaa	Ge	Tin	Naa	Kin	Naa
ता	ति	ट	ता	ति	ट	ता	ता	ति	ट	धा	गे	धिं	ना	गिं	ना
Taa	Ti	Ta	Taa	Ti	Ta	Taa	Taa	Ti	Ta	Dhaa	Ge	Dhin	Naa	Gin	Naa

The rules of *kaida* do not specify what the rhythmic relationship should be between our theme and the *theka*. For instance we could play it like this:

Theme

However, it could just as easily be played in double-time like this:

Although it is not specified by the rules of *kaida,* we would probably not wish to play this piece in quadruple-time. If we attempt to do so we will get something which looks like this:

धा ति ट धा	ति ट धा धा	ति ट धा गे	तिं ना किं ना
DhaaTiTaDhaa	TiTaDhaaDhaa	TiTaDhaaGe	TinNaaKinNaa
ता ति ट ता	ति ट ता ता	ति ट धा गे	धिं ना गिं ना
TaaTiTaTaa	TiTaTaaTaa	TiTaDhaaGe	DhinNaaGinNaa

Ch. 9. Compositional Theory - Cyclic Forms

Kaida certainly does not forbid us from starting in quadruple-time, however one usually does this only in extremely slow tempos. In this particular case, it is awkward because quadruple-time gives us only eight beats while *Tintal* is 16 beats. If we were to shift from quadruple time up to 8-times as our final desired tempo, this would give us only four beats. Although this would not violate any rules of *kaida* it would necessitate too many awkward gymnastics to make it work in 16 beats.

This introduction to the *kaida* plays an important function. It presents very clearly the *bols* that are going to be used. This can only be done if it is slower than the tempo in which one wishes to perform. Therefore the standard approach is to play the introduction at half of the tempo that wishes to perform the final piece.

There is another approach to our introduction which is sometimes found. One plays the theme in half the desired tempo, then one switches to 3/4th of the ultimate tempo for an intermediate introduction. Then one switches to full tempo. One advantage of this approach is that it is very beautiful. However, this intermediate introductory passage must, by necessity, be structured in a different fashion. Therefore, it may be considered by some to be stretching the rules of *kaida* a bit. Therefore this approach should be used only after some consideration.

At this point we may be getting a little confused. Let us step back and see what we have done up to now.

Theka

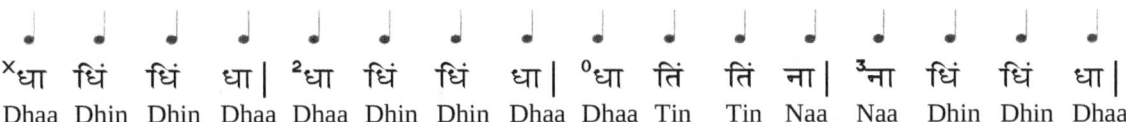

Theme

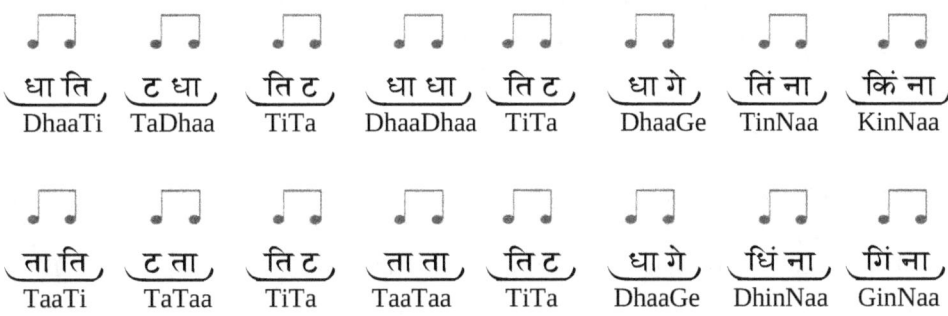

Theme in full tempo

Bharan

So we have constructed our *kaida* like this. We started with *theka*, then played the theme (introduction) at double-tempo. This particular tempo is chosen such that it will be half of what we really wish to play. Then we play it at the full tempo (i.e., quadruple-time). Since quadruple-time only produces eight beats for this *kaida*, we then play it one more time. This is referred to as *bharan*.

There is a certain controversy concerning the correct use of *bharan*. One school of thought considers this second iteration (*bharan*) to be an integral part of the *kaida*. Another school holds that it is only obligatory when the full tempo fails to complete a full cycle (as in this example). It is certainly not for us to settle the matter here. However, it is probably better to go ahead and always include it anyway.

From this point, it is a simple question of playing all of the variations in our chosen tempo (e.g., quadruple time). We need not repeat it here, it is understood.

There comes a time that we must resolve our *kaida*; we do this by performing a *tihai*. The *tihai* is a section that is played three times. *Tihai* is a very important part of Indian music; however we will postpone the discussion until later.

After the *tihai* is performed, we come back to the *theka* in the original tempo.

I am sure that we have lost many of our readers by this point. It may be helpful to go back and look at the whole performance written out in detail. Therefore, the performance goes like this:

Theka

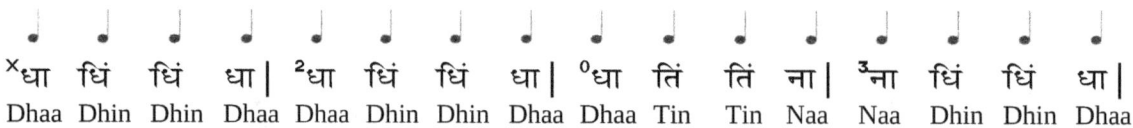

Theme

Ch. 9. Compositional Theory - Cyclic Forms

Theme in full tempo

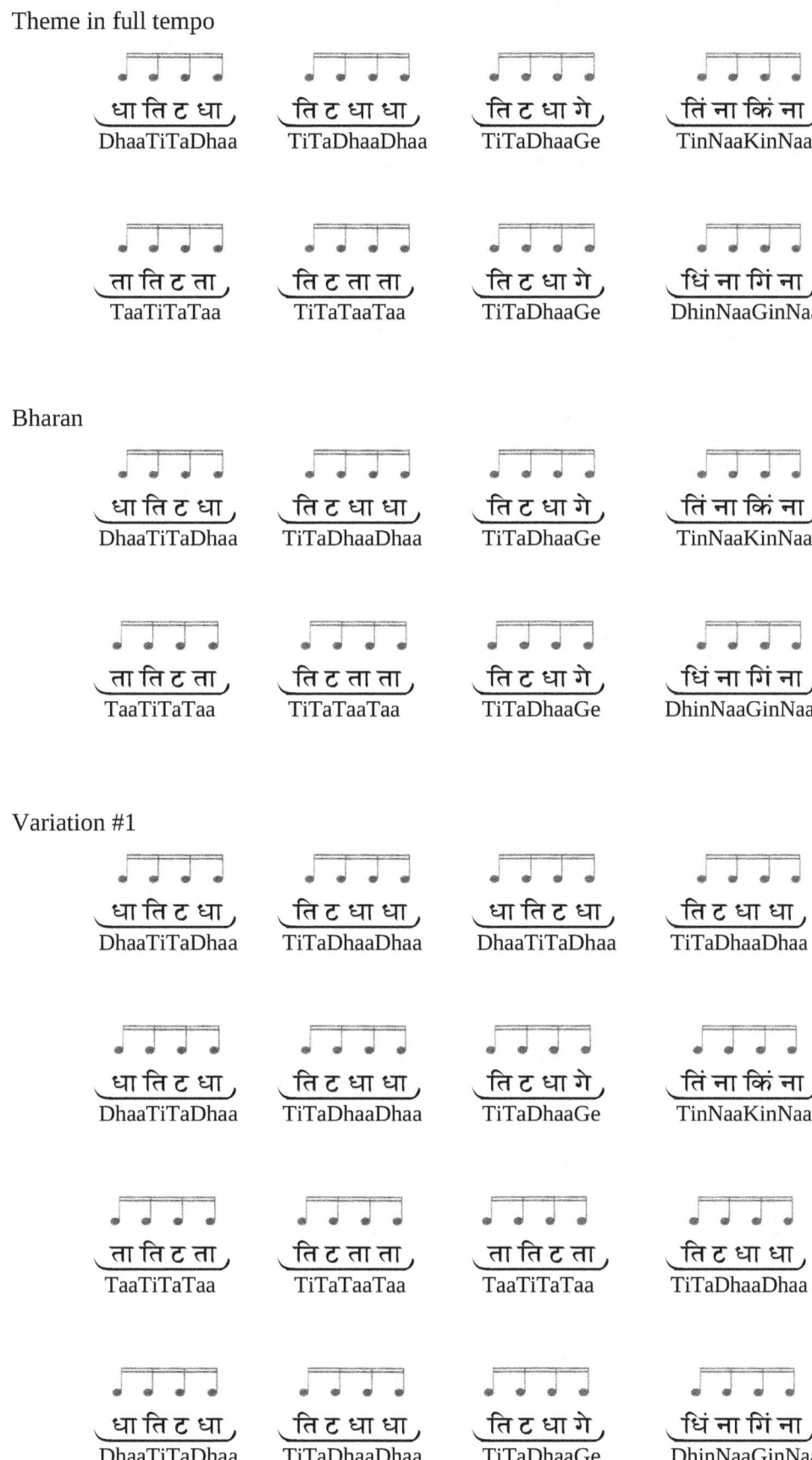

Bharan

Variation #1

Variation #2

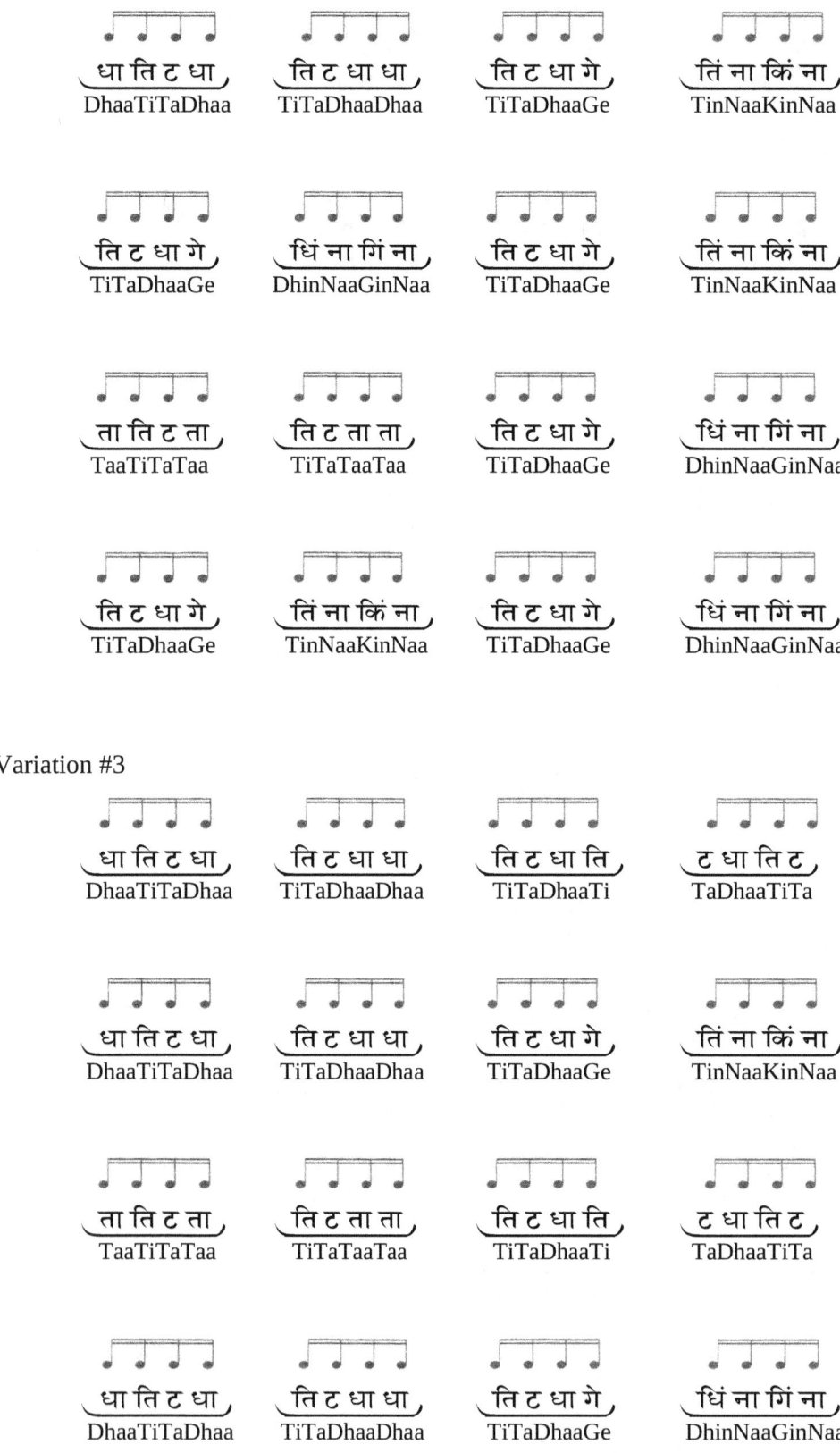

Variation #3

Ch. 9. Compositional Theory - Cyclic Forms

Variation #4

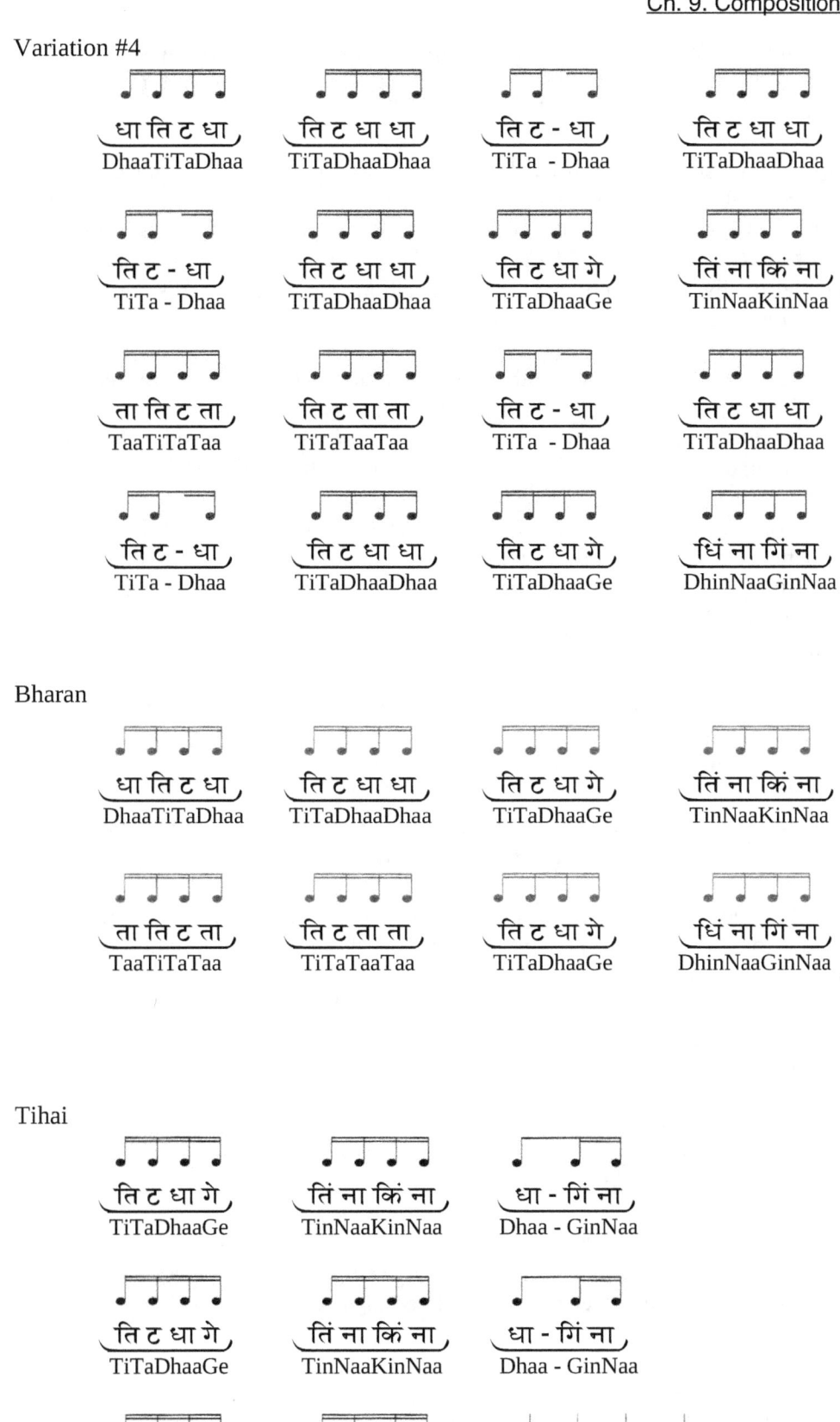

Bharan

Tihai

page 99

We may summarise the first rule of *kaida* quite simply. The overall form must be *theka*, introduction (i.e., theme at half the desired speed), theme at full speed, variations, *tihai*, return to *theka* in the original tempo. Let us now move to the second rule of *kaida*.

Kaida Rule #2 No New Bols - The second rule of *kaida* states that no *bols* may be introduced into the *kaida* that are not specified in the theme. (Although many musicians tend to ignore this rule these days.) We clearly would not wish to take this previous example and suddenly introduce *bols* like *DhiRaDhiRaKiTaTaKa* (धि र धि र कि ट त क) or *TiRaKiTa* (ति र कि ट) that were not used in the original theme. This rule should be fairly obvious and not need any explanation. However, there is one twist that needs to be addressed: the normal latitude of *bols*.

There is a normal latitude which is extended to tabla *bols*. The theory of *bols* allows a tremendous flexibility in the treatment of vowels. For example, the *bol Dhin* (धिं) is general considered equivalent to *Dhee* (धी), *Dhi* (धि), and *Dheen* (धीं) (there are two types of "n", one of which is considered a vowel). With this in mind, it is quite common to see alternate forms. So why do we have this flexibility?

Most of the languages of Northern India are not accented in the way that English is. Whereas English is accented by applying a stress, North Indian languages tend to accent by duration. For instance, we have long *oo* (ऊ) and short *u* (उ), etc. These linguistic characteristics often run counter to the musical requirements. Sometimes a musical requirement forces a particular *bol* to be long; but at other times short. It will be changed accordingly.

Kaida Rule #3 Logical Progression of Variations - The third rule of *kaida* states that all of the variations must proceed in a logical fashion. Yet there are many ways that we may proceed and still be logical. However the overall form is fairly consistent.

The variation is pivotal to the *kaida*; curiously it has no single accepted name. It may be referred to as *bal* (बल), *prastar* (प्रस्तार), *palta* (पल्टा), or a number of other terms.

The key to understanding the progression of variations, is to think of the *kaida* as being a poem in rhythm. As such, we must resort to the analogy of the rhyme. Let us turn to the limerick to refresh ourselves on the nature of rhyming patterns.

The limerick is wisdom poetical	A
In a form which is quite economical	A
But the good ones I've seen	B
Seldom are clean	B
And the clean ones seldom are comical	A

We see that the limerick is clearly based upon an AABBA rhyming pattern. The key word here is rhyming; this is not to suggest absolute equivalence. We will see later that this is an important point when applied to the *kaida*.

Let us look at rhyming patterns in our *kaida*:

Theme

धा	ति	ट	धा	ति	ट	धा	धा		ति	ट	धा	गे	तिं	ना	किं	ना	
Dhaa	Ti	Ta	Dhaa	Ti	Ta	Dhaa	Dhaa	**A**	Ti	Ta	Dhaa	Ge	Tin	Naa	Kin	Naa	**B**
ता	ति	ट	ता	ति	ट	ता	ता		ति	ट	धा	गे	धिं	ना	गिं	ना	
Taa	Ti	Ta	Taa	Ti	Ta	Taa	Taa	**A**	Ti	Ta	Dhaa	Ge	Dhin	Naa	Gin	Naa	**B**

Ch. 9. Compositional Theory - Cyclic Forms

Our theme clearly shows a pattern which reflects an ABAB rhyming structure. Let us now look and see how our *kaida* progresses from this in a logical fashion.

We see our first variation has the rhyming pattern AAABAAAB. It is shown here:

Variation #1

धा ति ट धा ति ट धा धा Dhaa Ti Ta Dhaa Ti Ta Dhaa Dhaa	**A**	धा ति ट धा ति ट धा धा Dhaa Ti Ta Dhaa Ti Ta Dhaa Dhaa	**A**
धा ति ट धा ति ट धा धा Dhaa Ti Ta Dhaa Ti Ta Dhaa Dhaa	**A**	ति ट धा गे तिं ना किं ना Ti Ta Dhaa Ge Tin Naa Kin Naa	**B**
ता ति ट ता ति ट ता ता Taa Ti Ta Taa Ti Ta Taa Taa	**A**	ता ति ट ता ति ट धा धा Taa Ti Ta Taa Ti Ta Dhaa Dhaa	**A**
धा ति ट धा ति ट धा धा Dhaa Ti Ta Dhaa Ti Ta Dhaa Dhaa	**A**	ति ट धा गे धिं ना गिं ना Ti Ta Dhaa Ge Dhin Naa Gin Naa	**B**

Our second variation has the form ABBBABBB. It may be seen like this:

धा ति ट धा ति ट धा धा Dhaa Ti Ta Dhaa Ti Ta Dhaa Dhaa	**A**	ति ट धा गे तिं ना किं ना Ti Ta Dhaa Ge Tin Naa Kin Naa	**B**
ति ट धा गे धिं ना गिं ना Ti Ta Dhaa Ge Dhin Naa Gin Naa	**B**	ति ट धा गे तिं ना किं ना Ti Ta Dhaa Ge Tin Naa Kin Naa	**B**
ता ति ट ता ति ट ता ता Taa Ti Ta Taa Ti Ta Taa Taa	**A**	ति ट धा गे धिं ना गिं ना Ti Ta Dhaa Ge Dhin Naa Gin Naa	**B**
ति ट धा गे तिं ना किं ना Ti Ta Dhaa Ge Tin Naa Kin Naa	**B**	ति ट धा गे धिं ना गिं ना Ti Ta Dhaa Ge Dhin Naa Gin Naa	**B**

Before we continue to look at the rest of the rhyming patterns, let us look at some variations that we could have done. We have performed AAABAAAB and ABBBABBB. It is very reasonable that at this point we could perform ABABABAB. This could be structured like this:

Possible Variation

धा ति ट धा ति ट धा धा Dhaa Ti Ta Dhaa Ti Ta Dhaa Dhaa	**A**	ति ट धा गे धिं ना गिं ना Ti Ta Dhaa Ge Dhin Naa Gin Naa	**B**
धा ति ट धा ति ट धा धा Dhaa Ti Ta Dhaa Ti Ta Dhaa Dhaa	**A**	ति ट धा गे तिं ना किं ना Ti Ta Dhaa Ge Tin Naa Kin Naa	**B**
ता ति ट ता ति ट ता ता Taa Ti Ta Taa Ti Ta Taa Taa	**A**	ति ट धा गे धिं ना गिं ना Ti Ta Dhaa Ge Dhin Naa Gin Naa	**B**
धा ति ट धा ति ट धा धा Dhaa Ti Ta Dhaa Ti Ta Dhaa Dhaa	**A**	ति ट धा गे धिं ना गिं ना Ti Ta Dhaa Ge Dhin Naa Gin Naa	**B**

Some musicians will even expand the size to accommodate further permutations. For instance we could expand the rhyming patterns to include structures such as AABAABABAABAABAB, ABAABAABABAABAAB, etc. This habit is not universally accepted, and the performance of such variations runs the risk of incurring the wrath of conservative elements within the audience.

One will notice in all of these structures, that each pattern must end in a "B" pattern. This is no accident. This "B" phrase functions as a sub-theme, or turn-around which is obligatory. We would never end a *kaida* in an "A" structure. We will discuss this sub-theme later.

Manipulations of large structures such as "A" and "B" are very limiting; therefore, we break them down to produce smaller structures. This is clearly illustrated in subsequent variations. For instance, we may derive structures such as *TiTaDhaa* (ति ट धा) and even merely *TiTa* (ति ट) by breaking down our "A" structure. The addition of these smaller patterns greatly expands the mathematical possibilities. Let us look at the subsequent variations:

Variation #3

धा ति ट धा ति ट धा धा									ति ट धा			ति ट धा			ति ट		
Dhaa Ti Ta Dhaa Ti Ta Dhaa Dhaa	**A**	Ti Ta Dhaa	**C**	Ti Ta Dhaa	**C**	Ti Ta	**D**
Dhaa Ti Ta Dhaa Ti Ta Dhaa Dhaa	**A**	Ti Ta Dhaa Ge Tin Naa Kin Naa	**B**
Taa Ti Ta Taa Ti Ta Taa Taa	**A**	Ti Ta Dhaa	**C**	Ti Ta Dhaa	**C**	Ti Ta	**D**
Dhaa Ti Ta Dhaa Ti Ta Dhaa Dhaa	**A**	Ti Ta Dhaa Ge Dhin Naa Gin Naa	**B**

Variation #4

Dhaa Ti Ta Dhaa Ti Ta Dhaa Dhaa	**A**	Ti Ta -	**E**	Dhaa Ti Ta Dhaa Dhaa	**F**
Ti Ta -	**E**	Dhaa Ti Ta Dhaa Dhaa	**F**	Ti Ta Dhaa Ge Tin Naa Kin Naa	**B**
Taa Ti Ta Taa Ti Ta Taa Taa	**A**	Ti Ta	**E**	Dhaa Ti Ta Dhaa Dhaa	**F**
Ti Ta -	**E**	Dhaa Ti Ta Dhaa Dhaa	**F**	Ti Ta Dhaa Ge Dhin Naa Gin Naa	**B**

The sub-theme is a very important part of the theme-and-variation structure. However, there is no agreement as to exactly how it is to be defined. Some *gharanas*, most notably the Punjab *gharana,* tend to define this sub-theme in much smaller terms. For instance, whereas we defined the entire "B" structure as our sub-theme (i.e., *TiTaDhaaGeDhinNaaGinNaa* (ति ट धा गे धिं ना गिं ना), it could just as easily have been defined as merely *DhinNaaGinNaa* (धिं ना गिं ना). This is well within the accepted structure of *kaida*.

There are a few observations that we can make about the overall form of the *kaida*. One will note that this *kaida* is in *Tintal*. Historically, all *kaidas* were in *Tintal*. However, today they may be performed in other *tals*. This raises some interesting questions concerning the overall structure. Let us take the form of an *Ektal kaida* as an example.

Ektal Kaida (Quadratic Form)

(6 beat structure)	**A**	(6 beat structure)	**B**
(6 beat structure)	**A**	(6 beat structure)	**B**

Ch. 9. Compositional Theory - Cyclic Forms

Ektal Kaida (Triadic Form)

(4 beat structure)	A	(4 beat structure)	A	(4 beat structure)	B
(4 beat structure)	A	(4 beat structure)	A	(4 beat structure)	B

We see that there are two philosophies concerning the generation of *kaidas* in *Ektal*. One philosophy holds that the quadratic structure is inherent to the *kaida* form. Therefore whenever a *kaida* is generated in any *tal*, it must maintain this quadratic structure. However, there are others who are of the opinion that the quadratic structure was merely a reflection of the structure of *Tintal*. This school of thought holds that any reasonable structure is acceptable, and that in the case of *Ektal*, a triadic structure is convenient. We are not going to pontificate on these matters; we merely bring out the fact that there are different opinions on this point.

This previous section dealt with the third rule of *kaida* which states that all variations must proceed in a logical mathematical fashion. This form is very similar to the rhyming patterns of a poem. We also saw that there is not merely one, but numerous logical processes which may be invoked. We also saw that the nature of the permutations first start with the manipulation of larger patterns. Later these patterns are broken down into smaller blocks. One may then continue to manipulate ever smaller and smaller blocks, until one has exhausted the artistically acceptable variations (or more likely, exhausted the audience.)

<u>Kaida Rule #4 Everything Played Twice</u> - The fourth rule of *kaida* states that everything must be played twice. If we looked at all of our previous variations we noticed that they were invariably constructed upon two symmetrical structures. Therefore if we had an ABBB structure, it had to be reflected by another ABBB structure. By the same token if there was an AAAB structure, it had to be reflected by another AAAB structure. This is a prime rule of *kaida*.

The first iteration is called the *bhari* (भरी) or *khuli*. The word *bhari* means "full". The name is derived from the fact that there is a preponderance of strokes with the full left hand (e.g., *Dhaa* धा, *Dhin* धिं, *Ga* ग, etc.).

The second iteration is called the *khali* (खाली) or *mundi*. The word *khali* literally means "empty", and refers to the absence of resonant left hand strokes.

The manner in which the left hand works is very interesting and important to the correct playing of *kaida*. (Please refer to the table below for illustration.) Note that the full left hand strokes are not maintained throughout the *bhari*. Rather at some point before the *khali* section, they drop out. This may be view as a kind of foreshadow. In the same way, the resonant left hand strokes are not eliminated throughout the *khali*. Rather at some midpoint, there is a return to the full resonant strokes. It is always amazing how little of the *khali* is characterised by the lack of open, resonant left hand strokes.

Bhari / Khali Sections

BHARI This section played with full resonant left hand											Left hand drops out			
धा	ति	ट	धा	ति	ट	धा	धा	ति	ट	धा गे	तिं	ना	किं	ना
Dhaa	Ti	Ta	Dhaa	Ti	Ta	Dhaa	Dhaa	Ti	Ta	Dhaa Ge	Tin	Naa	Kin	Naa
KHALI This section shows the *khali*								Return of resonant left hand						
ता	ति	ट	ता	ति	ट	ता	ता	ति	ट	धा गे	धिं	ना	गिं	ना
Taa	Ti	Ta	Taa	Ti	Ta	Taa	Taa	Ti	Ta	Dhaa Ge	Dhin	Naa	Gin	Naa

The manner in which the left hand returns in the *khali* is not specified in the rules of *kaida*. The example above shows about half of the *khali*, but it is not unusual for there to be only a couple of strokes. It is better to say that the rules of *kaida* merely say that the *khali* must be indicated; it does not actually specify what proportion of the *khali* must refrain from using open-left-hand strokes.

<u>Mixing Kaida with Other Forms</u> - We must not forget that *kaida* is a procedure. Therefore, if we take this procedure and apply it to other compositional forms, we get valid and interesting mixes. For instance, if we take *rela* and develop it according to the rules of *kaida*, we get a form known as *kaida-rela*. By the same token, if we take a *peshkar* and develop it according to the *kaida* procedure, we get a form known as *peshkar kaida*. These mixed forms will be discussed under the appropriate sections.

<u>Artistic License and Kaida</u> - In the real world, people do not always obey the laws of the land; in a similar fasion, musicians do not always obey the rules of *kaida*. Although I am personally against taking undue liberties with *kaida,* I do have an obligation to put before you the liberties that one may encounter.

There are many reasons why a musician may disobey the rules when presenting a *kaida*. One of which is ignorance. Some musicians are inadequately trained and may not truly understand the significance of *kaida*. This certainly cannot be condoned. There are, however, musicians who understand full well the rules of *kaida* and choose to ignore them. Their case is simple and at times compelling. *Kaida* by its very nature, is a mechanical process for generating theme-and-variation. As such, the beauty is often more cerebral than visceral. We could say that it has the same type of beauty as an elegant mathematical proof. Unfortunately such cerebral forms of beauty are often inaccessible to the average concert goer. Therefore, there has been a tendency in recent years for many artists to "spice it up" to make the *kaida* more appealing to the masses. This is often accomplished at the expense of running rough-shod over the fundamental rules. I realise that there are commercial pressures to do so.

The bottom line is that, as a student of music, you have a simple obligation. You must be completely conversant with the forms you are dealing with. If, after truly understanding such forms, you wish to take such liberties, then it is up to you.

Kaida is discussed in greater detail in the fourth volume of this series, *Focus on the Kaidas of Tabla*.

GAT

Gat is a very poorly defined term. It essentially refers to a class of *purbi* fixed compositions, as opposed to improvisations. It is so poorly defined that many types are cadential (e.g., *tipalli*) while the majority are cyclic. We include the *gat* here under cyclic form because it is the most common interpretation. *Gat* is determined by the *bols* which are used (Table 9.4). Such *bols* are typically from the *purbi* tradition (i.e., *Farukhabad, Lucknow,* and *Benares gharanas*). *Bols* such as *KiTaTaKa* (कि ट त क) and *DhaGeTiTa* (धा गे ति ट) are commonly used.

Table 9.4. Criterion for Gat	
Overall philosophy	-
Structure	-
Bol Type	Purbi
Function	-
Technique	-

Ch. 9. Compositional Theory - Cyclic Forms

Although the *gat* is very poorly defined, it has some subclasses which are very clearly defined. Some of the common subclasses are:

1) Ekhatthu (cyclic or cadential) - *Ekhatthu* is a *gat* which is played entirely with one hand.

2) Dohatthu (cyclic or cadential) - *Dohatthu* is a *gat* that uses two hands on a single drum.

3) Fard (cyclic) - A *gat* with only one internal structure.

4) Domukhi (cyclic) - A *gat* with two internal structures.

5) Tinmukhi (cyclic) - A *gat* with three internal structures.

6) Dupalli (cadential) - A *gat* with two internal structures, but at different *layakari*

7) Tipalli (cadential - A *gat* with three internal structures, but at different *layakari*

8) Chaupalli (cadential) - A *gat* with four internal structures, but at different *layakari*.

9) Lom-Vilom (cyclic) - A musical palindrome.

10) Gat-Kaida (cyclic) - A *kaida* that uses the *bols* of *gat*. This is very similar to the *banti*.

We would be justified in treating all of these under our section on *gat;* but since these subclasses are so well defined, we will treat them separately

Let us look at a *gat* that is reputed to be from Haji Sahib. Haji Sahib, otherwise known as Vilayat Ali Khan, was a great stalwart of the Farukhabad *gharana*.

Haji Sahib's Gat in Tintal (S. Dawood Khan, 1978, personal interview)

धिर धिर किट तक त क त ग धि न धि न त क त ग
DhiRa DhiRa KiTa TaKa Ta Ka Ta Ga Dhi Na Dhi Na Ta Ka Ta Ga

धिर धिर किट तक तग धिर धिर किट तक तग धिर धिर किट तक
DhiRa DhiRa KiTa TaKa Ta Ga DhiRa DhiRa KiTa TaKa Ta Ga DhiRa DhiRa KiTa TaKa

तिर तिर किट तक त क त ग धि न धि न त क त ग
TiRa TiRa KiTa TaKa Ta Ka Ta Ga Dhi Na Dhi Na Ta Ka Ta Ga

धिर धिर किट तक तग धिर धिर किट तक तग धिर धिर किट तक
DhiRa DhiRa KiTa TaKa Ta Ga DhiRa DhiRa KiTa TaKa Ta Ga DhiRa DhiRa KiTa TaKa

This last composition is fairly typical of the "pure" *gat*. By "pure", I mean a *gat* which is not one of the well defined sub-classes. This *gat* has a very well defined binary structure; in other words, it has a very clear *bhari / khali* arrangement. Although such *bhari / khali* structures are very common in the *gat*, they are not a requirement.

Table 9.5. Criteria for Peshkar	
Overall philosophy	Cyclic
Structure	-
Bol Type	Dhee - Kra Dhin Naa धी - क्र धिं ना etc.
Function	Opening piece
Technique	-

PESHKAR

Peshkar is a style which is defined by function and *bols* (Table 9.5). The word *"pesh"* literally means an introduction, and reflects its function as a traditional opening for tabla solos.

The term *Peshkar* is often applied to very different compositional forms. It is often applied to the opening improvisation for instrumental, or other classical forms. When it is used in this form the term is defined entirely by the function. Although this is an extremely common style of playing, it is also highly improvised. It is very much a reflection of a musician's individual style. It is therefore hard to make any definite statements about this style of *peshkar*.

The term "*peshkar*" is also applied to a classical form of theme-and-variation. Because it is a theme-and-variation, it bears a superficial resemblance to *kaida*; however, there are fundamental differences. *Kaida* for example, is defined entirely by the structure, with no concern for *bols* or function. *Peshkar* conversely, is defined by the *bols* and function, and not so much by the structure. (We will frequently use the *kaida* as a point of reference in our discussion of *peshkar*.)

Peshkar is defined by a particular set of *bols*; *Dhee - Kra Dhin Naa* (धी - क्र धिं ना), is a common example. Let us look at a simple *peshkar*:

Peshkar in Tintal (S. Dawood Khan personal interview 1976)

धिं - किड़ धिं धा ते   धा तिर किट धा ते   धा ते   धा धा तुं ना
Dhin - Kid Dhin Dhaa Te   Dhaa TiRa KiTa DhaaTe Dhaa Te Dhaa Dhaa Tun Naa

तिं - किड़ तिं ता ते   ता तिर किट धा ते   धा ते   धा धा धिं ना
Tin - Kid Tin Taa Te   Taa TiRa KiTa DhaaTe Dhaa Te Dhaa Dhaa Dhin Naa

Variation #1

धा घिड़ नाग धीं ना घिड़ नाग धीं ना   धा ते धा घिड़ नाग धीं ना
Dhaa GhiDa NaaGa Dhin Naa GhiRa NaaGa DheenNaa Dhaa Te Dhaa GhiRa NaaGa Dheen Naa

धा घिड़ नाग धीं ना धा ते   धा तुं ना धा ते   धा धा धिं ना
Dhaa GhiRa NaaGa DheenNaa Dhaa Te Dhaa Tun Naa Dhaa Te Dhaa Dhaa Dhin Naa

Variation #2

घिड़ नाग धी ना धा घिड़ नाग धीं ना   धा ते   धा ते   धा तुं ना
GhiRa NaaGa Dhee Naa Dhaa GhiRa NaaGa DheenNaa Dhaa Te Dhaa Te Dhaa Tun Naa

धा ते   धा तुं ना धा ते   धा तुं ना धा ते   धा धा धिं ना
Dhaa Te Dhaa Tun Naa Dhaa Te Dhaa Tun Naa Dhaa Te Dhaa Dhaa Dhin Naa

Ch. 9. Compositional Theory - Cyclic Forms

Pseudo Tihai

तक्	घिडां	- न	धा	तुं	ना	धिं	ना	धा	तुं	ना	धिं	ना	धा	तुं	ना
Tak	GhiDaan	- Na	Dhaa	Tun	Naa	Dhin	Naa	Dhaa	Tun	Naa	Dhin	Naa	Dhaa	Tun	Naa

तक्	घिडां	- न	धा	तुं	ना	घिडां	- न	धा	तुं	ना	घिडां	- न	धा	तुं	ना
Tak	GhiDaan	- Na	Dhaa	Tun	Naa	GhiDaan	- Na	Dhaa	Tun	Naa	GhiDan	- Na	Dhaa	Tun	Naa

×धा
Dhaa

The last example is fairly typical of both the structure and *bols* of *peshkar*. Let us make a few observations. One of the things that we see is that, like the typical *Tintal kaida*, it has a roughly quadratic/binary structure. But unlike the *kaida*, the symmetry is very weak, there is not necessarily any *bhari/khali* form. We also see that the variations do not progress in the way that they would in a *kaida*. Where *kaida* is based upon a process of permutation, the *peshkar* variations are based upon a process of substitution. One of the most interesting things is the pseudo-*tihai* at the end. If one is listening to it, it feels like a *tihai*, however it does not have the well defined triadic structure that we have come to expect in a *tihai*.

Let us look at another *peshkar*.

Peshkar in Tintal (Zakir Hussain, personal interview 1988)
Theme (play twice)

धा	-कृ	धा	ती	धा	तिर	किट	धा	ती	धा	धा	ती	धा	धा	तिं	ना
Dhaa	- Kra	Dhaa	Tee	Dhaa	TiRa	KiTa	Dhaa	Tee	Dhaa	Dhaa	Tee	Dhaa	Dhaa	Tin	Naa
-	-कृ	धा	ती	धा	तिर	किट	धा	ती	धा	धा	ती	धा	धा	तिं	ना
-	- Kra	Dhaa	Tee	Dhaa	TiRa	KiTa	Dhaa	Tee	Dhaa	Dhaa	Tee	Dhaa	Dhaa	Tin	Naa
-	ना	तिं	ना	किड	नाक	तिं	ना	तिं	ना	ना	ती	ना	ना	तिं	ना
-	Naa	Tin	Naa	KiDa	NaaKa	Tin	Naa	Tin	Naa	Naa	Tee	Naa	Naa	Tin	Naa
-	धा	गे	ना	धिं	ना	धा	धा	धिं	ना	-	धा	-	धा	धिं	ना
-	Dhaa	Ge	Naa	Dhin	Naa	Dhaa	Dhaa	Dhin	Naa	-	Dhaa	-	Dhaa	Dhin	Naa

Variation #1

धा	-कृ	धा	ती	धा	तिर	किट	धा	ती	धा	धा	ती	धा	धा	तिं	ना
Dhaa	- Kra	Dhaa	Tee	Dhaa	TiRa	KiTa	Dhaa	Tee	Dhaa	Dhaa	Tee	Dhaa	Dhaa	Tin	Naa
-	-कृ	धा	ती	धा	तिर	किट	धा	ती	धा	धा	ती	धा	धा	तिं	ना
-	- Kra	Dhaa	Tee	Dhaa	TiRa	KiTa	Dhaa	Tee	Dhaa	Dhaa	Tee	Dhaa	Dhaa	Tin	Naa
-	ना	तिं	ना	किड	नाक	तिं	ना	तिं	ना	ना	ती	ना	ना	तिं	ना
-	Naa	Tin	Naa	KiDa	NaaKa	Tin	Naa	Tin	Naa	Naa	Tee	Naa	Naa	Tin	Naa
-	धा	गे	ना	तिं	ना	धा	गे	ना	तिं	ना	धा	गे	ना	धिं	ना
-	Dhaa	Ge	Naa	Tin	Naa	Dhaa	Ge	Naa	Tin	Naa	Dhaa	Ge	Naa	Dhin	Naa

Variation #2

Dhaa - Kra	Dhaa	Tee	Dhaa TiRa KiTa	Dhaa	Tee	Dhaa	Dhaa	Tee	Dhaa	Dhaa	Tin	Naa
- KraDhaa	TeeDhaa	GeNaa	DhaaTee	DhaaGe	TinNaa	KeNaa	- Dhaa	Dhaa	Tee	Dhaa	Dhaa	Tin	Naa
-	Naa	Tin	Naa KiDa	NaaKa	Tin	Naa	Tin	Naa	Naa	Tee	Naa	Naa	Tin	Naa
-	Dhaa	Ge	Naa	Tin	Naa	Dhaa	Ge	Naa	Tin	Naa	Dhaa	Ge	Naa	Dhin	Naa

Variation #3 +Tihai

Dha - Kra	Dhaa	Tee	Dhaa TiRa KiTa	Dhaa	Tee	Dhaa	Dhaa	Tee	Dhaa	Dhaa	Tin	Naa
- KraDhaa	TeeDhaa	GeNaa	DhaaTee	DhaaGe	TinNa	KeNaa	- Dhaa	Dhaa	Tee	Dhaa	Dhaa	Tin	Naa
- Naa Tin Naa KiDa NaaKa TinNaa -	KraTaa	TiTaa	KeNaa	TaaTee	TaaKe	TinNaa	KeNaa
- KraDhaa TeeDhaa GeNaa DhaaTee DhaaGe DhinNaa GeNaa - Dhaa DhaaTee Dhaa - Dhaa DhaaTee Dhaa - Dhaa DhaaTee

×Dhaa

Let us make a few observations about the previous *peshkar*. Notice the similarity in the *bols* and flow of the piece as compared to the previous example. Also notice the same process of substitution was used to create the variations. But unlike the earlier *peshkar*, we see that totally unrelated *bols* may be used in the substitution process; this is different from the strict adherence to a basic set of *bols* as characterised in the *kaida*. Notice that there is a clearly defined *tihai* that resolves this particular *peshkar*. Even then, the *tihai* is simple, almost under-formed. When we listen to it, we find that it feels very much like the pseudo-*tihai* that we had in the first *peshkar*.

Let us continue our comparison of the *kaida* and the *peshkar*. Up to this point, we have been remarking upon the differences between *kaida* and *peshkar*. This is certainly a useful intellectual exercise, but we must not forget that these differences are not inherent to the two forms. As has already been mentioned, both *peshkar* and *kaida* are forms of theme-and-variation. We have also mentioned that *peshkar* is defined by function and *bols*, while *kaida* is defined by structure. Since these are not overlapping criteria, there is no reason why we cannot use the *bols* of *peshkar*, have it function like a *peshkar*, yet use the strict structure and procedure of the *kaida*. In such cases it is referred to as *peshkar-kaida* (or *kaida-peshkar*). An example is shown on the next page:

Peshkar Kaida (Yadav 1999b:73)

Dhee - Ga Dhin Taa Dhin Naa - KaDhaa Tit Dhaa - GaDhaa Dhin Naa - KaDhaa

Tee - Ka Tin Taa Tin Naa - KaTaa Tit Dhaa - GaDhaa Dhin Naa - KaDhaa

Variation #1

Dhee - Ga Dhin Taa Dhin Naa - KaDhaa Dhee - Ga Dhin Taa Dhin Naa - KaDhaa

Dhee - Ga Dhin Taa Dhin Naa - KaDhaa Tit Dhaa - GaDhaa Dhin Naa - KaDhaa

Tee - Ka Tin Taa Tin Naa - KaTaa Tee - Ka Tin Taa Tin Naa - KaTaa

Dhee - Ga Dhin Taa Dhin Naa - KaDhaa Tit Dhaa - GaDhaa Dhin Naa - KaDhaa

Variation #2

Dhee - Ga Dhin Taa Dhin Naa - KaDhaa Dhin Naa - KaDhaa Dhin Naa - KaDhaa

Dhee - Ga Dhin Taa Dhin Naa - KaDhaa Tit Dhaa - GaDhaa Dhin Naa - KaDhaa

Tee - Ka Tin Taa Tin Naa - KaTaa Tin Naa - KaTaa Tin Naa - KaTa

Dhee - Ga Dhin Taa Dhin Naa - KaDhaa Tit Dhaa - GaDhaa Dhin Naa - KaDhaa

Variation #3

Dhee - Ga Dhin Taa - Dhaa Dhin Taa - Dhaa Dhin Taa Dhin Naa - KaDhaa

Dhee - Ga Dhin Taa Dhin Naa - KaDhaa Tit Dhaa - GaDhaa Dhin Naa - KaDhaa

Tee - Ka Tin Taa - Taa Tin Taa - Taa Tin Taa Tin Naa - KaTaa

Dhee - Ga Dhin Taa Dhin Naa - KaDhaa Tit Dhaa - GaDhaa Dhin Naa - KaDhaa

Variation #4

धी ना - कधा, धा धा धिं ता - धा धिं ता धिं ना - कधा,
Dhee Naa - KaDhaa Dhaa Dhaa Dhin Taa - Dhaa Dhin Taa Dhin Naa - KaDhaa

धी -ग, धिं ता धिं ना - कधा, तित् धा - गधा, धिं ना - कधा,
Dhee - Ga Dhin Taa Dhin Naa - KaDhaa Tit Dhaa - GaDhaa Dhin Naa - KaDhaa

ती ना - कता, ता ता तिं ता - ता तिं ता तिं ना - कता,
Tee Naa - KaTaa Taa Taa Tin Taa - Taa Tin Taa Tin Naa - KaTaa

धी -ग, धिं ता धिं ना - कधा, तित् धा - गधा, धिं ना - कधा,
Dhee - Ga Dhin Taa Dhin Naa - KaDhaa Tit Dhaa - GaDhaa Dhin Naa - KaDhaa

Variation #5

धी ना कधा, तित् धा - गधा, तित् धा - गधा, धिं ना - कधा,
Dhee Naa KaDhaa Tit Dhaa - GaDhaa Tit Dhaa - GaDhaa Dhin Naa - KaDhaa

धी -ग, धिं ता धिं ना - कधा, तित् धा - गधा, धिं ना - कधा,
Dhee - Ga Dhin Taa Dhin Naa - KaDhaa Tit Dhaa - GaDhaa Dhin Naa - KaDhaa

ती ना कता, तित् ता - कता, तित् ता - कता, तिं ना - कता,
Tee Naa KaTaa Tit Taa - KaTaa Tit Taa - KaTaa Tin Naa - KaTaa

धी -ग, धिं ता धिं ना - कधा, तित् धा - गधा, धिं ना - कधा,
Dhee - Ga Dhin Taa Dhin Naa - KaDhaa Tit Dhaa - GaDhaa Dhin Naa - KaDhaa

Tihai

धी -ग, धिं ता धिं ना - कधा, धा - - -
Dhee - Ga Dhin Taa Dhin Naa - KaDhaa Dhaa - - -

धी -ग, धिं ता धिं ना - कधा, धा - - -
Dhee - Ga Dhin Taa Dhin Naa - KaDhaa Dhaa - - -

धी -ग, धिं ता धिं ना - कधा, | ˣधा
Dhee - Ga Dhin Taa Dhin Naa - KaDhaa Dhaa

We may summarise *peshkar* quite simply. It is an introductory section of a tabla solo. Although the word is sometimes applied to the introductory improvisation found in classical instrumental accompaniment, it is more correctly applied to a form of theme-and-variation. This theme-and-variation usually flows with a different form from *kaida*, but does not have to. When the *peshkar* follows a strict *kaida* format, it is called *peshakar-kaida*.

Ch. 9. Compositional Theory - Cyclic Forms

RELA

Rela is a very popular compositional type. It is characterised by a high speed manipulation of small structures (e.g. TiRaKiTa तिरकिट, KiDaNaKa किडनाक, etc.) *Rela* may be improvised or composed. It is defined by function and occasionally by the *bol*, but not by structure.

There is an interesting story as to the origin of the term "*rela*". According to this story, there was a king who was very much impressed with the sound of the railroad train. In India, a railroad train is called a *rel gadi* (रेल गाड़ी) He asked his court musician to compose a piece on tabla that would imitate this sound. The musician did so, and the king was so impressed that he declared that from that day henceforth, this should be called *rela*.

This is an amusing story, but one which is far from correct. The etymology of the term "*rela*" (रेला) is very simple. The Oxford - Hindi-English dictionary (McGregor 1997) gives three definitions for the word *rela*. 1) a rushing stream. 2) A rush, shoving, crowded attack. and 3) line or string of animals. The musical composition "*rela*" is very consistent with contemporary usage of the Hindi term. There is no need to invoke amusing, but unlikely etymologies.

There are two schools of thought as to the criteria used to define *rela*; some define it by *bol* and some by function (Table 9.6). Those who define *rela* by the *bol* (Stewart 1974) say that it is characterised by a preponderance of closed *bols* (e.g., TiRiKiTaTaKa तिरकिटतक) while those who define *rela* by its function say that it is an ultra-high speed tabla solo. There are so many *relas* with open *bols* that it is difficult to support the first definition. The only thing that we can say about the *bol* is that they must be *bols* which are capable of being played at high speeds (e.g., GiDaNaGa गिडनग, Dhin Na Ta Ka धिं न त क etc.).

Below is a *rela* which adheres to the "bolist" theory of *rela* definition:

Table 9.6. Criteria for Rela (two philosophies)

	Bol Definition	Function Definition
Overall philosophy	Cyclic	Cyclic
Structure	-	-
Bol Type	Closed bols	-
Function	High-speed solo	High-speed solo
Technique	-	-

Rela in Tintal (Yadav,1999b:254)

धा - तिर किट त क तिर किट
Dhaa - Ti Ra Ki Ta Ta Ka Ti Ra Ki Ta

धा - तिर किट त क तिर किट धा - तिर किट त क
Dhaa - Ti Ra Ki Ta Ta Ka Ti Ra Ki Ta Dhaa - Ti Ra Ki Ta Ta Ka

ता - तिर किट त क तिर किट
Taa - Ti Ra Ki Ta Ta Ka Ti Ra Ki Ta

ता - तिर किट त क तिर किट धा - तिर किट त क
Taa - Ti Ra Ki Ta Ta Ka Ti Ra Ki Ta Dhaa - Ti Ra Ki Ta Ta Ka

Most musicians hold that the *rela* need not be based upon closed *bols*; open *bols* are acceptable if they lend themselves to very high speeds. Below is an example:

Rela in 8 or 16 beats

धा - चि ड ना ग धिं न धिं न गिं ना
Dhaa - Ghi Da Naa Ga Dhin Na Dhin Na Gin Naa

ना ग धिं न धिं न गिं ना धा - चि ड ना ग तिं न तिं न किं ना
Naa Ga Dhin Na Dhin Na Gin Naa Dhaa - Ghi Da Naa Ga Tin Na Tin Na Kin Naa

ता - कि ड ना क तिं न तिं न किं ना
Taa - Ki Da Naa Ka Tin Na Tin Na Kin Naa

ना ग धिं न धिं न गिं ना धा - चि ड ना ग धिं न धिं न धिं ना
Naa Ga Dhin Na Dhin Na Gin Naa Dhaa - Ghi Da Naa Ga Dhin Na Dhin Na Gin Naa

One will notice in the previous examples that we did not bother to give variations. *Rela* per se, is not bound by any particular structure. If we use a formalised approach, it becomes similar to the *kaida*. These are referred to as *kaida relas*. Conversely, the most freeform *relas* are very similar to *laggis* and are referred to as *swatantra relas*. In practice, this is a broad continuum with *relas* falling very freely at any point in between. On the following page is a *kaida rela*:

Kaida Rela in Jhaptal

धा - ति ट गि ड ना ग धा - ति ट गि ड ना ग धिं न ता ग
Dhaa - Ti Ta Gi Da Naa Ga Dhaa - Ti Ta Gi Da Naa Ga Dhin Na Taa Ga

धा - ति ट गि ड ना ग धिं न ता ग तू - ना - कि ड ना क
Dhaa - Ti Ta Gi Da Naa Ga Dhin Na Taa Ga Too - Naa - Ki Da Naa Ka

ता - ति ट कि ड ना क ता - ति ट कि ड ना क तिं न ता ग
Taa - Ti Ta Ki Da Naa Ka Taa - Ti Ta Ki Da Naa Ka Tin Na Taa Ga

धा - ति ट गि ड ना ग धिं न ता ग धी - ना - गि ड ना ग
Dhaa - Ti Ta Gi Da Naa Ga Dhin Na Taa Ga Dhee - Naa - Gi Da Naa Ga

Bharan (optional)

धा - ति ट गि ड ना ग धा - ति ट गि ड ना ग धिं न ता ग
Dhaa - Ti Ta Gi Da Naa Ga Dhaa - Ti Ta Gi Da Naa Ga Dhin Na Taa Ga

धा - ति ट गि ड ना ग धिं न ता ग तू - ना - कि ड ना क
Dhaa - Ti Ta Gi Da Naa Ga Dhin Na Taa Ga Too - Naa - Ki Da Naa Ka

ता - ति ट कि ड ना क ता - ति ट कि ड ना क तिं न ता ग
Taa - Ti Ta Ki Da Naa Ka Taa - Ti Ta Ki Da Naa Ka Tin Na Taa Ga

धा - ति ट गि ड ना ग धिं न ता ग धी - ना - गि ड ना ग
Dhaa - Ti Ta Gi Da Naa Ga Dhin Na Taa Ga Dhee - Naa - Gi Da Naa Ga

Ch. 9. Compositional Theory - Cyclic Forms

Variation #1

धा - ति ट गि ड ना ग धा - ति ट गि ड ना ग धिं न ता ग
Dhaa - Ti Ta Gi Da Naa Ga Dhaa - Ti Ta Gi Da Naa Ga Dhin Na Taa Ga

धा - ति ट गि ड ना ग धा - ति ट गि ड ना ग धिं न ता ग
Dhaa - Ti Ta Gi Da Naa Ga Dhaa - Ti Ta Gi Da Naa Ga Dhin Na Taa Ga

धा - ति ट गि ड ना ग धा - ति ट गि ड ना ग धिं न ता ग
Dhaa - Ti Ta Gi Da Naa Ga Dhaa - Ti Ta Gi Da Naa Ga Dhin Na Taa Ga

धा - ति ट गि ड ना ग धिं न ता ग तू - ना - कि ड ना क
Dhaa - Ti Ta Gi Da Naa Ga Dhin Na Taa Ga Too - Naa - Ki Da Naa Ka

ता - ति ट कि ड ना क ता - ति ट कि ड ना क तिं न ता क
Taa - Ti Ta Ki Da Naa Ka Taa - Ti Ta Ki Da Naa Ka Tin Na Taa Ka

ता - ति ट कि ड ना क ता - ति ट कि ड ना क तिं न ता ग
Taa - Ti Ta Ki Da Naa Ka Taa - Ti Ta Ki Da Naa Ka Tin Na Taa Ga

धा - ति ट गि ड ना ग धा - ति ट गि ड ना ग धिं न ता ग
Dhaa - Ti Ta Gi Da Naa Ga Dhaa - Ti Ta Gi Da Naa Ga Dhin Na Taa Ga

धा - ति ट गि ड ना ग धिं न ता ग धी - ना - गि ड ना ग
Dhaa - Ti Ta Gi Da Naa Ga Dhin Na Taa Ga Dhee - Naa - Gi Da Naa Ga

Variation #2

धा - ति ट गि ड ना ग धा - ति ट गि ड ना ग धिं न ता ग
Dhaa - Ti Ta Gi Da Naa Ga Dhaa - Ti Ta Gi Da Naa Ga Dhin Na Taa Ga

धा - ति ट गि ड ना ग धिं न ता ग तू - ना - कि ड ना ग
Dhaa - Ti Ta Gi Da Naa Ga Dhin Na Taa Ga Too - Naa - Ki Da Naa Ga

धा - ति ट गि ड ना ग धिं न ता ग धी - ना - गि ड ना ग
Dhaa - Ti Ta Gi Da Naa Ga Dhin Na Taa Ga Dhee - Naa - Gi Da Naa Ga

धा - ति ट गि ड ना ग धिं न ता ग तू - ना - कि ड ना क
Dhaa - Ti Ta Gi Da Naa Ga Dhin Na Taa Ga Too - Naa - Ki Da Naa Ka

ता - ति ट कि ड ना क ता - ति ट कि ड ना क तिं न ता ग
Taa - Ti Ta Ki Da Naa Ka Taa - Ti Ta Ki Da Naa Ka Tin Na Taa Ga

धा - ति ट गि ड ना ग धिं न ता ग धी - ना - गि ड ना ग
Dhaa - Ti Ta Gi Da Naa Ga Dhin Na Taa Ga Dhee - Naa - Gi Da Naa Ga

धा - ति ट गि ड ना ग धिं न ता ग तू - ना - कि ड ना ग
Dhaa - Ti Ta Gi Da Naa Ga Dhin Na Taa Ga Too - Naa - Ki Da Naa Ga

धा - ति ट गि ड ना ग धिं न ता ग धी - ना - गि ड ना ग
Dhaa - Ti Ta Gi Da Naa Ga Dhin Na Taa Ga Dhee - Naa - Gi Da Naa Ga

Variation #3

धा - ति ट गि ड ना ग धिं न ता ग धा - ति ट गि ड ना ग धिं न ता ग
Dhaa - Ti Ta Gi Da Naa Ga Dhin Na Taa Ga Dhaa - Ti Ta Gi Da Naa Ga Dhin Na Taa Ga

धा - ति ट गि ड ना ग धा - ति ट गि ड ना ग
Dhaa - Ti Ta Gi Da Naa Ga Dhaa - Ti Ta Gi Da Naa Ga

धा - ति ट गि ड ना ग धा - ति ट गि ड ना ग धिं न ता ग
Dhaa - Ti Ta Gi Da Naa Ga Dhaa - Ti Ta Gi Da Naa Ga Dhin Na Taa Ga

धा - ति ट गि ड ना ग धिं न ता ग तू - ना - कि ड ना क
Dhaa - Ti Ta Gi Da Naa Ga Dhin Na Taa Ga Too - Naa - Ki Da Naa Ka

ता - ति ट कि ड ना क तिं न ता क ता - ति ट कि ड ना क तिं न ता क
Taa - Ti Ta Ki Da Naa Ka Tin Na Taa Ka Taa - Ti Ta Ki Da Naa Ka Tin Na Taa Ka

ता - ति ट कि ड ना क ता - ति ट कि ड ना ग
Taa - Ti Ta Ki Da Naa Ka Taa - Ti Ta Ki Da Naa Ga

धा - ति ट गि ड ना ग धा - ति ट गि ड ना ग धिं न ता ग
Dhaa - Ti Ta Gi Da Naa Ga Dhaa - Ti Ta Gi Da Naa Ga Dhin Na Taa Ga

धा - ति ट गि ड ना ग धिं न ता ग धी - ना - गि ड ना ग
Dhaa - Ti Ta Gi Da Naa Ga Dhin Na Taa Ga Dhee - Naa - Gi Da Naa Ga

Tihai

धा - ति ट गि ड ना ग धिं न ता ग धा - ति ट गि ड ना ग धिं न ता ग धा
Dhaa - Ti Ta Gi Da Naa Ga Dhin Na Taa Ga Dhaa - Ti Ta Gi Da Naa Ga Dhin Na Taa Ga Dhaa

(- - -)

धा - ति ट गि ड ना ग धिं न ता ग धा - ति ट गि ड ना ग धिं न ता ग धा
Dhaa - Ti Ta Gi Da Naa Ga Dhin Na Taa Ga Dhaa - Ti Ta Gi Da Naa Ga Dhin Na Taa Ga Dhaa

(- - -)

धा - ति ट गि ड ना ग धिं न ता ग धा - ति ट गि ड ना ग धिं न ता ग |×धा
Dhaa - Ti Ta Gi Da Naa Ga Dhin Na Taa Ga Dhaa - Ti Ta Gi Da Naa Ga Dhin Na Taa Ga Dhaa

This last *kaida-rela* had some things that were implicit, but not specified within the notation. In particular it should start with the *Jhaptal theka*, then follow with the theme in half the ultimate tempo, then proceed to the full speed in the manner shown above.

Let us contrast this formal development with the extremely freeform approach of the *swatantra rela*.

Ch. 9. Compositional Theory - Cyclic Forms

A *swatantra rela* is shown below:

Swatantra Rela in Dipchandi or Rupak

Theme

धा - ति र कि ट धा - ति र कि ट धा - धा - ति र कि ट त क ता - ति र कि ट
Dhaa - Ti Ra Ki Ta Dhaa - Ti Ra Ki Ta Dhaa - Dhaa - Ti Ra Ki Ta Ta Ka Taa - Ti Ra Ki Ta

ता - ति र कि ट ता - ति र कि ट धा - धा - ति र कि ट त क ता - ति र कि ट
Taa - Ti Ra Ki Ta Taa - Ti Ra Ki Ta Taa - Dhaa - Ti Ra Ki Ta Ta Ka Taa - Ti Ra Ki Ta

Variation #1

धा - ति र कि ट त क ति र कि ट धा - धा - ति र कि ट त क ता - ति र कि ट
Dhaa - Ti Ra Ki Ta Ta Ka Ti Ra Ki Ta Dhaa - Dhaa - Ti Ra Ki Ta Ta Ka Taa - Ti Ra Ki Ta

ता - ति र कि ट त क ति र कि ट धा - धा - ति र कि ट त क ता - ति र कि ट
Taa - Ti Ra Ki Ta Ta Ka Ti Ra Ki Ta Dhaa - Dhaa - Ti Ra Ki Ta Ta Ka Taa - Ti Ra Ki Ta

Variation #2

धा - ति र कि ट त क ति र कि ट धा - ति र कि ट त क ति र कि ट
Dhaa - Ti Ra Ki Ta Ta Ka Ti Ra Ki Ta Dhaa - Ti Ra Ki Ta Ta Ka Ti Ra Ki Ta

धा - धा - ति र कि ट त क ता - ति र कि ट
Dhaa - Dhaa - Ti Ra Ki Ta Ta Ka Taa - Ti Ra Ki Ta

धा - धा - ति र कि ट त क ता - ति र कि ट
Dhaa - Dhaa - Ti Ra Ki Ta Ta Ka Taa - Ti Ra Ki Ta

Variation #3

धा - धा - ति र कि ट त क ता - ति र कि ट
Dhaa - Dhaa - Ti Ra Ki Ta Ta Ka Taa - Ti Ra Ki Ta

धा - धा - ति र कि ट त क ता - ति र कि ट
Dhaa - Dhaa - Ti Ra Ki Ta Ta Ka Taa - Ti Ra Ki Ta

धा - ति र कि ट धा - ति र कि ट धा - ति र कि ट धा - ति र कि ट
Dhaa - Ti Ra Ki Ta Dhaa - Ti Ra Ki Ta Dhaa - Ti Ra Ki Ta Dhaa - Ti Ra Ki Ta

Tihai

धा - धा - ति र कि ट त क ता - ति र कि ट धा - - -
Dhaa - Dhaa - Ti Ra Ki Ta Ta Ka Taa - Ti Ra Ki Ta Dhaa - - -

धा - धा - ति र कि ट त क ता - ति र कि ट धा - - -
Dhaa - Dhaa - Ti Ra Ki Ta Ta Ka Taa - Ti Ra Ki Ta Dhaa - - -

धा - धा - ति र कि ट त क ता - ति र कि ट |×धा
Dhaa - Dhaa - Ti Ra Ki Ta Ta Ka Taa - Ti Ra Ki Ta   Dhaa

This last *rela* underscores the extreme flexibility of the *swatantra rela*. It is no surprise that this form lends itself easily to improvisation.

Let us recap what we have seen about the *rela*. We see that it is a type which is defined by the *bol*. They must be *bols* which may be played in high speeds. Although some are of the opinion that the *rela* should be made of closed *bols,* the majority of the musicians will admit readily to the use of open *bols* as well. If one adopts a formal approach to theme-and-variation, then the *rela* is usually referred to as *kaida rela*. However, if a more freeform approach is used, it is referred to as *swatantra rela*. It is the *swatantra rela* which lends itself very well to improvisation.

Table 9.7. Criteria for Laggi (two philosophies)

	Bol Definition	Function Definition
Overall philosophy	Cyclc	Cyclic
Structure	-	-
Bol Type	Open bols	-
Function	-	High-speed accompaniment for light music
Technique	-	-

LAGGI

Laggi is also a very popular compositional type. Some define it by function and others define it by *bol* (Table 9.7). Structure appears to have no part in its definition. *Laggi* is usually improvised and does not have a well defined system of theme-and-variation. *Laggi* is based upon a basic visceral appeal rather than the more cerebral approach of *kaida*. Traditional *laggis* are similar to the *rela*. However, the modern approach is simply to link folk patterns (like *kaherava*) at high speed. It must be noted that this latter approach is greatly frowned upon by the older generation of classical tabla players. Still, this lighter approach is emerging as being the common form.

There are numerous variations upon the *laggi*. *Rang*, *ladi*, and *rao* are but a few examples.

Let us look at a very simple example. This example uses open *Toon* (तूं) with *Ga* (ग) for the execution of *Dhin* (धिं). It also uses exaggerated modulations which are typical of the folk styles. This particular variation satisfies both the "bolists" as well as the functionalists in terms of their defining criteria.

<u>Laggi in Kaherava</u> (Bhavsar, 1990)
धा धिं ना धा ना धिं धा ना
Dhaa Dhin Naa Dhaa Naa Dhin Dhaa Naa

Below is another example of the "bolist's" approach to *laggi:*

<u>Laggi in Tintal</u> (Dutta 1984:33)
Theme
धा ती धा ना धा तूं ना ना ता ती धा ना धा तूं धा ना
Dhaa Tee Dhaa Naa Dhaa Too Naa Naa Taa Tee Dhaa Naa Dhaa Too Dhaa Naa

Ch. 9. Compositional Theory - Cyclic Forms

Variation #1

धा तु ना ना धा तू ना ना धा तू ना ना धा तू ना ना
Dhaa Tu Naa Naa Dhaa Too Naa Naa Dhaa Too Naa Naa Dhaa Too Naa Naa

धा ती धा ना धा तू ना ना ता ती धा ना धा तू धा ना
Dhaa Tee Dhaa Naa Dhaa Too Naa Naa Taa Tee Dhaa Naa Dhaa Too Dhaa Naa

ता तू ना ना ता तू ना ना ता तू ना ना ता तू ना ना
Taa Too Naa Naa Taa Too Naa Naa Taa Too Naa Naa Taa Too Naa Naa

धा ती धा ना धा तू ना ना ता ती धा ना धा तू धा ना
Dhaa Tee Dhaa Naa Dhaa Too Naa Naa Taa Tee Dhaa Naa Dhaa Too Dhaa Naa

Variation #2

धा तू ना धा तू ना धा तू ना धा तू ना धा ना तू ना
Dhaa Too Naa Dhaa Too Naa Dhaa Too Naa Dhaa Too Naa Dhaa Naa Too Naa

धा ती धा ना धा तू ना ना ता ती धा ना धा तू धा ना
Dhaa Tee Dhaa Naa Dhaa Too Naa Naa Taa Tee Dhaa Naa Dhaa Too Dhaa Naa

ता तू ना ता तू ना ता तू ना ता तू ना ता ना तू ना
Taa Too Naa Taa Too Naa Taa Too Naa Taa Too Naa Taa Naa Too Naa

धा ती धा ना धा तू ना ना ता ती धा ना धा तू धा ना
Dhaa Tee Dhaa Naa Dhaa Too Naa Naa Taa Tee Dhaa Naa Dhaa Too Dhaa Naa

Variation #3

धा तू ना धा तू ना धा ना तू ना धा तू ना धा तू ना
Dhaa Too Naa Dhaa Too Naa Dhaa Naa Too Naa Dhaa Too Naa Dhaa Too Naa

धा ती धा ना धा तू ना ना ता ती धा ना धा तू धा ना
Dhaa Tee Dhaa Naa Dhaa Too Naa Naa Taa Tee Dhaa Naa Dhaa Too Dhaa Naa

ता तू ना ता तू ना ता ना तू ना ता तू ना ता तू ना
Taa Too Naa Taa Too Naa Taa Naa Too Naa Taa Too Naa Taa Too Naa

धा ती धा ना धा तू ना ना ता ती धा ना धा तू धा ना
Dhaa Tee Dhaa Naa Dhaa Too Naa Naa Taa Tee Dhaa Naa Dhaa Too Dhaa Naa

Variation #4

धा तू ना धा ना तू ना धा तू ना धा तू ना धा तू ना
Dhaa Too Naa Dhaa Naa Too Naa Dhaa Too Naa Dhaa Too Naa Dhaa Too Naa

धा ती धा ना धा तू ना ना ता ती धा ना धा तू धा ना
Dhaa Tee Dhaa Naa Dhaa Too Naa Naa Taa Tee Dhaa Naa Dhaa Too Dhaa Naa

ता तू ना ता ना तू ना ता तू ना ता तू ना ता तू ना
Taa Too Naa Taa Naa Too Naa Taa Too Naa Taa Too Naa Taa Too Naa

धा ती धा ना धा तू ना ना ता ती धा ना धा तू धा ना
Dhaa Tee Dhaa Naa Dhaa Too Naa Naa Taa Tee Dhaa Naa Dhaa Too Dhaa Naa

Variation #5

धा ती धा तु ना धा ती धा तु ना धा ती धा ना तु ना
Dhaa Tee Dhaa Too Naa Dhaa Tee Dhaa Too Naa Dhaa Tee Dhaa Naa Too Naa

धा ती धा ना धा तु ना ना ता ती धा ना धा तु धा ना
Dhaa Tee Dhaa Naa Dhaa Too Naa Naa Taa Tee Dhaa Naa Dhaa Too Dhaa Naa

ता ती ता तु ना ता ती ता तु ना ता ती ता ना तु ना
Taa Tee Taa Too Naa Taa Tee Taa Too Naa Taa Tee Taa Naa Too Naa

धा ती धा ना धा तु ना ना ता ती धा ना धा तु धा ना
Dhaa Tee Dhaa Naa Dhaa Too Naa Naa Taa Tee Dhaa Naa Dhaa Too Dhaa Naa

Variation #6

धा ती धा तु ना धा ती धा ना तु ना धा ती धा तु ना
Dhaa Tee Dhaa Too Naa Dhaa Tee Dhaa Naa Too Naa Dhaa Tee Dhaa Too Naa

धा ती धा ना धा तु ना ना ता ती धा ना धा तु धा ना
Dhaa Tee Dhaa Naa Dhaa Too Naa Naa Taa Tee Dhaa Naa Dhaa Too Dhaa Naa

ता ती ता तु ना ता ती ता ना तु ना ता ती ता तु ना
Taa Tee Taa Too Naa Taa Tee Taa Naa Too Naa Taa Tee Taa Too Naa

धा ती धा ना धा तु ना ना ता ती धा ना धा तु धा ना
Dhaa Tee Dhaa Naa Dhaa Too Naa Naa Taa Tee Dhaa Naa Dhaa Too Dhaa Naa

Variation #7

धा ती धा ना तु ना धा ती धा तु ना धा ती धा तु ना
Dhaa Tee Dhaa Naa Too Naa Dhaa Tee Dhaa Too Naa Dhaa Tee Dhaa Too Naa

धा ती धा ना धा तु ना ना ता ती धा ना धा तु धा ना
Dhaa Tee Dhaa Naa Dhaa Too Naa Naa Taa Tee Dhaa Naa Dhaa Too Dhaa Naa

ता ती ता ना तु ना ता ती ता तु ना ता ती ता तु ना
Taa Tee Taa Naa Too Naa Taa Tee Taa Too Naa Taa Tee Taa Too Naa

धा ती धा ना धा तु ना ना ता ती धा ना धा तु धा ना
Dhaa Tee Dhaa Naa Dhaa Too Naa Naa Taa Tee Dhaa Naa Dhaa Too Dhaa Naa

Variation #8

धा ती धा ना तु ना धा ती धा ना तु ना धा ना तु ना
Dhaa Tee Dhaa Naa Too Naa Dhaa Tee Dhaa Naa Too Naa Dhaa Naa Too Naa

धा ती धा ना धा तु ना ना ता ती धा ना धा तु धा ना
Dhaa Tee Dhaa Naa Dhaa Too Naa Naa Taa Tee Dhaa Naa Dhaa Too Dhaa Naa

ता ती ता ना तु ना ता ती ता ना तु ना ता ना तु ना
Taa Tee Taa Naa Too Naa Taa Tee Taa Naa Too Naa Taa Naa Too Naa

धा ती धा ना धा तु ना ना ता ती धा ना धा तु धा ना
Dhaa Tee Dhaa Naa Dhaa Too Naa Naa Taa Tee Dhaa Naa Dhaa Too Dhaa Naa

Ch. 9. Compositional Theory - Cyclic Forms

Variation #9

धा ती धा ना तू ना धा ती धा ती धा ती धा ना तू ना
Dhaa Tee Dhaa Naa Too Naa Dhaa Tee Dhaa Tee Dhaa Tee Dhaa Naa Too Naa

धा ती धा ना धा तू ना ना ता ती धा ना धा तू धा ना
Dhaa Tee Dhaa Naa Dhaa Too Naa Naa Taa Tee Dhaa Naa Dhaa Too Dhaa Naa

ता ती ता ना तू ना ता ती ता ती ता ती ता ना तू ना
Taa Tee Taa Naa Too Naa Taa Tee Taa Tee Taa Tee Taa Naa Too Naa

धा ती धा ना धा तू ना ना ता ती धा ना धा तू धा ना
Dhaa Tee Dhaa Naa Dhaa Too Naa Naa Taa Tee Dhaa Naa Dhaa Too Dhaa Naa

Variation #10

धा ती धा ती धा ना तू ना ती धा ना ती धा ना तू ना
Dhaa Tee Dhaa Tee Dhaa Naa Too Naa Tee Dhaa Naa Tee Dhaa Naa Too Naa

धा ती धा तू ना धा ती धा तू ना धा ती धा ना तू ना
Dhaa Tee Dhaa Too Naa Dhaa Tee Dhaa Too Naa Dhaa Tee Dhaa Naa Too Naa

ता ती ता ती ता ना तू ना ती ता ना ती ता ना तू ना
Taa Tee Taa Tee Taa Naa Too Naa Tee Taa Naa Tee Taa Naa Too Naa

धा ती धा तू ना धा ती धा तू ना धा ती धा ना तू ना
Dhaa Tee Dhaa Too Naa Dhaa Tee Dhaa Too Naa Dhaa Tee Dhaa Naa Too Naa

Variation #11

ती धा ना ती धा ना तू ना ती धा ना ती धा ना तू ना
Tee Dhaa Naa Tee Dhaa Naa Too Naa Tee Dhaa Naa Tee Dhaa Naa Too Naa

धा ती धा तू ना धा ती धा तू ना धा ती धा ना तू ना
Dhaa Tee Dhaa Too Naa Dhaa Tee Dhaa Too Naa Dhaa Tee Dhaa Naa Too Naa

ती ता ना ती ता ना तू ना ती ता ना ती ता ना तू ना
Tee Taa Naa Tee Taa Naa Too Naa Tee Taa Naa Tee Taa Naa Too Naa

धा ती धा तू ना धा ती धा तू ना धा ती धा ना तू ना
Dhaa Tee Dhaa Too Naa Dhaa Tee Dhaa Too Naa Dhaa Tee Dhaa Naa Too Naa

Variation #12

ती धा ना ती ना ती ना ती ना ती ना ती धा ना तू ना
Tee Dhaa Naa Tee Naa Tee Naa Tee Naa Tee Naa Tee Dhaa Naa Too Naa

धा ती धा तू ना धा ती धा तू ना धा ती धा ना तू ना
Dhaa Tee Dhaa Too Naa Dhaa Tee Dhaa Too Naa Dhaa Tee Dhaa Naa Too Naa

तीं	ता	ना	तीं	ना	तीं	ना	तीं	ना	तीं	ना	तीं	ता	ना	तू	ना
Tee	Taa	Naa	Tee	Naa	Tee	Naa	Tee	Naa	Tee	Naa	Tee	Taa	Naa	Too	Naa

धा	तीं	धा	तू	ना	धा	तीं	धा	तू	ना	धा	तीं	धा	ना	तू	ना
Dhaa	Tee	Dhaa	Too	Naa	Dhaa	Tee	Dhaa	Too	Naa	Dhaa	Tee	Dhaa	Naa	Too	Naa

Tihai

तीं	धा	ना	तीं	धा	तू	ना	धा	तू	ना	धा	तू	ना	धा	तू	ना	धा
Tee	Dhaa	Naa	Tee	Dhaa	Too	Naa	Dhaa	Too	Naa	Dhaa	Too	Naa	Dhaa	Too	Naa	Dhaa

```
-  1  -  2  -  3  -
```

तीं	धा	ना	तीं	धा	तू	ना	धा	तू	ना	धा	तू	ना	धा	तू	ना	धा
Tee	Dhaa	Naa	Tee	Dhaa	Too	Naa	Dhaa	Too	Naa	Dhaa	Too	Naa	Dhaa	Too	Naa	Dhaa

```
-  1  -  2  -  3  -
```

तीं	धा	ना	तीं	धा	तू	ना	धा	तू	ना	धा	तू	ना	धा	तू	ना	ˣ धा
Tee	Dhaa	Naa	Tee	Dhaa	Too	Naa	Dhaa	Too	Naa	Dhaa	Too	Naa	Dhaa	Too	Naa	Dhaa

Let us review what we know about *laggi*. It is a rather poorly defined term, which encompasses equally poorly defined forms such as the *rang, ladi,* and *rao*. Some use structure to, define the *rela*, and others use the *bols*. The bolist's view states that *laggi* is defined by a heavy use of open right hand *bols*. This view is the more traditional one. The functionalists on the other hand, view *laggi* as being a fast aggressive assertion on the part of the tabla player in lighter styles such as *Kaherava* and *Dadra*. In practice, the functionalist view of *laggi* is really nothing more than a heavy use of fast *prakars and relas*.

Table 9.8. Criterion for Ekhatthu	
Overall philosophy	-
Structure	-
Bol Type	-
Function	-
Technique	One hand on one drum

EKHATTHU

Ekhatthu is a style which is defined entirely by technique (Table 9.8.) It is derived from the word "*ek*" (एक) which means "one" and "*haath*" (हाथ) which means "hand". In this style, one plays the entire composition with one hand, usually the right hand. The term *ekhatthu* really says nothing of the structure, function, *bol* or anything. However, since most *ekhatthus* are of the cadential class, we will put off a discussion until the next chapter.

DOHATTHU

Dohatthu, like the *ekhatthu*, is defined entirely by the technique (Table 9.9). Tabla normally has the left hand playing the *bayan* and the right hand playing the *dayan*. However when you raise one of the hands and bring it to the other drum, such that both hands are playing on the same drum, this is called *dohatthu*. The word "*dohatthu*" is derived from the word "*do*" (दो) which means "two", and "*haath*" (हाथ) which means "hand". Like the *ekhatthu*, the word *dohatthu* really says nothing about *bols*, structure, or anything. However, a large number of *dohatthus* are of the cyclic class, therefore we will give a discussion of them here. The *dohatthu* is also referred to as a *lalkila* composition.

Table 9.9. Criterion for Dohatthu	
Overall philosophy	-
Structure	-
Bol Type	-
Function	-
Technique	Two hands on one drum

<u>Dohatthu in Tintal</u> (Tisra Jati) (S. Dawood Khan, 1978, personal interview) The bold text represents the *dohatthu* section, which is played on the right hand drum only.

धा - न धा - न त की ट त की ट धा तिर कट धी कि ट गिं - त रा - न
Dhaa - Na Dhaa - Na Ta Kee Ta Ta Kee Ta Dhaa TiRa KiTa Dhee Ki Ta Gin - Ta Raa - Na

कत् - ति ट की ट गिं - त रा - न धा तिर कट धी कि ट क त ग दी गे न
Kat - Ti Ta Kee Ta Gin - Ta Raa - Na Dhaa TiRa KiTa Dhee Ki Ta Ka Ta Ga Dee Ge Na

ना गे न ना गे न त की ट त की ट धा तिर कट धी कि ट गिं - त रा - न
Naa Ge Na Naa Ge Na Ta Kee Ta Ta Kee Ta Dhaa TiRa KiTa Dhee Ki Ta Gin - Ta Raa - Na

कत् - ति ट की ट गिं - त रा - न धा तिर कट धी कि ट क त ग दी गे न
Kat - Ti Ta Kee Ta Gin - Ta Raa - Na Dhaa TiRa KiTa Dhee Ki Ta Ka Ta Ga Dee Ge Na

ना गे न ना गे न त की ट त की ट धा तिर कट धी कि ट गिं - त रा - न
Naa Ge Na Naa Ge Na Ta Kee Ta Ta Kee Ta Dhaa TiRa KiTa Dhee Ki Ta Gin - Ta Raa - Na

कत् - ति ट की ट गिं - त रा - न धा तिर कट धी कि ट क त ग दी गे न
Kat - Ti Ta Kee Ta Gin - Ta Raa - Na Dhaa TiRa KiTa Dhee Ki Ta Ka Ta Ga Dee Ge Na

Tihai

धा तिर कट धी कि ट क त ग दी गे न धा - - कत - -
Dhaa TiRa KiTa Dhee Ki Ta Ka Ta Ga Dee Ge Na Dhaa - - Kat - -

धा तिर कट धी कि ट क त ग दी गे न धा - - कत - -
Dhaa TiRa KiTa Dhee Ki Ta Ka Ta Ga Dee Ge Na Dhaa - - Kat - -

धा तिर कट धी कि ट क त ग दी गे न |^x धा
Dhaa TiRa KiTa Dhee Ki Ta Ka Ta Ga Dee Ge Na   Dhaa

DOMUKHI

Domukhi is a style of *gat* with two iterations of the theme. The word "*domukhi*" is derived from the word "*do*" (दो) which means "two" and "*mukh*" (मुख), which means "face", "mouth" or "voice". It is defined both by *bol* and structure. Since this is a *purbi* composition, it must use a *purbi bol* structure (i.e. *pakhawaj* inspired). It is of course also defined by the structure because it must also have a theme repeated twice. Its defining criteria is shown in Table 9.10.

Table 9.10. Criteria for Domukhi

Overall philosophy	-
Structure	Two iterations of theme
Bol Type	Purbi
Function	-
Technique	

Domukhi Gat (Dohatthu) in Tintal (Tisra Jati) (S. Dawood Khan, 1978, personal interview) (bold is two hands on dayan

धा गे ति ट कि ट धा तिर कट धी कि ट क त ग दी गे न   First theme *(mukhi)*
Dhaa Ge Ti Ta Ki Ta Dhaa TiRa KiTa Dhee Ki Ta Ka Ta Ga Dee Ge Na

ना गे न ना गे न ना गे ति ट कि ट
Dhaa Ge Na Naa Ge Na Naa Ge Ti Ta Ki Ta

धा गे ति ट कि ट धा तिर कट धी कि ट क त ग दी गे न   Second Theme *(mukhi)*
Dhaa Ge Ti Ta Ki Ta Dhaa TiRa KiTa Dhee Ki Ta Ka Ta Ga Dee Ge Na

There are a few comments which need to be made about the last example. One will notice that not only is this piece a *domukhi* but it is also a *dohatthu*. This is but a mere coincidence and should not be construed to be a necessary part of the *domukhi*. The technique of the last piece is simple; the bold text represents the *dohatthu* section, and is to be played on the right hand drum only.

TINMUKHI

Tinmukhi is the same as *domukhi*, except that the *tinmukhi* has the theme iterated thrice. Like the *domukhi*, it is defined by the use of *purbi bols* and a structure which shows a theme repeated three times. Its defining criteria is shown in Table 9.11. The next page shows an example:

Table 9.11. Criteria for Tinmukhi

Overall philosophy	Cyclic
Structure	Three iterations of theme
Bol Type	Purbi
Function	-
Technique	-

Tinmukhi Gat (Dohatthu) in Tintal (Tisra Jati) (S. Dawood Khan, 1978, personal interview)

धा गे ति ट कि ट धा तिर कट धी कि ट क त ग दी गे न   First theme (mukhi)
Dhaa Ge Ti Ta Ki Ta Dhaa TiRa KiTa Dhee Ki Ta Ka Ta Ga Dee Ge Na

ना गे न ना गे न ना गे ति ट कि ट
Naa Ge Na Naa Ge Na Naa Ge Ti Ta Ki Ta

धा गे ति ट कि ट धा तिर कट धी कि ट क त ग दी गे न   Second theme (mukhi)
Dhaa Ge Ti Ta Ki Ta Dhaa TiRa KiTa Dhee Ki Ta Ka Ta Ga Dee Ge Na

ना ग ना ग ना ग ना ग ना ग ना ग ना गे न ना गे न ना ग ना ग ना ग
Naa Ga Naa Ga Naa Ga Naa Ga Naa Ga Naa Ga Naa Ge Na Naa Ge Na Naa Ga Naa Ga Naa Ga

ना गे ति ट कि ट
Naa Ge Ti Ta Ki Ta

धा गे ति ट कि ट धा तिर कट धी कि ट क त ग दी गे न   Third theme (mukhi)
Dhaa Ge Ti Ta Ki Ta Dhaa TiRa KiTa Dhee Ki Ta Ka Ta Ga Dee Ge Na

A few words or in order about the last composition. The bold text represents the *dohatthu* section, which is played on the right hand drum only.

This whole chapter has dealt with the cyclic form. It is a basic artistic principle that transitions are effected with a cadential form, usually a *tihai*. Although it is not within the scope of this chapter to discuss these forms, we may mention that the following *tihai* could be used to resolve either the previous *domukhi* or the *tinmukhi*.

<u>Tihai</u> for either of the previous examples (tisra jati)

के तिर कट धी कि ट क त ग दी गे न ना ग ना ग ना ग
Ke TiRa KaTa Dhee Ki Ta Ka Ta Ga Dee Ge Na **Naa Ga Naa Ga Naa Ga**

घे घे घे घे घे घे घिं - त रा - न धा - -
GheGheGheGheGheGheGhin - Ta Raa - Na Dhaa - -

के तिर कट धी कि ट क त ग दी गे न ना ग ना ग ना ग
Ke TiRa KaTa Dhee Ki Ta Ka Ta Ga Dee Ge Na **Naa Ga Naa Ga Naa Ga**

घे घे घे घे घे घे घिं - त रा - न धा - -
GheGheGheGheGheGheGhin - Ta Raa - Na Dhaa - -

के तिर कट धी कि ट क त ग दी गे न ना ग ना ग ना ग
Ke TiRa KaTa Dhee Ki Ta Ka Ta Ga Dee Ge Na **Naa Ga Naa Ga Naa Ga**

घे घे घे घे घे घे घिं - त रा - न | ˣधा
GheGheGheGheGheGheGhin - Ta Raa - Na   Dhaa

In the previous *tihai*, the right hand *dohatthu* is indicated in bold. The left hand *dohatthu* is indicated in italics.

LOM-VILOM

Lom-vilom is a musical palindrome of the *gat* class. As such, if you say the *bols* from the end-to-beginning or beginning-to-end, it will be the same. It has two structures, an ascending structure known as the *arohi* and a descending structure known as the *avarohi*. The *lom-vilom* is defined by its structure. The defining criteria is shown in Table 9.12.

Table 9.12. Criteria for Lom-Vilom

Overall philosophy	Cyclic
Structure	Same backwards as forwards
Bol Type	-
Function	-
Technique	-

Lom-Vilom in Tintal (Das 1967:145)

Arohi

न ग दि ग त क त क धा - न धा - त क त
Naa Ga Dee Ga Ta Ka Ta Ka Dhaa - Na Dhaa - Ta Ka Ta

धा - घे घे न गि न न गि न क त धि धि क त
Dhaa - Ghe Ghe Na Gi Na Na Gi Na Ka Ta Dhi Dhi Ka Ta

Avarohi

त क धि धि त क न गि न न गि न घे घे -
Ta Ka Dhi Dhi Ta Ka Na Gi Na Na Gi Na Ghe Ghe -

धा त क त - धा न - धा क त क त ग दि ग न
Dhaa Ta Ka Ta - Dhaa Na - Dhaa Ka Ta Ka Ta Ga Dee Ga Na

MISCELLANEOUS FORMS

There are a number of other forms that we may wish to bring up here. These are minor forms. However by the term "minor", we do not wish to imply that they are unimportant. In most cases, these are forms that the majority of musicians tend to lump into one of the other larger categories.

Rao - In some ways *rao* is similar to *rela*, in other ways it is similar to *laggi,* and in other ways it is similar to *prakar*. The term does not seem to be very old. It has been suggested that it only goes back to the late 19th or early 20th century (Stewart 1974:157). These are fast forms of accompaniment used to accompany the *jhala* sections of instrumental pieces. Most consider them to be under the *laggi* class of compositions. Since they are insufficiently differentiated from the *laggi*, we will not discuss them any further.

Tar Paran - *Tar paran* is a form which is some ways cadential and in other ways it resembles a cyclic form. The cause for the ambiguity stems from the fact that it is not really clear whether it is the *tihai* or the body section that is important. The term "*rela*" was not used for *pakhawaj* compositions until relatively recently; therefore the term *tar paran* was preferred by many musicians to describe these *rela*-like compositions.

Parar - This is a form that is very similar to the *tar paran*. It has a quadratic form which is very similar to the *kaida*.

Ch. 9. Compositional Theory - Cyclic Forms

<u>Theka</u> - This is a form of theme-and-variation that is found in the *Benares* tradition. This should not be confused with the more usual definition of *theka*.

<u>Chalan</u> - The word *chalan* means to "move" or to "walk". There appear to be different interpretations as to what the form of *chalan* is. Most interpret this to be a form that has some of the characteristics of a *prakar*, and at the same time some of the characteristics of a *laggi*. Essentially, it is a small rhythm which is repeated to give a solid groove. This aspect makes it very similar to many interpretations of *laggi*. However, this basic groove is used as a basic foundation upon which more complex improvisations and elaborations may be built. This aspect makes it very similar to the *prakar*.

CONCLUSION

We have touched upon the topic of the cyclic form. These styles are based upon a continuous flow of rhythm. Common examples are *theka, prakar, kaida, rela,* and *laggi*. Inherent to this class is a feeling of balance and flow. However, there is also a class which is not based upon a continuous flow, but rather a cadence. This will be discussed in the next chapter.

WORKS CITED

Bhavsar, Jayant
1990   Personal Interview

Courtney, D.R
1998   *Fundamentals of Tabla*, Houston, TX Sur Sangeet Services.

Das, Ram Shankar (Pagaldas)
1967   *Tabla Kaumudi* (vol. 2). Gwalior, India: Ramchandra Sangeetalaya.

Dutta, Aloke
1984   *Tabla, Lessons and Practice.* Calcutta: Janabani Printers & Publishers.

Hussain, Zakir
1988   personal interview

Kapoor, R.K.
-no date- *Kamal's Advanced Illustrated Oxford Dictionary of Hindi-English.* New Delhi: Verma Book Depot

Khan, Shaik. Dawood
1976-1990 personal interviews

Pathak, R.C.
1976   *Bhargava's Standard Illustrated Dictionary of the Hindi Language*, Varanasi, India: Bhargava Bhushan Press.

Stewart, R. M.
1974   *The Tabla in Perspective.* Ann Arbor: University Microfilms International. (Ph.D. Dissertation).

McGregor, R.S.,
1997   *Oxford Hindi - English Dictionary*, Oxford, Oxford University Press.

Pathak, R.C.
1976   *Bhargava's Standard Illustrated Dictionary of the Hindi Language.* Varanasi, India: Bhargava Book Depot.

Yadav, B.L.
1999b   *Tabla Prakash*, Alahabad , India Sangeet Sadan Prakashan.

CHAPTER 10

COMPOSITIONAL THEORY (CADENTIAL FORMS)

The cadential philosophy of composition is very different from the cyclic. Where the cyclic form is characterised by a sense of balance and flow, the cadence is characterised by tension and imbalance. Such tension and imbalance naturally seeks a resolution. This resolution is usually on the *sam*, or first beat of the cycle. Therefore, the *sam* is part of the cadential form.

INCLUSION OF THE SAM

The *sam* is included in the cadential form; this creates some very interesting mathematics. For example, if one were to compare two *Tintal* compositions, both of which are one-cycle in length, but one is cyclic and the other is cadential, one would see something interesting. The cyclic form would be 16 *matras* while the cadential form would be 17 *matras*. It is obvious that *Tintal* must be 16 beats, so what happens to the extra beat.

There are three ways that one can visualise how the extra beat is handled; these are shown diagrammatically in Figure 10.1. All three approaches may be used within certain circumstance.

One common view is to consider the first beat of the *theka* to be completely replaced by the last beat of the cadential form. This is graphically illustrated in the upper portion of Figure 10.1. However, since most *thekas* start with *Dhaa* (धा) and most of our cadential forms end with *Dhaa* (धा), there are few situations where we may objectively observe this process. Nevertheless, it is subjectively obvious to even the most casual observer that the concluding *sam* is part of the cadential form and not the *theka*.

The process of replacing the first beat of the *theka* with the last beat of the cadence is objectively observable in one set of circumstances. We must look at situations where the *theka* does not start with *Dhaa* (धा). One of the most common examples is *Jhaptal*, which starts with *Dhin* (धिं). Let us look at a simple *mukhada* in *Jhaptal* to provide an illustration:

Simple Mukhada in Jhaptal

^Xधिं ना | ²धिं धिं ना | ⁰तिं धा धा |
Dhin Naa   Dhin Dhin Naa   Tin DhaaDhaa

³तिरकिट तकता - तिरकिट | ^Xधा ना | ²धिं धिं ना | ... etc.
TiRaKiTa   TaKaTaa -   TiRaKiTa   Dhaa Naa   Dhin Dhin Naa

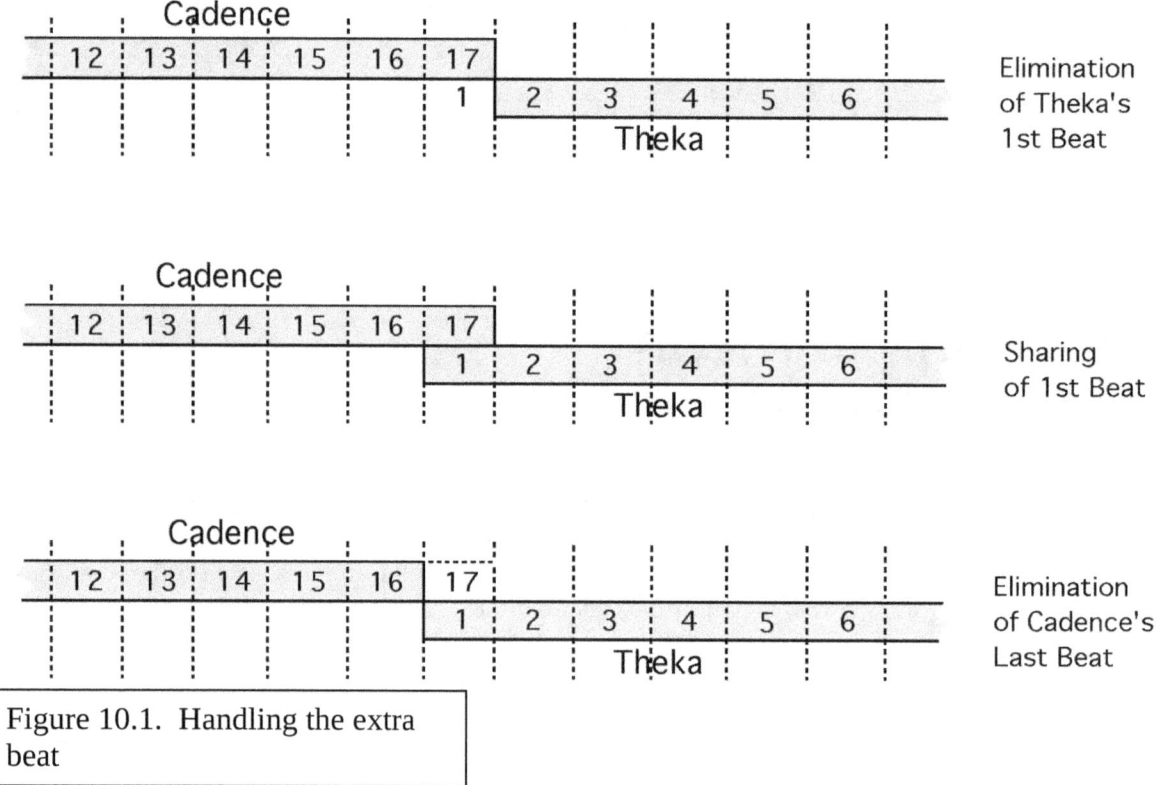

Figure 10.1. Handling the extra beat

This last example is based upon the simple *mukhada Dhaa-Dhaa-TiRaKiTaTaKaTaa-TiRaKiTaDhaa* (धा - धा - ति र कि ट त क ता - ति र कि ट धा). We saw that it began on the seventh beat and continued through to *sam*, effectively displacing all of the strokes in the last *vibhag* of the *theka*, including the *sam*.

Sometimes it is not the first beat of the *theka*, but the last beat of the cadential form which is eliminated. We may return to our *mukhada* to illustrate this process.

Simple Mukhada in Jhaptal

ˣधिं ना | ²धिं धिं ना | ⁰तिं धा धा |
Dhin Naa   Dhin Dhin Naa   Tin DhaaDhaa

³ति र कि ट, त क ता -, ति र कि ट, | ˣधिं ना | ²धिं धिं ना | ... etc.
TiRaKiTa   TaKaTaa -   TiRaKiTa   Dhin Naa   Dhin Dhin Naa

In this last example, the last stroke of the *mukhada* (i.e., *Dhaa* धा) was dropped. Thus, the *Dhin* (धिं) of the *theka* was able to express itself.

There is still another view; this view is to consider both strokes to be overlapping. This view works in most cases because most *tals* begin with *Dhaa* (धा), and most cadential forms end in *Dhaa* (धा). Therefore, it is very simple to merely consider the two strokes to be overlapping.

Ch. 10. Compositional Theory - Cadential Forms

We will see that these three ways of dealing with the extra beat are not handled consistently within the cadential form. The *mukhada* for instance, is rather weak and in a high percentage of cases will fail to replace the *sam* of the *theka*. On the other hand, other forms such as *tihai* demand this replacement. The matter is further complicated by the fact that some *tihais* do not end on *sam* but will end before, or even after the *sam*. These various considerations will be dealt with in greater detail later.

MATHEMATICS OF THE CADENTIAL FORM

You may be thinking that the extra beat of the cadential form will make for some interesting mathematics. Indeed, this is the case. This was introduced in the last chapter. Let us expand upon the math a bit.

Let us start with a basic introduction to the mathematics of the cadential form. In its simplest, the cadence has this form:

$$\text{number of beats to fill} = \frac{[(\text{number of units}) - \text{sam}]}{\text{layakari}}$$

Let us look at how this formula may be applied. Let us say hypothetically, that we wish to take the following *tihai* and play it in *chaugun*. The form of the *tihai* is:

तिरकिट धा - तिरकिट धा - तिरकिट धा
Ti Ra Ki Ta Dhaa - Ti Ra Ki Ta Dhaa - Ti Ra Ki Ta Dhaa
1 2 3 4 5   6 7 8 9 10   11 12 13 14 15 16 17

The application of the previous formula is simple. We see that it has 17 units. Remember that a cadential form includes the *sam,* so it is always one more than we might intuitively feel. Therefore, we must subtract the *sam* before anything else. This gives us the number 16 to place in our numerator. We now need to divide the entire thing by our *layakari*. We have already established that we wish to play in *chaugun;* therefore we place the number 4 in our denominator. This gives us the number 4 for the number of beats to replace. Therefore:

$$4 = \frac{[(17) - 1]}{4}$$

Therefore, we find that the previous *tihai* works very well in one *vibhag* of *Tintal*. It could be written like this:

... तिं ना | ³तिरकिट धा-तिर किटधा- तिरकिट | ˣधा धिं धिं धा... etc.
Tin Naa   TiRaKiTa Dhaa - TiRa KiTaDhaa - TiRaKiTa   Dhaa Dhin Dhin Dhaa

In many ways, our formula works very much like the formula for the cyclic form. We discussed this in some detail in the last chapter. Therefore, we need not go into this in any detail here.

THE VARIOUS FORMS

We have discussed the cadence in the most general terms. It is appropriate that we look at these specific forms in greater detail. In general, a cadence creates a sense of tension, which is resolved upon reaching the *sam*. Structurally, this may be accomplished in any of several ways.

One of the most common is by the use of a *tihai*. The *tihai* is a phrase that is repeated three times. *Tihais* may stand alone, but they are more likely to be placed within larger forms. These typically are our *tukadas*, *moharas*, and *uthans*. There is a variation of the *tihai* which has four phrases instead of three. This is known as *chauhai*. The *chauhai* is neither common, nor is it conceptually difficult; therefore we may ignore it in this work.

Sometimes our cadences do not need a *tihai*. Many times it is sufficient to simply raise the *bol* density to create the necessary sense of artistic tension. This is commonly found in our *dupallis*, *tippalis*, *chaupallis*, and our simple *mukhadas*.

Some forms may use either approach to resolve. That is to say that they may have a *tihai*, or they may utilise a simple increase in *bol* density to achieve the effect. This would be found in such forms as the *mukhada* or *paran*. This may seem confusing right now, but as we look into these in greater detail it shall become clear.

MUKHADA

The word *mukhada* literally means "face". There are two schools of thought concerning its definition. One group defines it by structure and function, while another group defines it solely on the basis of function (Table 10.1). Functionally, *mukhada* is an unobtrusive emphasis of the *sam*. Structurally, it is a very short piece, usually no more than a few beats, which resolves upon the *sam*. Virtually any *bol* may be used.

To the structuralist, the *mukhada* is nothing more than a mere "lick". It is a sudden increase in *bol* density for the few beats preceding the *sam*. At the *sam*, the *bol* density suddenly falls to the original level, or in some cases below it. The function is to create a musical tension which is relaxed at *sam*. A simple *mukhada* in *Tintal* is illustrated on the next page.

Table 10.1. Criteria for Mukhada (two philosophies)

Overall philosophy	Cadential	Cadential
Structure	Use single structure only to resolve on sam.	-
Bol Type	-	-
Function	Sharp emphasis of sam	Sharp emphasis of sam
Technique	-	-

Ch. 10. Compositional Theory - Cadential Forms

^xधा धिं धिं धा | ²धा धिं धिं धा | ⁰धा तिं तिं ना |
Dhaa Dhin Dhin Dhaa   Dhaa Dhin Dhin Dhaa   Dhaa Tin Tin Naa

³ता ता , तिर किट , तक ता - , तिर किट , | ^xधा
TaaTaa   TiRaKiTa   TaKaTaa -   TiRaKiTa   Dhaa

The functionalist takes a different view of the *mukhada*. To the functionalist, the structure is not important. What is important is the unobtrusive emphasis of the *sam*. Since there are differing views as to what constitutes "unobtrusive", one may find well developed compositional forms which are indistinguishable from *tukada*. These styles will be discussed in greater detail later.

FILMI / FOLK PICKUP

This is a style which is closely allied to the *mukhada*. The relevant criteria for its definition are function and structure (Table 10.2). Although it is structurally similar to the simple (structuralist) *mukhada*, it is functionally different, because it is found only in the lighter, non-classical genre. It is also different because the *mukhada* must be used to end a section, while the pickup may be used either to start or end.

Even though this is a common cadence, it does not have a broadly accepted name. This is due primarily to the low level of formal training which is found among many light and folk musicians. Nevertheless, the English word "pickup" is often used to describe it. It is also occasionally referred to as a "*toda*". Below is a very common "pickup" in a four beat version of *Kaherava tal*.

Table 10.2. Criteria for "Pickup"

Overall philosophy	Cadential
Structure	Simple line
Bol Type	-
Function	A transitional "lick" of light music
Technique	-

^xना के , न ना | ⁰के न , ना ड , | ^xsam
NaaKe   NaNaa   KeNa   NaaDa

TIHAI

The *tihai* (तहाई), sometimes called *tiya*, is the most typical of the Indian cadential forms. It is defined entirely by structure (Table 10.3). A *tihai* is essentially the repetition of a phrase three times. This triadic structure creates a rhythmic counterpoint which produces a strong sense of musical tension. The resolution on the *sam* provides the release. It is so important, that the majority of Indian cadences are based upon the *tihai* at some level. Below is an example of a typical *tihai*. In this example, the phrase *TiRaKiTa Dhaa* (ति र कि ट धा) is repeated three times. The last *Dhaa* (धा) of the last iteration corresponds to the first beat of the next cycle.

Table 10.3. Criteria for Tihai

Overall philosophy	Cadential
Structure	Triadic structure usually ending on sam
Bol Type	-
Function	-
Technique	-

³ तिरकिट धा - तिर किटधा - तिरकिट | ˣधा
TiRaKiTa Dhaa - TiRa KiTaDhaa - TiRaKiTa Dhaa

There are three philosophies for the resolution of a *tihai*. By all accounts, the most common is to resolve upon the *sam*. This is so common, that most works on the subject do not consider anything else. However, on a few occasions one may resolve before, or after the *sam*. When one resolves before the *sam*, it is called an *anagat tihai*. When one resolves after the *sam*, it is called *atit tihai*.

The phrases of the *tihai* (referred to as *palla*), may be linked in one of two ways. One way is to use a time interval between the three *pallas* (phrases). This is called a *damdar tihai*. The second approach has no gap between phrases. This is referred to as *bedam*. These two approaches are shown schematically in Figure 10.2.

Bedam Tihai - The *bedam tihai* has a number of interesting characteristics. An example of a *bedam tihai* is shown below:

Bedam Tihai in Tintal (Vashisht 1977:39)
ˣ तिट कत गदी गेन | ² धाती धाति टक तग |
TiTa KaTa GaDee GeNa DhaaTee DhaaTi TaKa TaGa

⁰ दीगे नधा तीधा तिट | ³ कत गदी गेन धाती | ˣधा
DeeGe NaDhaa TeeDhaa TiTa KaTa GaDee GeNa DhaaTee Dhaa

We see that the phrase *TiTaKaTaGaDeeGeNaDhaaTeeDhaa* (तिट कत गदी गेन धा ती धा), is repeated three times without any interval between. We may generalise the character of the *bedam tihai* in the following formula:

$$\frac{[(\text{number of beats to fill}) \cdot (\text{layakari})] + 1}{3} = (\text{number of units in palla})$$

The application of this formula is interesting. We have to fill one cycle of *Tintal*. Therefore the number of beats is 16; the tempo *(layakari)* is double-time, so it has a value of 2. The constant "1" is due to the fact that a 16 beat cycle actually resolves on the 17th beat (i.e., the first beat of the next cycle). If it was desired to resolve on a different beat from the *sam* then a different value would be used here. The "3" represents the basic triadic nature of the *tihai*. This formula shows that it takes 11 units to create one *palla* (phrase) for a *bedam tihai* in *Tintal*.

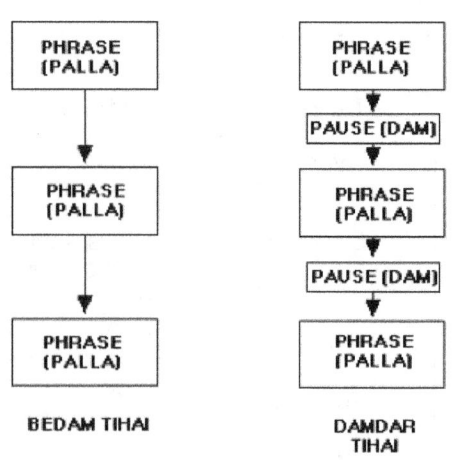

Figure 10.2. Damdar / bedam tihais

Ch. 10. Compositional Theory - Cadential Forms

$$\frac{(16 \cdot 2)+1}{3} = 11$$

<u>Damdar Tihai</u> - The *damdar tihai* has surprisingly different characteristics. The word "*dam*" literally means "breath", but has the secondary meaning of a very small unit of time (Kapoor-no date). For instance, the Hindi expression *"ek dam"* means "suddenly"; it does not imply a "gasp". A *damdar tihai* in a ten beat cycle known as *Jhaptal* is shown below.

<u>Damdar Tihai in Jhaptal</u> (Vashisht 1977:143)

^X धा गे ति र   कि ट त क |²धा   -   धा गे ति र |⁰ कि ट त क   धा |³   -   धा गे ति र   कि ट त क |^Xधा
DhaaGeTiRa KiTaTaKa Dhaa - DhaaGeTiRa KiTaTaKa Dhaa - DhaaGeTiRa KiTaTaKa Dhaa
                           (dam)   (dam)

In this example, the expression *DhaaGeTiRaKiTaTaKaDhaa* (धा गे ति र कि ट त क धा) is repeated three times with a pause in between. This form may be generalised by the formula:

[3 • (number of units in palla)] + [2 • (number of units in pause)] = [(number of beats to fill) • (layakari)]+1

If we apply the above formula to the above example, we see the following relationships. There are several constants in this formula. The "3" represents the basic triadic structure of the *tihai*, and the "2" represents the two pauses between the phrases. Again the "1" represents the resolution on the first beat of the next cycle. If we take the previous example of *DhaaGeTiRaKiTaTaKaDhaa* (धा गे ति र कि ट त क धा), we get nine for the number of units. Remember that the *dam* (pause) must be normalised to the same *layakari* as the phrase *(palla)*; therefore, the last *Dhaa* (धा) is actually *Dhaa - - -* (धा - - -), and the quarter note" -" becomes "- - - -". Therefore, the value of the pause *(dam)* is 7. An easy way to think of it is that one is normalising this composition so that the 16th note becomes the fundamental unit. Since this normalisation required a four-to-one shift, our *layakari* = 4 (i.e., *chaugun*). The entire *tihai* resolves in one cycle of *Jhaptal;* so the number of beats to fill + 10. Finally, after all the numbers are in place, we get [3(9)]+[2(7)]=[(10)(4)]+1. We see that this formula described the situation quite adequately.

<u>Filling the Pause</u> - It should be noted that the pause or *dam,* need not actually be a rest. It is common for *bols* to be thrown in to fill up the gap. The inclusion of *bols* in the *dam* is done for purely artistic reasons, and has no theoretical significance. Therefore, we may partially fill the pause of our previous example with TiRaKiTa (ति र कि ट), and we get something like this:

Damdar Tihai in Jhaptal

^X ध गे ति र   कि ट त क |²धा   ति र कि ट   ध गे ति र |
DhaaGeTiRa KiTaTaKa Dhaa   TiRaKiTa DhaaGeTiRa
                          (dam)

⁰ कि ट त क   धा |³   ति र कि ट   ध गे ति र   कि ट त क |^Xधा
KiTaTaKa Dhaa   TiRaKiTa DhaaGeTiRa KiTaTaKa Dhaa
                (dam)

page 133

It is very easy to say that filling the *dam* with strokes does not change the theoretical construction of the *damdar tihai*. In practice, this may blur the distinction between the two forms. Let us look at the example shown below in Figure 10.3:

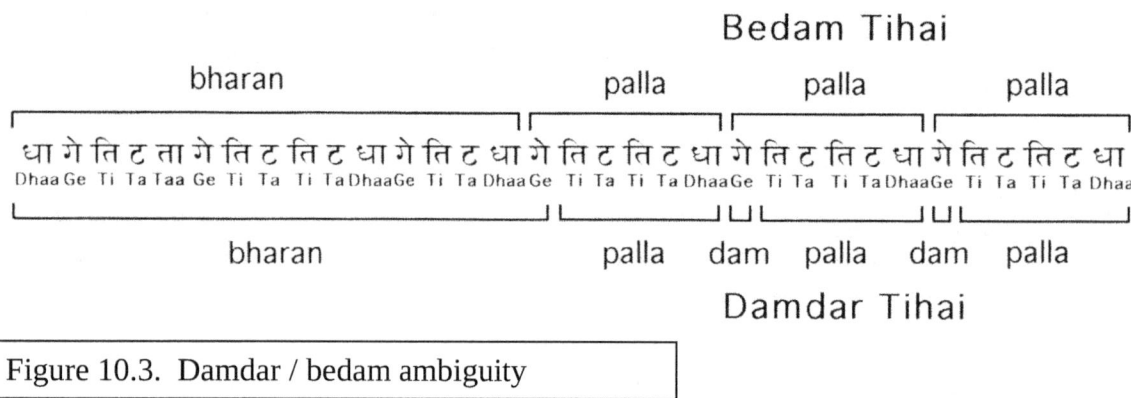

Figure 10.3. Damdar / bedam ambiguity

This example deserves some further attention, because it is a situation that will come up many times. We see in this particular case it is 33 units. This is a very normal number for a cadential form in *Tintal*. It is composed of a body (*bharan*) and a *tihai*; this much is totally clear. What is not clear is where the *bharan* ends and the *tihai* begins. This question, it turns out, is absolutely crucial in determining whether this *tihai* is *damdar* or *bedam*. If we look at it one way, we have a 16 unit *bharan* with a 17 unit *tihai*; this is the *damdar tihai* in the lower portion. This is an interpretation which most musicians would find comfortable, because there is a tendency to give importance to certain strokes according to their position within the *tal*. Therefore if this composition were performed in single time (quite likely in cases of *drut Tintal*), then we have a one cycle *bharan*, with a one cycle *damdar tihai*.

However, this is obviously not the only interpretation. The average concert-goer is not a professional musician and will not selectively weigh the beats according to their position within the *tal*. They will interpret them as they hear them. According to the upper interpretation, it produces a *bedam tihai* which starts, not on *sam*, but on the beat before *sam/khali*. This is certainly a legitimate interpretation.

The bottom line is simple; the common habit of filling the *dam* in a *tihai* may have profound theoretical as well as practical artistic implications. This is not to imply that it is bad, quite the opposite. It opens up totally new and powerful musical possibilities.

Attit Tihai - The *attit tihai* is a one which ends, not on *sam*, but at some point after the *sam*. We must admit that it is not very common. Indeed, its misapplication may even be interpreted by the audience as a mere mistake.

Anagat Tihai - The *angat tihai* is one which ends before the *sam*. This too is rare, and if improperly used, it also may be interpreted as a mere mistake.

Ch. 10. Compositional Theory - Cadential Forms

It is the norm for slow instrumental pieces to begin on the 12th beat, and resolve upon the *sam* (i.e., *masitkhani gat*). A common application of the *anagat tihai* would be to play your improvisation, then close your improvisation with an *anagat tihai* which resolves upon the 12th *matra*. At which point, you could immediately shift to some other entirely unrelated form to further resolve back to *sam*. The effect may be quite exciting.

<u>Sankirna / Sampurna Tihai</u> - Occasionally the expression *sankirna tihai,* or *sampurna tihai,* is encountered. These terms deal with the usage of *bols* in the resolution of a *kaida*. If the entire theme of the *kaida* is used, it is called *sampurna tihai*. Conversely, if only part of the theme is present, or if the theme is present in some altered form, the *tihai* will be called *sankirna tihai*. Since these terms are rare, and the implication so clear, we need not give an example.

There are other types of *tihais*. Some, like the *chakradar* and the *ginti tihais*, deserve special treatment. Therefore we will discuss them separately.

We have seen that the *tihai* is the most important structure for the north Indian cadence. Most of these forms have a *tihai* in them at some level. Essentially, the *tihai* is the repetition of a phrase three times. The last stroke of the last iteration should correspond to the first beat of the following cycle. The phrases may be contiguous *(bedam)*, or they may be separated by a pause *(damdar)*. Occasionally, terms such as *atit* (end after *sam*), *anagat* (end before *sam*), *sampurna* (full theme), or *sankirna* (fragmented theme) are encountered.

COMPLEX CADENTIAL STRUCTURE

It is appropriate that we take a few minutes to describe the basic complex cadential structure. It is a structure which is very common and shared by a large number compositional forms, such as *tukada, mohara,* most *parans,* and even some *mukhadas*. This form is a small body of material, followed by a *tihai*. This is graphically shown in Figure 10.4.

The relationship between the *tihai* and the body is interesting, but not always clear. The *tihai* section is the most obvious cadential element. It may be of any form of *tihai*, either *damdar* or *bedam*. It is the reason that this form is a cadence. The body, on the other hand, has a function and purpose that is at times vague. In some cases, it is nothing more than a *bharan*, or a small filler, to bridge a gap in the *tal*. At other times, it is very important in creating a sense of musical tension; therefore, the body is essentially a *mukhada* which is prefacing a *tihai*. If the body becomes very long and balanced, then it is as though it were a cyclic piece that uses a *tihai* to resolve it. All of these forms exist, and the exact function of the body must be considered on a case-by-case basis. Since this form is so common, we may use the term "complex cadential form" anytime we wish to invoke this model.

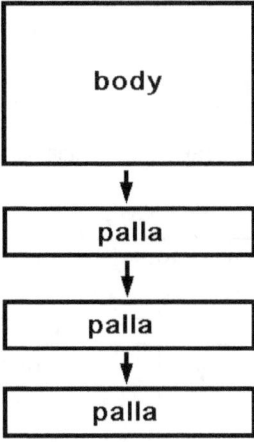

Figure 10.4. Complex cadential structure

Table 10.4. Criteria for Mohara	
Overall philosophy	Cadential
Structure	Short body with tihai
Bol Type	-
Function	Modest assertion from tabla player in classical styles
Technique	-

MOHARA

The *mohara* is a useless term. The literal meaning of the word *mohara* is "the vanguard of an army" (Kapoor no date). But there is such disagreement as to what a *mohara* is for tabla, that there is no way we can use the term in any meaningful fashion. The only thing that we can say with any certainty is that it is of the *paran* class.

There are competing ideas as to what the *mohara* is. One school has *mohara* being virtually indistinguishable from the *mukhada*. This approach is alluded to by earlier scholars (Stewart 1974), but really pushed by Shepherd (Shepherd 1976). In such an approach, the *mohara* need not have a *tihai*. However, most people opine that it is structurally of the complex cadential class. This appears to be the dominant opinion.

Below is an example *mohara*. This example has a clear structure; it is of two parts (e.g., complex cadential structure). The first part is a small body of material; the second part is a *tihai*. The body acts as an introduction to the *tihai*.

Mohara (Shepherd 1976:174)

^xधा धिं धिं धा | ²धा धिं धिं धा | ⁰धा - तिं ना, किट त क ता - तिर, किट त क ति र कि ट,
Dhaa Dhin Dhin Dhaa Dhaa Dhin Dhin Dhaa Dhaa - TinNaa KiTaKaTaa - TiRa KiTaTaKaTiRaKiTa

त क त क ति र कि ट, | ³धा - - - ति र कि ट, त क त क ति र कि ट,
TaKaTaKaTiRaKiTa Dhaa - - - TiRaKiTa TaKaTaKaTiRaKiTa

धा - - - ति र कि ट, त क त क ति र कि ट, | ^xधा
Dhaa - - - TiRaKiTa TaKaTaKaTiRaKiTa Dhaa

There is also little agreement as to the length of the *mohara*. Although a *muhkada* will be less than one cycle, most *moharas* are one to three cycles in length. Since most *parans* also have the same structure, there are many compositions which may be considered either *paran* or *mohara*.

CHAKRADAR

The *chakradar* is a special form of *tihai*. It may be thought of as three *tihais* joined together. Since a *tihai* is a part of the *paran* or *tukhada,* it may also be three *parans* joined together. Indeed, it is possible to simply string three complex cadences together to create a *chakradar*. The *chakradar* is defined entirely by the structure (Table 10.5).

Table 10.5. Criteria for Chakradar	
Overall philosophy	Cadential
Structure	Three tihais joined together
Bol Type	-
Function	-
Technique	-

The origin of the term "*chakradar*" is interesting. The expression "*chakra*" means variously a "wheel", a "round", a "cycle", a "rotation", etc. The term "*dar*" means "a thing that posses the qualities of something". For instance, "*zamin*" means "land" and a landowner is a "*zamindar*". The term for a small unit of time roughly corresponding to a "breath" is a "*dam*", and *tihais* which have that small pause are "*damdar*". In the same manner, the literal meaning of the word "*chakradar*" is a composition that has a "rolling" quality. Indeed, that is exactly the case. When one listens to a *chakradar,* one expects it to resolve immediately, but it does not. It just keeps rolling along for a long time before reaching resolution.

There a numerous forms of the *chakradar*. The most common structures are shown in Figure 10.5. If we look at this illustration, we see that there are four basic forms. These are: a) *Chakradars* which consist of a *palla* repeated nine times. b) Three complex cadential structures linked together, c) Two complete *pallas*, an incomplete *palla,* two more complete *pallas*, and incomplete *palla* followed by three complete *pallas* d) Three complex cadential forms with the first two having incomplete ending *pallas*.

Below is a *chakradar* that follows the structure shown in Figure 10.5a.

<u>Chakradar</u> (Zakir Hussain, Personal Interview, 1988)

^X तिरकिट धा-तिर किटधा- तिरकिट | ²धा- तिरकिट धा-तिर |
  TiRaKiTa Dhaa-TiRa KiTaDhaa- TiRaKiTa   Dhaa- TiRaKiTa Dhaa-TiRa

⁰ किटधा- तिरकिट धा- | ³तिरकिट धा-तिर किटधा- तिरकिट | ^Xधा . . .
  KiTa Dhaa- TiRaKiTa Dhaa-   TiRaKiTa Dhaa-TiRa KiTaDhaa- TiRaKiTa   Dhaa

A more developed and more common structure is shown in Figure 10.5.b. This is the most common structure. We see that this is really nothing more than three complex cadences strung together. An example is shown on the next page:

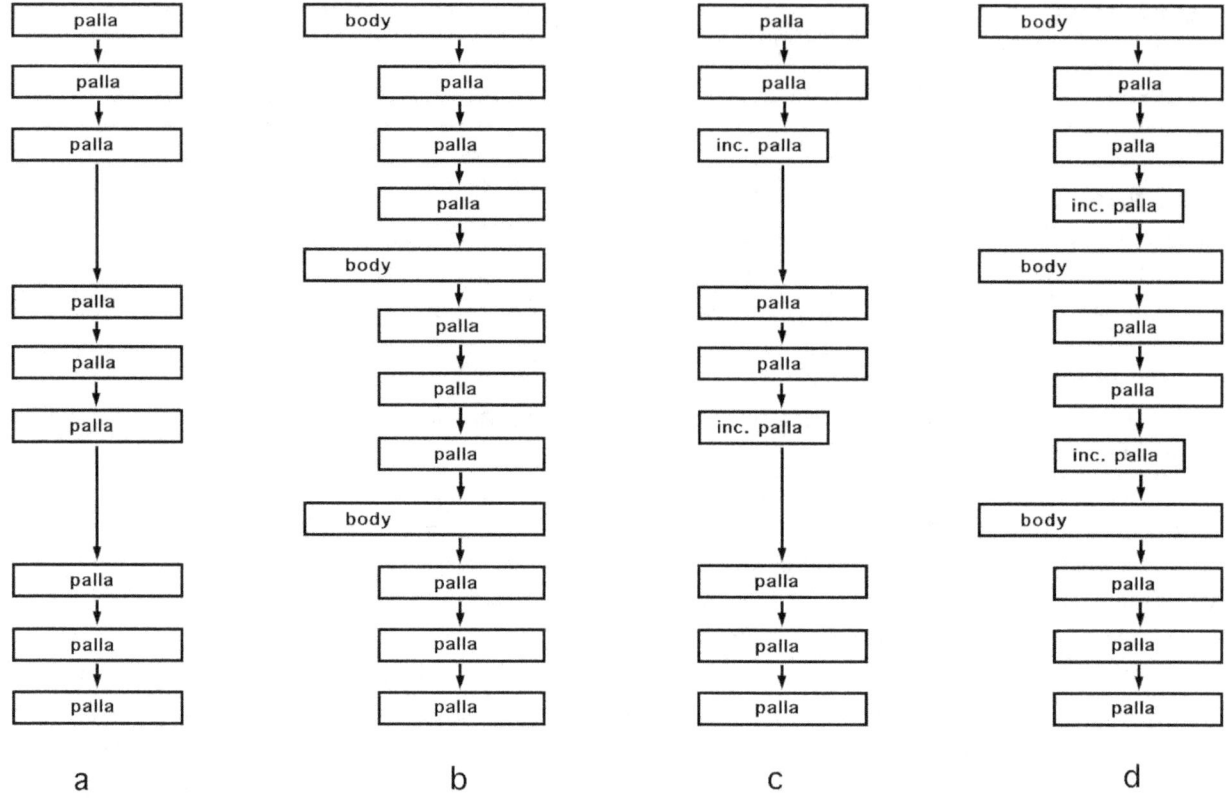

Figure 10.5. Various types of chakradar

Chakradar in Tintal (Sharma 1975:164)

× धा - धा - तिरकिट धिं - तिरकिटतक धिरकिटतकतिर किटतकधेत् - त -|
   Dhaa - Dhaa - TiRaKiTa Dhin - TiRaKiTaTaKa DhiRaKiTaTaKaTiRa KiTaTaKaDhet - Ta -

² तिरकिटधिरकिट तिरकिटधेत् - त - तक्कड़ां धातक् | ⁰ कड़ांधा तक्कड़ां धा
  TiRaKiTaDhiRaKiTa TiRaKiTaDhet - Ta - TakKdaan DhaaTak KdaanDhaa Tak Kdaan Dhaa

  धा - धा - तिरकिट |³ धिं - तिरकिटतक धिरकिटतकतिर किटतकधेत् - त -
  Dhaa - Dhaa - TiRaKiTa Dhin - TiRaKiTaTaKa DhiRaKiTaTaKaTiRa KiTaTaKaDhet - Ta -

  तिरकिटधिरकिट |× तिरकिटधेत् - त - तक्कड़ां धातक् कड़ांधा |² तक्कड़ां धा
  TiRaKiTaDhiRaKiTa TiRaKiTaDhet - Ta - TakKdaan DhaaTak KdaanDhaa TakKdaan Dhaa

× धा - धा - तिरकिट धिं - तिरकिटतक |⁰ धिरकिटतकतिर किटतकधेत् - त -
  Dhaa - Dhaa - TiRaKiTa Dhin - TiRaKiTaTaKa DhiRaKiTaTaKaTiRa KiTaTaKaDhet - Ta -

  तिरकिटधिरकिट तिरकिटधेत् - त - |³ तक्कड़ां धातक् कड़ांधा तक्कड़ां |×धा
  TiRaKiTaDhiRaKiTa TiRaKiTaDhet - Ta - TakKdaan DhaaTak KdaanDhaa TakKdaan Dhaa

Ch. 10. Compositional Theory - Cadential Forms

The structure shown in Figure 10.5.c is particularly good at creating a sense of musical tension. An example is shown below:

<u>Bedam Chakradar in Rupaktal</u> (Leake 1993:159)

⁰धा - ति र	कि ट त क	तक्	¹क्ड़ां धा	² धा - ति र	कि ट त क	⁰तक् क्ड़ां धा
Dhaa - TiRa	KiTaTaKa	Tak	Kdaan Dhaa	Dhaa - TiRa	KiTaTaKa	Tak Kdaan Dhaa

¹धा - ति र	कि ट त क	²तक् क्ड़ां
Dhaa - TiRa	KiTaTaKa	Tak Kdaan

⁰धा - ति र	कि ट त क	तक्	¹क्ड़ां धा	² धा - ति र	कि ट त क	⁰तक् क्ड़ां धा
Dhaa - TiRa	KiTaTaKa	Tak	Kdaan Dhaa	Dhaa - TiRa	KiTaTaKa	Tak Kdaan Dhaa

¹धा - ति र	कि ट त क	²तक् क्ड़ां
Dhaa - TiRa	KiTaTaKa	Tak Kdaan

⁰धा - ति र	कि ट त क	तक्	¹क्ड़ां धा	² धा - ति र	कि ट त क	⁰तक् क्ड़ां धा
Dhaa - TiRa	KiTaTaKa	Tak	Kdaan Dhaa	Dhaa - TiRa	KiTaTaKa	Tak Kdaan Dhaa

¹धा - ति र	कि ट त क	² तक् क्ड़ां	⁰तिं
Dhaa - TiRa	KiTaTaKa	Tak Kdaan	Tin

Let us look at the form indicated in Figure 10.5.c in greater detail. Essentially one takes a simple *tihai* and plays it. However when one reaches the final *Dhaa* (धा), the entire *tihai* starts again. This continues for a total of three times, and it only finishes at the third iteration. In a sense, this amounts to dropping a beat from two of the *pallas*. Therefore, these *pallas* are incomplete. This is a very attractive approach, and is the easiest of the *chakradars* to perform. It also is very well suited to improvisation. If one is in the middle of the first *tihai* and it appears that the music is going to take a different direction, one need not complete the *chakradar*. One merely has to play the final *Dhaa* (धा), thus completing the *tihai* at the *sam*. One may then move on to something else.

Just as we have strung three simple *tihais* together by removing their last beat (of the first two); so too we can create a *chakradar* by stringing three complex cadential structures together in the same fashion. This process is illustrated in Figure 10.5.d. An example is shown on the next page:

Chakradar in Tintal (S. Dawood Khan 1978, Personal; interview)

धा गे तिट ता के तिट किड धा तिट ता के तिट
DhaaGe TiTa TaaKe TiTa KidDhaa TiTa TaaKe TiTa

किड धा तिट किड धा - न धा ता -
KidDhaa TiTa KidDhaa - Na Dhaa Taa -

धिर धिर किट तक ता - तिर किट तक तक् - किट धा
DhiRaDhiRa KiTaTaKa Taa - TiRa KiTaTaKa Tak - KiTa Dhaa

धिर धिर किट तक ता - तिर किट तक तक् - किट धा
DhiRaDhiRa KiTaTaKa Taa - TiRa KiTaTaKa Tak - KiTa Dhaa

धिर धिर किट तक ता - तिर किट तक तक् - किट
DhiRaDhiRa KiTaTaKa Taa - TiRa KiTaTaKa Tak - KiTa

धा गे तिट ता के तिट किड धा तिट ता के तिट
DhaaGe TiTa TaaKe TiTa KidDhaa TiTa TaaKe TiTa

किड धा तिट किड धा - न धा ता -
KidDhaa TiTa KidDhaa - Na Dhaa Taa -

धिर धिर किट तक ता - तिर किट तक तक् - किट धा
DhiRaDhiRa KiTaTaKa Taa - TiRa KiTaTaKa Tak - KiTa Dhaa

धिर धिर किट तक ता - तिर किट तक तक् - किट धा
DhiRaDhiRa KiTaTaKa Taa - TiRa KiTaTaKa Tak - KiTa Dhaa

धिर धिर किट तक ता - तिर किट तक तक् - किट
DhiRaDhiRa KiTaTaKa Taa - TiRa KiTaTaKa Tak - KiTa

धा गे तिट ता के तिट किड धा तिट ता के तिट
DhaaGe TiTa TaaKe TiTa KidDhaa TiTa TaaKe TiTa

किड धा तिट किड धा - न धा ता -
KidDhaa TiTa KidDhaa - Na Dhaa Taa -

धिर धिर किट तक ता - तिर किट तक तक् - किट धा
DhiRaDhiRa KiTaTaKa Taa - TiRa KiTaTaKa Tak - KiTa Dhaa

धिर धिर किट तक ता - तिर किट तक तक् - किट धा
DhiRaDhiRa KiTaTaKa Taa - TiRa KiTaTaKa Tak - KiTa Dhaa

धिर धिर किट तक ता - तिर किट तक तक् - किट | ˣधा
DhiRaDhiRa KiTaTaKa Taa - TiRa KiTaTaKa Tak - KiTa Dhaa

Ch. 10. Compositional Theory - Cadential Forms

Nohhaka - It is clear that within the structure of a *tihai* there may be any number of *Dhaas* (धा). If it specifically has nine *Dhaas* (धा) culminating on *sam,* then it is sometimes referred to as a *nohhaka*.

Nohhaka Dhaa in Tintal (S. Dawood Khan, 1978, personal interview)

धि र धि र कि ट त क ता - ति र कि ट त क तक् कडां - - न धा
DhiRaDhiRa KiTaKa Taa - TiRa KiTaKa Tak Kdaan - - Na Dhaa

कडां - - न धा कडां - - न धा
Kdaan - - Na Dhaa Kdaan - - Na Dhaa

धि र धि र कि ट त क ता - ति र कि ट त क तक् कडां - - न धा
DhiRaDhiRa KiTaKa Taa - TiRa KiTaKa Tak Kdaan - - Na Dhaa

कडां - - न धा कडां - - न धा
Kdaan - - Na Dhaa Kdaan - - Na Dhaa

धि र धि र कि ट त क ता - ति र कि ट त क तक् कडां - - न धा
DhiRaDhiRa KiTaKa Taa - TiRa KiTaKa Tak Kdaan - - Na Dhaa

कडां - - न धा कडां - - न |ˣधा
Kdaan - - Na Dhaa Kdaan - - Na Dhaa

Farmaishi Chakradar - *Farmaishi chakradar* is a term that one will run across periodically. The *farmaish* may be thought of as being somewhat a cross between a challenge and an encore. This is where the audience demands or requests some particular piece or style. *Farmaishi chakradars* have a structure which is indistinguishable other *chakradars*. Therefore the term is meaningless, so we will not go into any detail here.

Kamali Chakradar - The term *"kamali chakradar"* means a "wondrous *chakradar*". This is essentially meaningless, as the *kamali chakradars* are indistinguishable from other *chakradars*. Therefore, we will not discuss it further.

Chakradar Paran - This is a *paran* which uses the *chakradar* structure. (See the discussion of *paran* for further information.)

Let us recap what we have seen in the *chakradar*. This is essentially a *tihai* in which each of its *pallas* itself contains a *tihai*. They may be either simple *tihais,* or they may be more complex cadences (e.g., *paran, tukhada*). Some are easy to construct, while others require some very sophisticated mathematics. The artistic effect is one of rolling; when the listener expects a resolution, it just continues until it finally resolves at some later time.

PARAN

Paran (परन) is a common type cadence; it is defined both by function and *bol* (Table 10.6). Functionally, it is a heavy assertion on the part of the tabla player in the classical styles. The *bols* are invariably powerful, open strokes from the *pakhawaj* tradition. There are many types of *parans*. Forms such as the *lalkila paran, tar paran, bol paran* etc., are but a few sub-forms of this major class of compositions.

Table 10.6. Criteria for Paran	
Overall philosophy	Cadential
Structure	-
Bol Type	Pakhawaj
Function	Assertion from tabla player in classical styles
Technique	-

The origin of the term *paran* is obscure, but it is believed that it is a corruption of "*parhant*". *Parhant* is the recitation of *bols* in a *kathak* dance recital. This could imply that the *paran* was a composition whose *bols* were so beautiful that it was suitable for a special recitation.

It is certain that the *bols* are the defining criterion of *paran*, with function acting as a strong second. The *bols* invariably reflect open, resonant strokes derived from the *pakhawaj* tradition. *Bols* such as *TiTaKaTaGaDeeGeNa* (ति ट क त ग दी गे न), *DhuMaKiTaTaKa* (धु म कि त त क), or *DhaaGeTeTe* (धा गे ते टे) are most common. Functionally, the *paran* is an aggressive display of virtuosity on the part of the tabla player. It may be used in *kathak* dance, tabla solos, but not in light or folk genre. It may be used whenever the "trading off" places control in the hands of the tabla player, but may be inappropriate for general accompaniment due to its tendency to overpower the main vocalist / instrumentalist.

Although structure is not a defining criterion for *paran,* we may make a few observations. Usually it is structured in a complex cadential form. However, there are cases where no *tihai* is present.

A typical example of a *paran* in *Jhaptal* is shown below:

Paran in Jhaptal (Mridangacharya / Shankardas 1977: 26)

^X घिं - ति र कि ट त क, ता गे ते ट | ² ते टे क धा, के ट ता गे, ते ट ते ट |
Ghin - TiRaKiTaTaKa   TaaGeTeTa   TeTeKaDhaa   KeTaTaaGe   TeTaTeTa

⁰ का - ति र कि ट त क, ता गे - दि, | ³ ग न ना गे, ना - गे - ति र कि ट,
Kaa - TiRaKiTaKa   TaaGe - Di   GeNaNaaGe   Naa - Ge - TiRaKiTa

त क ता - क - ते - , | ^X ते त ग न, ता गे ते ट |
TaKaTaa - Ka - Te -   TeTaGaNa   TaaGeTeTa

² घे - घे - ति र कि ट, त क ता क त्, ति र कि ट त क ता - , |
Ghe - Ghe - TiRaKiTa   TaKaTaaKat   TiRaKiTaTaKaTaa -

⁰ कि ट त क ग दि ग न, धा - - धा, | ³ कि ट त क ग दि ग न, धा - - धा, कि ट त क ग दि ग न | ^Xधा
KiTaKaGaDiGaNa   Dhaa - - Dhaa   KiTaTaKaGaDiGaNa   Dhaa - - Dhaa   KiTaTaKaGaDiGaNa   Dhaa

Ekhatthu Paran - An *ekhatthu paran* is one which is played only with one hand. This is discussed separately under heading of *Ekhatthu*.

Lalkila Paran - A *lalkila paran*, sometimes known as *dohatthu paran,* uses both hands on a single drum. Refer to the *dohatthu* heading for a further discussion.

Bol Paran - A *bol paran* uses words of Sanskrit, Hindi, or Persian in place of usual syllables. This style is very commonly used in *kathak* dance performances. On the next page is a *bol paran* in praise of the Lord Shiva.

Ch. 10. Compositional Theory - Cadential Forms

Bol Paran in Ada Chautal (14 matras)(Garg 1994:378)

first iteration

				Words
ˣजयकै लासी	²अविना शी सुख	⁰राशी सदा र	³हे गं गा तट	
jaykai laasi	avina shee sukha	raashi sada ra	hegang ga tata	
धा गे दिं ता	ग दि ना - धा - क त	दिं ता क ता - ग	दिं ता ता - ति ट	Technique
DhaaGe DinTaa	GaDiNaa - Dhaa - KaTa	DinTaa KaTaa - Ga	DinTaa Taa - TiTa	

			Words
⁰काशी खा तभं	⁴ गवृष भसं ग	⁰शी शगं गशिव	
kaashi kha tabhang	gavrisha bhasang ga	shee shang gashiva	
दिं ता दि ग न ता	- ग दि ग ग दिं - ता	धेत् - त धा - न क त	Technique
DinTaa DiGaNaTaa	- GaDiGa GaDin - Taa	Dhet - TaDhaa - NaKaTa	

			Words
ˣशं कर धा शं	²कर धा शं कर	⁰धा	
shan kara dhaashan	kara dhaa shan kara	dhaa	
दिं - ग ड़ धा दिं	ग ड़ धा - दिं - ग ड़	⁰धा	Technique
Ding - GaRa DhaaDin	GaRaDhaa - Ding - GaRa	Dhaa	

second iteration

					Words
जयकै	³ लासी अविना	⁰ शी सुख राशी	⁴सदा र हे गं	⁰गा तट	
jaykai	laasi avina	shee sukha raashi	sada ra hegang	gaa tata	
धा गे	दिं ता ग दि ना -	धा - क त दिं ता	क ता - ग दिं ता	ता - ति ट	Technique
DhaaGe	DinTa GaDiNa -	Dhaa - KaTa DinTaa	KaTaa - Ga DinTaa	Taa - TiTa	

				Words
काशी	ˣखा तभं गवृष	²भसं ग शी शगं	⁰ गशिव	
kaashi	khaa tabhang gavrisha	bhasang ga shee shang	gashiva	
दिं ता	दि ग न ता - ग दि ग	ग दिं - ता धेत् - त धा	- न क त	Technique
DinTaa	DiGaNaTaa - GaDiGa	GaDin - Taa Dhet - TaDhaa	- NaKaTa	

			Words
शं कर	³धा शं कर धा	⁰शं कर धा	
shan kara	dhaashan kara dhaa	shan kara dhaa	
दिं - ग ड़	धा दिं ग ड़ धा -	दिं - ग ड़ धा	Technique
Ding - GaRa	DhaaDin GaRaDhaa -	Ding - GaRa Dhaa	

third iteration

				Words
⁴जयकै लासी	⁰ अविना शी सुख	ˣराशी सदा र	² हे गं गा तट	
jaykai laasi	avinaa shee sukha	raashi sadaa ra	hegang gaa tata	
धा गे दिं ता	ग दि ना - धा - क त	दिं ता क ता - ग	दिं ता ता - ति ट	Technique
DhaaGe DinTaa	GaDiNaa - Dhaa - KaTa	DinTaa KaTaa - Ga	DinTaa Taa - TiTa	

			Words
⁰काशी खा तभं	³ गवृष भसं ग	⁰ शी शगं गशिव	
kaashi khaa tabhang	gavrisha bhasang ga	shee shang gashiva	
दिं ता दि ग न ता	- ग दि ग ग दिं - ता	धेत् - त धा - न क त	Technique
DinTaa DiGaNaTaa	- GaDiGa GaDin - Taa	Dhet - TaDhaa - NaKaTa	

			Words
⁴शं कर धा शं	⁰कर धा शं कर	ˣधा	
shan kara dhaashan	kara dhaa shan kara	dhaa	
दिं - ग ड़ धा दिं	ग ड़ धा - दिं - ग ड़	धा	Technique
Ding - GaRa DhaaDin	GaRaDhaa - Ding - GaRa	Dhaa	

Let us make a few observations about the previous example. The technique used is a hodgepodge of *pakhawaj bols* and general *purbi* material. It is performed in a very powerful fashion as befitting a *kathak* recital. Structurally this *paran* is a *chakradar*. However, the *bol paran* may be in any structural form; a linear structure like a *sath* or *fard*, a *tihai*, or a complex cadential structure would also be acceptable. This particular piece is notated in *Ada Chautal*, yet it would also work very well in *Rupak, Dipchandi, Dhammar,* or *Tivra tal*. If only a single iteration is made, we see that it takes 19 *matras*; therefore a single iteration would work very well in *Matta tal*.

The *bol paran* is commonly named according to the particular wordings. For instance, one will hear terms thrown about such as *Ganesh stuti, Shiva stotram, holi paran, Radha/Krishna paran*, etc. It is impossible to go over all the different names that the various *bol parans* may be called. However, if one has even the slightest familiarity with either Hindi or Sanskrit, the exact meaning is always clear.

Namaskari Paran / Salami Paran - The *namaskari paran* or *salami paran* has two meanings. According to one definition, it is similar to *bol paran;* however, instead of merely speaking, one raises the hand (or hands) in a characteristic greeting. For a *namaskari paran,* one will raise both hands, and bring them together in the form of a *namaskar*. For a *salami paran,* it is the same except that only the right hand need be brought to the forehead in the gesture for *salam*. Both of these forms may be used in tabla solos and *kathak* dance recitals.

There is another definition of the *salami/namaskari paran* that doesn't have anything to do with the tabla player. In this form, it is the accompaniment while the *kathak* dancer performs the customary greeting. These compositions are indistinguishable from the rest of the complex cadential material (i.e., *mohara, paran, tukada* etc.); so the term becomes meaningless for the tabla player.

Farmaishi Paran - A *farmaishi paran* is used in encores. Again, the term is nearly meaningless, as this says almost nothing which may be objectively discerned. It has been suggested (Feldman 1995) that the structure is such that the first *Dhaa* (धा) of the first iteration falls on the *sam*. The second *Dhaa* (धा) of the second iteration falls on the *sam,* and the final *Dhaa* (धा) of the final iteration falls on the *sam*. Unfortunately, the large number of exceptions to this rule, coupled with the fact that this is a very usual *chakradar* structure make us question the utility of this term.

Tar Paran - A *tar paran* is one which is used with instruments such as sitar or *sarod,* and has a structure which is consistent with these instrumental styles. It has been suggested (Stewart 1974:158), that these forms are more like the modern *rela,* and should therefore be considered cyclic forms.

Kamali Paran - A *kamali paran* is one which is considered "wondrous". This too, is a meaningless expression, as it is not tied to any objectively discernible characteristic.

Misc. Parans - It would be impossible to cover all of the miscellaneous designations for *parans* that crop up. One will encounter terms such as *nalikayantra, chakrakriti, mayur, saudanani,* and a host of others. These terms are in some cases idiosyncratic to particular musicians; in some cases they are feeble attempts to apply ancient and obsolete principles to the music. Whatever the reason for their coming into being, their lack of broad acceptance, and the consequent idiosyncratic nature of their definitions, mean that they may be ignored.

We may summarise the *paran* as a cadence which is derived from the *pakhawaj* tradition. Both etymology and contemporary usage indicate that *kathak* has had a major influence on its development. It is defined primarily by *bol* and function, with structure playing a negligible part. Many different types of *parans* have developed over the years. Unfortunately many of the commonly used terms such as *kamali paran* or *farmaishi paran* are essentially meaningless.

EKHATTHU

Ekhatthu is a style which is determined entirely by the technique (Table 10.7). It is the playing of an entire composition with just a single hand. There is nothing about the *ekhatthu* which suggests structure, *bol*, or function. However the simple fact that only one hand is used means that long complex forms may not be executed in such a way as to maintain the listener's interest. Therefore, it is common to find the *ekhatthu* used to play relatively short cadential forms. Anything within the complex cadential format is the norm, usually a *paran* or *tukada*. Below is an example of an *ekhatthu mukhada* which is played only with the right hand:

Table 10.7. Criteria for Ekhatthu

Overall philosophy	-
Structure	-
Bol Type	-
Function	-
Technique	Single hand

Ekhatthu Mukhada in Tintal (S. Dawood 1978, Personal; interview)

दीं दीं नाना त्रक दिं न दिं न ना ति ट ता
Deen Deen NaaNaa TraKa DinNa DinNa NaaTi TaTaa

ति ट ता न ना -न ता दीं नाना ति ट
TiTa Taa NaNaa - Na Taa Deen NaaNaa TiTa

ति ट ता न ना -न ता ति ट ति ट ता न ना -न ता
TiTa Taa NaNaa - Na Taa TiTa TiTa Taa NaNaa - Na Taa

ति ट ति ट ता न ना -न |˟ता
TiTa TiTa Taa NaNaa - Na Taa

DOHATTHU

The *dohatthu*, also referred to as the *lalkila* composition, is merely the lifting of one of the hands and playing both hands on a single drum. It may be any style imaginable. The *dohatthu* was discussed in the last chapter.

TUKADA

The word *tukada* literally means "a piece". There are two schools of thought as to the definition of *tukada*. According to a small number of musicians, *tukada* is defined entirely by the *bols*, specifically closed *bols* such as TiRaKiTa. Yet according to most people, it is defined according to structure (Table 10.8). The structuralists contend that a *tukada* is a short piece which has a small body or introduction culminating in a *tihai*. This makes it identical to most *moharas* and *parans*. The "bolists" contend that it is defined by the use of pure tabla *bols*. One consequence of this latter philosophy is that there are a few cases where the *tihai* is left off (Sharma 1973:31). *Tukada* may be used in any style except for extremely light, or folk music.

Table 10.8. Criteria for Tukada

Overall philosophy	Cadential
Structure	Very small introductory passage followed by tihai
Bol Type	-
Function	-
Technique	-

If we place the academic considerations aside, the basic defining quality is simple; the *tukada* must be small. Even the name *tukada* implies something which is not too long. If the *tukada* is long, it is sometimes called *toda* (H. Shrivastava 1973:84). Very closely allied to the *tukada* is the *pirmal,* which is found exclusively in the dance forms.

Below are two examples of the *tukada*. It is interesting to note that neither of these forms conforms to the "bolists'" concept of the *tukada*. The extreme variety of *bols* present in the vast majority of *tukadas* indicate that the *bol* definition may be effectively discounted.

Tukada in Tintal (Yadav 1999a:9

^X धा गे ते टे, ता गे ते टे, धा गे ते टे, क डा - न | ² धा गे ते टे, धा - क डा, - न धा -, क डा - न |
DhaaGeTeTe TaaGeTeTe DhaaGeTeTe KarDaa - Na   DhaaGeTeTe Dhaa - KarDaa - NaDhaa - KarDaa - Na

⁰ क डा - न, धा धा, धा क डा - न | ³ धा धा, धा क डा - न, धा धा, | ^X धा
KarDaa - Na DhaaDhaa Dhaa KarDaa - Na   DhaaDhaa Dhaa KarDaa - Na DhaaDhaa Dhaa

Kathak Dance Tukada in Tintal (Anju Babu 1988, personal interview)

तत् तत् तूं तूं तीग् धा, दी ग दी ग, थेई - तत् तत् तूं तूं तीग् धा, दी ग दी ग, थेई -
Tat Tat Toon Toon TeegDhaa DeeGaDeeGa Thei - Tat Tat Toon Toon TeegDhaa DeeGaDeeGa Thei -

तत् तत् तूं तूं तीग् धा, दी ग दी ग, थेई -
Tat Tat Toon Toon TeegDhaa DeeGaDeeGa Thei -

तीग् धा, दी ग दी ग, थेई तीग् धा, दी ग दी ग, थेई तीग् धा, दी ग दी ग, थेई
TeegDhaa DeeGaDeeGa Thei TeegDhaa DeeGaDeeGa Thei TeegDhaa DeeGaDeeGa Thei

UTHAN

The word *uthan* (उठान) literally means "rising". This is a type of *paran* or *mohara* which is used in the Benares *gharana* to open a tabla solo. This style is defined by function and structure (Table 10.9).

Table 10.9. Criteria for Uthan

Overall philosophy	Cadential
Structure	Complex cadence
Bol Type	Purbi
Function	Open tabla solos in Benares Gharana
Techniquque	-

Ch. 10. Compositional Theory - Cadential Forms

Uthan in Tintal (Yadav 1999a:93)

^x DhaaGe TeTe TaaGe TeTe DhaaGe Di NaaGe TeTe |

² DhiTa TaGin -Na DhiTa TaGin -Na DhiTa Taa |

⁰ DhiTa DhiTa TaGin -Na Dhaa - DhiTa DhiTa |

³ TaGin -Na Dhaa - DhiTa DhiTa TaGin -Na |

^x DhiTa DhiTa TaGin -Na Dhaa - DhiTa DhiTa |

² TaGin -Na Dhaa - DhiTa DhiTa TaGin -Na |

⁰ DhiTa DhiTa TaGin -Na Dhaa - DhiTa DhiTa |

³ TaGin -Na Dhaa - DhiTa DhiTa TaGin -Na | ^x Dhaa

DUPALLI

A *dupalli* is a type of *gat* that has two sections (Table 10.10.). However, unlike an ordinary *gat* that is cyclic and symmetrical, the *dupalli* is cadential and asymmetric. The second section is in a higher speed than the first section. There is no *bhari/ khali* structure, and the two sections need not be the same. The only requirement is that both sections have similar set of *bols* and a similar feel.

Table 10.10. Criteria for Dupalli	
Overall philosophy	Cadential
Structure	Binary structure with increasing tempo
Bol Type	-
Function	-
Technique	

Dupalli in Tintal (Yadav 1999b:235)

^xTi Ta Ka Ta | ²Ga Di Ga Na | ⁰Dhaa Dhaa Dhaa TiTa | ³KaTa GaDi GaNa DhaaDhaa | ^xDhaa

TIPALLI

The *tipalli* is a common cadential *gat*. It is essentially a triadic composition where each of the three sections is in an increasing *layakari* (tempo). *Tipalli* is defined by its structure (Table 10.11). Below is a *tipalli* in *Tintal* which was given to me by my teacher, the late Shaik Dawood Khan.

Table 10.11. Criteria for Tipalli

Overall philosophy	Cadential
Structure	Triadic structure with increasing tempo
Bol Type	-
Function	-
Technique	-

Tipalli in Tintal (Ustad Shaik Dawood Khan, 1978 personal interview)

× दिंग् - ग , दिंग - ग , तकीट , तकीट |
Ding - Ga Ding - Ga TaKeeTa TaKeeTa

² धा - तिरकिट , धीकिट , कतग , दीगीन | (triple)
Dhaa - TiRaKiTa DheeKiTa KaTaGa DeeGeeNa

⁰ धा - तिरकिटधी - , किटकत , घेद्दी , किटतक | (quadruple time)
Dhaa - TiRaKiTaDhee - KiTaKaTa DhedDee KiTaTaKa

³ दिंग् - गदिंग - ग , तकीटतकीट , धा - तिरकिटधी - कि - ट - , कतगदीगीन | ×धा (sextuple)
Ding - GaDing - Ga TaKeeTaTaKeeTa Dhaa - TiRaKiTaDhee - Ki - Ta KaTaGaDeeGeeNa Dhaa

CHAUPALLI

Chaupalli, like the *dupalli* and the *tipalli*, is a cadential *gat* that has multiple sections. In the case of the *chaupalli*, it has four sections, with each one increasing in tempo. Like the *dupalli* and the *tipalli*, each phrase need not be identical; but should be merely similar in feel and *bol*. *Chaupalli* is defined by the structure (Table 10.12.)

Table 10.12. Criteria for Chaupalli

Overall philosophy	Cadential
Structure	Quadratic structure with increasing tempo
Bol Type	-
Function	-
Technique	-

Chaupalli in Tintal (Garg 1994:603)

×तिटकत | ²गदिगिन |
Ti Ta Ka Ta Ga Di Gi Na

⁰धा तिट , कत , गदि |
Dhaa TiTa KaTa GaDi

³ गिन , तिटकत , गदिगिन
GiNa TiTaKaTa GaDiGiNa

तिटकतगदिगिन | ×धा
TiTaKaTaGaDiGiNa Dhaa

AMAD

The *amad* is a form which is used primarily in the *kathak* dance tradition (Table 10.13). A characteristic *amad* is shown below. *Amad* is defined by its characteristic *bols*, structure, and function. There are a very few *bols* which occur in very specific ways. It is so specific that the *amad* is very easy to recognise. Structurally, the *amad* consists of a body and a *tihai*. Many times the *tihai* is not really a *tihai* in the strict sense, but a set of *bols* which gives a feel of a *tihai*. Functionally, it is an opening piece for a *kathak* dance. Here is a typical example.

Table 10.13. Criteria for Amad

Overall philosophy	Cadential
Structure	Body and tihai
Bol Type	Specific kathak bols
Function	Opening of kathak performance
Technique	-

Amad in Tintal (Shrivastava 1973:124)

^Xधा त क थूँ | ²गा - धा गे | ⁰दिं ग ता - | ³धा दिं ता - | ^Xधित ता किड़ धा |
Dhaa Ta Ka Thoon   Gaa - Dhaa Ge   Din Ga Taa -   Dhaa Din Taa -   Dhet Taa KiRa Dhaa

²तक् का थूँ गा | ⁰तकि टत का - | ³तिट कत गदि गन |
Tak Kaa Thoon Gaa   TaKi TaTa Kaa -   TiTa KaTa GaDi GaNa

^Xता थेई तत थेई | ²आ थेई तत थेई | ⁰थेई तत थेई थेई | ³तत थेई थेई तत | ^Xथेई
Taa Thei TaTa Thei   A Thei TaTa Thei   Thei TaTa Thei Thei   TaTa Thei Thei TaTa   Thei

SATH AND FARD

Sath and *fard* are virtually identical. They are *pakhawaj* based cadential *gats* with only a single structure (Table 10.14).

The term *sath* refers to a disruption of the normal "trading off" that is found in a typical performance of Indian vocal or instrumental. One plays the *sath* at the same time that the main performer is improvising. The object is to both resolve on the *sam* at the same time. The *sath* is defined by *bol* and by function. The function is to create tension by disrupting the normal process of trading off. Musical tension is also created by the powerful *pakhawaj bols*. The *sath* is in the borderline between a cadential form and a cyclic form. If one drops the last *Dhaa* (धा), and repeats the composition, it has a form very similar to a *fard*, which is cyclic. If one goes ahead and plays the *sath* to conclusion, then it is a cadence somewhat similar to the simple *mukhada*, except longer.

Table 10.14. Criteria for Sath

Overall philosophy	Cadential
Structure	single body
Bol Type	Pakahwaj bols
Function	Create tension by disrupting normal "trading off"
Technique	-

Fard is indistinguishable from *sath*. The word *fard* means a "split" or a "tear" (McGregor 1997). Since it is very common for *gats* to have two or more sub-structures, the implication is that if one takes an existing *gat*, and merely plays one of the structures, then it is *fard*. However, it appears that in practice modern *fards* bear little resemblance to the more ordinary binary *gats*.

Sath in Chautal (S. Dawood Khan, 1981 personal interview)

धा	-	तेद्	-	धा	-	कि	ट	त	की	ट	त	का	-	की	ट	ग	दी	गे	न		bol
Dhaa	-	Ted	-	Dhaa	-	Ki	Ta	Ta	Kee	Ta	Ta	Kaa	-	Kee	Ta	Ga	Dee	Ge	Na		
धा	-	*तक्*	-	*धा*	-	*ति*	*र*	*क*	*ट*	*त*	*क*	*ता*	-	*क*	*ट*	*ग*	*दी*	*गे*	*न*		technique
Dhaa	-	*Tak*	-	*Dhaa*	-	*Ti*	*Ra*	*Ka*	*Ta*	*Ta*	*Ka*	*Taa*	-	*Ka*	*Ta*	*Ga*	*Dee*	*Ge*	*Na*		

ना	ग	ति	ट	त	की	ट	त	का	-	कि	ट	त	की	ट	त		bol
Naa	Ga	Ti	Ta	Ta	Kee	Ta	Ta	Kaa	-	Ki	Ta	Ta	Kee	Ta	Ta		
ना	*ग*	*ति*	*ट*	*कि*	*ट*	*त*	*क*	*ता*	-	*ति*	*र*	*क*	*ट*	*त*	*क*		technique
Naa	*Ga*	*Ti*	*Ta*	*Ki*	*Ta*	*Ta*	*Ka*	*Taa*	-	*Ti*	*Ra*	*Ki*	*Ta*	*Ta*	*Ka*		

का	-	धु	म	की	ट	त	क	ग	दी	गे	न	ˣधा		bol
Kaa	-	Dhu	Ma	Kee	Ta	Ta	Ka	Ga	Dee	Ge	Na	Dhaa		
ता	-	*ग*	*दी*	*त*	*ट*	*क*	*त*	*ग*	*दी*	*गे*	*न*	*धा*		technique
Taa	-	*Ga*	*Dee*	*Ta*	*Ta*	*Ka*	*Ta*	*Ga*	*Dee*	*Ge*	*Na*	*Dhaa*		

It has not been my desire to talk of technique in this volume. This was the subject of *Fundamentals of Tabla*. However, this composition deserves special attention. You will see in the preceding piece that it was written in two parts. The first piece is the *bol*, while the second half, in italics, represents the technique. I have taken the first half which are the *pakhawaj bols,* and translated them into the more accessible tabla *bols*. I must stress that although you play the lower set of *bols,* you must recite the upper set. When one becomes comfortable with *pakhawaj bols,* it becomes second nature. However, this may require some practice.

Table 10.15. Criteria for Ginti Tukada

Overall philosophy	Cadential
Structure	-
Bol Type	Counting aloud the number of revolutions
Function	-
Technique	-

GINTI TUKADA

The *ginti tukada*, variously called *ginti paran*, or *ginti tihai*, is a very traditional *kathak* dance composition (Table 10.15). This is no different from the usual complex cadence, except for one thing. The *ginti tihai* has a large number of rounds. Unlike the *chakradar,* which is set usually at nine rounds without the requirement of equal timing, the *ginti* may have dozens of rounds, each one is usually the same. This is very exciting when performed with a *kathak* dancer. However, for any other purpose, it tends to get tedious. The primary characteristic is that the *bol* itself contains the counting. Below is a *ginti tukhada* which is built around 51 rounds in the *tihai*:

Ginti Tukada (counting 51 rounds)(may not start on sam) (Anju Babu 1988, personal interview)

तत् तत् थेई - तीग् धा दी ग दी ग थेई - तत् तत् थेई - तीग् धा दी ग दी ग थेई -
Tat Tat Thei - TeegDhaa DeeGaDeeGa Thei - Tat Tat Thei - TeegDhaa DeeGaDeeGa Thei -

तीग् धा दी ग दी ग थेई - तीग् धा दी ग दी ग थेई - तीग् धा दी ग दी ग थेई - कत् कत्
TeegDhaa DeeGaDeeGa Thei - TeegDhaa DeeGaDeeGa Thei - TeegDhaa DeeGaDeeGa Thei - Kat Kat

तीग् धा दी ग दी ग थेई - तीग् धा दी ग दी ग थेई - तीग् धा दी ग दी ग थेई - कत् कत्
TeegDhaa DeeGaDeeGa Thei - TeegDhaa DeeGaDeeGa Thei - TeegDhaa DeeGaDeeGa Thei - Kat Kat

[तीग् धा दी ग दी ग]51 times + थेई
    TeegDhaa DeeGaDeeGa   Note - Do not say   "TeegDhaaDeeGaDeeGa" but instead count the rounds.

CONCLUSION

We have seen that the cadence is very important in Indian music. The very nature of the Indian cadence moves toward a specific point of resolution, usually the *sam* (the first beat of the cycle). Common forms are the *paran, mukhada, mohara, tukada, tihai,* and a host of others, which were briefly discussed in this chapter.

The cadence and the cyclic forms alternate in a process which drives the music forward. It is nearly an endless process of establishing a stable "groove", then breaking it up with a cadence, only to reestablish a new "groove", is the dynamic process which lies at the very heart of the music. Without it, the music can have no soul.

We saw in this chapter that there is a large degree of confusion concerning nomenclature. This confusion was created by the different subtraditions, coupled with the low educational level among practising musicians in the 19th century. This confusion can be minimised by realising that many of these forms are defined using totally different criteria. In general these four criteria are: 1) Structure, 2) Function / style, 3) *Bol* (mnemonic/ stroke), and in very rare cases 4) Technique (e.g., one handed/ two handed techniques).

WORKS CITED

Babu, Anju
1988 personal interview

Courtney, D.R
1998 *Fundamentals of Tabla*, Houston, TX, Sur Sangeet Services

Feldman, Jeffrey M.
1995 *The Tabla Legacy of Taranath Rao*, Venice CA, Digitala

Hussain Zakir
1988 Personal interview

Garg, Laxminarayan
1994 *Katha Nritya*, Hathras India: Sangeet Karyalaya

Kapoor, R.K.
no date *Kamal's Advanced Illustrated Oxford Dictionary of Hindi- English*. Delhi, India: Verma Book Depot.

Khan, S. Dawood Khan
1976-1990 personal interviews

Leake, Jerry
1993 *Indian Influence (Tabla Perspective), Series A.I.M. Percussion Text* (Second Edition). Boston: Rhombus Publishing.

Mrdangacharya, Bhagavan Das and Ram Shankar Das (Pagaldas)
1977 *Mrdang-Tabla -Prabhakar* (vol. 2). Hathras, India: Sangeet Karyalaya.

Sharma, Bhagavat Sharan
1973 *Tal Prakash*. Hathras, India: Sangeet Karyalaya.
1977 *Tal Shastra*. Alighar, India: B. A. Electric Press.

Shepherd, F. A.
1976 *Tabla and the Benares Gharana*. Ann Arbor: University Microfilms International. (Ph.D. Dissertation).

Shrivastava, H. C.
1973 *Kathak Nrtya Parichay*. Allahabad, India: Sangeet Press.

Stewart, R. M.
1974 *The Tabla in Perspective*. Ann Arbor: University Microfilms International. (Ph.D. Dissertation).

Vashisth, Satya Narayan
1977 *Tal Martand*. Hathras, India: Sangeet Karyalaya.

Yadav, B. L.
1995 *Tabla Prakash* (volume 1) Allahabad, Sangeet Sadana Prakashan,
1999a *Tabla Prakash* (volume 2) Allahabad, Sangeet Sadana Prakashan,
1999b *Tabla Prakash* (volume 3) Allahabad, Sangeet Sadana Prakashan,

CHAPTER 11

IMPROVISATION

This chapter deals with improvisation. There are basic forms and underlying rules which govern the subject. We can discuss the general philosophy, techniques, and the various issues which arise.

There is one point which is an undercurrent through out this chapter; this point is simplicity. Improvisation is as simple as walking or talking or riding a bicycle. Even the basic tricks involved are simple.

WHAT IS IMPROVISATION?

It should be a very easy question to say what improvisation is. In practice, it can be a very difficult question. From the Western standpoint, all classical Indian music is improvised; because it does not use a printed score. Unfortunately, this is an over simplification which fails to fully reflect the real situation.

Improvisation has been compared with speech. Although conversations proceed in an unscripted way, they are subject to rules of grammar and communication which are instinctively understood by the participants (Bel & Kippen 1992). Even the social interactions that occur in a performance closely follow those of a conversation (Cooper 2018). We will look at many of these forms in this chapter.

Improvisation is a mixture of three things. There is memorised material that has been passed down from the teacher. There is memorised material which has been picked up by one's self; and there is impromptu material. Let us see how these three approaches may be used.

Improvisation involves a lot of material which has been passed down from one's teacher. This may seem like a contradiction, for if it is memorised, how can it be improvisation? Although the material is memorised, it is not specified as to exactly where or how it should be played. Therefore, the element of individual artistry comes into play when making such decisions. Although this is a small contribution, this is the first place that the student begins to approach the subject.

There is also material which one has picked up oneself. These may be rearrangements of traditional material, material that was once impromptu, but has now been committed to memory, or material which has been inspired from listening to other musicians. Whatever the source, there is a great amount of individual artistry involved in this process. The selection and modification of material, as well as the decision as to when to use it, takes a great amount of artistic maturity.

Impromptu material is the highest form of improvisation. It is usually a one time affair. It springs forth from the artist in a form that never was, and in all likelihood, never will be again. This is the ultimate form of artistic expression, which takes many years of experience.

In practice, these three forms of material blur together. It should blur together such that the audience is not able to tell whether a piece is improvised or memorised. This is necessary for producing a seamless performance.

LEARNING TO IMPROVISE

It is difficult to learn to improvise. Obviously it cannot be taught, at least not in the manner that one would learn fixed compositions. Learning to improvise, must be done by practising and playing with other musicians in a variety of performance situations. We will now give a brief roadmap of the steps one will pass through while learning how to improvise.

There is one constant in one's efforts to learn to improvise; this is listening. The first thing to do is listen to the music; the next thing to do is to learn to listen to the musician. This may appear to be the same; but it is not. Every musician relates to their music differently. Some musicians use their music; some abuse their music. Some are guided by their music; and others carefully lead theirs. Some make love with theirs; while other have a platonic relationships. The possible relationships with one's music are as varied as the personalities of the performers. With practice, it is possible to listen to a performance, and enter the mind of the performer. This gives very valuable insights into potential avenues of improvisation.

The next step to learning improvisation is to learn to accompany. If you are a rank beginner, it can be difficult even to play a basic *theka*. You will start to absorb the first elements of improvisation, as you experiment with such issues as where to start, when to start, how to start, when to speed up, and how to stop. However after a while, one will start moving in and out of the various *prakars*. Initially these *prakars* will be memorised. Yet simple memorisation does not tell you when or how to use them. A considerable amount of individual artistry is required just for these simple decisions; all of which must be made on the fly.

Next, one begins to experiment with some of the flasher material. If one is learning to accompany classical musicians, such material may be *mukhadas*, *tukadas*, *parans,* or any of a host of fixed forms which have been memorised. In a similar manner, if one is learning to accompany light music singers, then it will involve learning how to use the carefully memorised *laggis* and pickups.

This stage of learning can be quite daunting. I believe that this is the most difficult stage of one's studentship. It is very much like learning a language by memorising phrases and sentences. It is functional up to a point, but not the same as having fluent knowledge of the language. In the same fashion, the stage where all the musical material is practised and memorised, is probably the most difficult. This is because there is not yet that visceral understanding of the music.

The final stage of learning to improvise is where one finds oneself unconsciously generating material. Suddenly, *prakars* that have never been practised or learned, come into being. Suddenly *mukhadas* and *relas* begin to come with a minimum of thinking. From here, it gets easier. Time is on your side. If you keep playing year in and year out, you will get to the final stage.

When one reaches the final stage, improvisation is like walking. It is totally unconscious and effortless. When you start a performance, you do not really know what you are going to do. As you are performing, you do not have any awareness as to what you are doing; and when it is finished, you do not have any clear memory of what you just did. It is as though your whole body and mind were placed in auto-pilot for the duration of the performance. If you listen to its recording, you will find yourself thinking to yourself, "Where did that come from?" This is the state in which all elements of material from the guru, one's own material, and impromptu material, have totally blended together in a harmonious whole.

So these are the various stages that you pass through when you are learning to improvise. When one reaches the stage where improvisation is totally effortless, one is said to be *taiyar*. The word "*taiyar*" literally means "ready".

WHEN TO IMPROVISE
The question of when to improvise is dependent on a number of factors. These factors include such diverse considerations as the musical style, the nature of the performance, and the musical responsibilities of that instant. It even has a lot to do with the personality of the musician you are playing with.

The musical style determines both the extent of one's improvisations, as well as the type of improvisations allowed. For instance if one is doing "copy" film songs, virtually no improvisation is allowed. One simply has to get a recording and go over it many times to commit it to memory. It is then spit out, as-is. On the other hand, lighter forms such as *git, gazal qawwali*, etc., give greater scope for improvisation. Typically, theses styles revolve around *prakars* of *Kaherava* or *Dadra* with occasional pickups, *laggis,* and small *tihais*. Classical instrumental accompaniment also offers a great scope for improvisation. This usually is in slow and fast *Tintal*. Typical improvisations revolve around *prakrars*, *parans*, *mukhadas,* and *gats*. Classical vocal accompaniment offers the least scope for improvisation. Tradition dictates that it is the responsibility of the tabla player to simply "keep the *theka*". However, improvisation within the *prakar* is the norm, and an occasional *mukhada*, or *tukada* may always be slipped in, if it is done discretely. A tabla solo would appear to offer the maximum scope for improvisation. This is not the case. If the level of improvisation is too high, the solo will appear to be unstructured and undisciplined. Tabla solos are generally a large number of fixed compositions that are interspersed with improvisation. If there is a dearth of fixed compositions, the performer will be perceived as lacking in *"taleem"* (i.e., untrained) or undisciplined.

The nature of the performance will also determine the nature and extent of one's improvisations. If one is dealing with an audience that is unaware of the nuances of the music, it is often necessary to "play to the peanut gallery". You throw in a lot of flash and gimmicks, because you know that the more cerebral material will be lost to them. On the other hand, if you are dealing with a sophisticated audience who truly understands the intricacies of the music, then you will do best by avoiding this. Audiences of connoisseurs, are very quick to turn upon an artist that they deem to be engaging in too much gimmickry. If they should turn upon you, it is a hard lesson to learn!

The musical requirements of the moment play a tremendous role in determining what improvisations one may take. These requirements change, literally, second by second. This is a situation that truly challenges a musician.

One example of how the musical requirement changes, depends upon who is keeping time. In a classical instrumental piece for example, there is an alternation of these duties. There are times when the tabla player is "keeping the *theka*", and the main instrumentalist (e.g., sitar, sarod, santur, etc.) performs their improvisations. There will be a reversal of roles, which will be triggered by the main instrumentalist returning to the *gat* (main theme). It is at this point the main instrumentalist starts to keep time, while the tabla player is free to perform much more aggressively. In both roles, there is scope for improvisation, but the nature of one's improvisations will be different. For instance, when you are keeping the *theka*, you are free to improvise around the *prakar*. You are even free to throw in an occasional *mukhada*. However, you must not engage in improvisations that will compromise the basic flow of the *theka*. If you do so, you run the risk of confusing the main instrumentalist. If you do that, you are derelict in your duty as an accompanist.

The nature of one's improvisation also depends upon where you are in the cycle. If you are somewhere near the beginning or middle, then improvisations should not break the flow of the *theka*. This is not to say that you should refrain from any syncopation; this only means that improvisations should not break the feeling of flowing. However, if one is nearing the *sam*, it is often a musical requirement to improvise in such a way that it has a cadential quality. This may be a simple matter of adding a few strokes to increase the *bol* density, thus raising the level of musical tension. This may also involve a slight, and nearly imperceptible increase in tempo.[1] Or it may be the introduction of some formal *mukhadas* or *tihais*. These cadential improvisations are acceptable as one approaches the *sam*. This is why we say that the musical requirements literally change second-by-second.

The nature of one's improvisations also depends upon social circumstances. The same social stratification that one finds in day-to-day life extends to the stage. For instance, if one is accompanying an extremely senior artist, then there is a tendency for the tabla player to be quite reserved. Obviously, this does not make for an exciting performance. Conversely, if the tabla player is socially or professionally higher than the main performer, there is a tendency for the tabla player to overshadow the main performer. This may go down well with the "peanut gallery", but this is far from a desirable situation.

There is a tendency for performers to pair up when they are of comparable age, professional, and social position. This was not always the case. In the last century, tabla players came from the lowest levels of Indian social structure. Although the main musicians were seldom much higher, there was enough of a difference that it pressured tabla players to simply keep the *theka*. Today, caste and community are becoming less of an issue; but there are still tendencies for musicians to "pair off" along similar lines.

The artistic views of the main performer are also factors in determining acceptable levels of improvisation. Sometimes more conservative performers demand that the tabla player be more restrained. On the other hand, some performers encourage a greater degree of improvisation.

The bottom line is simple; developing professional relationships is very much like getting married. Once one has established this relationship, it may continue for the rest of one's professional lives. It is even to a point that if your regular partner chooses another tabla player for a performance, there will be gossip. It may seem silly, but it is a part of the social world which surrounds the profession.

---

[1]Many artists are unaware that they do this, but they do. Refer to the section on "Rubato" in Chapter 4 - *Tempo*.

Ch. 11. Improvisation

In this section, we discussed the myriad considerations that one faces when deciding when to improvise. There are an unfathomable mixture of stylistic, artistic, technical, and psychological issues at involved. In general, we may say that one develops a professional relationship with a small number of performers, one then works from there. Classical vocal provides little scope for improvisation. Film songs are basically "paint by number", and give virtually no scope for individual artistry. The maximum improvisation is allowed in instrumental accompaniment.

HOW TO IMPROVISE

It is difficult to really say how to improvise. It all boils down to one's frame of mind. Normally, when you start to play, you will fall back upon a fairly fixed routine. Then you start to immerse yourself into the music. The mental state is very similar to what one encounters in the various states of meditation. Through constant attention to the music, you reach a point where you are not playing the music, but merely following it. It is a curious feeling of detachment. It is as though you are listening to the music, rather than performing it. From this point, everything will simply flow along on its own.

This is all well and good, but you did not buy this book as an introduction to altered states of consciousness. (Although at times you have probably questioned what frame of mind induced you to buy this book to begin with.) You probably bought it because you want some easy concrete tools to help you. Let us look into some of these now.

Every musician has a "bag of tricks" that helps them with improvisation. These tools are as varied as the individual personalities. However, we can give a few of them here. They are presented "as is" with no particular order or justification. Look into them, and if you find them useful, then you can use them. If not, that is still ok.

<u>Multiple Use of Mukhadas</u>. To attempt to memorise different *mukhadas* for each *tal*, is a difficult and unnecessary undertaking. Just a few *mukhadas* may be used for virtually any *theka*. Let us take a simple example: *Dhaa - TiRaKiTaTaKa* (धा - ति र कि ट त क). See below, how this *mukhada* may be used in a variety of contexts.

Tintal

^Xधा धिं धिं धा | ²धा धिं धिं धा | ⁰धा तिं तिं ना | ³धा तिर किट तक |
Dhaa Dhin Dhin Dhaa Dhaa Dhin Dhin Dhaa Dhaa Tin Tin Naa Dhaa TiRa KiTa TaKa

Rupak Tal

⁰तिं तिं ना | ¹धा तिर | ²किट तक |
Tin Tin Naa Dhaa TiRa KiTa TaKa

Dadra

^Xधा धिं धा | तिर किट तक |
Dhaa Dhin Dhaa TiRa KiTa TaKa

Kaherava

^Xधा गे ना ती | ⁰धा तिर किट तक |
Dhaa Ge Naa Tee Dhaa TiRa KiTa TaKa

Jhaptal

^Xधिं ना | ²धिं धिं ना | ⁰तिं धा | ³तिर किट तक |
Dhin Naa Dhin Dhin Naa Tin Dhaa TiRa KiTa TaKa

Use Few Building Blocks - Extremely complex solos may be constructed of very simple building blocks. Let us take for example what we can do with only two building blocks; these are shown below. Let us assign a numeric value to them.

$$\underset{\text{Dhaa - Ti Ra Ki Ta}}{\text{धा - ति र कि ट}} = 3$$

$$\underset{\text{Dhaa - Ti Ra Ki Ta Ta Ka}}{\text{धा - ति र कि ट त क}} = 4$$

Let us say that we were working with *Tintal*, therefore one possibility would be to construct something based upon 3+3+3+3+4. In other words:

धा - ति र कि ट धा - ति र कि ट धा - ति र कि ट धा - ति र कि ट धा - ति र कि ट त क
Dhaa - Ti Ra Ki Ta Dhaa - Ti Ra Ki Ta Dhaa - Ti Ra Ki Ta Dhaa - Ti Ra Ki Ta Dhaa - Ti Ra Ki Ta Ta Ka

Let us say we were working in *Rupak tal*. We could construct something around 3+4, therefore:

धा - ति र कि ट धा - ति र कि ट त क
Dhaa - Ti Ra Ki Ta Dhaa - Ti Ra Ki Ta Ta Ka

Rupak does not have to use only 3+4. It could just as easily been 4+3, or:

धा - ति र कि ट त क धा - ति र कि ट
Dhaa - Ti Ra Ki Ta Ta Ka Dhaa - Ti Ra Ki Ta

We could continue to describe this process to excruciating detail. However, I think that the process is so simple, we need not give any more examples.

Simple Bedam Chakradars from Tukadas - For any *tal*, a simple *bedam chakradar* may be constructed by stringing three complex cadences together as long as, 1) A single iteration is not less than one cycle 2) The complex cadences work in that *tal* and 3) The last *Dhaa* (धा) is dropped for all phrases except the last. This structure was described in the last chapter, so we need not go into detail here.

Jhaptal tukadas present a special case. Any *Jhaptal tukada* when played thrice, becomes a *Tintal chakaradar*. Let us say that a typical *Jhaptal thukada* is 11 *matras* long. If it is played three times, it comes to 33 *matras*, or two cycles of *Tintal* with the *sam*. As a practical matter, you may wish to practice this a bit beforehand, because longer material may introduce concerns as to how much pause (*dam*) to place between the three iterations.

Two Times at Double Tempo - Any expression may be played twice at double tempo without changing the mathematics. In many cases, this can be used to generate new material from old. For example, let us look at this *prakar* of *Jhaptal*.

Jhaptal

धिं ना | धिं धिं ना धिं धिं ना | तिं ना | धिं धिं ना धिं धिं ना |
Dhin Naa DhinDhin NaaDhin DhinNaa Tin Naa DhinDhin NaaDhin DhinNaa

We see that the second and the fourth *vibhags* were created simply by taking the normal *Dhin Dhin Naa* (धिं धिं ना), and playing them twice at double time. This process is very good at giving a texture to one's improvisations without requiring complex math.

<u>Any Cadential Material in Any Tal with Bharan</u> - Any *tihai, paran, tukada*, or any cadential material may be performed in any *tal* with the appropriate *bharan*. This is a very good way to stretch your material so that you can play in more *tals*. Let us say that you have a *Tintal tukada* that fits in one cycle (i.e., 17 *matras*). You could play it in *Rupak tal* very simply with this process. All you need to do to play this is to increase the size to 22 beats (i.e., 3 cycles of 7 *matras* with the *sam*). Therefore, all you need to do is improvise for 5 *matras* (remember our simple building blocks), then play the *Tintal tukada*, and it will come to *sam*.

There is one word of warning about this process. It may be done elegantly and beautifully, or it may be done in a forced and awkward fashion. This is of course where artistry comes in. As a general rule, the *bols* should be consistent with the composition that you are using.

Let us review some of what we have seen about the "tricks" that musicians have. We have only touched upon the more common ones. There are many others, most of which are tied to particular *tals* or circumstances. For instance, virtually all ordinary *Ektal* material may be played in *Tintal* simply by shifting to *adi lay*, or *Tintal chakradars* are constructed by stringing *Jhaptal tukadas* together. The number of tricks are innumerable, and something specific to each individual musician.

CONCLUSION

I am sure that you can appreciate the difficulty in writing about improvisation. Improvisation is inextricably linked to the inspirational aspect of music. It is that indefinable soul that separates music from mere ordered sound.

Still, we have seen that there are a few basic guidelines that can be followed. In general, we see that for each moment of the performance, there are appropriate improvisations. There are times that we are allowed to be aggressive, and there are other times that we must be more subdued.

Every musician has a "bag of tricks" which helps them in improvising. Some of these tricks are general purpose; but most are limited to specific styles or *tals*. We were able to cover some of the more common ones.

Still, there should be one picture to emerge from this chapter which may not have been clear in the earlier chapters; I am referring to simplicity. In the process of reading about the material, one may get the false impression that tabla is so very complicated. This is not really so. It is simple, and in almost every case the most effective performances are the simple ones.

WORKS CITED

Bel, Bernard & Jim Kippen
1992 "Modelling Music with Grammars: Formal Language Representation in the Bol Processor", *Computer Representations and Models in Music.* pg. 207-238. Academic Press.

Cooper, Alexander
2018 *Musical Connectivity in Sitar and Tabla Performance.* Doctoral Dissertation. University of Edinburgh.

CHAPTER 12

PHYSICS OF THE TABLA

This chapter deals with the physics of the tabla. So what do we mean by the physics of the tabla? In a nutshell, we are talking about how the tabla works. We will start with a simple overview. This reacquaints us with basic concepts, most of which we learned back in our school days. We will next move into the topics of interference, standing waves, and the modes of vibration. These will be for membranes in general, and the tabla in specific.

Unfortunately, our knowledge of how the tabla works is very incomplete. It has been a neglected field for a long time. Even the early pioneers such as C.V. Raman, were forced to make only a quick overview of the *dayan*, and then move on. We know almost nothing as to how the *bayan* works. We know almost nothing of the affects of the cavity upon the *dayan*. With this apology, we will proceed.

GENERAL OVERVIEW OF THE PHYSICS

Let us start with a general review of a few basic concepts in physics.

Phase - The concept of phase is a very important and very simple concept. Let us imagine a couple that are living together with a joint bank account. (We do not specify their genders or the nature of their relationship; because it is none of our business.) Imagine too, that they are both employed, earn salaries, and spend money from this joint account. Let us also imagine that they both receive a salary only once a month. In such a situation, the balance of the joint bank account will be highly dependent upon when each individual is paid.

Let us imagine that both individuals are paid on the first of each month. In which case, the bank balance will fluctuate greatly as each individual simultaneously deposits money into the account, then spends it at the same time. We would say that their financial activity is "in phase".

Now let us imagine that one member is paid on the first, but the other is paid on the 15th of each month. In this case the deposits of one individual offsets the expenditure of the other, Therefore, there will be considerably less fluctuation in the bank balance. This is said to be "out of phase".

This is very significant. Both individuals spend money and receive salary at the same frequency, But the condition of their bank balanced is strongly affected by the phase relationship of their salaries. This additive or subtractive mechanism according to the phase, is at the base of much that happens in the physical world around us.

Interference - Interference is another important concept. Fortunately, it too is not difficult. It deals with the way that waves interact with each other.

Imagine yourself in a pleasant situation. You are sitting on the bank of a peaceful pond one summer morning. Between sips of your favourite drink, you are amusing yourself by tossing pebbles into the pond. Each pebble produces a series of circular waves emanating from the spot where the pebble entered the water.

Now imagine what happens when you toss two pebbles into the water in different places. In this case, both pebbles produce their own series of expanding waves. Unlike bricks or passengers on a crowded train, waves can pass through each other, and even occupy the same space at the same time. However, they do influence each other; they can enhance each other or diminish each other in the same way that the activity of our previous couple's bank account was subject to the phase of their financial activity. Therefore, when the troughs interact, they deepening each other, and when the waves interact, they enhance each other. This is an example of interference.

Let us modify this scenario a bit. Let us imagine that there is a large concrete wall in the water. Now if one tosses a single pebble into the water, the waves strike the concrete wall and reflect back in the opposite direction. There is now interference between the original wave and the reflected version of itself.

Standing Waves and Resonance Modes - Let us turn to a situation that every musician has encountered. You are in a venue that does not have good acoustics (basically like the majority of your venues). The bass player is doing their thing, but you only hear a particular note coming from the hall. Of all the notes the bass player is playing, there is only that one note ringing through the hall.

This is a standing in wave. The sound goes out into the audience, and bounces off a wall. As it bounces of a wall, there is interference as it interacts with itself. The sound continues to travel to the opposite wall, where it again is reflected; again there is the same interference. At a few, (very very few) frequencies, these interference patterns will line up to create a standing wave. These possible frequencies represent what are known as a resonance modes. This is what is happening when the bass player happens to hit one of these notes.

In this example, a resonance mode was excited by playing a particular note. But there is another way to evoke this vibrational mode.

An alternate way of invoking this mode is a bit more colourful. Imagine an altercation in the crowd and two people decide to settle their differences "the old fashioned way". One of them pulls out a gun and starts shooting. At that point the entire auditorium is acoustically excited (actually the audience would be excited too.) But only the frequencies that correspond to various resonance modes will produce standing waves.

These last two scenarios showed two ways of producing standing waves. The first example was based upon finding a resonant frequency by continuously playing a corresponding note on the electric bass. The second way revolved around a single impulse which excited the entire auditorium, after which only the stable resonance modes could be heard.

Both of these approaches may be found in the real world. The former is the basis of sympathetic vibration, and is the way that the sympathetic strings of a sitar work. Curiously, this way of exciting a vibrational mode requires such a precise matching of the frequencies, that it is not found that often., The more common manner of exciting a vibrational mode is with a powerful impulse (i.e., the gunshot, plucking of strings, striking a membrane). This latter approach is extremely common and is found in everything from pianos, to MRI diagnostic machines, and more importantly for us, the tabla.

Simple Vibrational Modes of Strings - Let us change the medium from air to a musical string. We apply a powerful impulse to the string by plucking it. (This is analogous to the gunshot.) This sends waves traveling down the string until they meet an obstruction. This obstruction may be either a fret of a bridge; the results will be identical.

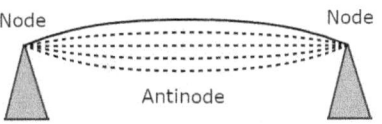

a. First vibrational mode of string

Upon meeting the obstruction, the waves are reflected back upon themselves. The waves travels to the opposite end, where they again encounter an obstruction. This sets up a back and fourth motion of the waves. Again, at certain frequencies the interference patterns line up. These are standing waves in a string.

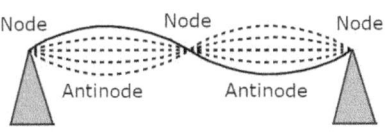

b. Second vibrational mode of string

We learned about vibrational modes through the vibrating string in our school days. This is illustrated in Figure 12.1. Figure 12.1.a illustrates the first vibrational mode of a string. Figure 12.1.b illustrates the second vibrational mode. Figure 12.1.c illustrates the third mode. This series continues indefinitely.

The node is the portion of the string that does not move. The two endpoints are inherently nodes; this is because they are held firmly in place by the two bridges. From here on, the only possible vibrational modes are those that have nodes on each end. We see in Figure 12.1.b and 12.1.c, that there may be other nodes in the middle as well. The second mode for instance, has a node in the dead centre of the string, while the third mode has two nodes in between. If you have ever seen anyone play a guitar by harmonics, they always place their fingers at the points of the nodes which correspond to the desired note.

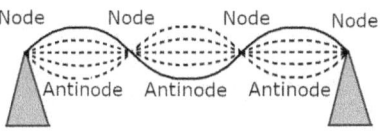

c. Third vibrational mode of string

Figure 12.1. Resonance modes of string

The antinode conversely, is the place where there is maximum movement. These modes may be emphasised by striking at the antinodes.

We may return to a practical example for this. A guitar will produce a mellow sound, deficient in upper vibrational modes, by strumming closer to the centre. Conversely, it will produce a brighter sound, one that is richer in overtones, by striking closer to the bridge.

We have described common ways that a string can vibrate; however, we have not discussed the frequencies at which these modes operate.

It turns out that there is a very simple relationship between the modes, and the frequencies of the sounds they produce. The first order vibrational mode will have a frequency that is f. The second vibrational mode has a frequency of $2f$; the third vibrational mode has a frequency of $3f$, etc. This simple and convenient arrangement is summarised in Figure 12.2.

At this point one should realise that we have just laid out a physical foundation for the harmonics that were discussed in Chapter 2 - *Timbre*.

THINGS TO REMEMBER

1) The various ways that something can vibrate are called modes.
2) The antinodes are the parts that move the most.
3) The nodes are the parts that do not move.
4) If the frequencies of the various modes have an integral relationship with each other (i.e., 1x, 2x, 3x, etc.) they are called harmonic.
5) If the frequencies of the various modes do not show this simple relationship, they are called inharmonic.

VIBRATIONAL MODES AND NODES

Let us now look at the various modes, nodes, antinodes, and the frequencies of drum skins. It is not very likely that drums were discussed in your high school physics classes. They are considerably more complicated than strings. However, easy or not, we are going to jump in.

As was the case with strings, the vibrational modes of drum skins are defined by their nodes. There are three possible nodes for vibrating membranes. There are nodal circles, nodal diameters, and nodal points.

<u>Nodal Circles</u> - The simplest nodal circle is shown in Figure 12.3. This is a single circle where the membrane is anchored to the shell. Other nodal circles are also possible.

The movement of the skin in the mode shown in Figure 12.3 is very simply visualised. The skin will move downward as shown in the figure. After a very brief period, the skin will then move back up. It passes through the resting position, but continues up until it resembles a hill. Again, after a brief period the membrane moves back down to its earlier condition. This simple up-and-down motion continues indefinitely.

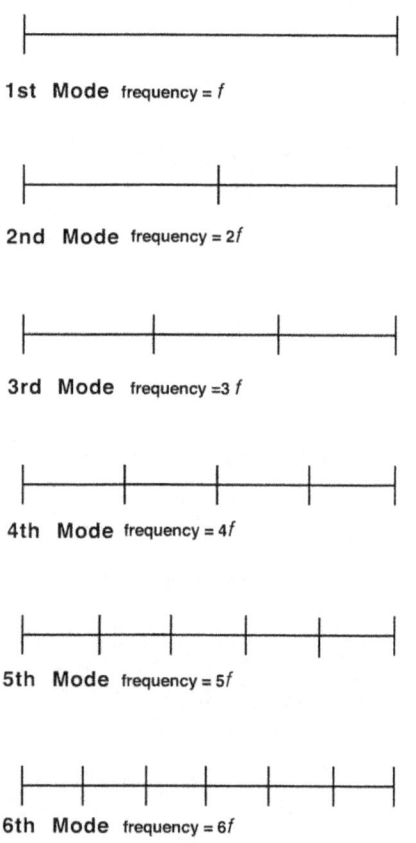

Figure 12.2. Harmonics and the resonance modes of a string

There is an easy way to portray this vibrational mode. It is common to schematically represent it by its node, which in this case is a simple circle. This is shown in Figure 12.4.

Let us look at another example of a nodal circle. Figure 12.5 shows a vibrational mode that has two nodal circles. This mode is considerably more difficult to visualise. In this example we see that when the inner portion of the circle moves upwards, the outer portion moves downward. Conversely, when the inner portion moves downward, then the outer portion moves upwards. Again, this motion continues indefinitely. The vibrational mode that uses two nodal circles is schematically illustrated in Figure 12.6.

Ch. 12. Physics of the Tabla

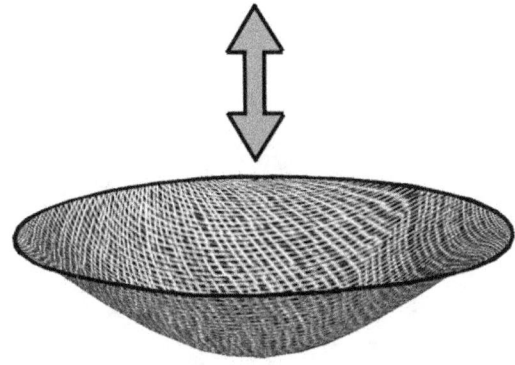

Figure 12.3. Simple vibrational mode of a drumskin with a single circular node

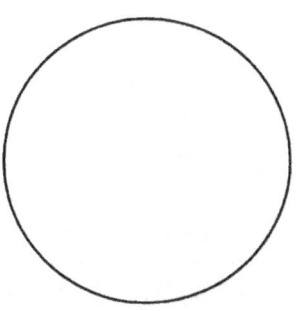

Figure 12.4. Simplest vibrational mode represented as a single circle

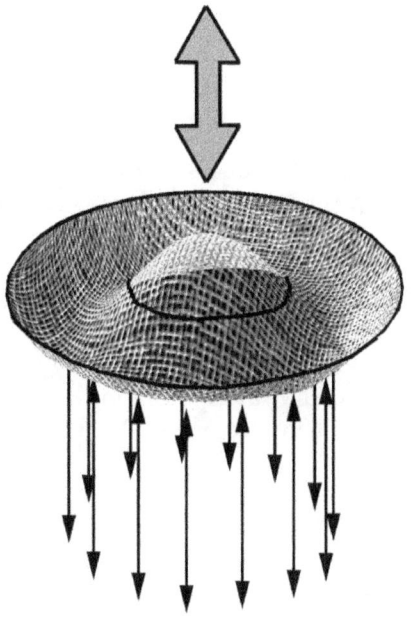

Figure 12.5. Vibrational mode with two circular nodes

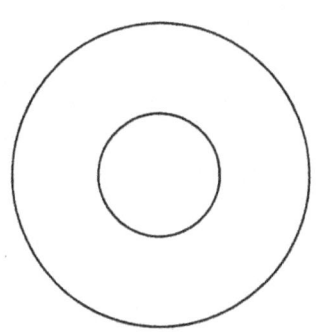

Figure 12.6. Vibrational mode represented as two circles

It is possible to have other nodal circles for a membrane. However, the practical limit for the *dayan* appears to be three.

<u>Nodal Diameters</u> - Nodal diameters are nodal lines that bisect the drumhead. The simplest real world example is shown in Figure 12.7. Notice that this is not just a nodal diameter, but it also contains a nodal circle. In the real world, the skin is locked onto the drumshell; therefore, there will always be at least one nodal circle on a drum.

page 165

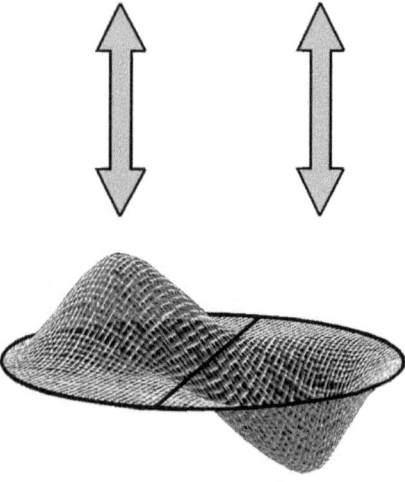

Figure 12.7. Vibrational mode with one circular node and one nodal diameter

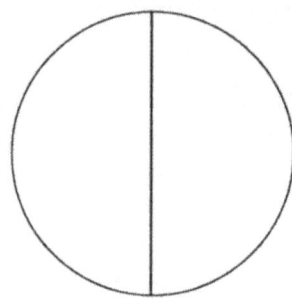

Figure 12.8. Vibrational mode with one circular node and one nodal diameter is represented as a circle and a diagonal line

Figure 12.7 shows how the nodal diameter behaves. We see that when one side of the membrane rises, the other side falls. Conversely, when the first side falls, the opposite side rises. This is referred to as dipolar resonance. This is not too difficult to visualise.

The vibrational mode with one nodal diameter and one nodal circle is schematically shown in Figure 12.8.

<u>Nodal Points</u> - A nodal point is a single point that remains stationary in a vibrating membrane. Conventional views on the subject say this is not relevant to the tabla. Therefore, we will not discuss the topic here.

A SIMPLE EXPERIMENT

There is a very simple experiment which helps us observe the nodes of the *dayan*, it can be visualised by its Chladni pattern (Figure 12.9)[1]. This works very easily for the mode shown in Figure 12.7. First, one sprinkles some powder on the *dayan*. Then one strikes it using the *Tin* (तिं) stroke. This usually requires several strokes to give the powder ample opportunity to migrate to portions of the membrane which exhibit the minimum agitation (nodes). One can then observe the nodal diameter.

It should be noted that the Chladni pattern of other resonance modes will also be produced. However, their expression may be minimised by keeping the *Tin* (तिं) as soft and as clean as possible.

Let us consider what is happening here. *Tin* (तिं) emphasises a mode that has one nodal circle, and and one nodal diameter. The two halves of the drum vibrate vigorously; this causes the powder to bounce around. In the process, the powder will gravitate to the nodes, because that is where the movement is minimal. The powder will then line up across the drum. It is important to note that the ring finger determines the position of this node. In a similar manner, striking *Tin* (तिं) on or near the antinode enhances the expression of this mode.

---

[1]Ernst Chladni (1756-1827) was a pioneer in the field of acoustics. He developed this technique using metal plates. However, over the last two centuries it has been adapted to a variety of other situations.

A   **B**   **C**

Figure 12.9. Producing Chladni pattern for (1,1) resonance mode of tabla.
a) sprinkle powder b) play Tin several times c) observe resultant pattern

NORMAL VIBRATIONAL MODES

Table 12.1, shows a list of normal vibrational modes for a circular membrane[2]. Let us look at this chart in greater detail.

The first column shows a schematic of the arrangement of the nodes. By now, we should be very comfortable in visualising the modes by their schematic representation (i.e., Figures 12.4, 12.6, & 12.8).

The next column is the standard designation of the modes. This is expressed in the form of (m,n). In this form, m represents the number of nodal diameters while n represents the number of nodal circles. For example, the vibrational mode illustrated in Figures 12.5 and 12.6 has two nodal circles and no nodal diameters. Therefore, it would be expressed as (0,2) and is illustrated by the 4th entry in Table 12.1. For another example, the vibrational mode illustrated in Figure 12.7 would be referred to as mode (1,1), because it has one nodal diameter and one nodal circle; this is the second entry in Table 12.1. With these examples, the significance of the first and second columns should be very clear.

The third column represents the relative frequencies for an ideal membrane. Let us say that a membrane has a vibrational mode (0,1) that has a frequency of 100 Hz (cycles per second), then the frequency of (1,1) will be 159.4 Hz, the frequency of the mode (2,1) has a frequency of 213.6 Hz, etc.

If we look at the frequency values that are shown in Table 12.1, something becomes very clear. These values are definitely inharmonic. The frequencies produced by our idealised drumhead do not show the regular, simple ratios that a vibrating string would show.

The fact that membranes tend to exhibit inharmonic spectra is musically very significant. Indian music has very stringent requirements for pitch. A drum producing an unpitched sound would probably not find much favour among classical Indian musicians.

It turns out that there is a way around this inharmonic quality. The key to this may be seen by comparing our idealised model to the real world.

---

[2] These vibrational modes are an idealised construct and are derived from theory rather than being derived empirically. Their forms and frequency ratios are derived from the wave equation for a thin membrane written as:

$$\frac{\partial^2 z}{\partial t^2} = \frac{T}{\sigma}\nabla^2 z = c^2 \nabla^2 z$$

where T is the tension, σ is the mass per unit area, and c is the wave velocity. For our purposes, the solutions are usually expressed as Bessel functions of order m, and the zeros of these functions give the frequencies of the various vibrational modes. The m and n of table 12.1 correspond to the nth zero of the Bessel function of order m (Rossing 1991).

Table 12.1. Resonance Modes of an Idealised Drumhead		
Schematic	Mode	Rel. Freq.
○	(0,1)	1.000
⊘	(1,1)	1.594
⊕	(2,1)	2.136
◉	(0,2)	2.296
✳	(3,1)	2.653
⊚	(1,2)	2.918
✴	(4,1)	3.156
⊕	(2,2)	3.501
◎	(0,3)	3.600
✱	(5,1)	3.652
✴	(3,2)	4.060
✴	(6,1)	4.154

In the real world, factors such as air loading, skin stiffness, and a host of other variables, may change the frequency values of these modes. This is very significant, because if random factors can influence the frequency values, then conscious design considerations may be even more effective. Therefore, it should be possible to tame the vibrational modes, and make them behave in a manner which is much more harmonic.

The alteration of the frequencies of these modes is exactly what happens during the manufacture of the *dayan*. It is made in such a way that various modes are coaxed into producing frequencies other than those predicted from our idealised membranes. This was shown in Chapter 2 - *Timbre*.

HARMONICS, VIBRATIONAL MODES, AND NODES OF THE DAYAN

Let us now look at the resonance characteristics of the *dayan*. So far we have reviewed the basics of nodes, antinodes, and vibrational modes. Armed with these concepts, we can see how things really work.

The first thing to recognise is that the sound of the *dayan* is said to be harmonic in nature. This means that the various overtones have simple, integral relationships to the fundamental. (We saw in Chapter 2, that this was an oversimplification.)

Another point to keep in mind is that for every harmonic, there must exist at least one resonance mode to support it. However, we may have several modes working together to create a single harmonic.

Earlier in this chapter, we discussed vibrational modes, and then mentioned the relative frequencies of their vibrations. It is appropriate for us to take the reverse approach in the next section. We will look at the harmonic structure, and then look at the vibrational modes that support them.

Harmonics of Dayan - There are several questions which arise. The first to be addressed is, "How many harmonics are there in the *dayan*?" This is a very good question; unfortunately, we do not have a good answer. A different question is, "How do the harmonics relate to the vibrational modes?" This too does not always bring forth a clear answer. However, we will do our best to answer these questions in this section.

First of all, how do we define our harmonic spectrum? If we require a strict integral relationship (i.e., f, $2f$, $3f$, $4f$, etc.), then the *dayan* clearly fails. With such a strict definition, there will be no harmonics at all! But few people would accept such a strict definition.

Let us look at the spectrogram in Figure 2.16 in Chapter 2, to see how many harmonics we may find. In this graph the intensity is denoted by how dark the line is. The frequency is denoted on the vertical axis, and the time is denoted in the horizontal axis. We see a number of spectral lines clearly illustrated; we have labelled seven. One may even argue the existence of up to 10 or more; although admittedly this is stretching things a bit. Clearly the higher harmonics are weak, very unstable, and have very poor numerical relationships to the fundamental. We can safely discount the upper harmonics as being largely insignificant. But this still does not tell us how many harmonics there are.

It turns out that the easiest thing to do is to fall back upon convention. Generally, five harmonics are considered. We will bow to this convention. But remember, this is a mere simplification, and one should really say that there are five "significant" harmonics.

But where did this convention come from? This convention goes back to the pioneering work of C.V. Raman (Raman 1920). Raman had only the crudest scientific equipment, and five harmonics were all that he was able to see. Today, we have very sensitive spectrum analysers, which can measure things that were unthinkable in Raman's day. But one thing does not change; Raman was not able to see these other harmonics, because they were very weak and insignificant. Even looking at these harmonics with our modern equipment, we still find that these upper harmonics are weak and insignificant. With that being said, let us now look at the five significant harmonics, and their resonance modes.

<u>The Fundamental</u> - The fundamental is the lowest frequency that is generated in a harmonic series. In the *dayan*, this is the sound that is produced by the *Toon* (तू) stroke (Fleischer 2004). One lightly and quickly strikes the centre of the drum with the index finger to elicit this harmonic.

The resonance mode that creates the fundamental is very simple. It is the (0,1) mode; this has a single nodal circle (i.e., the rim of the drum), and no nodal diameters. This mode is very easy to visualise. It was graphically illustrated in Figure 12.3-12.4. It is also the first mode shown in our series in Table 12.1.

<u>The Second Harmonic</u> - In a harmonically correct tone, the second harmonic is an overtone that has a frequency of twice the fundamental. In the case of the tabla, we can only say that it is approximately twice the frequency of the fundamental (see Chapter 2 - *Timbre*).

The second harmonic in the *dayan* is generated by the (1,1) vibrational mode. This mode has one nodal circle and one nodal diameter. This mode was described earlier in Figures 12.7-12.8; it is also the second mode shown in Table 12.1. Although this mode is a bit more complicated, the illustration should make it clear.

<u>Third Harmonic</u> - The third harmonic is considerably more complicated than either the fundamental or the second harmonic. There are five vibrational modes that have been shown to be responsible for this harmonic. These are illustrated in Figure 12.10 (Rossing 1991).

The vibrational modes responsible for the third harmonic are mixed; there are both normal modes (Bessel), and combination modes. One of the normal modes is the (0,2) mode. This was described in great detail in Figures 12.5-12.6; this is also the fourth entry in Table 12.1. Another normal mode that is responsible is the (2,1) mode which is the third entry in Table 12.1. Curiously enough, there are a number of other modes responsible for the third harmonic which are not predicted by our Bessel functions, and not normally found in simple drums. These combination modes are the last three shown in Figure 12.10.

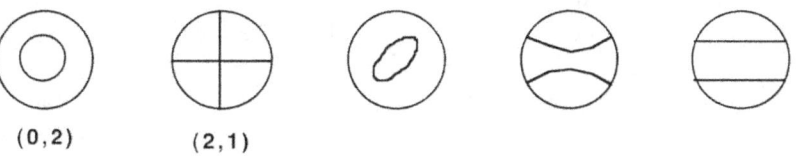

Figure 12.10. Vibrational modes of the third harmonic

Fourth Harmonic - The fourth harmonic introduces a higher level of complexity in the vibrational modes. The vibrational modes responsible for this harmonic are shown in Figure 12.11. Two of the normal modes are described by our mathematics and are found in other drums. These are the (1,2) mode and the (3,1) mode. These correspond to the sixth and fifth examples in Table 12.1, respectively. There are three more combination modes; these are shown in the last three examples in Figure 12.11 (Rossing 1991).

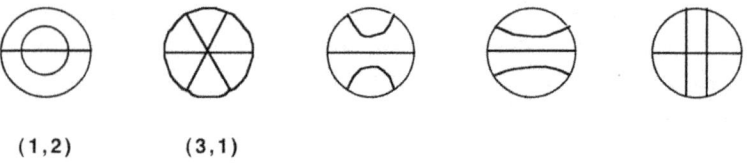

(1,2)   (3,1)

Figure 12.11. Vibrational modes of the fourth harmonic

Fifth Harmonic - The fifth harmonic involves an even greater degree of complexity of the vibrational modes. These modes are illustrated in Figure 12.12. The first three modes are normal modes and similar to what we have found in other drums. However, the last mode is a combination mode, and is not found on most drums (Rossing 1991).

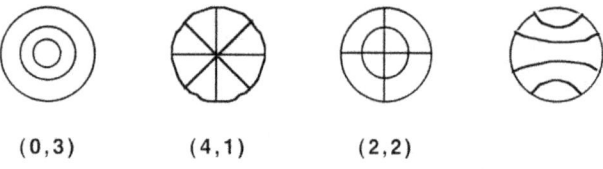

(0,3)   (4,1)   (2,2)

Figure 12.12. Vibrational modes of the fifth harmonic

This section showed that the tabla is able to take a membrane whose spectrum is very inharmonic, and alter the vibrational modes to produce a spectrum which approximates a harmonic spectrum. However, we did not discuss how this happens. The most important mechanism for altering these vibrational modes is a process known as loading.

LOADING

Loading has tremendous influence over the way that the skin vibrates. Loading is the process of artificially increasing the mass of the resonator. This increase in mass translates to a lowering of the frequency at which the resonator vibrates.

Let us start with a very simple analogy. As a child we used to play with a simple toy made by passing kite string through a button and making a loop. One loop of the string would go in to one hand and the other length would go into the other. The button would be set spinning, while we alternately pulled and released the string. The button would spin one direction, then stop, then spin in the other direction, only to stop and return once more. This simple little toy could thus be made to spin indefinitely. We called them whirligigs; but I imagine that they were known by a host of other names. As would so often happen, we would use different sizes and different weight buttons. Heavier disks would operate much more slowly than the smaller, lighter ones.

Loading reduces the resonant frequency by increasing the mass of the resonator. This is really not much different from the way that heavier guitar strings will vibrate at a lower pitch than smaller, lighter ones.

The same process of loading is seen in the tabla. The *syahi* is a very massive application that loads the skin, and thus lowers the frequency. This is represented by the simple model shown in Figure 12.13. In this model, we see that a mass is stretched between two springs. These springs act to bring the mass back to the resting position. As we increase the mass, the resonant frequency decreases. This is exactly what happens with the tabla.

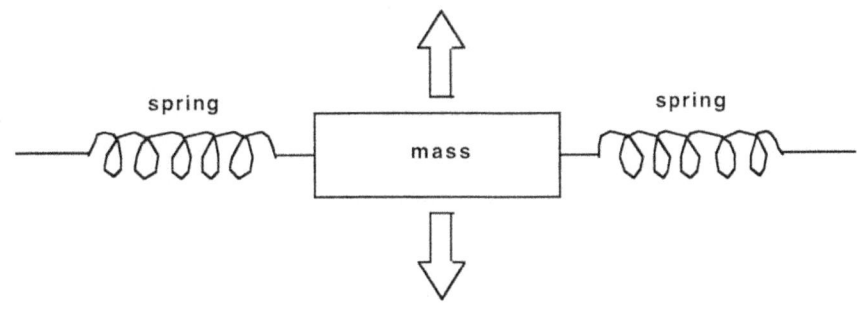

Figure 12.13. Increasing the mass lowers the frequency of vibration

The brilliant thing is that the different vibrational modes are not affected equally. By adjusting both the thickness and the contour of the syahi, certain modes may be affected more than others. It has been empirically observed that making the centre thicker than the edge, affects the fundamental more. Conversely, making the edge thicker affects the higher harmonics.

DAMPENING

Dampening is another important factor that influences the way that the head vibrates. Dampening is the process of introducing some mechanism to mute the vibrations in some way to drain off the energy. If one sets a pendulum swinging, it will not swing forever, but will eventually die down. It dies down because the pendulum is dampened by such factors as air friction and mechanical effects in the string.

There are a number of dampening factors in the tabla. The friction of air is one. Wood porosity and mechanical forces in the skin are also factors. These are nearly random, and are common with other drums. However, there is one dampening factor that is engineered into the tabla (both drums) that is absolutely brilliant. Tabla is made with special dampeners woven into the drumhead. The outer annular membrane (*chat*) is visible, but a similar dampener is located beneath the main membrane. (See Volume 3 of this series, *Manufacture and Repair of Tabla* for more information.) Therefore, the main resonating membrane (*maidan*) is sandwiched between the two annular membranes (the *chat* and the *bharti*). This arrangement is shown diagrammatically in Figure 12.14.

This is a brilliant scheme because its dampening is not felt equally across the spectrum. The upper order vibrational modes are significantly more affected than the lower ones. Let us look at the spectrogram in Figure 2.16 (Chapter 2) to see this in greater detail. In this spectrogram we saw that many of the higher harmonics were initially strong. This may be seen even in the 5th harmonic or higher (the strength is indicated by the relative darkness in the graph). Even though they were initially strong, they did not sustain. Although a lower sustain in the upper order vibrational modes is not confined to the tabla's *dayan*, here it is particularly pronounced.

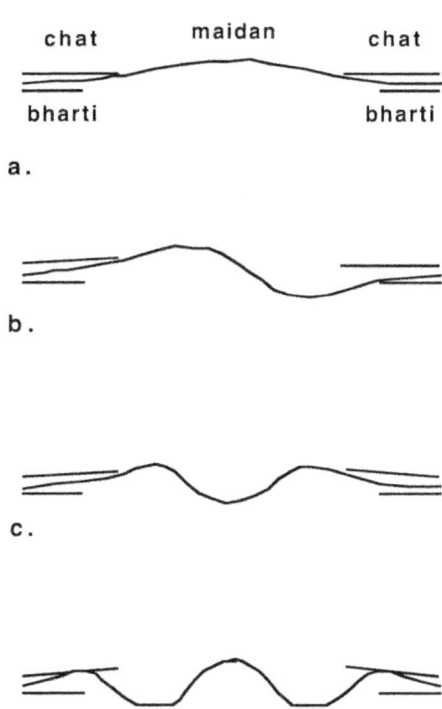

Figure 12.14. The higher order vibrational modes are dampened more than the lower order modes

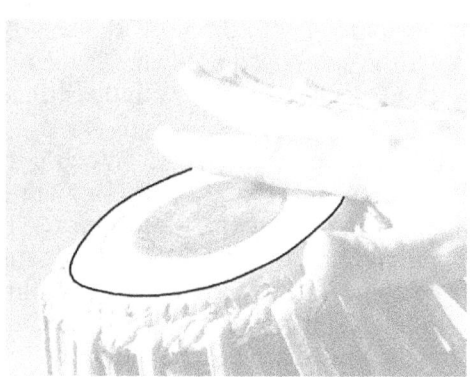

Figure 12.15. Tun (तुं) shows a major expression of the (0,1) vibrational mode

Figure 12.14 shows why the upper order vibrational modes are dampened more than the lower order modes. A lower order mode is shown in Figure 12.14.a. We see that the antinode is located at a considerable distance from the *chat* and the *bharti* (dampeners). However, as we move into progressively higher modes, the antinodes shift towards the edge. At some point, the antinodes may even be under the *chat*. It is obvious that the dampening affect on these higher order modes will be extreme.

There is a simple musical reason that necessitates this dampening. The higher order modes produce overtones which give a much sharper, but musically indistinct pitch. Indian musicians feel that dampening these unmusical modes gives a tone which is more pleasant.

PHYSICS AND THE TECHNIQUE OF THE DAYAN

The physics of the *dayan* is reflected in performance technique in two ways. It is reflected in the muting of the (0,1) mode by the last two fingers of the right hand. It is also reflected in the emphasis of other modes by the striking of the drum in particular fashions. We may look at these in greater detail.

Suppression of the (0,1) Mode - The suppression of the (0,1) mode is probably the most profound reflection of how the physics of the *dayan* influences the technique. We saw in our previous examination of the spectra (Chapter 2 - *Timbre*), that the lowest frequency component is particularly problematic due to the fact that it isn't in tune with the rest of the *dayan*. Although the rest of the spectra show a strong harmonic quality, the "fundamental" is sharp.

The sharp quality of the (0,1) mode is easily demonstrated without any equipment. One simply has to take a well tuned *dayan,* and compare the musical pitch of *Toon* (तुं) (Figure 12.15), *Tin* (तिं), and *Naa* (ना). Convention says that the *dayan* will use *Tin* (तिं) or *Naa* (ना) to tune to. However, when we play *Toon* (तुं) we find that it is approximately one step higher than the tonic. Therefore, if the tabla is tuned to *Sa,* then the *Toon* (तुं) stroke produces *Re* (the natural 2nd).

The way musicians deal with this problem is to mute the lowest vibrational mode (i.e., the 0,1 mode). This is done by placing the ring finger against the skin of the drum.

The consequence of this finger position is profound. Only the vibrational modes which have nodes running under the ring finger will be present. A few examples are shown in Figures 12.16-12.20. These are only a few examples; one can see many more.

<u>Striking Positions and the Antinodes</u> - The most efficient way to evoke particular modes is to strike as close to the antinodes as possible. This is most apparent in strokes which emphasise the lower order modes, such as *Toon* (तूं) or *Tin* (तिं). As a practical matter, the positions of the antinodes are less well defined in strokes which emphasise the higher order vibrational modes (e.g., *Naa* ना). For this, one simply strikes the rim very forcefully. This has the "shotgun" approach of exciting the upper order vibrational modes with considerably less specificity than one finds in the lower order modes.

HARMONICS, VIBRATIONAL MODES, AND NODES OF THE BAYAN

At this time, the physics of the *bayan* is not well understood. I am aware of only one work that was intended to address the issue. This was the work of B.S. Ramakrishna in 1957.

The basic problem seems to be that early investigators were using analysis approaches that had been worked out for the *dayan*. Vibrational modes of a circular membrane provide a workable model for the *dayan*, but they just don't work well for the *bayan*. So much of the physics of the *bayan* depends upon what is happening with the air inside the drum, and much less on what the skin is doing.

I have always felt that the closest analogue to the *bayan* is the passive radiator speaker design. Even this sometimes seems very remote. Perhaps one of you will take up the challenge and fill in the gaps.

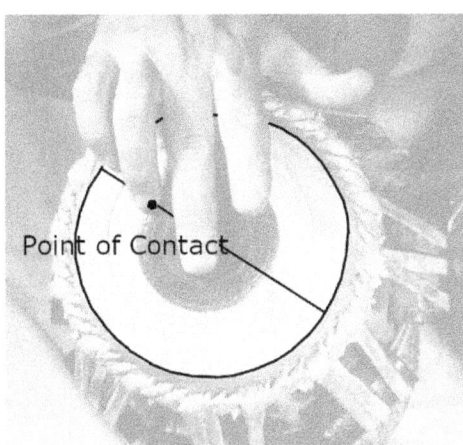

Figure 12.16. The (1,1) mode has a node running beneath our ring finger

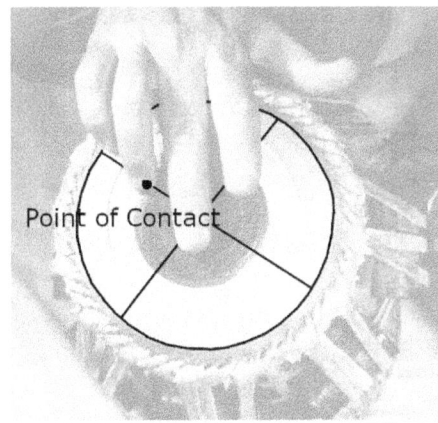

Figure 12.17. The (2,1) mode has a node running beneath our ring finger

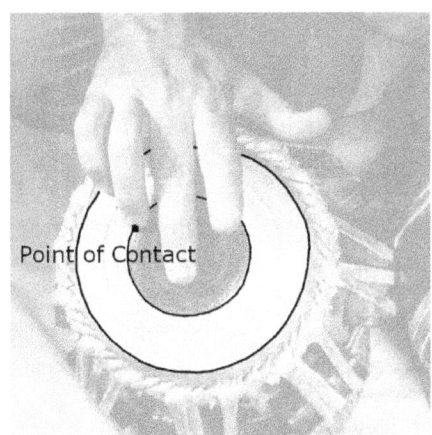

Figure 12.18. The (0,2) mode has a node running beneath our ring finger

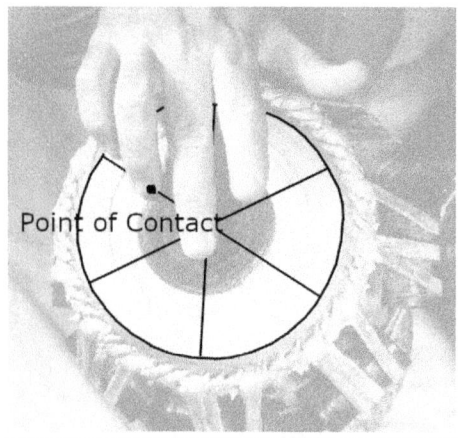

Figure 12.19. The (3,1) mode has a node running beneath our ring finger

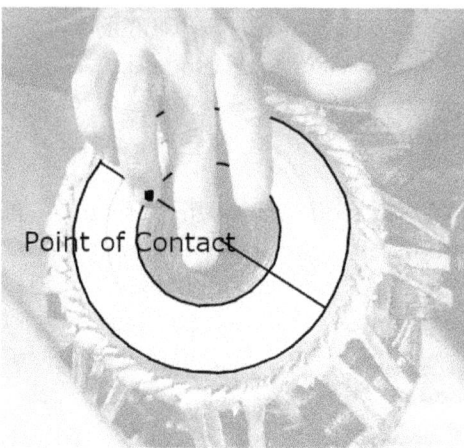

Figure 12.20. The (1,2) mode has a node running beneath our ring finger

CONCLUSION

We briefly reviewed what is known of the physics of the tabla. In the final analysis, we really do not know very much. Large parts of what we think we know have been imported from other common drums, but the tabla is clearly not a common drum. This approach leaves many loose ends.

One area where there needs to be a lot of work is the topic of the cavity. It is obvious that it must exert an affect on both the *bayan* as well as the *dayan*. But exactly what that is, isn't clear. I spent about two years experimenting with the cavity of the *dayan* in a vain attempt to understand what this. Other than being able to demonstrate that the sustain of the *dayan* could be influenced by what was happening here, my efforts went nowhere. I was hampered by limited funds (and even more limited intelligence). I hope that someone with deeper pockets, and more smarts than I, will be able to address this.

Another area that should be looked into is the topic of nodal points. Conventional views on the subject say that nodal points play no part in the physics of the *dayan*. However, the nearly universal technique of keeping the ring finger positioned on the surface of the *dayan*, simply screams that the concept of the nodal point should not be ignored.

There is also the question of modes. Previous investigators (Rossing, et al.) identified vibrational modes which were not predicted by the Bessel functions. Yet beyond a brief description of their nodes, there really is very little that we know about them.

The physics behind the bayan is even more baffling. There has been very little effort to understand its physics; and what we think that we know seems to me to be unsatisfying.

As we draw this chapter to a close, I must throw down the gauntlet to anyone with the capacity to address these deficiencies. I am unable to due to my own limitations. (By the time you read this, there is a good chance I will be dead.)

If you can, please do so.

WORKS CITED

Cohen, Hirsh and George Handelman
1957 "On the Vibration of a Circular Membrane with Added Mass", *Journal of Acoustical Society of America*. Vol. 29 No 2, pp. 229-233

Courtney, David R.
1999 "Psychoacoustics of the Musical Pitch of Tabla", *Journal of the Sangeet Research Academy*. Calcutta, India, Vol 13, No1 October.

Fleischer, Helmut
2004 "Vibration and Sound of the Indian Tabla", *Proceedings of the Joint Congress CFA/DAGA 04, Societé Française d'Acoustique, Paris, 1073*. Vol. 1074.

Fletcher, N.H. and T.D. Rossing
1991 Physics of Musical Instruments. New York: Springer-Verlag: New York.

Ramakrishna, B.S. and M.M. Sondhi
1954 "Vibrations of Indian Musical Drums Regarded as Composite Membranes", *Journal of Acoustical Society of America*. Vol 26 No 4. pp. 523-529.

Ramakrishna, B.S.
1957 "Modes of Vibration of the Indian Drum Dugga or Left-Hand Thabala", *Journal of the Acoustical Society of America*. Vol. 29, Number 2, 234-238.

Raman, C.V.
1935 "The Indian Musical Drums" *Proc. Indian Academy of Science*. Vol. A1 pp1 79.

Raman C.V. and S. Kumar
1920 "Musical Drums with Harmonic Overtones", *Nature* (London) vol 104, pp 500.

Rossing, Thomas D.
1991 "Musical Instruments", *Encyclopedia of Applied Physics* (Vol 11). New York: VCH Publishers (pp 157).
1992 "Acoustics of Drums", *Physics Today*. New York. American Institute of Physics. March 1992 vol. 45, no 3, pp.40-47.

T. Sarojini and A. Rahman
1958 "Variational Method for the Vibrations of the Indian Drums", *Journal of Acoustical Society of America*. Vol 30 pp. 191-196.

CHAPTER 13

ACOUSTIC FIELDS AND MICROPHONES

Let us begin this chapter with something that every tabla player has encountered. Your instrument will sound one way in one room, but it will sound different on stage, or even in another room. You hear a tabla one way when you walk into a performance, but as you move around the room, it sounds different. Furthermore, just listening to the sound of the tabla as it comes off a sound system is totally different from the way it sounds to your ears.

The fact that one is unable to hear the tabla as being the same throughout the auditorium is disconcerting. You are a performing artist, and it is only natural that you want to present the best sound possible. But how can you do this if you cannot even get a consistent feel for the sound. Although there are many reasons for this, one factor is the concept of acoustic fields.

In order to get a grasp on what is happening here, we need to refer back to some earlier chapters. Chapter 2 - *Timbre*, acquainted us with the acoustic and psychoacoustic nature of the sounds of the tabla. Chapter 12 - *Physics of the Tabla* acquainted us with what was happening inside the tabla to make those sounds. This chapter will acquaint us with what happens to the air as the sound leaves the tabla. This will be through the concept of acoustic fields. We will pay particular attention to the way fields influence both the choice of microphones, as well as their placement.

There is one topic which is central to our discussion. If we are going to understand acoustic fields, we must first be comfortable with the inverse square law.

INVERSE SQUARE LAW
The topic of the inverse square law is crucial to our understanding of acoustic fields. This describes the manner in which sound intensity will decrease with distance.

Let us illustrate the inverse square law with a simple example. Let us say that you are celebrating with some firecrackers (i.e., *pathake*, or squibs). If you are in your own garden, you will find that moving a few metres away from the firecracker will greatly decrease the volume. It is intuitive that moving away from the sound source reduces the volume. Now let us imagine the same celebration, but now the firecrackers are located a half kilometre away. At this point, you can move all around the garden, and it will not make any difference in the loudness the explosions.

Think of the significance of this last example. It is the same firecracker, and the same few metres movement in the garden. But if these few metres are near the source of the sound, the change in volume is more. Conversely, if the same few metres change is located far from the source, the decrease in sound may be imperceptible.

Let us formalise what we understood intuitively from the last example. The inverse square law states that a physical quantity is inversely proportional to the square of the distance. We can express this as:

$$\text{intensity} \propto \frac{1}{\text{distance}^2}$$

We could continue down this line, but we will not. It would lead us into arcane calculations involving the speed of sound in air at different temperatures, wave fronts, and other complex material.

Let us cut through this and get right down to the bottom line. The inverse square law for sound states that every time one doubles the distance from a sound source, the sound is four times less[1]. If we express this in a way which is easier for most musicians, we get:

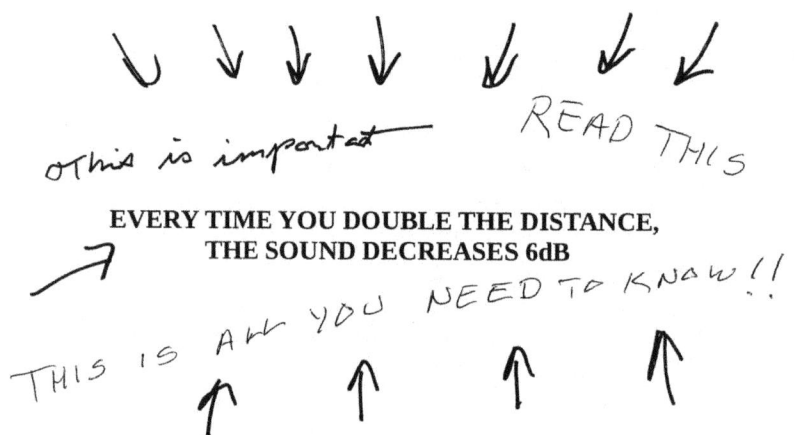

EVERY TIME YOU DOUBLE THE DISTANCE, THE SOUND DECREASES 6dB

IS THE INVERSE SQUARE LAW REALY A "LAW"?

Physicists are smart and we are all simple minded musicians, therefore if scientists say it is a "law", then it must be true - right?

From the standpoint of a tabla player in real world conditions, the inverse square law is not really a "law" at all. It will fail more often than it will work.

There are two presumptions of the inverse square law which cause it to fail. Firstly, it presumes that the sound source is a single point of infinitesimal dimensions. The second presumption is that there will be nothing in the environment which will act upon the sound in any way (i.e., no people, no walls, no ceiling, no floor, etc.)

ACOUSTIC FIELDS

Acoustic fields are greatly defined by how well they adhere to the inverse square law. Where is this law applicable? Where does it fail? How does it fail? These are the questions which are pivotal to understanding the subject.

How many fields are there? That is a good question that does not have a good answer. There are different interpretations. As a general rule, there are three overall approaches to fields. There is a two-field approach that is preferred by physicists; there is a three-field approach which is preferred by audio

---

[1] For those who might want some clarification, this works for both sound intensity level (dB SIL) and sound pressure level (dB SPL).

Ch.13. Acoustic Fields & Microphones

engineers; and there is a third approach used by marketers of "near field" speakers. Unfortunately, the latter has been completely obfuscated with improperly used terminology and marketing bullshit. If you are coming into this with what you "learned" from near field speakers, you had better forget it all, and start over.

TWO-FIELD APPROACH

In a physics course, they are likely to tell you that there are two acoustic fields. There is a near field and a far field (Figure 13.1).

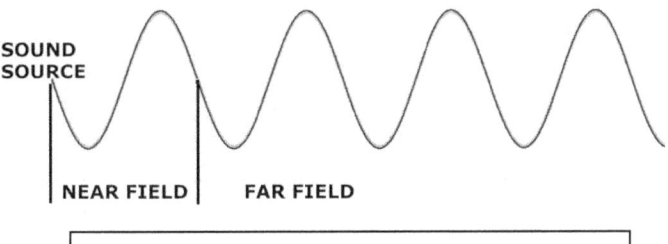

Figure 13.1. The two acoustic fields.

The far field is that which is located some distance from the source of sound. It begins roughly one wave-length from the source of the sound and continues out to infinity. This field behaves according to the inverse square law. Conversely, the near field is that which surrounds the source of the sound. It extends roughly one wavelength from the source. It is characterised by a much more complicated behaviour, one that is not subject to the inverse square law.

The key word in the last two paragraphs is "roughly". There isn't a precise boundary between the two fields, and can vary tremendously according to the situation. Many would suggest that two wavelengths would be a better definition.

This two field approach is what they teach in school, so it must be true - right?

Mmmmmm...., this isn't really very useful and borders on being incorrect. This may be interesting for those with deeply held reductionist world views, for it gives us a model of what is happing at a very fundamental level. But on a practical level, it perpetuates the same erroneous presumptions that plague the inverse square law (i.e., single point sound source, and an uncluttered 3-dimensional space.) Furthermore, it introduces a new erroneous assumption, that is that there will be a single distance corresponding to the wavelength. In practice, the various components of the sound of musical instruments have wave-lengths which stretch from about 20 feet to less than an inch. For the tabla, most of the wavelengths run from about 11 feet to about 2 inches.

It is clear that we need to have a more realistic and practical approach to acoustic fields.

THREE FIELD APPROACH

The three-field model is more common among the engineering fields. It provides a series of "rules of thumb", which have served musicians and sound engineers for a long time. The three fields are represented in a highly simplified form in Figure 13.2. This represents a room with a small stage, and a tabla on the stage.

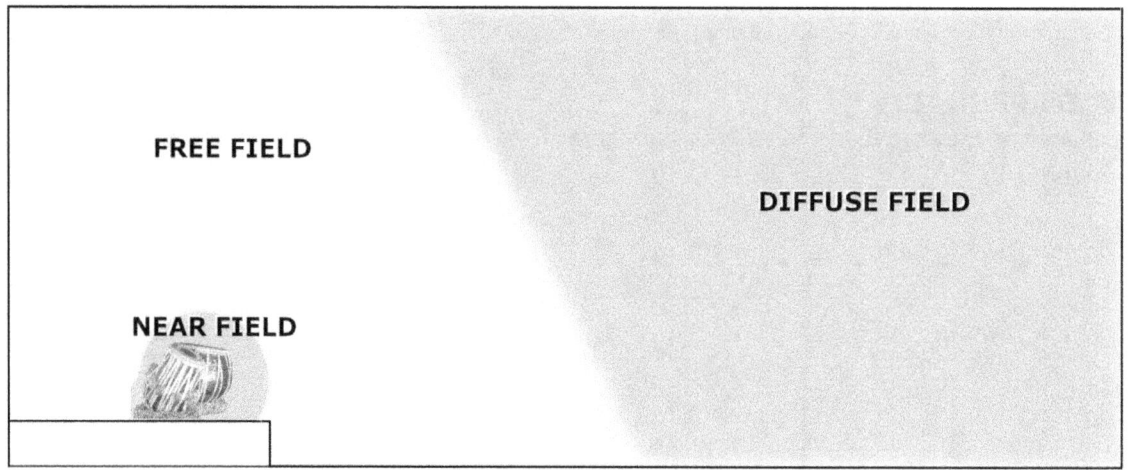

Figure 13.2. The three acoustic fields.

Near Field – The tabla has a near field which extends from the surface of the drums to a distance of about 1-2 feet[2]. Within this field the inverse square law has no applicability. Sound should not be considered as emanating from the instrument, but rather a complex movement as air sloshes-around. Most modern recordings and almost all present day sound reinforcement systems, place the microphone within the near field.

Free Field - The free field is the field that extends from about 1-2 feet from the tabla to some distance into the room/auditorium. It behaves in a manner somewhat similar to the "far field" of the two-field model. This field is defined by the fact that the inverse square law kicks in and starts to work (at least sort of). There are minimal sound reflections from walls, floor, etc., so any listener sitting within this field is actually listening to the tabla. Recordings of Indian film music from the 1950s often recorded the tabla from within its free field. In open air performances, the entire audience may be considered to exist in the free field.

Diffuse Field - If we move further into the auditorium, we will reach the diffuse field. It is a point where the volume of sound no longer decreases with an increase in distance. There, we are listening to the auditorium rather than the sound coming from the tabla. The is known as the "diffuse field" or occasionally "reverberant field", and is characterised by a collapse of the inverse square law. Listening to music within the diffuse field is normal for most well made auditoriums; the sound of a well designed hall greatly contributes to its overall enjoyability. But one seldom wishes to place a microphone in the diffuse field. The concept of the diffuse field is really only applicable to auditoriums and indoor performance situations; because outdoor venues do not have a diffuse field.

This is only the briefest introduction to the topic of fields. Let us look at how they are of concern to the tabla player.

---

[2]The International Electrotechnical Commission defines the near sound field as "sound field near a sound source where instantaneous sound pressure and particle velocity are substantially out of phase" (IEC 801-23-29).

Ch.13. Acoustic Fields & Microphones

NEAR FIELD

The near field is the most important to the tabla player. In this field, things behave in an apparently erratic fashion. There is a lot movement of air which is not reflected in the production of sound. But as far as the tabla is concerned, it is not really erratic, and there are things happening that we should be aware of.

Let us look at the near field behaviour of the two lowest order vibrational modes. There are other modes as noted in the previous chapter, but since these higher order vibrational modes do not have any influence over our choice of microphones or their placement, we will not discuss them here.

(0,1) Vibrational Mode – This is the most fundamental vibrational mode of the *dayan*. As its name implies, it has a single nodal circle around the rim, with no nodal diameters. This mode is easily evoked by playing the *Toon* (तूं) stroke. The movement of the drum-skin was illustrated in the last chapter in Figure 12.3.

The movement of air is illustrated in Figure 13.3, and the manner in which sound is produced is illustrated in Figure 13.4. You will notice that Figure 13.3 is the same as Figure 12.3. This is not a mistake, because in this case, the movement of air and the movement of the skin are the same. This mode introduces no real concern for microphone placement.

(1,1) Vibrational Mode - The (1,1) vibrational mode is the second most basic mode for any drum. By definition, the (1,1) mode it is a dipole resonance source characterised by a single circular node, and a single nodal diameter. It is responsible for the second harmonic of the *dayan* spectra. The movement of the skin in this mode was shown in the previous chapter in Figure 12.7.

This mode is the most important to the tabla player. It conveys the majority of information concerning the pitch of the *dayan*. It also is a major concern when choosing microphone placement. It is so important to us that we will spend considerable time on it.

It is interesting to note that the movement of the skin, the movement of air, and the projection of sound in this mode do not correlate. The movement of the skin is shown in the last chapter in Figure 12.7, while the movement of the air is shown in Figure 13.5.

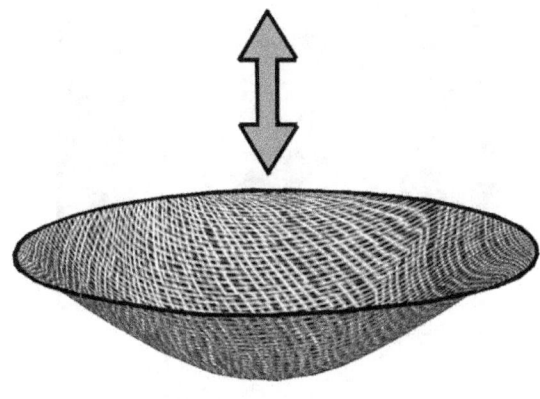

Figure 13.3. Movement of air within the (0,1) vibrational mode

Figure 13.4. Projection of sound from the (0,1) vibrational mode.

One of the most obvious effects is the way that it moves air from one side to the other. This action does not radiate a sound outward. This movement is illustrated by the double pointed arrow in the centre of Figure 13.5. This lateral movement of air requires considerably less energy than radiating sound outwards. Since very little energy is expended in the production of sound, this mode can maintain itself for a long time. A major portion of the sustain of the *dayan* is due to this resonance mode.

This lateral "sloshing" of air suppresses the projection of sound into the environment. But this action is limited to the area that is in the immediate vicinity of the node. As we move away from this node, the sound is able to leak out in opposite directions. This action is illustrated by the two side arrows of Figure 13.5. This is the sound that we actually hear in the *dayan*.

The manner in which the (1,1) vibrational mode leaks sound into the environment creates two lobes of sound projection. This is illustrated in Figure 13.6. These two lobes are comparable with one exception; they are exactly 180° out of phase. This is to be expected from the dipolar nature of the (1,1) resonance mode.

We only discussed the near field behaviour of the two lowest order vibrational modes. There are other vibrational modes which were covered in the last chapter, *Physics of the Tabla*. But these other modes have significantly less influence over the near field behaviour than the (0,1) and (1,1) vibrational modes. Therefore, we will not go into them here[3].

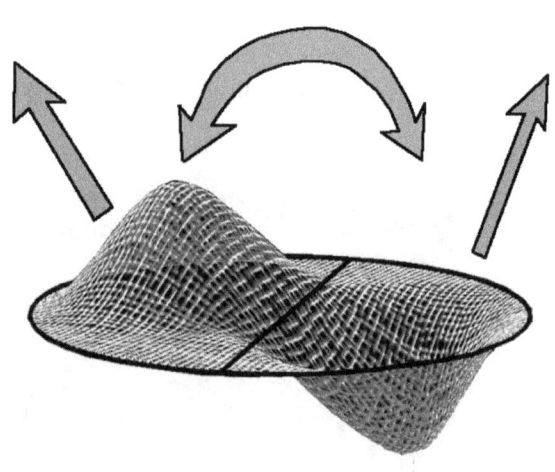

Figure 13.5. Movement of air within (1,1) vibrational mode.

Figure 13.6. Two lobes of sound projected from the (1,1) mode

---

[3] One must remember that the air will move around the drum in a fashion that reflects all of the vibrational modes combined. Just as the air tends to move between the antinodes of the (1,1) mode, in a similar fashion, air moves around between the antinodes of different vibrational modes. The interplay of the various modes is reflected in the complex manner in which sound is ultimately projected from the *dayan*.

MICROPHONE PLACEMENT AND THE NEAR FIELD

Microphones and near fields are a natural match. Microphones are the tools of choice for analysing the behaviour of air in the near field in the laboratory (Bader et al. 2009). Therefore, understanding what is happening here is going to greatly impact the practical aspect of microphone placement on stage.

The microphone placement for the *bayan* does not have any complicated considerations. There are strokes of the *Ga* (ग) class, and strokes of the *Ka* (क) class. The major portion of the sound of *Ga* (ग) is around 100Hz; this has a wavelength of about 11 feet! Moving the microphone a few inches doesn't seem to make much difference. Strokes of the *Ka* (क) class, are essentially white noise, and do not depend upon any resonance modes. Moving the microphone closer to the *bayan* makes them louder, while moving the microphone further makes them softer. As a general rule, keeping the microphone closer to the *bayan* produces a more balanced sound.

But microphone placement for the *dayan,* on the other hand, is more complicated. For this, we need to consider the near field behaviour of the various vibrational modes.

As a practical matter we need to concentrate on the (1,1) mode. The higher order vibrational modes of the *dayan* [i.e., (3.1), (4,1), (2,2), etc.] function on a scale which is too small to consider. On the other hand, the lowest order (0,1) vibrational mode, only expresses itself during the *Toon* (तूं) stroke. The relatively low incidence of this stroke, means that we do not have to give this too much consideration. But the (1,1) vibrational mode is constantly being evoked in every resonant stroke of the *dayan*. Therefore, it has a disproportionately greater influence over the quality of sound of the *dayan*. Since this is our major concern, our discussion of microphone placement will concentrate upon this mode.

There are three common ways to mic the tabla. These are shown in Figure 13.7. Figure 13.7-a shows a single microphone placed within a few inches of both drums in the centre. This is the most common arrangement, and has been popular for at least 50 years. Figure 13.7-b shows a dual microphone arrangement; this is the most popular dual microphone arrangement. Figure 13.7-c shows a dual microphone setup, but with the two microphones crossed in the centre.

The sound produced by these three microphone arrangements is remarkably different, especially for the sound of the *dayan*. The reason for these difference may be seen by viewing them from the top. This is shown in Figure 13.8.

A

B

C

Figure 13.7. Common microphone placements. a) Single mic in centre. b) Common two mic placement c) Crossed two mic placement

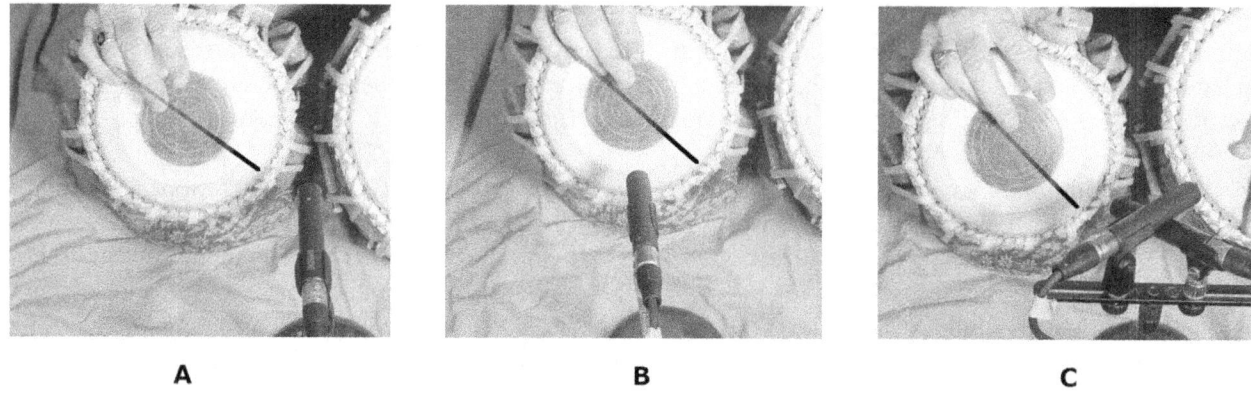

Figure 13.8. Nodal diameter of (1,1) mode in relation to common microphone arrangements. a) Single mic in centre. b) Common two mic placement c) Crossed two mic placement

Figure 13.8 shows the nodal diameter of the (1,1) mode, in relation to the various microphone configurations. Figure 13.8a shows that with the single microphone arrangement, the node tends to point directly at the microphone. Conversely, the microphone placement in Figure 13.8b is considerably off the node. The crossed microphone in Figure 13.8c, has the microphone again pointing at the node.

The expression of the second harmonic from the (1,1) mode will vary considerably due to microphone placement. In situations where the microphone lines up with this node (Figure13.8a and Figure 13.8c), there will be a marked suppression of the second harmonic. Yet in situations where the microphone is well off the node (Figure13.8b), the second harmonic will express itself clearly.

The obvious question is, "Which one is better?" This question does not have a simple answer; because it is an artistic consideration rather than a technical one. In situations where we would like a very sonorous sound with a long sustains and a clearly defined pitch, we might go with the two microphone configuration shown in Figure 13.8b. Classical vocal concerts, especial of the *kheyal*, are situations where this might be appropriate. However, the majority of cases require a sharper more defined sound. This would call for microphone arrangements such as 13.8a or 13.8c.

As a general rule, we want to place our mics in such a way as to suppress the second harmonic. This will be the case for both stage and recording. "Why", one may ask? The answer has to do with audience expectations.

The single microphone configuration shown in Figure 13.8a, has defined audience's expectations of what the tabla is supposed to sound like for the last half century. In contrast, older recordings (e.g., Bade Gulam Ali Khan, Allaudin Khan), tended to record the tabla in its free field. This showed a greater expression of the second harmonic in the tabla's sound. But very few people will listen to these recordings and say; "Wow! What fantastic tabla!"[4]

This would indicate that the obvious choice for a dual mic setup should be the arrangement in Figure 13.7c and 13.8c. But this arrangement is dependent on the availability of some form of a dual microphone adapter. One example is shown in Figure 13.9. Unfortunately, you cannot expect every venue to have these. Therefore, a more accessible alternative is the arrangement shown in Figure 13.10.

---

[4]This is of course an oversimplification. There are numerous technical and artistic reasons why the tabla in these early recordings does not generate the same visceral appreciation as contemporary recordings.

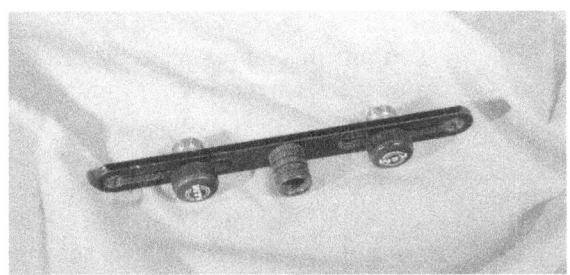

Figure 13.9. Dual microphone adapter

Figure 13.10. Alternative dual microphone arrangement

The microphone setup in Figure 13.10 is not intuitive; but in light of what we know about the (1,1) vibrational mode, makes perfect sense. For this arrangement, the microphone is placed very close to the *dayan*, just barely out of the range of our hands. It is aligned perfectly with the (1,1) node, therefore there will be a marked suppression of the second harmonic. The *bayan* on the other hand, is very intuitive. The mic is merely located as close to the *bayan* as possibly without interfering with the movements of our hands. This arrangement produces a well defined, crisp sound, with very good rejection of feedback.

There is still another dual microphone approach which is worthy of our discussion. Figure 13.11 shows a stereo condenser microphone. Superficially, it resembles any other microphone, but when the headbasket (windscreen) is held up to the light, we can see that there are not one, but two capsules (Figure 13.12). In this case, they have their axes located at a 90°. It can be used for the tabla in a fashion shown in Figure 13.13.

Figure 13.11. Stereo microphone (MXL V67Q) (Marshall Electronics undated)

The stereo microphone has many advantages. The very small form factor is very convenient, and does not take up a lot of stage real estate. It also produces the classic tabla sound of a single microphone, but with power and control of a dual mic setup.

However, there are caveats. Stereo microphones tend to be designed for free field/ diffuse field recordings in auditoriums. Therefore, they may not be able to handle the higher sound pressure levels (SPL) that we find with the tabla. If you wish to use this approach, always look at the microphone's maximum SPL rating, and make sure that it is sufficiently high for your purposes. Another consideration is the microphone's durability. This is especially important when one is intending to use it for stage.

Figure 13.12. Dual capsule

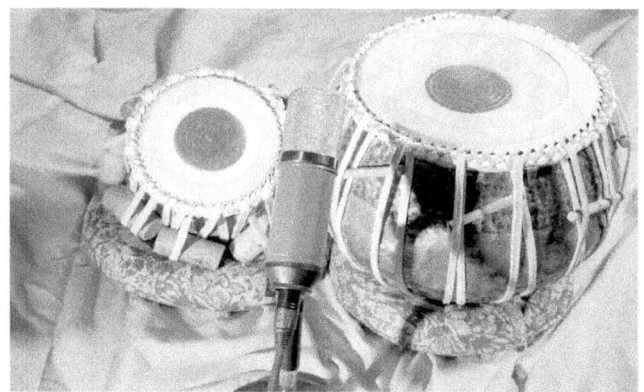

Figure 13.13. Stereo microphone placement

<u>Extraneous Elements</u> - The near field of your tabla is like an artist's canvas. You are in control of it by virtue of your performance, your microphone selection, and your microphone arrangement. But let us extend this artist analogy. How would you feel if you were a painter, and insects kept flying into your canvas and becoming lodged in the wet paint? This obviously would be annoying. Unfortunately, dealing with extraneous elements which encroach upon the near field of your tabla is a constant problem, especially in a live performance.

I will confine myself to unwanted extraneous sounds here. (Although on one occasion I did have a large boa constrictor crawl into my lap in the middle of a performance.) In a stage performance, there are generally two kinds of extraneous sounds that we must contend with. The most pesky and ubiquitous is the sound from the speakers; this can cause feedback. But there are also problems stemming from being forced to sit too close to other musicians, or from external entities such as generators or other equipment. These extraneous elements can be addressed by proper selection of microphones, attention to stage layout, and other approaches. Although they are very important, they are not connected with the physics of the near field, so we will not address them here.

Let us move on and discuss the free field.

FREE FIELD

As previously mentioned, the free field is that portion of the room where reflected sounds are negligible. It is generally considered to be synonymous to both the far field that one may find in laboratory condition, or a direct field. It is characterised by a general adherence to the inverse square law. It begins at the distance in which microphones stop exhibiting peculiar responses according to their placement, and ends at the point in which room reverberations start to dominate.

There are many things that are of concern for us in the free field. Speaker placement, recording, sound, and video are just a few. Unfortunately, many things that happen here may be beyond our control.

<u>Speakers</u> – The most important thing that happens in our free field is the placement of speakers. The speakers themselves have their own near, free, and a diffuse fields. This introduces many concerns as feedback becomes a very likely possibility. This however, is a different topic and will be discussed in Chapter 14 - *Sound Reinforcement*.

<u>Microphones</u> – It is not very often that microphone placement will be done in the free field. There will be sound reflections, people coughing, babies crying, and other unwanted sounds to spoil the recording. Still such situations do arise.

One common example of microphone placement in the free field is to be found in halls that are designed specifically for classical performances and plays. These often have omnidirectional microphones suspended from the loft over the stage. They generally work acceptably; but you may have no control over these. Therefore we will not discuss them.

In some situations, it may be practical to have your own omnidirectional mics. Sometimes these mics are regular microphones that offer an omnidirectional option (Figure 13.14). Sometimes they are dedicated omnidirectional microphones. Generally the only place where these microphones may be placed and work acceptably, is if they are placed onstage. This is often impractical.

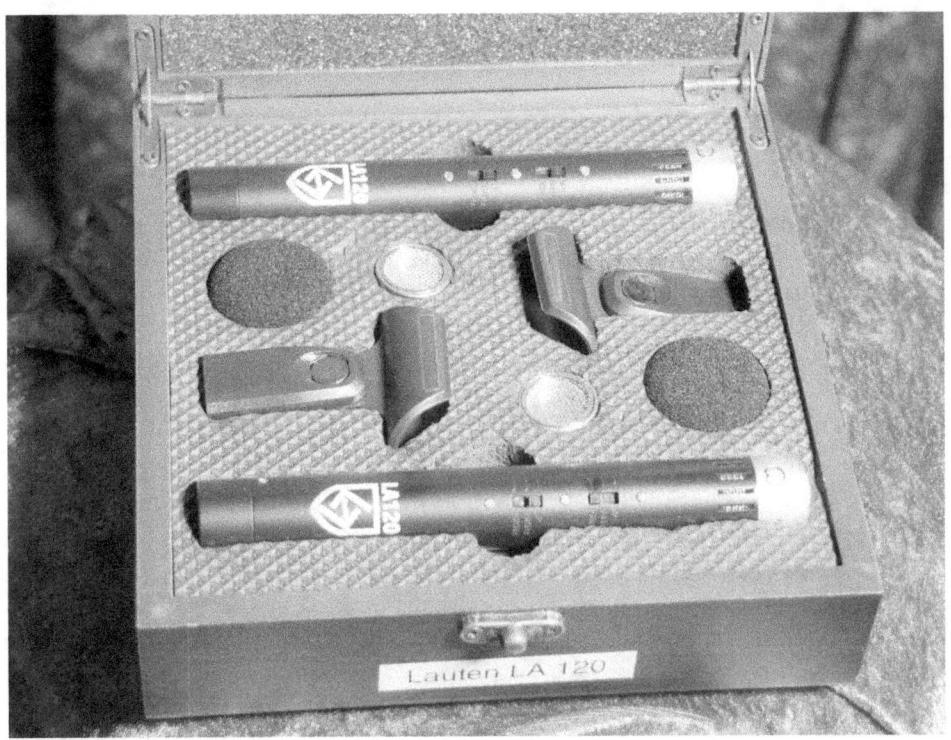

Figure 13.14. Microphones with interchangeable capsules usually offer omnidirectional options (Lauten Audio 2016)

A very common case of free field placement of the mic is in the case of videography. Obviously the ideal would be for the camera to tie directly into the mixing board for a direct connection. This too may be impractical or impossible. In many cases, you will be forced to use whatever mic is in the camera; this is the worst approach, but unfortunately very common.

Anyone who has ever tried this realises that the sound on the video is terrible. It comes out cavernous and excessively reverberant. This may be surprising, because it didn't sound that way when we were sitting in the audience.

Why was the sound so different in the auditorium compared to what was on the video?

The Haas Effect – The Haas effect also known as the "precedence effect", describes how the brain gives priority to the first incidence of a sound, while suppressing subsequent ones. It is named after Dr. Helmut Haas, who described this in his 1949 doctoral dissertation (Haas 1949)[5].

---

[5] Although this bears Haas' name, it is based upon a substantial amount of previous work. Earlier research includes the work of Lothar Cremer (Cremer 1948), Hans Wallach (Wallach et al. 1949), and I. Langmuir (Langmuir et al. 1944). It was even described as early as 1851 by Joseph Henry in his *On The Limit of Perceptibility of a Direct and Reflected Sound*. (Henry 1851).

The practical part of this is simple. If a sound comes to one's ears, any similar sound will not be perceived for a period of approximately 50 msec.

To understand the reason for the Haas effect, we have to look at the evolutionary pressures under which humans developed. In the real world, sound reflections are everywhere. Imagine the consequences of missing the sound of an approaching predator simply because it was being overwhelmed with a lot of sonic garbage.

This effect and its implications, strongly underscore the difference between real world and ideal conditions. The Haas effect most strongly manifests itself in the way that the brain suppresses room reflections of a sound. But in an ideal free field, there are no room reflections.

The Haas effect has tremendous implications for both the listening and the recording of music within the free field. We must always presume that anything recorded here will sound cavernous compared to what we are hearing with our ears.

Is there anything that we can do to cut down on these echoes? Well there is, at least sort of.

Shotgun Mic - The shotgun microphone (Figure 13.15) offers a way to record in the free field, while minimising extraneous noises. It does this by having an extremely directional pickup pattern. But shotgun microphones are generally designed for voice, not music; therefore there may be problems. To begin with, the directionality only tends to work in the mid to upper frequencies, but at the lower frequencies where the *bayan's* resonant sounds are, this directionality is quite poor. Furthermore, even the directionality of the mid and upper frequencies, is often obtained at the expense of linearity in its frequency response. The bottom line is, that this may suit your needs; but then perhaps it may not. You will have to try it, and decide for yourself.

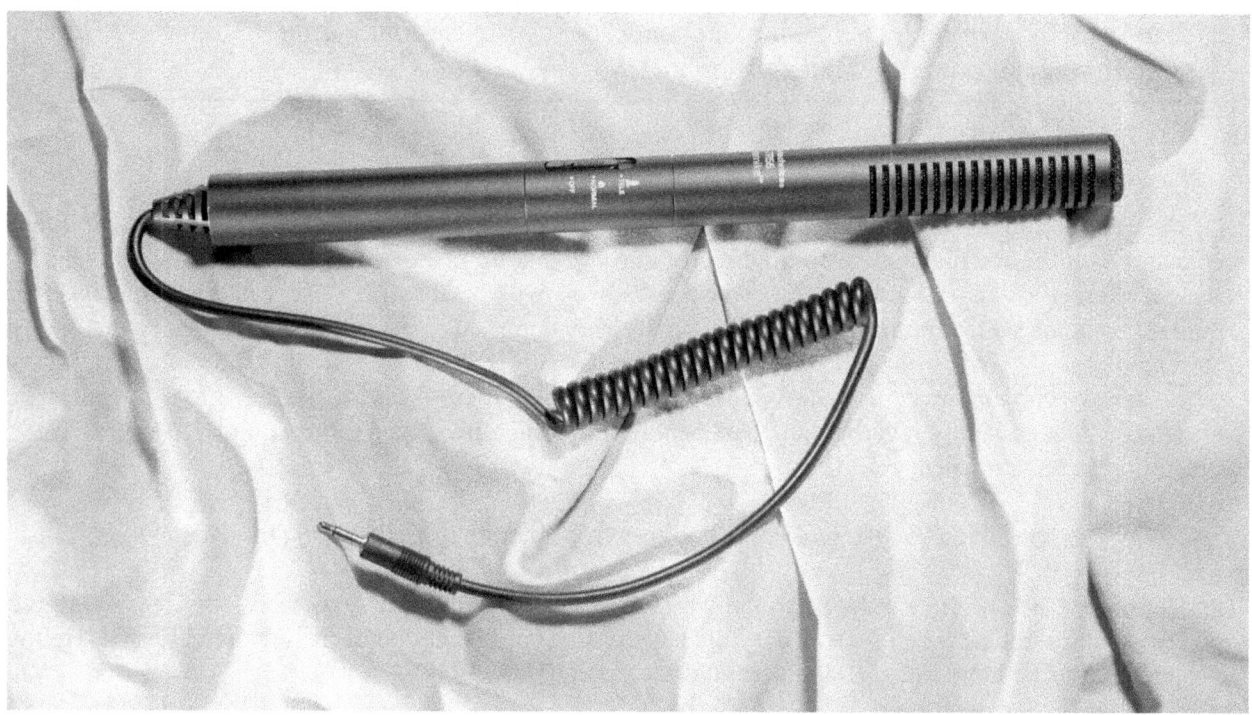

Figure 13.15. Shotgun microphone (Audio Technica undated)

Ch.13. Acoustic Fields & Microphones

DIFFUSE FIELD

As previously mentioned, the diffuse field is that area of the hall/auditorium where the reflected sounds dominate.[6] The inverse square law collapses. It is an area of the hall where sound comes from almost random directions, with apparently random changes of energy. (It isn't really random, but a reflection of the resonance characteristics of the hall.) On balance, these random variations in sound energy average out to the extent that proximity to the original sound source is irrelevant.

The diffuse field is a very important topic for many people. A considerable amount of work has been done over the years concerning modelling and measurements of diffuse field acoustics (e.g., Melchior 2009). But we will not discuss this any further here. This is a book on tabla, not auditorium design. As a musician who just comes into a venue for one night, there is nothing that you can do. If it is good, then that is great, if it is bad, well, that is just the way it is.

It is good to reiterate that diffuse fields are generally absent in open air performances.

CONCLUSION

As a practical matter, there are three fields in a typical concert or recording situation. They have tremendous impact on microphone selection and placement. These fields are defined according to their level of adherence to the inverse square law. The free field is defined as being that region where the law expresses itself. Once one goes out into the auditorium at some point, it will fail. This failure of the inverse square law is due to the direct sound from the instrument being overwhelmed by reverberant acoustical energy in the auditorium. In the other extreme, the inverse square law fails when one gets too close to the musical instrument. The source of such failure reflects the fact that the instrument is not a single point of infinitesimal size. As such, there are complex motions of air that do not conform to the production of sound.

In spite of their very different behaviours, there is no precise boundary between these three fields. As a practical matter, the near field of the tabla can be considered to extend roughly 1-2 feet from the tabla; while the boundary between the diffuse field and the free field is dependent upon the auditorium. By definition, the diffuse field starts at the point where the reverberant sound in the auditorium is equal to the direct sound coming from the instrument. Open air venues have no appreciable diffuse field.

WORKS CITED

Audio-Technica
undated   *ATR55*. Matsushita:Audio-Technica

Bader, Rolf, Malte Münster, Jan Richter, and Heiko Tim
2009   "Microphone Array Measurements of Drums and Flutes", *Musical Acoustics, Neurocognition and Psychology of Music: Current Research in Systematic Musicology, at the Institute of Musicology, University of Hamburg - Volume 25*. University of Hamburg. Austria: P. Lang.

Cremer, L.
1948   *Die wissenschaftlichen Grundlagen der Raumakustik*, Bd. 1. Hirzel-Verlag Stuttgart.

Haas, Helmut
1949   *Über den Einfluss eines Einfachechos auf die Hörsamkeit von Sprache;* Doctoral Dissertation.
1951   "Uber den Einfluss eines Einfachechos auf die Horsamkeit von Sprache", *Acustica*, 1, 49–58.

---

[6]There are several definitions that have precise meanings. The "diffuse field" is specified by the International Electrotechnical Commission (IEC 801-23-31) as, "Sound field which in a given region has statistically uniform energy density, for which the directions of propagation at any point are randomly distributed." The "diffuse field distance" is the point at which the diffuse field begins. The definition given by (IEC 801-31-17) says that it is; "That distance from the acoustic centre of a sound source at which the mean-square sound pressure of the direct sound, in a specified direction, is equal to the mean-square sound pressure of the reverberant sound in the room containing the source."

International Electrotechnical Commission
2022   *Glossary*. https://std.iec.ch/glossary. Accessed August 20, 2022.

Henry, Joseph.
1851   "On the limit of perceptibility of a direct and reflected sound", *Proceedings American Association Advancement of Science*. Vol. 5. 1851.

Langmuir, I., Schaefer, V. J., Ferguson, C. V., & Hennelly, E. F.
1944   "A study of binaural perception of the direction of a sound source", *OSRD Report 4079, PB number 31014*, Office of Technical Services, U. S. Department of Commerce.

Lauten Audio
2016   *Lauten 120 Small Diaphragm Condenser Microphone Pair*. CA: Lauten Audio.

Marshall Electronics
undated *MXL V67Q Stereo Manual*. El Segundo, CA:Marshal Electronics.

Melchior, F., Z.. Kuang, D. deVries, & S.Brix
2009   "Spherical Array Systems - On the Effect of Measurement Errors in Terms of Perceived Auralization Quality", *Proceedings of the NAG/DAGA*.

Wallach, H., Newman, E. B., & Rosenzweig, M. R.
1949   "The precedence effect in sound localization", The American Journal of Psychology, 62, 315–336.

CHAPTER 14
SOUND REINFORCEMENT

The process of augmenting the acoustic environment of the venue with an electronic sound system is known as sound reinforcement. To put it simply, the sound system allows yourself to be heard. For a musician, there is no other technical aspect of the stage as important as the sound system.

Proper sound has historically been the biggest obstacle to the development of major musical productions. In the *Natya Shastra* (circa 200 BCE), the sage Bharata warns against constructing theatres too large. One of the major reasons is that the performers cannot be adequately heard. (Bharata Muni, Natya Shastra, circa 200 BCE)

Today, we have electronic sound systems. It would be impossible to have a major performance today without one. In its simplest form, the function of the sound system is to pick up the weak sounds from the instruments, usually with a microphone, amplify it, and feed it out to the auditorium with the speakers. It actually does much more; so let us look at the system in greater detail.

We will begin with an overview of the system. An idealised sound reinforcement system is shown in Figure 14.1. We see that it is composed of the microphones, mixer, effects, equalizer, main amplifier, the main speakers, monitor amplifier, and monitor speakers. The function of the microphones is to pick up the sound waves and convert them into electrical signals. These signals must be blended together into a single signal to be sent to the auditorium. This process of blending the various signals and gently massaging the sound, is performed by the mixer. The mixer sends three different signals out; effects, main, and monitor. The main signal must be sent to the equalizer. This equalizer is designed to do two things 1) compensate for deficiencies in the complex chain of electronic and acoustical devices; and 2) to compensate for deficiencies in the hall acoustics. The equalized signal is then sent to the power amplifier(s) which boost the current to a point where it can power the speakers. The speaker's job is to convert the electrical energy into the sound that the audience hears. Do not forget that there is another chain of signals coming off of the mixer; this is our monitor chain. The function of the monitor is to allow the musicians on stage to be able to hear what each other is doing. The third signal coming off the mixer is sent to the effects.

This system is called an "electro-acoustic chain" (Courtney 1986). The above example is just a basic schematic, for there are many variations. In some cases, major components are merged together. For instance, it is common to see the mixer, equalizer, and power amplifier merged into one device. This is called a "powered mixer". It is also common to find the monitor speakers and the monitor power amplifiers merged into one unit. These are called a "powered monitors". Conversely, it is also common to find these sections further divided. For instance, large shows rarely use a single power amplifier, but use banks of amplifiers that feed massive arrays of speakers. The signals which feed such arrays are commonly processed by limiters, crossovers, and a host of other specialised devices.

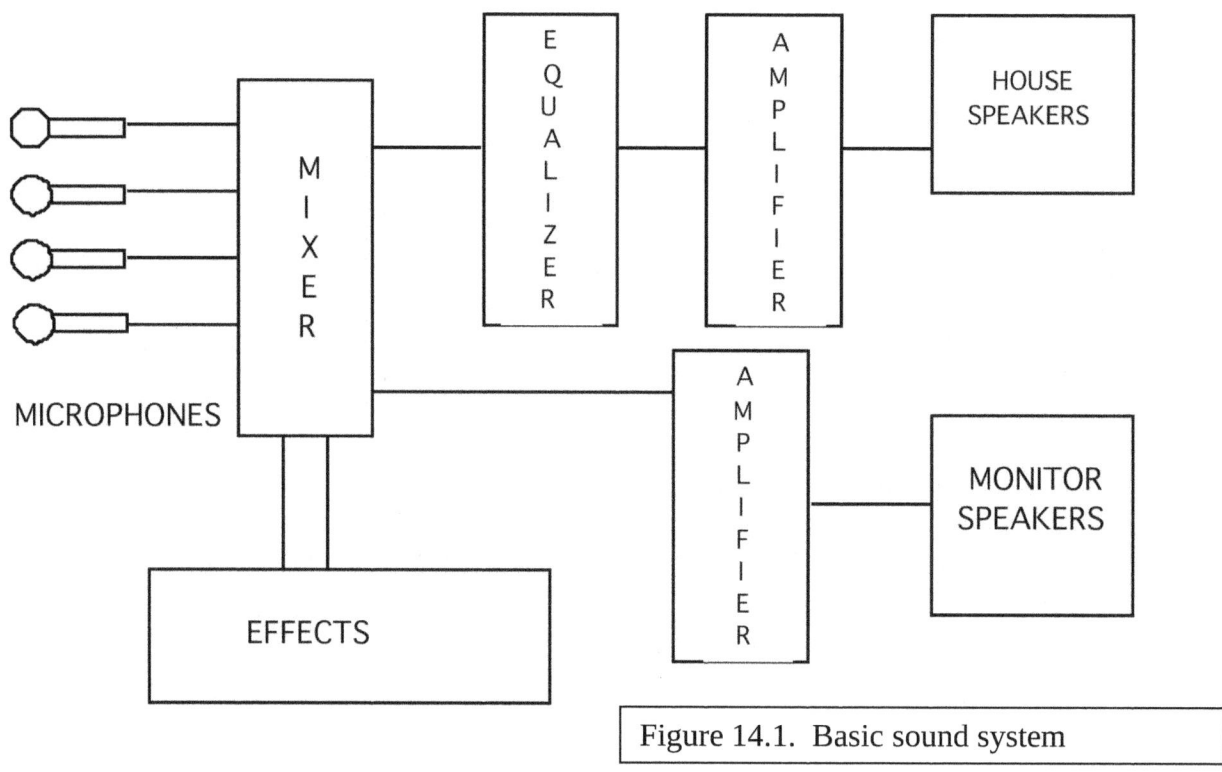

Figure 14.1. Basic sound system

Microphone - The microphone is the first stage of our electro-acoustic chain. The function of which is to convert acoustic information into electrical information. This process is referred to as transduction (Stark 1996:5). Microphones have numerous characteristics which must be properly understood. The three characteristics that we will look at are the mechanics of the transducer, the pickup pattern, and the method by which the microphone connects to the mixer. Let us first look at the process of transduction.

Microphones can transduce the sound in any of several ways. There are the carbon, piezoelectric, dynamic, ribbon, and condenser approaches. However, in this work we will only discuss the dynamic and the condenser. As a tabla player these are the only technologies that we are likely to use on the stage.

The dynamic microphone is one of the oldest mic transducers in existence. In spite of its age, it has very good sound quality, and remains one of the most popular approaches to microphone design. It is especially popular for the stage work. The most common implementation is called the "moving coil" microphone. In this design, a small lightweight coil is attached to a diaphragm. As the diaphragm moves, it propels the coil through a magnetic field, thus generating a small current. The principal is very simple, but the actual design of these microphones is very sophisticated.

In the majority of cases, your stage microphone will be a dynamic microphone. They have exceptional durability and a good sound. There is only one inherent weakness to the dynamic microphone; they have poor high frequency response. However, modern materials and advanced designs have largely overcome this problem.

The condenser microphone is another popular design. It is the preferred technology for studio work, but not as popular on the stage. It consists of a diaphragm that has a static charge. This conductive diaphragm is situated very near a fixed plate which is also charged. The membrane moves back and forth near the stationary plate; therefore, the entire system resembles a condenser (capacitor) with continually varying capacitance. This produces an extremely low-level signal which must be amplified by a small circuit located in the microphone itself. The condenser microphone is the most complicated of any of the commonly available microphones. Early designs were very delicate; however, modern designs are robust enough for stage use. Their strongest advantage is that they have truly superb high frequency characteristics. This advantage has made them very popular.

The condenser microphone requires a source of power to operate. There are two approaches as to how this power is to be supplied. Older designs required a small cell (battery) to be placed in them. Unfortunately, these mics tended to self destruct due to leakage of the cells. A much more practical approach was to have the mixer supply the power. In decades past this was problematic, because most stage mixers could not supply this power. Today, the universal support of phantom power has eliminated this problem.

So how well does the condenser microphone work with tabla? There are very few high frequency components to the sound of tabla; therefore, condenser microphones do not really have an opportunity to shine. But since the problems associated with condenser microphones have largely been addressed, they have become satisfactory mics for both stage and studio. But there is one thing to consider. Condenser microphones are generally designed for studio work. As such, they often have a much poorer off axis rejection than mics specifically designed for stage.

Off axis rejection? What does this mean? This brings us to the second aspect of stage mics. We discussed the method of transduction; but we also need to consider the pickup pattern.

The concept of the pickup pattern is simple. All microphones have an inherent direction; this is called the axis.[1] But not all microphones behave in the same way around this axis. The manner in which a microphone picks up sound is referred to as the "pickup pattern"

There are three general pickup patterns. If a microphone has an equal sensitivity to sound coming from all directions, then it is said to be omnidirectional. If it is sensitive to sound coming only from the front axis, then it said to be directional. Sometimes microphones have equal sensitivity from both front and back but reduced sensitivity from the other sides; this is called bidirectional, or "figure-8". These three basic patterns; omnidirectional, bidirectional, and directional will now be discussed in greater detail.

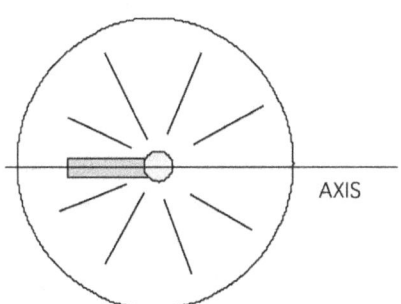

The omnidirectional microphone has a response which is equal in all directions. This is represented in Figure 14.2. These microphones have excellent fidelity, all at a fairly low cost. However, their inability to isolate individual instruments and their tendency to feedback, limits their usefulness on stage. They have some use for dramatic presentations, but are nearly useless for musical performances. (The omnidirectional mic was briefly mentioned in the last chapter.)

Figure 14.2. The omnidirectional microphone

---

[1] In the next few pages, we adopt a convention of having the axis running along the same axis as the body of the mic. This need not be the case in real life. The axis of the capsule, not the body, determines the microphone's performance. Frequently, this is perpendicular to the axis of the body. Always be attentive to the orientation of the capsule within the headbasket (wind-screen).

The bidirectional microphone is different from both the omni and the directional mic. It has a pickup pattern which is roughly equal in two directions (Figure 14.3). However it tapers off drastically as one moves perpendicular to the axis. The most common bidirectional microphone is the ribbon microphone. Bidirectional microphones offer only a limited utility on stage, because they are prone to feedback.

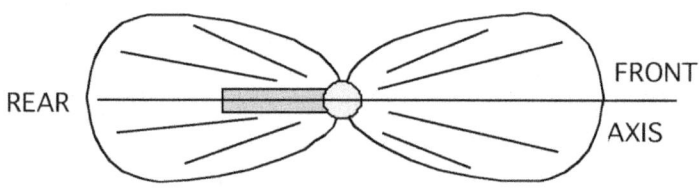

Figure 14.3. The bidirectional microphone

Directional microphones are the most common stage mics. Their maximum sensitivity is directly on the axis. They are simple to operate. One simply has to point it at the source of the sound, and they will work nicely (Figure 14.4)

One thing to keep in mind, is that the directionality of any directional microphone is frequency-dependent. It still exhibits a degree of off axis sensitivity at the low frequencies. Middle and higher frequencies, on the other hand, tend to be rejected when they come off-axis. This gives rise to something called the "proximity effect". Proximity effect is a boost in the bass response which occurs as you get close to the source of the sound. It is not necessary for us to go into detail as to why directional microphones exhibit this characteristic. It is sufficient to realise that this does occur, and will affect the overall tone of your instrument. Therefore, if you are engaging in any close-micing, and the sound appears excessive on the bass side, try backing the microphone off a few inches. This will usually take care of the problem. However, due to the general tendency to boost the bass anyway, proximity effect will not be a problem for the tabla.

All directional microphones do not have the same response pattern. Terms like cardioid, super cardioid, hypercardioid, and the shotgun, are thrown about loosely, often overlapping. Each has its own character. However, a complete discussion is beyond the scope of this book. Check other sources for greater detail.

There is another characteristic of microphones which is extremely important; that is the method by which it connects to the mixer. There are two common forms. One of which is called "single-ended", also referred to as "unbalanced"; and the other is called the "balanced" connection, or in technical terms a "differential" connection.

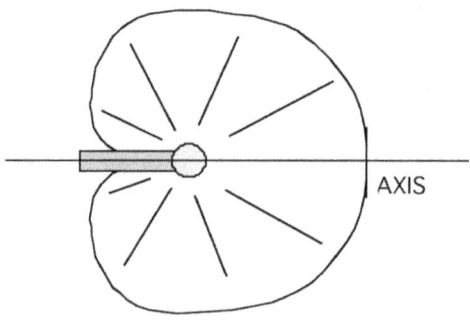

Figure 14.4. The cardioid directional microphone

The difference between a balanced and an unbalance connection is its ability to handle noise. By "noise" we are not referring to sound, but electromagnetic interference from the environment. The balanced connection gives us an ability to reject interference which an unbalanced connection cannot.

We can tell whether our system is balanced or unbalanced by looking at the connector. A microphone that uses a balanced connection uses an XLR connector. (Figure 14.5). Conversely, the common unbalanced connector is a 1/4" plug shown in Figure 14.6.

The 1/4" TS connector has been a standard for audio for over a century. The central conductor is the signal carrier, and the outer sheath is the ground. This type of plug was once common for telephone switchboards. This style of plug is generally referred to as being "TS" or "Tip-Shield". The simple quarter inch connector of this pattern, is inherently an unbalanced connection. Today, this connector, or its 3.5mm cousin, is found only in the lowest quality microphones.

Figure 14.5. XLR Connectors (balanced)

Figure 14.6. 1/4" TS Connectors (unbalanced)

Undoubtedly the "Rolls Royce" of microphone connectors is the XLR connector (Figure 14.5). The XLR connector has four conductors. There is a "plus", "minus", "ground", and "shield". The terms plus and minus are fairly arbitrary, and do not actually represent any standard phase. The shield and the ground are obvious. The separation of the shield from the ground, allows the XLR connection to support a variety of grounding topologies. This reduces the likelihood of ground loops developing. In the event that ground loops do occur, the balanced configuration gives us tools to break these loops (Stark, 1996)

Caution should be used when purchasing cables or mics with XLR connectors. For many years the XLR connector has been considered the mark of superior engineering; but some unscrupulous manufacturers have misused this reputation. Manufacturers have been known to use the XLR in an unbalanced configuration by hardwiring one of the signal carriers to ground. Another consideration is that sometimes the shield and the ground are hardwired together. This is not be a major problem in most configurations. However, this may leave one susceptible to "ground loops" (60/50 Hz hum induced through improper signal grounding), in some grounding topologies.

In spite of these caveats, a properly implemented XLR connection in a balanced configuration, is the best way to connect your microphone to the mixer.

I have not wanted to talk about particular brands and models; however, I must make an exception here. There are three microphones that I would like to discuss; the Shure SM-57, the Shure SM-58, and the Shure Beta 56.

The SM-57 and SM-58 are shown below. The SM-57 is shown in the left side of Figure 14.7 and the SM-58 is shown in the right side. These two microphones are considered the basic workhorse of the stage, and have been for over 60 years. Since they are so common, it is in your best interest to be familiar with them. They are extremely flexible, and very reasonably priced. Although the SM-58 is primarily a vocal microphone and the SM-57 is primarily an instrumental microphone, they are general enough in operation to be used for any application. The first thing that you will notice about them is that they do not have a switch. A non-musician friend of mine once remarked that it seemed strange that this feature was absent. I made it very clear that the lack of a switch was itself a professional feature. When you are setting up a program with a dozen microphones, you have many things to worry about. You do not need the added duty of having to run around, and see which switches are on or off.

Figure 14.7. Shure SM-57 (Shure 2006) and Shure SM-58 (Shure undated)

Undoubtedly the strongest asset of these microphones is their ruggedness. Once I was away in another city doing a performance. At that time, I had all of my microphones in a leather bag (bad habit), and I ran over my microphone bag with the car. This bag had different microphones of different costs and styles. My SM-57s and SM-58s came out with nothing more than bent headbaskets (windscreens), while my other microphones were a total loss. Although it is not the fanciest microphone, you will never go wrong micing your tabla with an SM-57 in stage situations.

There is one other stage microphone that is worth mentioning. This is the Shure Beta 56 (Figure 14.8). It is not a ubiquitous microphone like the SM-57 or the SM-58, but it is well worth getting for your own use. It has a good sound, an amazingly low profile, and the legendary Shure indestructibility. The only problem that I have encounter is that there is sometimes an inadequate clearance between the XLR connector and the screw mount. This problem is easily addressed simply by switching to a different XLR cable.

Microphone Stands - Most people do not give much attention to microphone stands. It is perceived as such an ordinary thing that one tends to take it for granted. Unfortunately, as I have worked various venues over the years, I have found that improper stands is one of the most common problems. The issue is that one plays tabla sitting on the ground, while many venues presume that artists will be standing. One very quickly learns that if you are going to play tabla, you had better carry your own stands! I have found four acceptable stands; these are shown in Figure 14.9.

There is one issue with microphone stands that one needs to be careful about. There are different standards as to how the stand connects to the microphone/microphone clip. In the old days, this was not an issue, because you simply bought what was locally available. However after globalisation, everything is available everyplace. Therefore, competing standards is something that you have to be aware of.

There are two common threads; there is the 5/8" and the 3/8". The 5/8' is the standard in the US for microphone stands while the 3/8th" is the European standard. These are shown in Figure 14.10. Adapters are available which allow one to change from one thread to another.

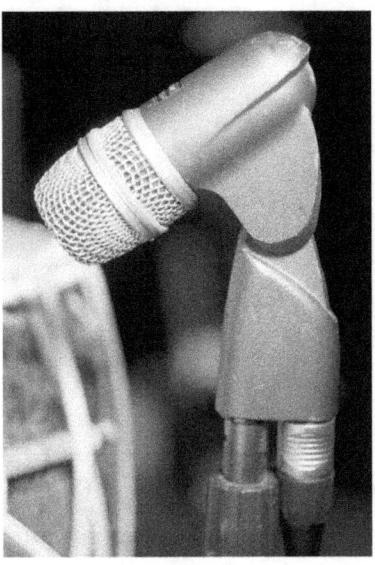

Figure 14.8. Shure Beta 56 (Shure 2005)

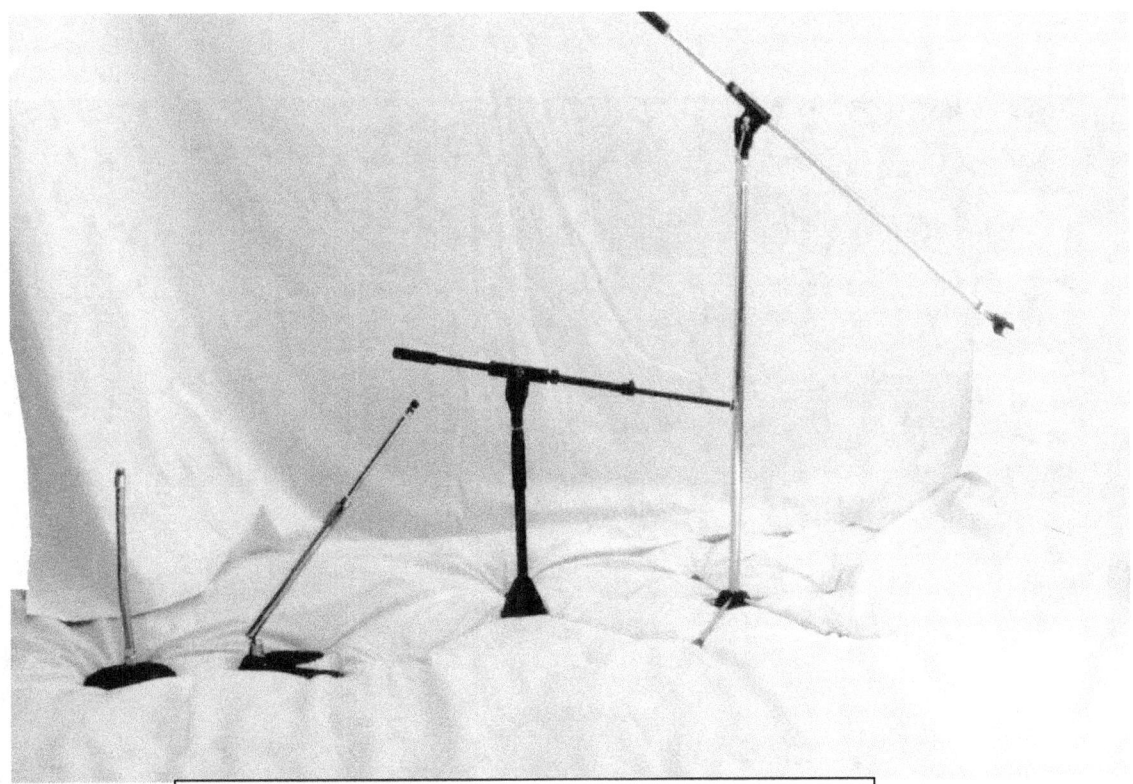

Figure 14.9. Microphone stands for the tabla

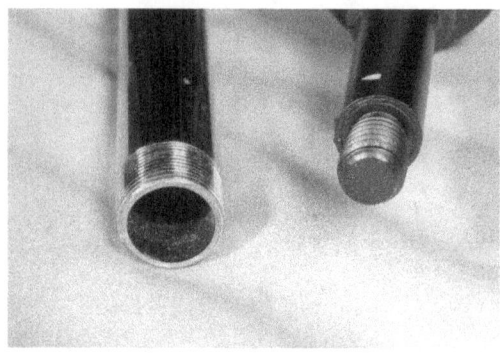

Figure 14.10. Different threads for stands. Lft.) 5/8" Rt.) 3/8"

<u>The Mixer</u> - The mixer is the most important artistic section of the sound reinforcement system. The other sections are largely technical, but the mixer is the sound man's (or woman's) paint palette. This is where the artistry of the sound-person really shines.

There are several jobs which are performed at the mixer. The main one is to balance the various musical signals until the overall artistic effect is achieved. However, the tone of the various instruments as well as the overall tone of the performance is controlled from here.

Mixers may be called different things throughout the English speaking world. Although "mixer" is the most common, very large versions may be referred to as the "board" or "console", while the largest of all may be referred to as a "desk".

My own mixer is a Soundcraft Signature 22; it is shown in Figure 14.11. However, I do not want to direct the discussion to any particular model, therefore we will deal with an idealised mixer shown in Figure 14.12.

The first step to understanding an analogue mixer, is to understand the overall layout. In particular, we need to be familiar with the flow of the signals. A general pattern for the signal flow is shown in Figure 14.13. Virtually all mixers, from the simplest to the most complex, tend to follow this basic pattern. There are three overall sections. There are the channels, the buses, and an area for miscellaneous functions.

Figure 14.11. Author's mixer (Soundcraft undated)

Ch. 14. Sound Reinforcement

Bus - Let us start by discussing the bus. The overall topology of the bus is very simple, and is shown in Figure 14.14.

The term "bus" is derived from the term "busbar". Historically the busbar was a very large, low impedance bar, rod, or heavy gauge wire. In old analogue electronics, they were used for grounding and power distribution. The term "busbar" is in reference to the large bars that are suspended from the celings of buses, and run down the isles, upon which the standing passengers grab hold. Since the various devices that attached to the bars are analogous to the people on the bus, it acquired the name "busbar".

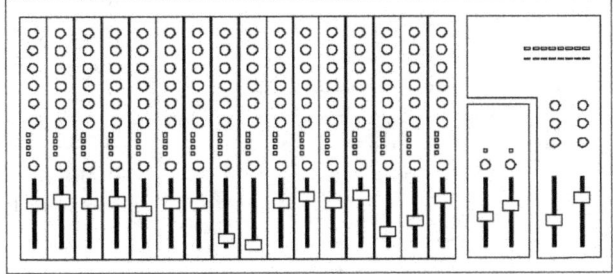

Figure 14.12. Idealised mixer

The bus is interesting in several ways. The most fundamental is that this topology does not have any inherent input or output. A signal may be placed upon the bus at any point, and similarly, it may be extracted from any point.

In an analogue mixer, the function of the various buses is to aggregate the signals from their various channels, and prepare them to be sent out. Common ways of extracting the signal from the buses are the master effects send out, submaster, and the master.

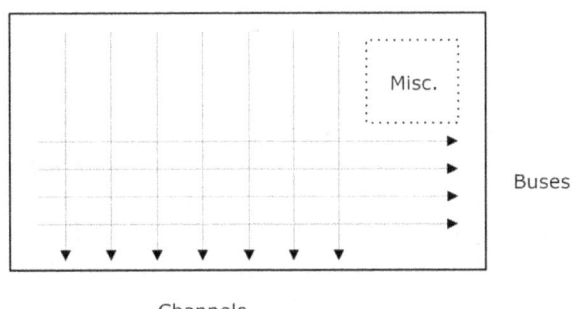

Figure 14.13. General signal flow in a mixer

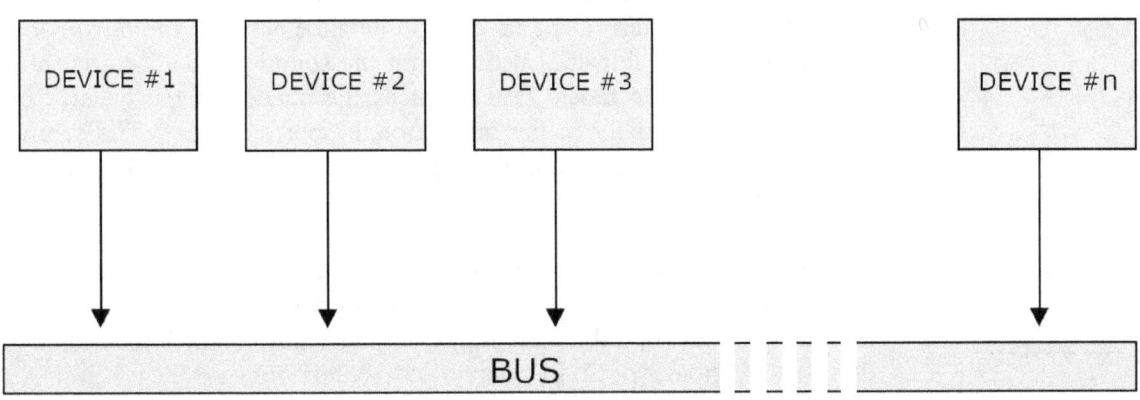

Figure 14.14. Bus topology

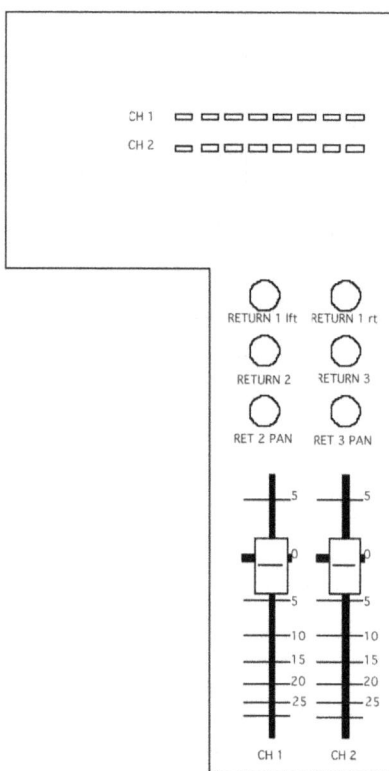

Figure 14.15. The master faders

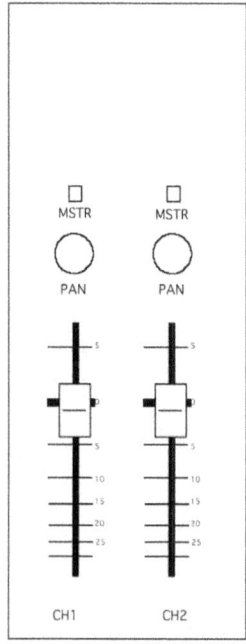

Figure 14.16. The submaster

Master Section/ Misc. - The master section and its adjacent misc section is the heart of the mixer. It extracts signals from the master buses, and misc. sources, mixes them, and outputs them. In the idealised mixer shown in Figure 14.12, it is represented by the inverted "L" shaped block at the far right hand portion of the mixer. This is blown up and shown in Figure 14.15.

As the name implies, the master section is hardwired to accept signals which are placed upon the master bus. This is usually two buses, one for the left channel and one for the right. However, in some large mixers there may be more.

The master section has a number sections, but the master faders are the most important. In a performance situation, these two faders control the overall sound to the venue. In some smaller setups, the functions may be split such that one fader controls the house while the other controls the stage monitors.

Other Functions in the Master / Misc. Sections - The master and misc. sections have a number of other functions and controls that we need not go into here. For instance, there may be some type of multi-band equalizer, master effects sends, effects returns, headphone levels, foldback microphone inputs, USB inputs, WiFi controls, bluetooth controls, or any of a variety of other functions. The possibilities are too great to go into them here, for they may change from brand to brand, or model to model.

Submasters - Submaster buses are very important to a mixer; they are second only to the master bus. In our idealised mixer shown in Figure 14.12, it is represented by the small square that is second from the right. It is blown up and shown in Figure 14.16.

The value of the submaster to the tabla player is easily demonstrated. Let us say that you are onstage with a two microphone setup to mic your tabla. Let us further say that the left and right hand microphone channels feed into a submaster. Once the correct balance between the *dayan* and the *bayan* has been established, at that point the sound person can control both drums with a single fader. This reduces the chance of the balance being thrown off accidentally in the middle of the performance. The submaster allows us to take very complex mixes, and use only a few faders to control everything.

The submasters are flexible and can be used for other purposes as well. It is very common to use it to feed the monitors. (We will discuss the monitors later.) The submaster may also be used for recording. This will be discussed in greater detail in Chapter 15 - *Recording*.

Ch. 14. Sound Reinforcement

Channel Controls and the Signal Chain - The channel controls are where most of the artistic decisions have to be made. In order to understand how channel controls work we must familiarise ourself with concept of the signal chain.

The signal chain represents a topology which is fundamentally different from that of the bus. This is shown diagrammatically in Figure 14.17. Unlike the bus, the signal chain has well defined inputs and outputs. The output of one device will feed directly into the input of the next device. This will continue through n number of devices, until the end of the chain is reached.

Figure 14.18 shows our idealised channel control; let us look at the various sections.

The top knob is referred to as the trim. This is the first stage for controlling the levels. Its purpose is to adjust the level to get the signal "in the ballpark". This is necessary, because different devices have widely varying signal levels. The trim brings the signal to some comfortable level where the next stage of electronics can handle it.

The next three controls are the equalizer. We already mentioned that the master section may have a multi-band EQ as well. The equalizer in the master/misc. section is generally for compensating for deficiencies in the venue or speakers; while the equalizers in the channel strips are generally used for artistic effect.

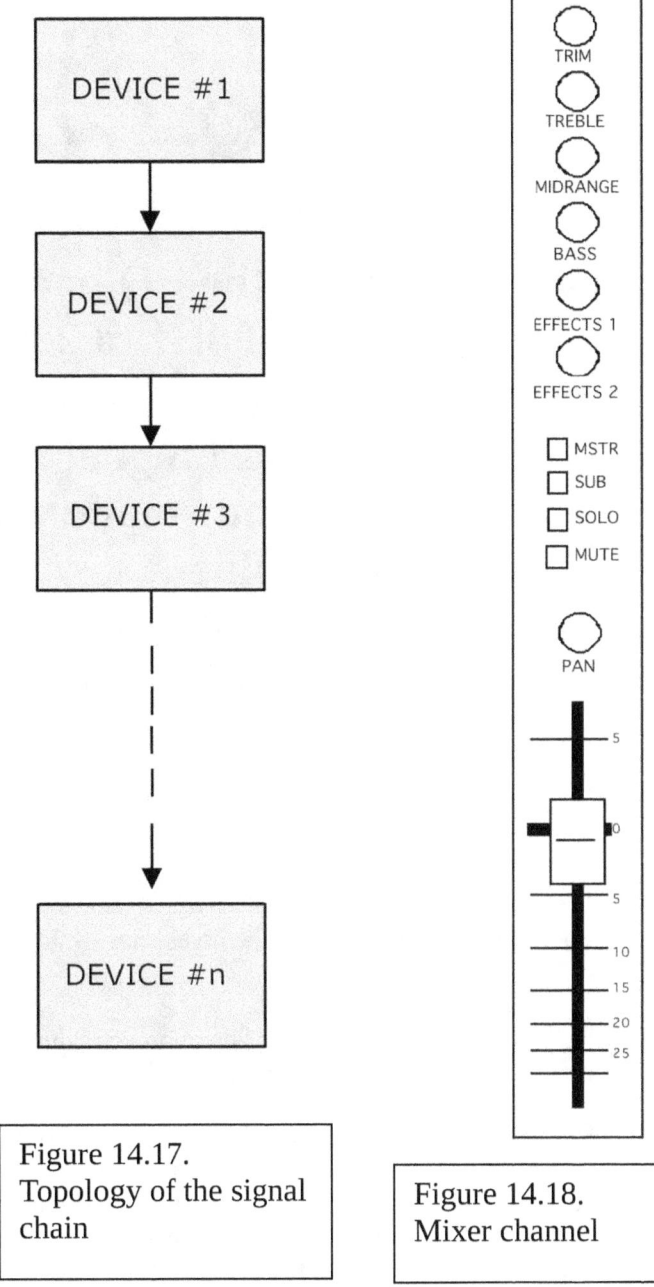

Figure 14.17. Topology of the signal chain

Figure 14.18. Mixer channel

The next bank in Figure 14.18 shows our effects-send. The purpose of this is to send signals to the aforementioned effects buses. This particular example has two, but there may be any number. The effects-send may be tailored to perform a variety of functions; but the most common is to send a signal to a reverberator. In fact, many times this will be marked specifically "reverb". The effects-send may also be used to send a signal to the stage monitor amplifier.

The next group of buttons are commonly referred to a channel-assign. The function of the channel-assign is to determine what happens to the signal from the channel control. The illustration here is a very simple example; it allows you to assign this channel to either the submaster bus or the master bus. You may decide not to send the signal to either, or you could send it to both.

EQ SECRET FOR TABLA!!
Boost the EQ in a band that extends from 100Hz to 200Hz to bring out the bayan. Furthermore, if you have the boost higher at 180Hz than 100Hz, then your modulations will be richer and bolder.

There are additional controls as well. These include solo, mute, and pan controls. These are all very important, but there seems to be no aspects of their operation which is of particular importance to the tabla.

Digital Mixers - The digital mixer is an approach which is rising in popularity. The analogue mixer is still the most popular, but the digital mixer deserves some discussion.

It is always said the "form follows function". But many times something becomes so ingrained into culture that forms are retained, even though they may not be the most compatible with newer technologies. This is definitely the case with digital mixers. They still retain the overall layout of traditional analogue mixers, even though there is no reason for them to do so. However, in some situations there is a break with the customary forms.

The remote controlled mixer is the most radical break from a traditional mixer layout. The traditional analogue mixer does not work very well with very large venues. Everything that is important happens on the stage. But this is the worst place for the sound-person to run the sound. The ideal location for the sound person is in the audience. But locating the sound-person a great distance from the stage has very obvious disadvantages due to long cable lengths.

Remote controlled mixers have a tremendous advantage in large venues. These are usually controlled by some type of computer tablet. Since the sound-person is no longer tethered to one position by cables, they are free to move around the auditorium with their tablet and make the necessary adjustments. There are a number of remote controlled mixers on the market. One example is the Soundcraft Ui24R (Soundcraft undated). This is shown in Figure 14.19.

Ch. 14. Sound Reinforcement

Figure 14.19. Remote controlled mixer (Soundcraft Ui24R)

External Effects / Reverb - There are a variety external effects that may be used in a typical Indian performance. Generally we need to talk about reverberation, compression, and equalization. Of these, equalization is so important that we will discuss it separately.

The digital delay / reverb (reverberation) is the most standard. The function of which is to add richness to the overall sound. Today, these units generally do more than mere reverberation; therefore they are more often referred to as "digital effects". One example is shown in Figure 14.20.

The amount of reverb used is dependent upon the size of the venue. Large auditoriums are naturally reverberant, and the addition of further reverberation makes everything sound muddy and indistinct. The only time that one might wish to add any reverb for a tabla would be in small intimate house gatherings. For any medium sized venue, the normal procedure is to add reverb to the main instrument or voice, but leave it off the tabla. Reverberation is not as complimentary to the tabla, as it is for other instruments.

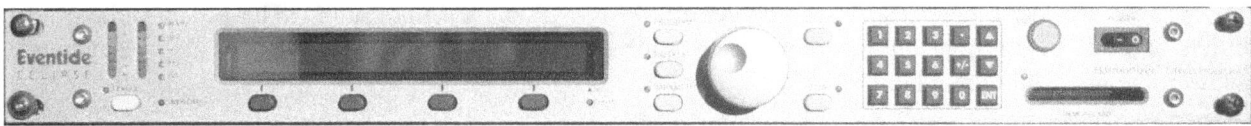

Figure 14.20. Digital effects unit (Eventide Eclipse)(Eventide 2018)

page 203

The compressor is another ubiquitous effect. A compressor may be thought of as being a sophisticated automatic gain control. They may be good for some instruments, but not the tabla. In stage performances, they are more likely to cause you problems than to help you. They increase the likelihood of feedback.

In passing, we should mention that there are a number of other effects on the market. There are harmonisers, subharmonic synthesisers, exciters, and a host of others. These are not commonly used, but if your artistic vision includes them, go for it.

Equalization - Equalization is very important for any live performance. We showed the equalizer as a stand alone unit schematically Figure 14.1. An example is shown in Figure 14.21. In an absence of a stand alone unit, one may use the on-board EQ of our mixer. Although this is very important for getting a good sound, there are no real issues which are specific to the tabla. Therefore we will not go into them further.

Figure 14.21. Graphic equalizer

Amplifier - The amplifier takes the line level signal and produces a signal of sufficient power to drive the speakers. There are numerous issues that come into play in our amplifier. Fortunately, most of these can be ignored. There is just one area which cannot be ignored; power.

If we review the basic setup as shown in Figure 14.1, we see that there are two limbs of amplification. One of these is for the monitors, and one for the house. They fulfil two different functions, so there will be very different power requirements.

The monitor amplifier does not have to be very powerful. For a classical Indian performance 75 to 150 watts would be more than enough.

The house system should be significantly more powerful. However, it is impossible to say exactly how much. A small room would probably do quite well with 100-200 watts while a very large outdoor venue would run into the thousands. The numbers are greatly affected by room acoustics, speaker efficiency, the kind of music you play (i.e., how much deep bass you have), and how loud you want the music to be. In general, an amplifier rated in the hundreds of watts is a ballpark figure.

There are many other aspects of power amplifiers which are important. These can include such things as built in limiting, output impedance, number of channels, amplifier classes, etc,. But it isn't appropriate to go into these here.

Ch. 14. Sound Reinforcement

<u>Speakers</u> - The speakers are some of the most important pieces of your sound system. Good speakers go a long way towards making good sound. A basic speaker is shown in Figure 14.22. We see that in its simplest form, we have a large magnet with a coil around it. This coil is free to move back and forth over the magnet. This coil is attached to a cone made of paper, plastic, or some other light-weight material. There must also be an enclosure to direct the sound into the audience.

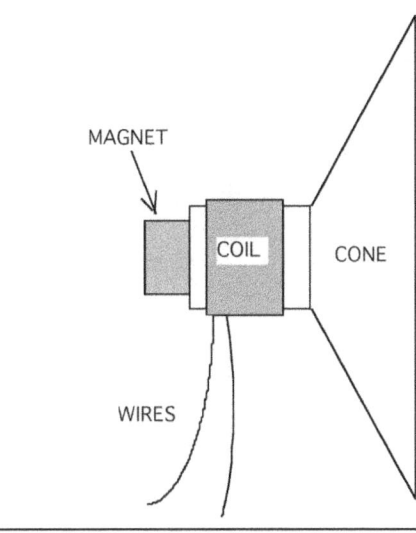

Figure 14.22. Basic speaker

If you are buying speakers for your personal gear, and you only play tabla in classical situations (i.e., no deep bass)

YOU DON'T NEED SPEAKERS THAT GO BELOW 80HZ!!!

Going down further is nice on paper, but it is terrible in real world situations. Extending below 70-80 Hz increases the size, decreases the efficiency, increases the cost, and more importantly, it greatly increases the weight! You will have to lug this from venue to venue for a long time; it will really take a toll on your back!

Microphone / Speaker Arrangement - We should talk about arranging the speakers and mics. Microphone arrangements and microphone choices were discussed at great length in Chapter 13; but we did not deal with the topic of their relationship to the speakers. This is a very important consideration in the setup phase of a program.

The most important thing to remember is to not have the axis of your microphone pointed anywhere near the axis of your speakers. This is illustrated in Figure 14.23. This arrangement is very prone to feedback.

A better arrangement is shown in Figure 14.24.

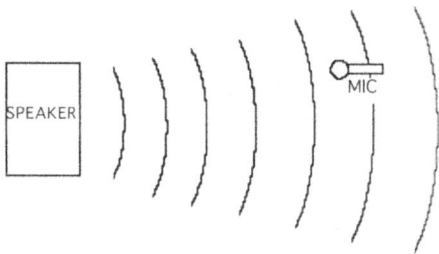

Figure 14.23. Improper speaker / mic arrangement

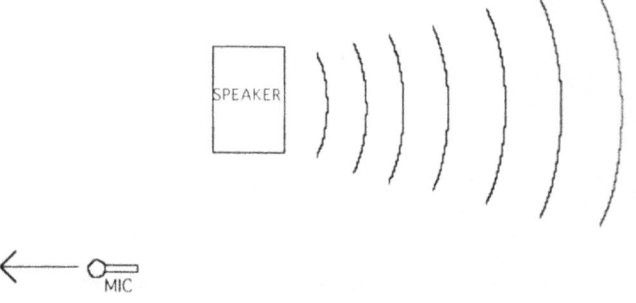

Figure 14.24. Proper speaker / mic arrangement

Speaker stands are very important. Low frequencies have the ability to move around objects, but high frequencies do not. Therefore, you should raise the speakers to a position where everyone in the audience can see them. A line-of-sight is an indication that there are no obstructions. A typical speaker and stand is shown in Figure 14.25.

Portable Systems - Any serious musician will have a portable system. This will vary tremendously from artist to artist according to budget and one's artistic and technical inclinations. Such systems are usually designed to support small to medium sized venues.

The most important investment for your system is going to be the cases (Figure 14.26). Do not forget that your cases are your best insurance against damage. Any seasoned professional will tell you that transporting equipment back and forth between venue and home takes a tremendous toll. Typically, you will have sunk thousands of dollars into your equipment, so it makes no sense to try and save money on the cases.

Figure 14.27 is a typical portable system. Everything is integrated into a single unit. It contains an 8-channel mixer, graphic EQ, and two power amplifiers. There is a front cover to protect everything during transportation. There are also the speakers and stands shown in Figure 14.25. The microphones are Shure SM-57's, SM-58s, (Figure 14.7), and a Shure Beta 56 (Figure 14.8). (There is no need to go into details, because your system will probably be different.) All in all, it is a very basic yet flexible system, that will handle most of the programs that a musician has to give. In the situations where such a system is inadequate, one is invariably dealing with a high budget program. Therefore, renting more equipment should not be a problem.

Ch. 14. Sound Reinforcement

Figure 14.25. Speaker and stand

Figure 14.26. Cases

Figure 14.27 Integrated powered mixer (Soundcraft 2003)

FINAL WORDS ABOUT SOUND SYSTEMS

R.T.F.M.!!!

WORKS CITED

Bharata Muni (translated by a board of scholars)
200 BC (circa) *Natyashastra Shastra* Sri Satguru Publications, Delhi.

Courtney, David
1986   "New Sounds from Old Sources", *Experimental Musical Instruments*. Vol II, No. 4, pg.10-15.

Eventide Inc
2018   *Eventide Eclipse User Manual*. Little Ferry, NJ Eventide Inc.

Lord, William H.
1991   *Stagecraft 1; A Complete guide to Backstage Work*, 2nd Edition. Meriwether Publishing Ltd. Colorado Springs, CO.

Oxford University Press.
1937   *Oxford Universal English Dictionary on Historical Principals. Volume 4 Sol - Tol*, Doubleday, Doran and Co, 1937.

Shure Inc.
2006   *Model SM57 User Guide*. Niles, IL:Shure Inc.
2005   *Model Beta 56 A User Guide*. Niles, IL:Shure Inc.
undated   *SHURE- SM58 - Vocal Microphone*. Eppingen, Germany: Shure Europe GmbH.

Soundcraft
2003   *Great Sound Made Easy -Gigrack*. Northridge, CA: Harman International Industries Limited. Northridge, CA: Harman International Industries Limited.
2017   *Soundcraft Ui Series User Guide v1.1- For Soundcraft Ui24R*. Northridge, CA: Harman International Industries Limited.
undated   *Soundcraft Signature User Guide: For Soundcraft Signature 16, 22 & 22MTK*. Hertfordshire, UK: Harman International Industries Limited.

Stark, Scott Hunter
1996 *Live Sound Reinforcement*, Mix books, Emeryville, CA.

CHAPTER 15
RECORDING

This chapter deals with the topic of recording the tabla. This chapter is primarily oriented to the practicing tabla musician or music student who is just wanting to get started in recording. Most of the important information has already been covered. Microphone placements were discussed in Chapter 13 - *Acoustic Fields & Microphones,* and the basics of transduction and the electronic chain were discussed in Chapter 14 - *Sound Reinforcement.* Nevertheless, there are a few loose ends which need to be addressed.

LINEARITY

The engineering of recording equipment has been dominated for over a century by the concept of linearity. In simple terms, this means that whatever goes into our electro-acoustic chain should come out without being distorted. We can equate the engineering concept of "linearity" with the audiophile's concept of "high fidelity". There are two main areas for which we look for a linear response; one of these is in frequency response, and the other is in our signal transfer characteristics.

<u>Frequency Response</u> - We can visualise the concept of a linear frequency response with the following example. Let us imagine a "black box". At this point it isn't important what the box does. We are only concerned that it has an input and an output. To this black box we will input a pink noise signal. Pink noise is a random signal which has an equal amount of energy per octave.[1] A black box that is perfectly engineered, will have the output of the black box the same as our input (Figure 15.1). Hence this device is said to have good linearity as per its frequency response. If we graph the frequency response, it will look like a straight line covering the audio spectrum (Figure 15.2).

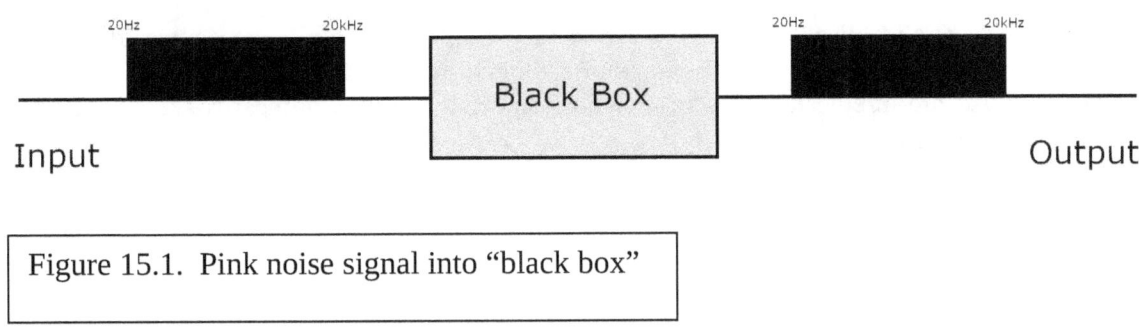

Figure 15.1. Pink noise signal into "black box"

---

[1] Pink noise should not be confuse with white noise. Conceptually they are both very similar; however pink noise has an equal amount of energy per octave, while white noise has an equal amount of energy per Hz. Pink noise is much closer to the way that we hear sound. The lions' share of frequencies are located at the upper octave of our range of hearing (i.e., 10,000 Hz -20,000Hz), but with very few frequencies in the lowest octave 20Hz-40Hz. Due to this imbalance, white noise sounds very treble heavy to our ears, while pink noise sounds more balanced.

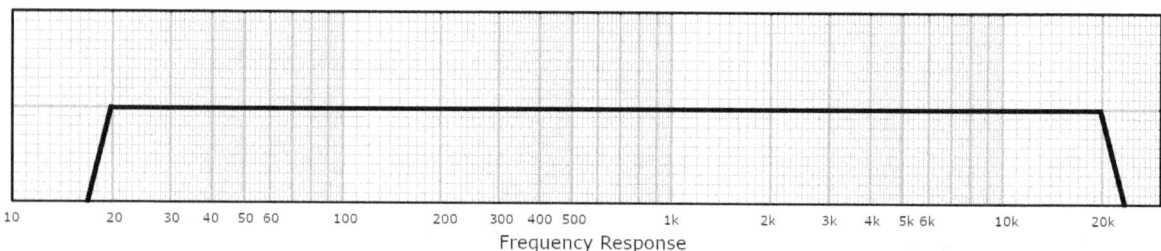

Figure 15.2. Perfectly linear frequency response across the audio spectrum

Signal Transfer - Signal transfer characteristics are another area where engineers look for a linear response. The example below is a black box to which we input a signal. In an ideal device, the output will follow the input (Figure 15.3). If we graph the output as a function of the input, an ideal black box has a linear signal transfer function as shown in Figure 15.4.

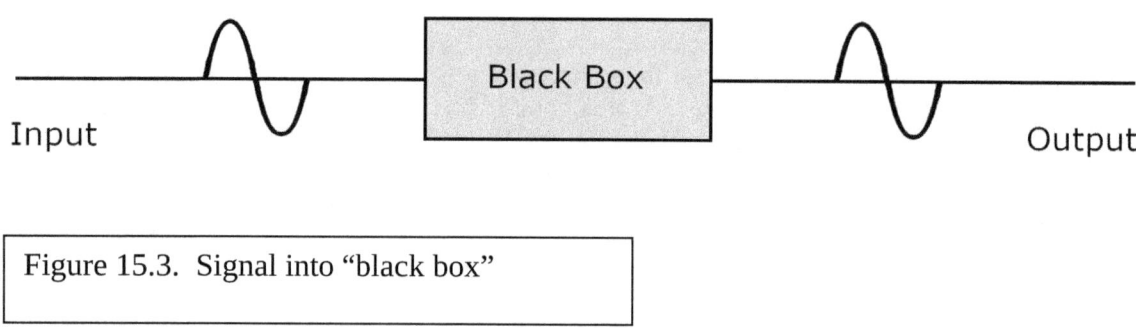

Figure 15.3. Signal into "black box"

These last two were idealised examples. In the real world, completely linear devices do not exist. But we do not always want them. The entire nature of analogue signal processing, and by extension their software equivalents, are predicated on there being some type of nonlinearity. We use these nonlinearities for artistic effect.

Let us change the subject.

VACUUM TUBES

The vacuum tube, more correctly known as the thermionic valve, is very important to modern recording. This is often not appreciated by people outside of the field. Most will automatically equate it with obsolete technology.

Ch. 15. Recording

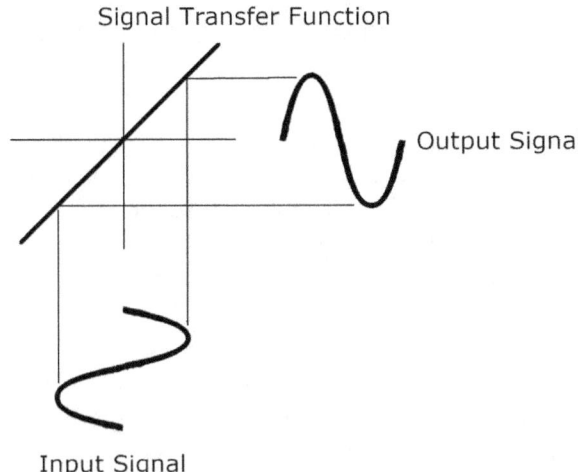

Figure 15.4. A perfectly linear signal transfer function.

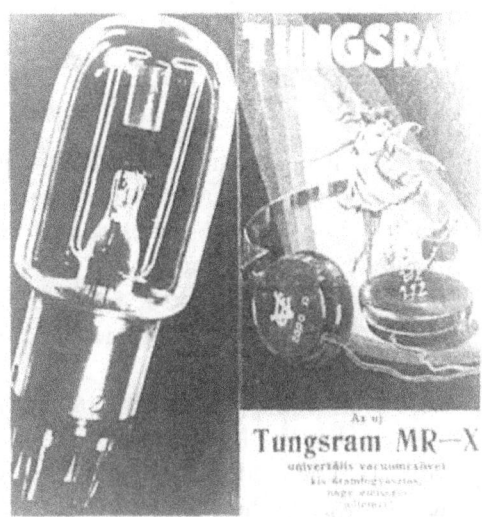

Figure 15.5. Early vacuum tube (1917)

The tube has an interesting history. It was invented at the turn of the 20th century. The earliest form was a simple diode that was invented by John Ambrose Fleming in 1904. However, its simplicity limited its utility. This was enhanced by Lee De Forest, who added a grid to control the electron flow; this was in 1906. Within a couple of decades, it became a ubiquitous item (Figure 15.5). It was a revolutionary device which created the modern field of electronics.

But the vacuum tube was far from ideal. It had numerous practical problems, such as extreme inefficiency and a limited lifespan. More fundamentally, it had poor poor signal transfer characteristics[2]. It would be some decades before it was replaced by solid state devices which had much "better" characteristics.

Let us change the subject again.

AESTHETICS OF SPOILAGE

People like spoiled things. It is a basic human aesthetic. Wine (spoiled grape juice) is more valued than grape juice. Yoghurt and cheese command more respect than milk. Old torn bluejeans command a much higher price than new, unbleached, un-torn versions. The list of spoiled items that have a higher value than the unspoiled ones is too numerous to even try to enumerate.

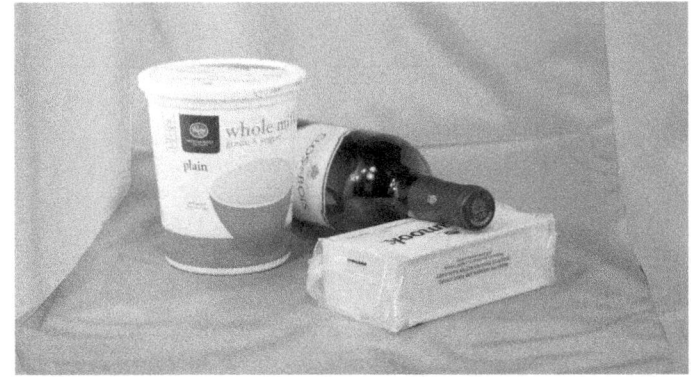

Figure 15.6. Spoiled foods – Yoghurt, wine & cheese

---

2 Nonlinear signal transfer is usually referred to as harmonic distortion. The reasons for this will become clear later.

WHERE IS THIS GOING?
Linearity, vacuum tubes, wine, cheese? The reader will certainly be justified in wondering where all of this is going.

These disparate subjects actually tie together. Today, there is a conflict between our dominant technologies, and what consumers of music actually want. For some decades, we have been able to make equipment with very high levels of performance. Yet the public balks whenever the sound is "too good" from a purely technical standpoint. The public has made it very clear that they are looking for a particular sound. This sound will not be produced unless we spend a considerable amount of time and money in either employing older technologies, or at least emulating them with software?

How did it happen that the public became attached to an antiquated sound? History gives us the answer. For the last hundred years, people have been listening to music as it was filtered through some type of electronic medium. We are entering the fourth generation of humans who have seldom heard real unfiltered music in their life. The electronic media has moulded people's tastes to the extent that a late 1960's sound is the default sound for what music is supposed to sound like. If another sound is desired, the tendency is to start with this sound, and then process it further. If you are going to record your tabla, you must be very cognisant of this fact.

To obtain the sound that the public wants to hear, you will need some basic tools. These will be your friends in the studio. Conversely, there is a studio tool that will be of extremely limited use.

THE TABLA'S FRIENDS IN THE STUDIO
1) The vacuum tube
2) The equalizer
3) The compressor
4) The microphone

THE ENEMY
The reverberator

THE VACUUM TUBE
The first question you may be asking yourself is, why the vacuum tube is so important for a good recording of tabla. The easy answer is that vacuum tubes distort the signal in a way that people have grown accustomed to, and have come to like. But for a more detailed answer, we have to look into the concept of harmonic distortion.

The reason why the vacuum tube is so important for getting the right sound, revolves around "harmonic distortion". This concept brings us back to the topic of signal transfer characteristics, that was illustrated in Figures 15.3 and 15.4 In particular, we must look at nonlinearities of the signal transfer characteristics.

Harmonic distortion is linked to the process of saturation. Saturation is one of the most basic nonlinearities for any electronic device.

This is easily visualise with a *reductio ad absurdum* situation. Let us imagine an amplifier that has a gain of 1000. Let us say that we put a signal of 1 volt into this amplifier. Now with a gain of 1000, that means that the output of the amplifier would have to be 1000 volts! This is of course preposterous. The output of the amplifier will only track the input up to a certain point. If the input signal reaches a point where the amplifier can go no further, then any further increase will have no affect, until it falls to a level where the amplifier can resume tracking. This is known variously as "saturation" or "clipping". An example of a saturated sine wave is shown in Figure 15.7.

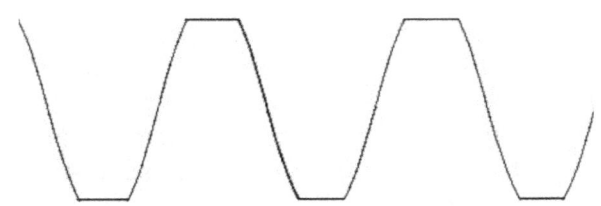

Figure 15.7. Hard saturated sine wave

A saturated signal contains harmonics that did not exist in the original signal. This is why it is referred to as harmonic distortion.

Most modern solid state devices maintain an excellent linearity right up to the point where the saturate. This is known as "hard saturation". From an engineering standpoint, this is very good. From an artistic standpoint, this is terrible.

This is bad for two reasons. On one hand, the purely linear response is uninteresting and is not what the public has become accustomed to. But worse still is that when most solid state devices do saturate (hard saturation), they generate a lot of odd harmonics (3x, 5x, 7x, etc)[3]. People hate odd harmonics!

Conversely, vacuum tubes exhibit what is known as "soft saturation". This is derived from a nonlinear signal transfer function as shown in Figure 5.8 (Chaffee 1933). In this example, notice that the peaks are rounded off rather than simply cut off.

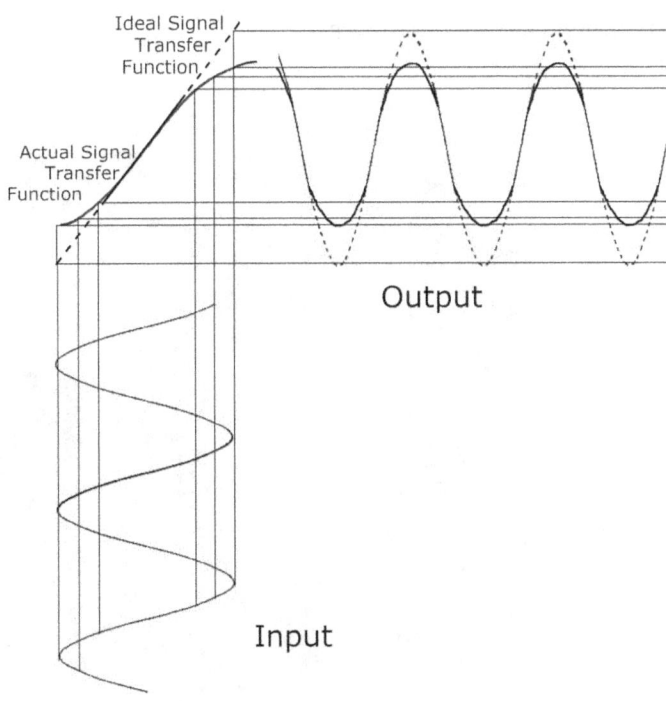

Figure 15.8. Non-linear signal transfer function of soft saturation

---

3 The key expression here is "most solid state devices". A very notable exception is the FET (Field Effect Transistor). The FET exhibits nonlinear characteristics which are very reminiscent of the vacuum tube. It is for this reason that they have found great favour among microphone manufacturers.

Soft saturation is very desirable. Where hard saturation generates large amounts of unpleasant odd harmonics, soft saturation generates even harmonics (2x, 4x, 6x, etc.). People love the sound of even harmonics, and their addition gives a feeling of vibrance to the music. This is the general principle behind many exciters. This is felt in vacuum tube equipment at low levels, long before the music shows hard saturation. This helps create the "classic sound" that the public likes.[4]

Vacuum tube saturation is especially good for the tabla. It is easily seen that the effects of the vacuum tube are most pronounced upon the musical peaks. The sound of the tabla is characterised by many peaks. Furthermore, by rounding off theses peaks it produces an additional effect known as "tube compression". The combination of tube compression and its addition of even harmonics, is especially complimentary to the tabla.

It is a common approach in high end recording setups that just about everything should go through a vacuum tube at some point. But there are two things to keep in mind:

1) Good vacuum tube equipment is very expensive.
2) Inexpensive vacuum tube equipment is generally crap.

This places the fledgling recording musician in a precarious position. Almost everyone seeks that high end, warm, and at times slightly crunchy sound that the vacuum tube is famous for; but few people are comfortable with the high costs associated with such equipment. This leads many musicians into buying equipment that has tubes in it, but due to cost considerations, the vacuum tubes are implemented in a way that is totally unacceptable.

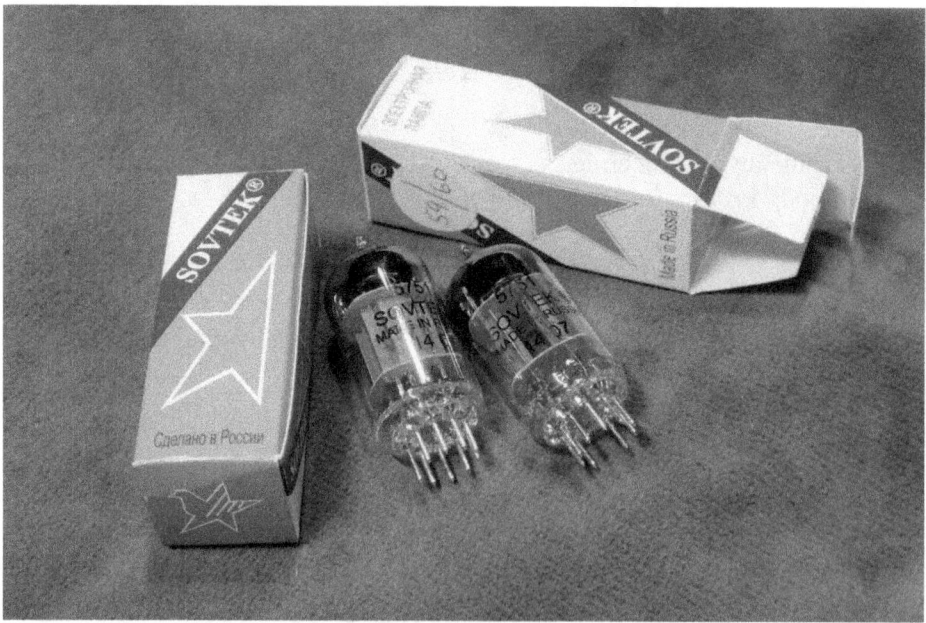

Figure 15.9. Vacuum tubes of modern manufacture

---

4   Equating the "classic sound" entirely to the harmonic distortion of vacuum tubes is a bit of an oversimplification. There are also the effects of transformers and magnetic tape. But the effects of the tube appear to be the main contributors to this sound. It is also an aspect which lends itself well to the modern studio.

How does one tell whether a device uses tubes correctly, or if it is just a marketing gimmick. Here are a few rules of thumb.

The first way to identify a poor implementation is to see if there is a special knob that is marked "Tube", "Warmth", or something similar. Any such knob indicates that the main signal is not passing directly through the tube, but that the tube is implemented in a side chain. In theory this should work, but in practice, I have never seen this do anything other than inject noise into the signal path.

Another warning sign is when the vacuum tube is clearly shown, but with an LED illuminating it from behind. The fact that the tube is visible means that it is a marketing ploy. This in itself is not necessarily bad, but the fact that they are forced to illuminate it from behind is very bad. The warm glow of the filament (a.k.a. heater) should be sufficient do the job. The lack of a glowing filament indicates that they are not powering the tube enough for a proper operation.

Virtually all of the low cost vacuum tube recording equipment is junk. One has to get into mid-range equipment before one gets really usable vacuum tube devices.

I am hesitant to make specific recommendations on equipment; but I will. I have found the ART PRO MPA II to be particularly impressive (Figure 15.10). It is a microphone preamplifier (ART undated). It is a very good microphone preamp. At the time of writing, it has a street price of about $500 USD[5]. This will certainly be more than many people would like to pay for a two channel preamp. But other tube preamps worth considering tend to be twice this amount.

Figure 15.10. ART PRO MPA II – Tube based pre-amplifier

The discussion of vacuum tubes is easily summarised. We have shown that a well implemented vacuum tube circuit can be a very valuable tool for getting good recordings of music, especially the tabla. The vacuum tube acts in a complex manner to improve the sound. On one hand it acts as an exciter by generating pleasant even harmonics that were not present in the original signal. In the process, it also creates "tube compression" by reducing the amplitude of the peaks that will be present in the sound of the tabla. But we have been intentionally vague as to specific equipment. This is because it may be implemented in the microphone, preamp, or virtually any analogue processing equipment we have in our signal path.

---

5   I am writing this in summer of 2022CE. By the time you are reading this, $500 might just buy you a *dosa*. But right now it is a lot of money.

THE EQUALIZER

The equalizer was discussed extensively in the last chapter. As previously mentioned, it can be used for both artistic purposes as well as addressing deficiencies in room acoustics. It can also be used as an analytical tool (Modak 1989). It is very important for getting a good sound, but we really have nothing to add here. It was discussed at some length in Chapter 14.

THE COMPRESSOR

The compressor is particularly useful in getting a good sound when recording the tabla. Some readers may find this statement curious, because we specifically warned against its use on stage.

The operation of a compressor is easy to comprehend. Imagine a small demon who sits in front of a volume control of an amplifier. Whenever the sound gets too loud, our demon turns the volume down. When the sound becomes too soft, our demon increases the volume. Therefore, the levels may be kept relatively constant. This is the reason why a compressor is also known as a "levelling amplifier". (No, "Levelling" is NOT the name of the demon.)

The original purpose of the compressor was to keep the levels of a signal within a certain range to accommodate the limited dynamic range of the old tape recorders. However, when properly used it can produce profoundly beautiful effects, especially for the tabla.

The effect of a compressor on the recording of tabla is shown in Figure 15.11. The first thing to notice is that the peaks have been levelled out in the compressed signal below. More importantly from an aesthetic standpoint, is the way that *Ga* has been boosted and its sustain increased. It is this last effect which is the most beautiful.

There is just one thing to keep in mind. In order to obtain this effect, the compressor must be very precisely set. Due to tremendous variability in the way that different compressors behave, it is impossible to give specifics. But as a general rule, you have to be running very fast; your attack and release times should be measurable in milliseconds, rather than seconds.

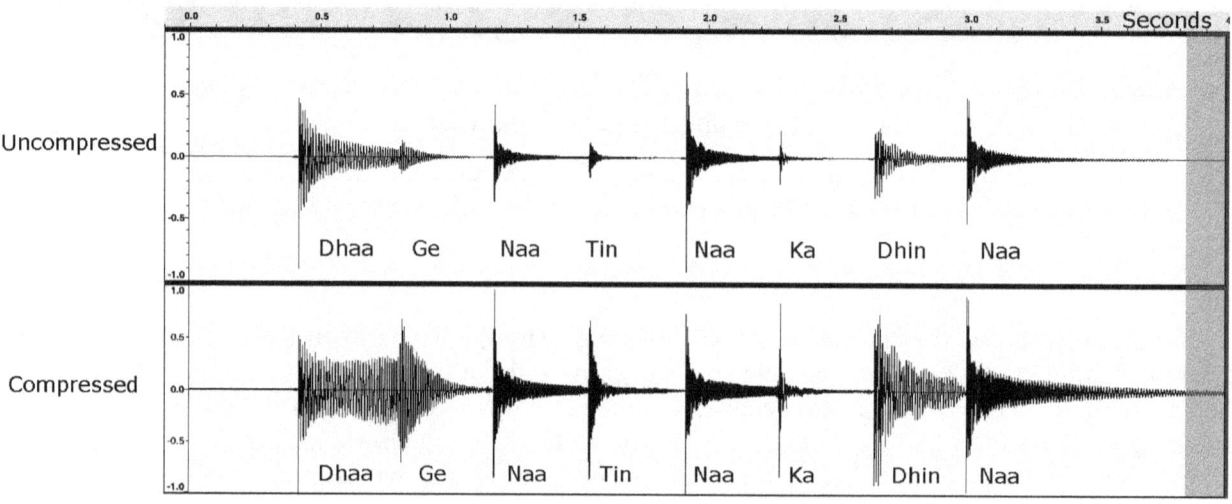

Figure 15.11. Comparison of an uncompressed signal with a compressed one

There are many compressors on the market. Once you become familiar with the idiosyncrasies of your particular model, I believe they all should work well for the tabla. However, a model that is worth noting is the ART PRO VLA II. Like its preamp cousin discussed earlier, this too is vacuum tube based. It has a street price of about $500. Admittedly, this is about twice the price of many other compressors, but the superb implementation of vacuum tubes more than makes up for its increased price. Comparable vacuum tube based compressors tend to cost much more.

Figure 15.12. ART PRO VLA II – Tube based audio compressor (ART 2007)

THE MICROPHONE

Microphones and microphone placement has been discussed extensively in earlier chapters. There are very few things which need to be added.

The main thing to realise is that there are studio microphones, and there are stage microphones; the two are not the same. The main considerations for stage microphones are a robust construction and excellent off axis rejection (feedback resistance). Curiously, a good quality of sound is of only tertiary importance for the stage mic. Conversely, a studio microphone has sound quality as the prime consideration. Consequently many studio microphones are too delicate for stage use. As a reflection of these different criteria, most stage microphones tend to be dynamic mics, while most studio microphones are condenser mics. One will even find ribbon mics in use in the studio; but these are generally too delicate for stage work.

There is one microphone which is the benchmark for all studio mics; this is the Neumann U87. It is a German microphone which has been around for more than half a century. It has such a reputation for performance, that virtually all other studio microphones are held up to this as a comparison. Just as the Shure SM-57 and Shure-SM58 are synonymous with stage work, the U87 is synonymous with studio work.

Could we say that the U87 is the workhorse for the recording studio today? Not very likely; it is far too expensive to be considered a workhorse. At the time of writing, it has a street price of over $3600 USD.

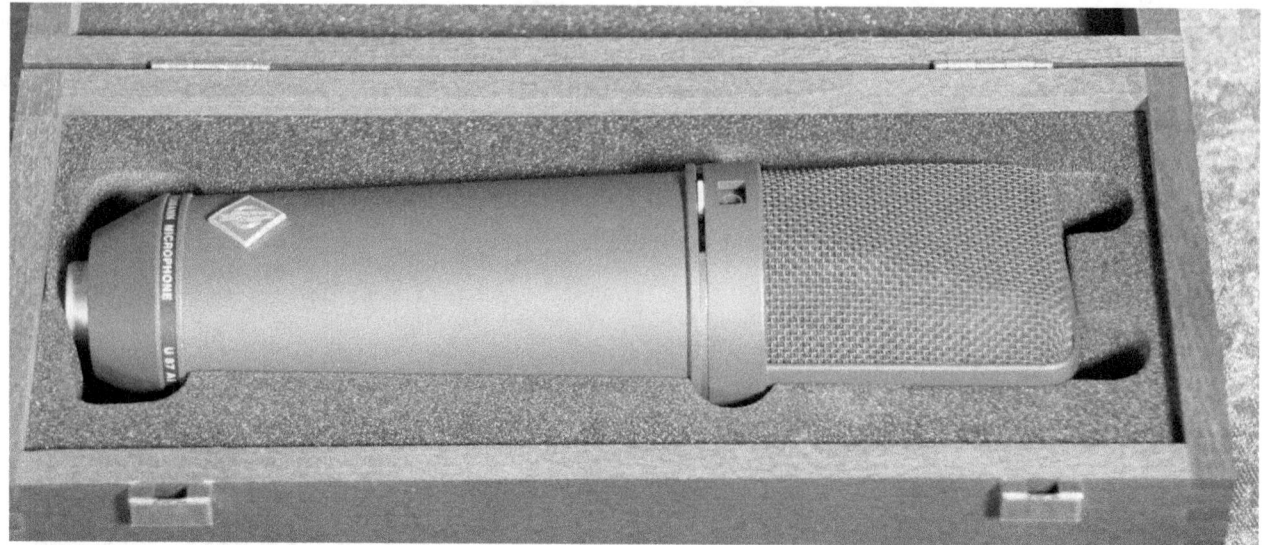

Figure 15.13. Neumann U87 Ai
(Neumann undated)

There is a lot of flexibility in microphone choices. I have had good results with an a couple of vacuum tube (valve) based Sterling ST69s (Sterling undated); these yield a very classic 1960's sound that is very reminiscent of the old records of Alla Rakha. Unfortunately at the time of writing, they are unavailable. I have also had good results with the Bluebirds (the older versions, before BLUE became just another purveyor of Chinese mics.)(BLUE undated) Even a budget friendly MXL V67Q (Marshall undated) does a very good job of micing the tabla.

The bottom line is simple; these days microphones are very good. The 1960s and 1970s were a golden period for microphones, and the patents on their critical technologies have expired. Therefore, everyone is free to copy them. If you have a good ear and are sensitive to mic placement, you can produce very good recordings without spending a lot of money.

THE REVERBERATOR
As mentioned earlier, the reverberator (a.k.a. "reverb"), is no friend of the tabla. Unless you are intentionally trying to get a cavernous echoey sound for some artistic effect, you should use this effect at an absolute minimum.

CLOSING REMARKS ON ANALOGUE EQUIPMENT
One cannot help but notice that the preceding discussion concerning analogue equipment was extensive. A large selection of analogue processors is one of the things that separates a professional studio from a typical home studio (fig 15.14). But this gets to be very expensive very quickly.

The discussion of expensive analogue equipment should not be construed as a "let them eat cake" attitude. There is a reason for this extensive treatment of the subject. If you are unable to afford stand-alone hardware, you will be dealing with software plugins which mimic the same. Plugins are a budget friendly alternative to dedicated analogue hardware. The concepts will be the same, so is imperative that you understand them.

DIGITAL AUDIO

Now we must discuss the computerised aspect of the recording process. The majority of your work will be in this realm, so this is of prime importance.

The entire concept of digital audio is predicated upon the process of digital sampling. Figure 15.15 shows an analogue signal that we wish to digitise. After it is digitised, we get a series of binary numbers which have the values as shown in Figure 15.16 (Courtney 1986).

Digital sampling functions in two directions; one of which is time (i.e., sampling rate) and the other is signal intensity (i.e., bit depth).

The sampling rate is the first factor. As the name implies, it is a reflection of how many times a second a sample is taken. There are a number of sampling rates in common use in digital audio, but 44.1k, 48k, 88.2k, 96k, 176.4k and 192.0k are the most common[6].

The other factor for digitising audio is the bit depth, also known as quantization. This is represented by the height of the blocks in Figure 15.16. Imagine a voltage range that the digitiser is capable of responding to. Bit depth is the number of discrete steps the digitiser uses to describe this voltage range. The numbers are very large, so instead of quoting the numbers directly, one uses the number of bits it takes to specify these discrete steps. The oldest bit depth in use today is 16-bits (65,536 discrete steps). If there is a standard, this is it, because this is what was used by audio CDs. Other bit depths in common use are 24-bits (16,777,216) and 32-bits (4,294,967,296).

Figure 15.14. Typical effects rack

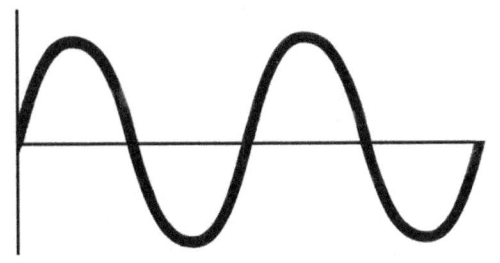

Figure 15.15. Signal to be digitised

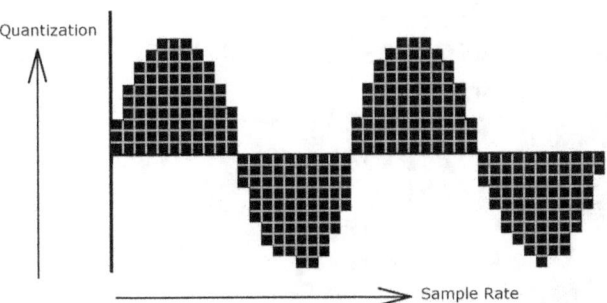

Figure 15.16. Digitised Signal

---

6   What does "k" mean? That is an interesting question that does not have a single answer. The most common interpretation is that it is short for kHz (kilohertz). Yet there is another school of thought that posits that it stands for ksps (kilo-samples-per-second). Either way it means the same thing.

This brings us to the question as to what are the best settings. In the old day it was best to do all your work in 16-bit / 44.1k. This was the standard for CDs. Working in other formats could actually increase the audible noise once it was converted to standard format. Today, the "standard format" isn't so standard, so it is normal to work with as high resolution as is comfortable. One can then convert the bit-depth / sample rate as necessary.

DIGITAL HARDWARE

What kind of hardware do we need? There really isn't much that I can write about this. Get the biggest fastest computer you can afford (Huber & Runstein 2017). Get an interface (digitiser) that has the number of channels you can afford (notice I didn't say want). If you are on a strict budget, you can plug your microphones directly into the digitiser (interface). You can expand the analogue section later.

We could go into considerable number of pages discussing this, but the bottom line would be the same.

DAW

The centre of your work in recording will be in the DAW. This stands for Digital Audio Workstation. Yet there are a number on the market, and most of them are really pretty good.

Intuition says that you get the most powerful DAW, with the most features that you can afford. Fortunately, this is not the case. Most DAWs allow you to expand their capability by the addition of plugins. Therefore, one has numerous options to grow, even with budget friendly software.

PLUGINS

Plugins are really where your recording power is. The DAW may be viewed as a shell to support these. Plugins come in several formats; AAX, VST, and AU, are the most common ones. You must know what formats are compatible with your DAW. Be aware that just because your DAW supports a particular format of plugin, occasionally other factors such as your hardware environment enter the picture. Do not forget to do your homework in this regard.

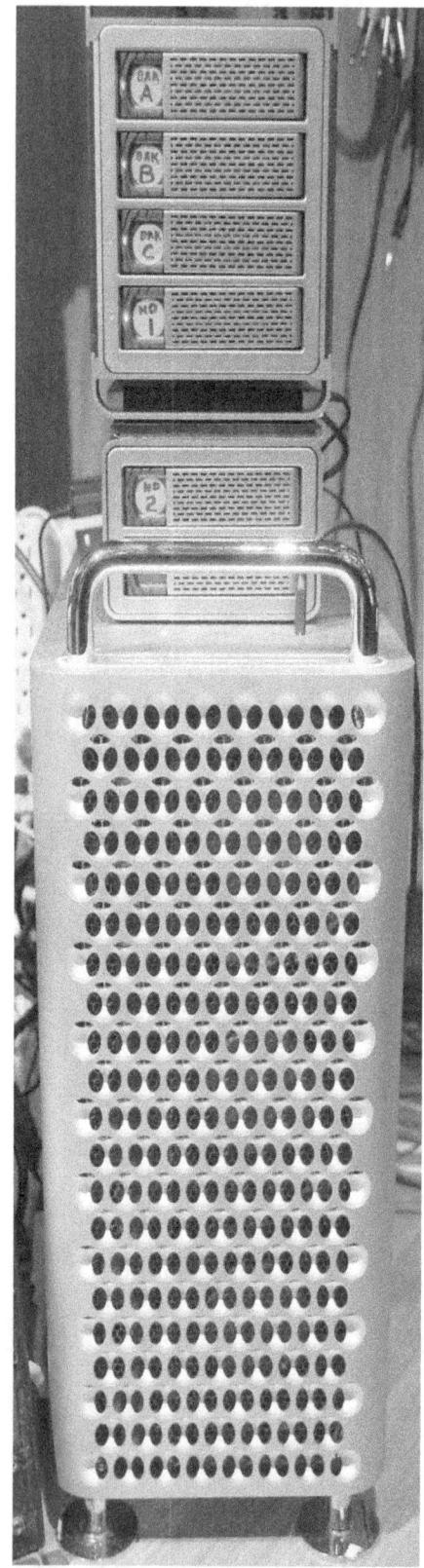

Figure 15.17. Author's computer MacPro Tower, 27TB (5-HDs, 4-SSDs), 8-core 3.5GHz, 96 GB RAM

A WORD OF WARNING!

Copy protection is a fact of life today. This is reasonable because it is a very involved and expensive proposition to develop DAWs and audio plugins. This is OK, and we are all familiar with a variety of licensing and software activation procedures. But within the field of audio software, there is a particularly aggressive and intrusive activation scheme that should be avoided. It is in the form of iLOK.

Stay away from iLOK, and its cousins JUCE, and PACE. They are so aggressive and so unreliable that any software purchased that utilises this scheme will be an unnecessary source of headaches. Before you buy any software, always check and see if any of these schemes are incorporated. If they are, you probably should look for alternatives.

There is very good professional software out there that does not abuse their customers in this fashion. My personal favourite is MeldaProduction. They have a full line of professional software at very reasonable prices. Their software, like all professional software does have activation protocols, but they are very customer friendly, and will not be a source of frustration.

WORKS CITED

ART
2007   *Pro VLA II Professional Two Channel Vactrol/Tube Leveling Amplifier*. Virginia Beach, VA:ART-Allied Research and Technology.
undated   *PRO MPA II ART PRO MPAII Microphone Preamplifier*. Virginia Beach, VA:ART-Allied Research and Technology.

BLUE
undated   *Bluebird*. Baltic Latvian Universal Electronics.

Chaffee, E. Leon
1933   *Theory of Thermionic Vacuum Tubes: Fundamentals - Amplifiers - Detectors*. New York: McGraw-Hill Book Company.

Courtney, David
1986   "New Sounds from Old Sources", *Experimental Musical Instruments*. Vol II, No. 4, pg.10-15.

Huber, David M & Robert E. Runstein
2017   *Modern Recording Techniques*. 9th Edition. Milton Park, UK:Routledge.

Marshall Electronics
undated   *MXL V67Q Stereo Manual*. El Segundo, CA:Marshal Electronics.

Modak, H.V.
1989   "Use of Graphic Equaliser in Musical Acoustics", *Journal of the Acoustical Society of India*. Calcutta, Acoustical Society of India.

Neumann.Berlin
undated   *Bedienungsanleitung / Operating Instructions - U 87 Ai*. Berlin Germany: Neuman.

Sterling Audio
undated   *Studio Microphone Operational Guide*. Sterling Audio.

CHAPTER 16
STAGE LIGHTING

Lighting plays an important part of any performance. Some think that lighting is just a method of making sure that the performers can be seen; this is far from the fact. Lighting is an integral part of the artistic experience. It is a vast area in itself, too vast to be covered in a book on tabla. Nevertheless, there are a few points which must be covered. Let us start with the basics.

HISTORY OF STAGE LIGHTING

The first written records of stage lighting appear in India. The *Natya Shastra* (circa 200 BCE) makes considerable mention of stage lighting. In the *Natya Shastra,* stage lighting is called *"vidyut"* (विद्युत्) which literally translated means "to illuminate". Unfortunately, details of the techniques used to illuminate these early stages are scarce.

Lighting was used in Europe as an integral part of the theatrical experience for a long time. In the middle ages, the Italian, Serilo, used lighting extensively for effect (Penzel 1978). Crude lenses were fashioned from flasks filled with coloured water, behind which were placed candles for an artistic effect. He also experimented with metallic pans and trays in order to project the weak lights of the era. All of this was in addition to crude burning lamps for general illumination. A tremendous innovation occurred in 1775 when David Garrick placed a row of candles in the stage and screened them from the audience.

Over the centuries, stage lighting went through many improvements. Much of this was driven by advances in various illuminants (camphene, kerosine, gas). Lighting based upon flammable substance reached its peak with the introduction of the limelight (Abulafia 2015). But the first hints of a revolution in stage lighting go back to the first electric light. This was the carbon arc which was invented at the turn of the 19th century, and first used on stage in the Paris Opera House in 1846. But the real revolution had its origin in the invention of the incandescent bulb. Numerous people were responsible for its development (e.g., Grove, Kinnersley, DeLaRue, et al.)(Schroeder 1923). The first patent on an incandescent lamp was taken by Frederick De Moleyns back to 1841; but the first commercially available incandescent bulb goes back to Joseph Swan in Great Britain (Chirnside 1979). In 1878 Edison introduced his version of the incandescent bulb; it was his version which ultimately proved to be the more commercially successful light bulb.

The electric (incandescent) light bulb quickly gained acceptance in the theatrical world. In 1880 and 1881, a series of experiments was performed at the Paris Grand Opera. From then on, it rapidly began to be seen on stages in Europe and America. The rapid acceptance was driven by safety issues. Electrified theatres were far less likely to burn down than the old gas-illuminated establishments.

But the incandescent bulb had problems, most notably their extreme inefficiency. It would be more than a century before more efficient alternatives would arise.

Figure 16.1. LED (lft) Incandescent bulb (rt)

Today the majority of stages have replaced their old bulbs with LEDs (Figure 16.1). This is short for "Light Emitting Diode". The LED goes back to the early 1960s, but the early versions were expensive, and were unable to handle the high power required for illumination. Today these problems have largely been taken care of.

REFLECTORS / LENSES

Reflectors and lenses were very important in the development of stage lighting. They helped control a simple problem which was inherent to all early forms forms of illumination. This problem was the rapid reduction in intensity of light as one moved away from the light source.

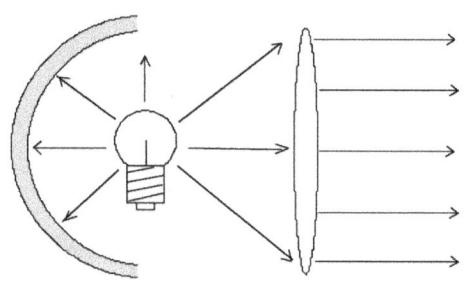

Figure 16.2. Reflector and lens

Figure 16.2 shows a typical arrangement. The reflector was placed at the rear of the light assembly. In the front of the light is the lens which controls the dispersion of the light. Reflectors and lenses are substantially less important today. The LED is directional by its very nature.

COLOURED ILLUMINATION

There must be a way to alter the colour. There are two approaches, one for incandescent bulbs, and another for LEDs

Obtaining a coloured light from an incandescent bulb is basically one of filtration. These bulbs tend to emit a white (or whiteish) light; therefore obtaining a coloured light is a process of filtering out the unwanted wavelengths. Historically, this was done either by tinting the glass bulb, or affixing some type of filter to the light's enclosure. But the use of gels or other filters has almost disappeared on modern stages. The incandescent bulb is highly inefficient, and placing filters on them just makes them more so.

LEDs are the preferred approach to obtaining a coloured light. LEDs tend to be coloured as per their very nature. The colour is usually determined by the semiconducting materials from which they are manufactured.

The problem with LEDs is not how to obtain a colour, but how to obtain a white light. The answer is that they don't. They give the illusion of white light by mixing different colours, usually red, green, and blue, to produce a white light. This common deception allows the production of almost any hue, simply by varying the amount of these three colours.

CONTROLLERS / DIMMERS

So far we have discussed how to create, direct, and colour the light; yet we have not discussed how to control the brightness. This may be done in a variety of ways.

Over the years, many different forms have been introduced. One of the oldest was the simple resistance dimmer. One simply inserted a variable resistor into the path of the current. Unfortunately, they were very large and consumed a lot of power.

Ch. 16. Stage Lighting

Many techniques were introduced to address the problems inherent to the resistive dimmers. They included such things as variable transformers and magnetic amplifiers. Most of these approaches are no longer being marketed. They have largely been replaced with electronic dimmers.

The electronic dimmer revolutionised stage lighting. It works in a variety of ways, usually by cutting the power on and off in very fast intervals. This approach requires the use of very fast, high power electronic switches. They are usually some form of a thyristor. Many are available, yet their names may vary according to their internal structure (e.g., TRIAC) or their manufacturer (e.g., GE's Silicon Controlled Rectifier).

Electronic dimmers have advantages and disadvantages. They are very compact; being compact allows many channels to be economically placed in a single unit. They lend themselves well to microprocessor control; this makes possible "smart" controllers with their multitude of programmable features. They are incredibly efficient; they dissipate a surprisingly small amount of heat. All of these advantages are balanced against one notable disadvantage; they have significant limits as to how much power they can handle. Do not exceed the rated value!

Today most stage lighting is controlled by multiple devices; there is a controller and a number of dimmer packs. A typical arrangement is shown in Figure 16.3. The controller is the central control; it contains the microprocessor, faders, and other things necessary for the user interface. It does not actually handle any substantial power, rather it generates a control signal which is sent to separate dimmer packs. These dimmer packs are designed to handle several channels of power for the lighting. However, they do not have any significant user interface.

Compatibility is a major consideration with this approach. There are many manufacturers and not every controller can communicate with every dimmer pack. Furthermore a dimmer that will work with incandescent bulbs does not necessarily work with LEDs. Additionally, not every LED is dimmable. Make sure that each component is compatible. If you are setting your own lighting system up, make sure that you research things thoroughly before investing your money!

We have covered the basic forms of incandescence, LEDs, reflectors, lenses, coloured filters, and dimmers. However, we still need to know more about stage lighting.

STAGE LIGHTS AND EFFECTS

There is a wide variety of lighting that the performing tabla player may choose from to enhance the performance. We will now look at some of the major ones.

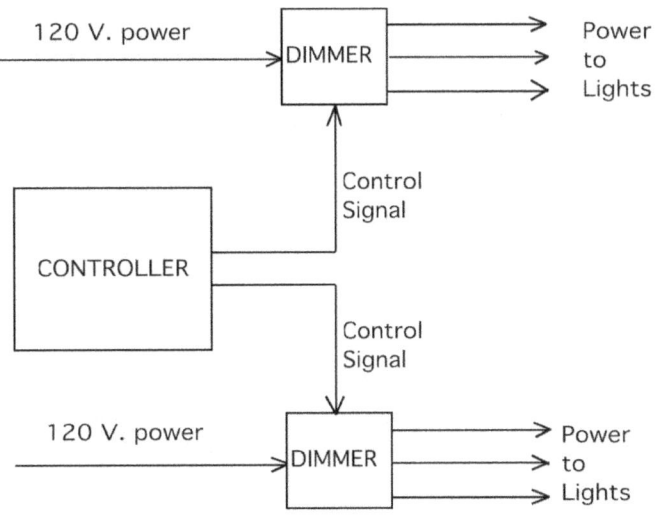

Figure 16.3. Controller / dimmer setup

Spot (spotlight) - The spotlight, variously called spot, ellipsoidal spot, or simply ellipsoidal, is a basic piece of stage lighting (Figure 16.4). It is often referred to as ellipsoidal due to the nature of the lenses and reflectors. The spotlight is characterised by an extremely hard edge that results from the extremely precise focusing characteristics of the reflectors and lenses. They are very bright and work well at great distances. Therefore, they

Figure 16.4. Ellipsoidal spotlight

Figure 16.5. Typical gobo

are often located in the back of the auditorium. A common usage is to have a person in the rear of the auditorium whose job is to follow the performers with the spotlight; this type is called a "follow spot". Since Indian musicians usually do not wander around the stage, a follow spot would commonly be set at the beginning of a program and left unattended. Spotlights have the advantage that the edge can be as hard or as soft as desired. If a soft edge is desired, one simply has to defocus the spotlight. One can also contour the shape of the beam.

Gobo Projector - This is actually an insignificant variation upon the ellipsoidal spot. The only real difference is in function. Whereas the ellipsoidal spot is usually used for illumination, the gobo is used to project an image onto the backdrop, floor, or any suitable flat surface. This is done by some minor modifications to the ellipsoidal spot. In its simplest form, one simply drops a "gobo" (fig 16.5) into a special holder and inserts it into the ellipsoidal spot. Additionally, one often drops a metal plate with a hole in it into the gel holder in front of the lens. This plate is called a "donut". This improves the image clarity by acting somewhat like an "f-stop" on a camera.

The gobo can be used for remarkably stunning effects. An example is shown in Figure 16.6; in this picture there is an illuminated pattern behind the statue. The projected image may be made to be any colour by simply placing a gel anywhere along the beam path. The concept of the gobo is similar to the slide projector; however, since a metal template is used instead of a slide, much greater intensities of light may be used.

Lasers - The laser is an interesting stage effect. The laser has an effect which is similar in many ways to the gobo. However where the gobo is a static effect, the laser is very dynamic and lends itself well to synchronising with the audio content of the performance.

Pars - The par, also referred to as a "par-can" or sometimes imply a "can", is an outgrowth of the automobile headlight. Originally they were an incandescent technology only, but today LED versions are very popular.

The par became very popular because it was a model of simplicity. It consisted of nothing more than a lamp, a housing (called a "can"), a socket, a wire, gelholder, and optional barndoors. There were no mechanical focusing arrangements, no external reflectors, lenses, or anything. The simplicity came from the fact that the reflector, lenses, and filament were all integrated into the same bulb. It was virtually maintenance free. Since the design of the par lamp was but a mere modification of the automobile headlamp, it was extremely shock resistant. The par can became the light of choice for portable light systems. A conventional par can is shown in Figure 16.7.

Figure 16.6. Typical gobo application

The par can was so popular that their form factor was maintained in LED versions. Since the LED par cans are not based upon the incandescent bulbs, there is no reason to maintain this form factor; but consumers' tastes can not be ignored. An LED par can is shown in Figure 16.8.

<u>Video Lighting</u> - The video light panel offers an LED option which musicians would do well to consider (Figure 16.9). Functionally, they are comparable a par can, but without the conventional form factor. They are small, light, robust, and reasonably economical. There are only two considerations that one needs to be cognisant of. The first potential problem is that their mounting arrangement is sometimes not compatible with musician's gear. Secondly, they sometimes lack the ability to change their colours. Nevertheless, it is not hard to find video lights with these features if one takes the time to search.

Figure 16.7. Conventional Par can

<u>Other Devices</u> - The combination of inexpensive microprocessors, combined with inexpensive LEDs, has opened up unfathomable artistic possibilities. It is difficult to even approach the myriad of devices offered by manufacturers such as Chauvet, U'King, Missyee, American DJ (ADJ), and a host of others. When you are setting up your personal system, it is important to research the field and see what meets both your budget and your artistic sense.

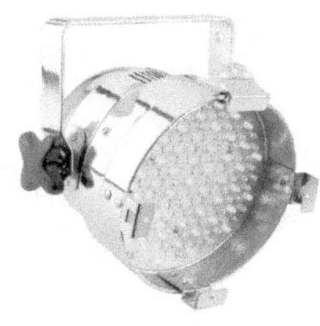

Figure 16.8. LED Par can

Figure 16.9. Video light

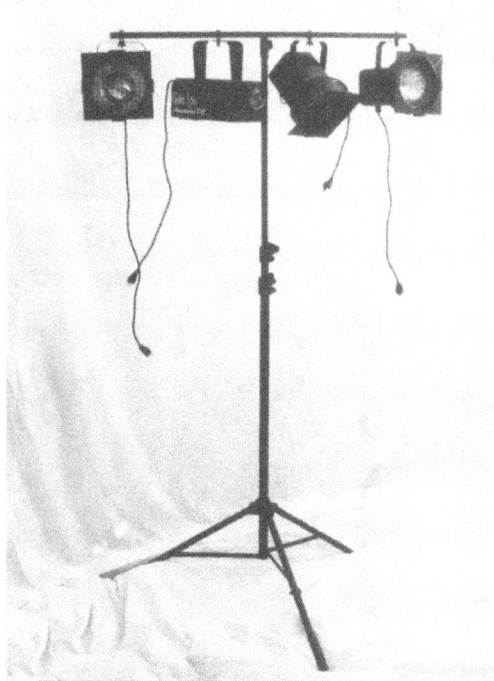

Figure 16.10. Lighting tree (ADJ 2018)

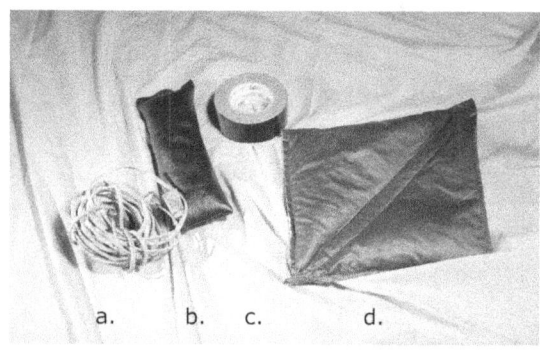

Figure 16.11. IMPORTANT!
a) Extension cord b) Sandbag c) Duct Tape d) Sandbag

Tree - A portable lighting system is necessary for today's musician. An important part of this is the lighting tree. House systems have the convenience of being mounted on battens. However, the batten is part of the theatre and cannot be moved. The tree is a lightweight and convenient way to position par cans and lighting effects. A typical lighting tree arrangement is shown in Figure 16.10.

MISC. ITEMS

Sandbags, extension cords, duct tape - Don't forget them (Figure 16.11). If you are a new student to the tabla you are probably wondering why I would waste time in a book on *tabla*, talking about these things. But if you have spent years as a performing musician, you are silently and knowingly nodding your head saying to yourself "yes", and remembering awkward situations that you have been in for forgetting them

The extension cord (Figure 16.11a) is obvious in its purpose. Unfortunately, it is too easy to forget this. The consequences of such an oversight are easy to imagine.

The sandbag is an extremely important item for the performing musician (Figure 16.11b & 16.11d). Unfortunately, it is also one of the most neglected. Their uses are myriad, but most commonly they are used to place on the legs of the lighting tree to stabilise it. Figure 16.11b is a general purpose sandbag, while the one in Figure 16.11d is designed specifically for stabilising the legs of the lighting tree. The term "sandbag" is actually a misnomer. The use of sand tends to leak and create a mess on stage; it is better to use very small pebbles.

Duct tape is also important for a myriad reasons (Figure 16.11c). But one of the most important reasons, yet least recognised by by those outside the profession, is the need to tape down cables that run across the ground. This is ESPECIALLY important for cables that run across the threshold of a door. If you attempt to give a program in a venue, and you neglect to do this, you will never be invited back.

COLOUR TEMPERATURE

Before we close this chapter, the topic of colour temperature is one that we should briefly touch upon. Although it is a very important topic for videographers, it of minimal importance for stage work.

The concept of colour temperature reflects the fact that there isn't such thing as white light. Rather there are different shades of white. The shades of white are expressed in terms of degrees above absolute zero (degrees Kelvin or simply "K"). The reasons for this reflect arcane concepts of idealised black body radiators.

All that we really need to know are the numbers we will encounter. Incandescent bulbs will tend to have an orangish hue to them; their values tend to be around 2500K. As the colour temperature increases, the hue starts shifting toward blue. Fluorescent bulbs have a strong bluish hue, and consequently a high colour temperature of 5000-6000K.

One should be VERY careful about the description on various light sources. For marketing reasons, the orangish bulbs tend to be described as "warm light ", while the bluer bulbs are designated as "cooler" lights. This is in spite of the fact that the "warmer lights" have a lower colour temperature than the "cooler lights".

If we simply wish to illuminate the stage, we really do, not care about the colour temperature. The human eye can accommodate almost anything. However, when we mix different bulbs of different colour temperatures, it becomes very noticeable. Do not mix colour temperatures unless this is really an effect you are trying to attain.

CONCLUSION

Lighting is something which any performing artist should be attentive to. The audience will not be privy to the arcane aspects of *kaida, rela, prakar,* or any of the other things that you have spent so much time studying. However, they will react to the overall feel of the performance. Presentation is VERY important, of which proper lighting is an important component.

WORKS CITED

Abulafia, Y.
2015. *The Art of Light on Stage: Lighting in Contemporary Theatre* (1st ed.). Routledge.
https://doi.org/10.4324/9781315691305

ADJ
2018   *LTS-6: User Manual*. ADJ Product LLC USA, Los Angeles, ADJ.

Bharata Muni (translated by a board of scholars)
200 BC (circa) *Natyashastra Shastra* Sri Satguru Publications, Delhi.

Chirnside, R.C.
1979   "Sir Joseph Swan and the invention of the electric lamp", *Electronics and Power*, vol. 25, no. 2, pp. 96-, February 1979, doi: 10.1049/ep.1979.0079.

Lord, William H.
1991   *Stagecraft 1; A Complete guide to Backstage Work*, 2nd Edition. Meriwether Publishing Ltd. Colorado Springs, CO.

Oxford University Press.
1937 *Oxford Universal English Dictionary on Historical Principals. Volume 4 Sol - Tol*, Doubleday, Doran and Co, 1937.

Penzel, Frederick
1978 *Theatre Lighting Before Electricity.* Wesleyan University Press, 1978. Project MUSE, doi:10.1353/book.77792.

Schroeder, Henry
1923 *History of the Electric Light*. Smithsonian Instituter, Baltimore, Lord Baltimore Press.

CHAPTER 17
STAGECRAFT

This chapter deals with the stagecraft. The *Oxford Universal Dictionary* (Oxford University Press 1937: 1993) defines stagecraft as "that part of the art of dramatic composition which is concerned with the conditions of representation on the stage". For a musician, this translates to all aspects of the live performance separate from the actual musical material. Strictly speaking, Chapter 14 - *Sound Reinforcement* and Chapter 16 - *Stage Lighting*, should be under this topic as well. However, their inclusion would have made this chapter unwieldy; therefore they were given their own chapters.

The various aspects of stagecraft are especially important for a modern tabla player. The philosophy of the live performance has undergone quite a change in the last hundred years. In the old days, the musician's duty was simply to play music; but today, if one adopts this simplistic attitude towards the live performance, then one is bound to fail. If a person wishes to listen to music, they put on some recorded music. Today's audiences don't go to a live performance to listen to music, they go to participate in an event. The nature of the event involves numerous extra-musical activities and skills.

Why do people go to a live show? Many ladies go to have an opportunity to show off their new jewellery or new *sari*. Most go to socialise with friends whom they do not meet often. Many people go to concert, especially classical concerts, simply to create the image of one who is cultured. Listening to the music is but one of many reasons. More difficult to describe is that very real, but intangible, group experience.

These statements may at first seem cynical, but I assure you that they are not. They are merely realistic assessments of the modern situation. If one is going to present a successful program, one must be sensitive to what these requirements are, and provide an atmosphere that is conducive to meeting them.

Your ability to interact with stage crew, as well as your reputation as a performing artist, will be determined in part by how well you understand the material in this chapter!

INDIAN STAGECRAFT
India has an incredibly rich tradition of stagecraft. Panini, the famous grammarian of the sixth century BCE, mentions the *Natya Sutras* of Silalin and Krsasva. Unfortunately, these works have not survived to the present. Some centuries after the *Natya Sutras*, the famous Bharata wrote his famous *Natya Shastra*. This treatise is the oldest surviving text on stagecraft in the world.

With such an ancient tradition of stagecraft, one would expect that this field in India would be highly developed; unfortunately this may or may not be he case. Both Indian and Occidental traditions went through declines at some point in their histories. However, the reemergence of the theatre and the formalisation of classical music in the European renaissance pushed stagecraft to new highs. The great *Vedic* theatrical tradition of Bharata was reduced to simple street *"tamashas"*. Even the classical music, although highly developed from a musical standpoint, is completely divorced from this once great tradition. Certainly, there are traditions such as the *Kathakali* of Kerala which maintain the strong attachment to the old *Vedic* traditions; but the average Indian will live their entire life without ever seeing such a performance. Furthermore, the pedagogic traditions of both north and south India place great emphasis on musical proficiency, but generally make no reference to the mechanics of the presentation. This once great tradition of indigenous Indian stagecraft came close to extinction. But things are changing. The technical aspects of stagecraft in India are becoming comparable to whatever is found internationally, especially in the urban areas.

THE STAGE AND AUDITORIUM

The theatre is one of the most important tools that a tabla player must master. We do not normally think of the auditorium as a tool; but that is exactly what it is. A good theatre is one of the largest and most complex machines devised by man. From the front, it appears to be just another piece of architecture, but from the back the sophisticated nature of the technology is very clear. Like any other piece of sophisticated technology, it did not develop overnight, but is the product of many centuries of evolution.

There is an interesting story concerning the invention of the first theatre. This is found in the *Natya Shastra* written by Bharata about two thousand years ago.

It appears that Bharata was commissioned to perform the first play. All of the actors, musicians, and dancers, were assembled and given gifts by the Gods appropriate to their various roles. This play was a depiction of a great battle where the Gods defeated the demons. Needless to say, the demons were very unhappy about the nature of the play, and set about to disrupt the performance. They used supernatural powers to interfere with the movements of the dancers, and to disrupt the memory and voice of the various players. When God (Brahma) saw the disruption of the play, he intervened and banished the demons. However, it was clear that the demons were regrouping in order to, again, disrupt the performance. Thereupon, God declared that a special hall endowed with all of the correct characteristics should be constructed. This was the first theatre.

The *Natya Shastra* goes into considerable detail concerning the construction and layout of a theatre. It warns that the theatre should not be too large or the performers will not be adequately seen or heard. It also goes into great detail about a myriad of points that today we would consider to be mere superstition. It is interesting to note that many of the things that we associate with a theatre today are described in great detail in this work. Bharata goes into detail in discussing the importance of the stage, the layout of the greenroom, and the stability of the foundation. However, many of the things that we expect in a theatre, such as elaborate settings, were conspicuously absent. Even today, settings are generally absent in traditional Indian theatre (e.g., *Kathakali*).

As hoary as the traditional Indian theatre is, there is no doubt that modern performance venues in India are clearly following the European mould. Therefore, we will spend much of this chapter looking at the contemporary (i.e., Western) theatre.

There are five types of theatres (DiBenedetto 2012). There is the proscenium, the thrust, the arena, the black box, and the found space. These will be discussed in greater detail.

THE PROSCENIUM

The most widely used form of theatre in the world is the proscenium style. This form is shown in Figure 17.1. The proscenium is easily recognised from the audience; it is an architecture that is reminiscent of a frame. In the old days, proscenia were very ornately decorated; this further enhanced the frame-like quality. Today, they tend be simple and functional.

The function of the proscenium is to create a technological and psychological performance space. It is technologically important because it is a front for all of the rigging and machinery which supports a modern performance. This machine is very important, and will occupy a major portion of this chapter. The proscenium is psychologically important because it creates a performance space.

The theatre is composed of several areas. These are shown in Figure 17.2.

The Auditorium - One of the most important sections is the auditorium. This is the area in which the audience sits and listens to the performance. This is the first thing that the audience is going to encounter, and is important in determining the ambience. Important qualities of the auditorium are such obvious amenities as heating, air conditioning, and illumination; these are so obvious that they scarcely deserve mentioning. Less obvious are the psychological qualities of the ambience.

Figure 17.1. The Proscenium is common in India as well as in the West. (Taylor 1890)

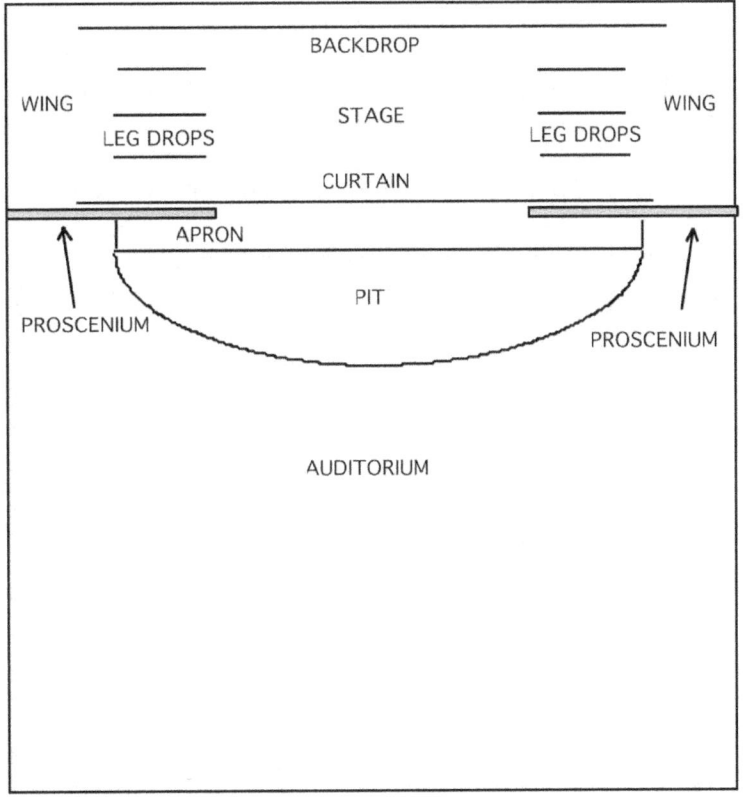

Figure 17.2. Layout of modern theatre

The Stage - The second area of the theatre is the performance space. In traditional theatres, the performance space is located behind the proscenium, well behind the curtain line. However, modern theatres tend to bring the performance space into the audience, well in front of the proscenium. Many modern theatres are designed to accommodate this. This is called a "thrust stage". Sometimes the orchestra pit can rise up and join with the main stage to form an extension of the stage.

There are conventions regarding the nomenclature of the stage and its various parts. Figure 17.3 shows the parts of the stage. Today, the audience tends to slope such that the rear seats are higher than the front. But in the old days, the stages used to slope towards the audience, while the audience was flat. Since the part of the stage close to the audience used to be lower than the part of the stage close to the backdrop, they have come to be called "downstage" and "upstage" respectively. The terms left and right are in reference to the performers; so if you are facing the audience, your left will be called stage left and your right will be called stage right.

Backstage - The third area of the theatre deals with the various mechanical considerations. This area is usually called "backstage", although such a term is actually a misnomer. These are primarily the areas on each side of the stage (the wings), the backdrop, the area behind the backdrop, and finally, the area above the stage (the fly space or loft).

The wings are the areas on either side of the stage. Typically, the rigging and lighting are controlled from here. In many smaller stages, the sound may also be controlled from here. There is usually very little behind the backdrop. Many theatres use this space as a convenient way to move from one wing to another. However, some theatres are designed to make use of back projection upon the backdrop, in which case this area is off limits.

Finally, there is the loft or fly space. This is the area above the stage. I have seen lofts that are as high as a five story building; usually they are much smaller. The fly space contains a complex system of pulleys, rigging, beams, and lighting. We will go over some of the important parts.

Located within the loft are the batten. These are large poles, originally of wood, but today usually made of steel. A batten is a general utility device for attaching scenery, props, or anything imaginable. It is raised or lowered by a complex system of rigging. If one has any stage decoration or special lighting, it can simply be clamped or tied to a batten and raised or lowered as required. Keep this in mind!

There are a number of curtains in a modern theatre (Figure 17.4). The most prominent is the main curtain or the house curtain (not shown). This tends to run from both sides of the proscenium and meet in the centre. Behind the house curtain on both sides of the stage are a series of long narrow curtains; these are called the leg drops. They serve the important function of obscuring the wings and backstage without interfering with the movement of performers either on, or offstage. The pair which are located closest to the audience are called tormentors. There is a similar set of curtains which run horizontally above the stage. They serve to obscure the battens, lighting, and rigging. If it is located in front of the house curtain it is called a valance while those located behind the main curtain are called teasers.

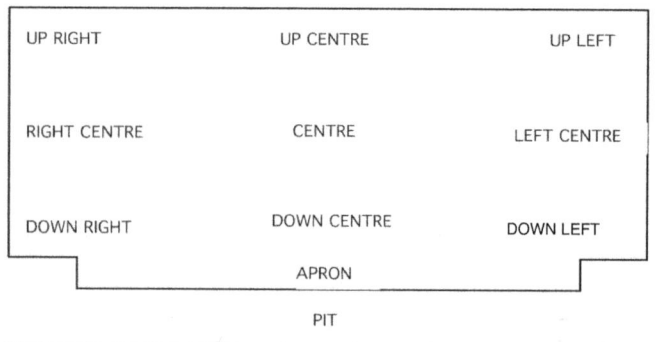

17.3. Parts of the stage

The house curtain deserves special attention. It defines an imaginary line which cuts across the stage, called a curtain line. This line is of prime importance when setting up. Many people like to open the curtain to make a dramatic start of the performance; but if one sets up the dais on the curtain line, then this will be impossible. Many people like to have the performance on the apron; in which case, the main curtain actually function as a backdrop. Again, for this to work, it is important to know where the curtain line is. Sometimes you may wish to set up on the curtain line and only partly close the house curtain. This allows the house curtain to frame an area of the stage which is smaller than that framed by the proscenium. By defining a smaller performance space, it is possible to make a much more efficient use of it. Again, it is vitally important to be aware of where your curtain line is.

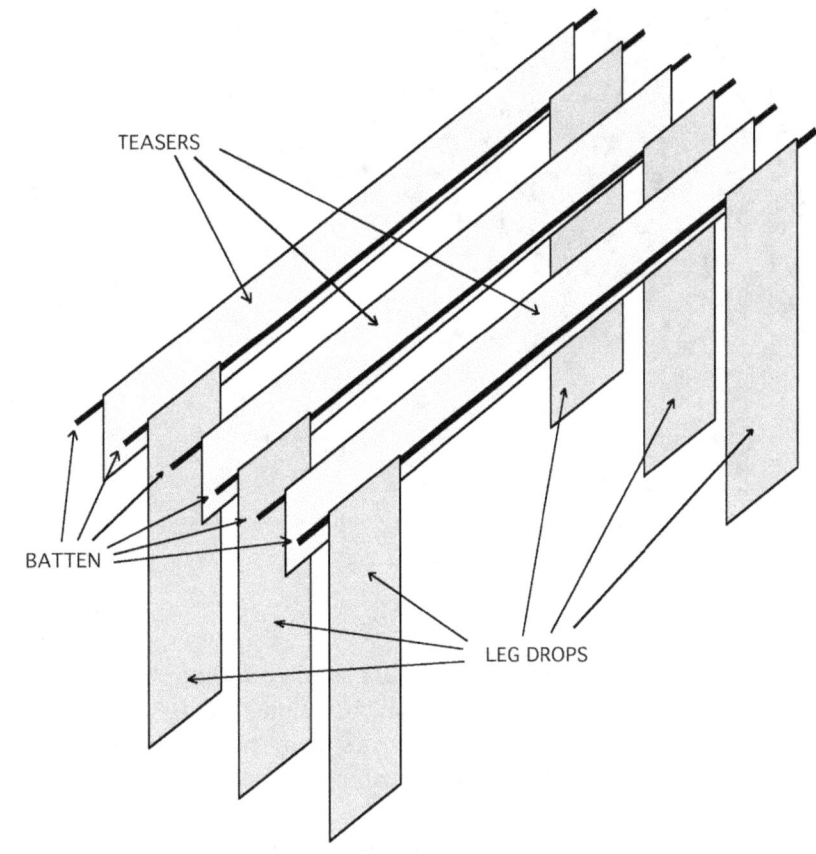

Figure 17.4. Stage curtains

We may summarise this section briefly. The three parts of the theatre (i.e., auditorium, stage, and backstage) each have important functions which must be understood. The auditorium provides the ambience for the attendees, the stage is your performance space, while the backstage, wings, etc. are important for the mechanical functions of a performance. When the function and nomenclature of the various aspects of the theatre are understood, it makes it easier for any tabla player to manage a performance.

OTHER THEATRE STYLES
The proscenium style of theatre is the most common, but there are other forms which we will encounter on occasion. We are specifically talking about the thrust, the arena, the black box, and the found space.

The thrust stage is a semicircular stage with a minimal backstage (Figure 17.5). This style of stage is very good from the standpoint of being able to interact with the audience. It is moderately easy to light. Unfortunately, it is a very hostile environment to work from the standpoint of feedback in the microphones.

The arena performance space, otherwise known as a "theatre in the round", has the audience completely surrounding you. No, No, No, No, 'nuff said!

Figure 17.5. Thrust stage

The black box overlaps with the found space. Both are performance spaces that are not specifically designed for performances. Although they can be very satisfying from an artistic standpoint, they can be challenging from a technical standpoint.

SAFETY

Theatres are dangerous places. When we think of dangerous places to work, we first think of mines, refineries, or similar places. It is easy to forget that historically theatres and stages were extremely dangerous. We would not think of wandering in a park on a cliff in the dark without railing; however as performers, we think nothing of running onto a dark stage with the risk of falling off the stage into the pit. Electrical machinery is also a safety issue. Theatres may only be a single building, but they might consume as much electricity as a small town. Furthermore, there may be tonnes of lights, battens, and other miscellaneous equipment hanging over your head. Over the years many people have perished in fires, been electrocuted, crushed by falling objects, or fallen to their death.

Fortunately today's stages are much safer. The early replacement of gas with electricity, extremely tight building codes, and the introduction of standards specifically designed for theatres, have brought fatalities to a minimum. Still, theatres can only be safe if we remember a few basic points.

The first rule is that smoking is prohibited on stages. This has nothing to do with cancer; it has do to with fire ordinances. Smoking in a theatre poses hazards which are not found in other places. For instance, there is a tendency for dust to accumulate around the rigging. This dust may act like tinder, and catch fire very easily. There is also a lot of fabric on the stage. They may be chemically treated to make them less susceptible to fire, but this is generally only good for a few years.

Learn the fire exits and try and maintain a sense of orientation. If the lights go out, and one only has the emergency lighting, it is easy to become disoriented.

Be aware of high voltages. The wings of most stage are wired with very high voltage equipment. This is much higher power than we ever find in the homes, so common sense is required. Most modern theatres are constructed in a way that keeps this equipment out of your way. But I have seen some older theatres, especially in India, where high voltage equipment was dangerously accessible.

Stay away from the rigging. Unlike the electrical and fire situation, where periodic inspections generally can assure safety, there is no way to know how well the rigging is set. One day a particular line can be correctly counter-balanced, and the next day it can be changed so that it becomes batten heavy. Messing around with the rigging can kill someone.

The bottom line is simple; do not be lulled into a false sense of security. Like the airline industry, the present level of stage safety was purchased at the cost of human lives. Complacency is the first step toward an accident. Do your job, but be careful!

Ch. 17. Stagecraft

TABLA AND THE PERFORMANCE SPACE

One of the first things to consider in setting up a program is the performance space. The performance space may be compared to a blank canvas that a painter uses. If a painter selects a canvas, they have a duty to fill it. In the same way, if you have a performance space, it is your duty to utilise it.

Proscenium - In a traditional theatre, the performance space is defined by the proscenium; this has both advantages and disadvantages. On the positive side, the proscenium creates an ambience of dignity, class, and perhaps even a touch of grandeur. However, many proscenia are designed around large stages to accommodate many performers with complex sets. Chances are you will not be able to do justice to this. There are two ways to work with the proscenium, you can expand the size of your performance, or you can reduce the size of your performance space.

One way to work with large stages is to expand your artistic content. Plants and stage decorations work quite well to fill up the space. Backdrops and gobos also work well; the gobo / ellipsoidal spot is economical, portable, and able to project a large image upon any white backdrop. One may even festoon a backdrop with colourful *saris* for a nice effect. All of this works well, as long as the proscenium is not too big. If it is, then you must think about reducing your performance area.

A reduction in the artistic space is the most common way to handle very large stages. The performance space is defined artistically and psychologically, and not necessarily defined by the proscenium. Therefore, there are numerous tools at our disposal.

A good use of lighting is probably the most powerful tool that you have to create a smaller performance space. A spotlight is a very traditional tool. By keeping the auditorium as dark as possible, and having only a small area of the stage lit, then the performance area shifts from the proscenium to just that small area which is illuminated. In practice, one does not have to use a "spot" in the strict technical sense. This same effect can be obtained by using well directed pars, floods, or anything else.

A small platform, known as a dais, is an excellent way to redefine one's performance space. This platform is the norm in India, but you may not have access to it in the West. Fortunately, a dais is the most easily improvised of structures. The easiest way to implement one is to simply have a large strong piece of plywood and lay it on top of milk crates, cinder blocks, or any other suitable support. When the whole thing is covered in bed sheets, no one can tell whether it is improvised or *pakka*.

Curtains are another way to reduce the area of your performance space. You can set the performance area to sit right on the curtain line. Then if you partially close the curtains from either side, it has the effect of broadening your tormentors (i.e., the leg drops closest to the audience). Therefore, your performance area is framed by the curtains to be a substantially smaller area than the proscenium.

The process of filling up the space or redefining a smaller space were treated as though they were mutually exclusive approaches to this problem. In practice, both approaches may be used together with satisfactory results. Let us see how these approaches can be used.

Let us first look at what not to do. Figure 17.6 shows very clearly the problems encountered when one is dealing with a large stage. In this example, the artists were simply dumped in the middle of a large stage without any attention to the artistic space or its utilisation. Lighting the entire stage worsened the feeling of under-utilisation of the stage. There was a carpet placed upon the stage which could have been used to help narrow the performance space. Unfortunately, this carpet was invisible to the audience, so the artistic advantage was nil. Because of inattention to details, the performance space defaulted to the proscenium, yet the artists were not capable of utilising this.

Figure 17.6. Poor use of proscenium stage

Figure 17.7. Better use of proscenium stage

A better use of a large stage is shown in Figure 17.7. In this case we see a combination of utilisation and performance space limiting techniques used. If one looks at the backdrop, we see that this curtain has been decorated with crepe paper. This is a very popular method of decoration in India, but one which is very rare in the US. This had the effect of utilising the back area of the stage. Although this area was utilised to some extent, the primary approach was the narrowing of the performance space. This was done with a strongly lit dais. The rest of the stage was kept in darkness. This had the effect of using the dais to define the performance space instead of the proscenium.

Thrust Stage - The thrust stage is especially well suited to the Indian performance (Figure 17.5). It is extremely conducive to artist / audience interactions. If the thrust stage is part of a large theatre, then it functions to remove the proscenium as a defining element in determining the size of your artistic space.

Lighting is sometimes an issue with the thrust stage. There is a tendency to place stage lighting in the loft above the stage. If the theatre was not specifically designed for a thrust stage there may be inadequate provisions for lighting.

Undoubtedly the biggest problem with the thrust stage involves sound reinforcement. The act of moving the performance space into the audience has the undesirable effect of placing the microphones in an area which is usually covered by the house speakers. This creates a situation where feedback is a common problem.

Black Boxes, Found Spaces and Home Performances - Many performances are in areas that were never designed to be theatres. This may be for private house performances, schools, churches, or other small institutions. Again, one of the major issues is the definition of one's performance space. This is surprisingly easy to accomplish. The first thing to do is shift chairs, lights, and other furniture to a position where a space is intuitively felt. Next, place a rug or sheet down on the ground. Traditionally, this was done for simple cleanliness; but today it is a device to help define the performance area, and create a focal point. Next, place strong lighting to illuminate this area. Several par cans or video lights work very well. Ellipsoidals also work well if they have a wide angle (typically 30° - 50° for a small house program).

Ch. 17. Stagecraft

STAGE MANNERISMS

Stage mannerisms are another consideration. In the old days, the mark of a good tabla player was a poker face and minimum movements of the body. To a great extent, this was a business tactic, because the tabla player was hired by the main artist. It was politically appropriate not to detract from the main musician, or else one would not be asked for another program. Today, the tabla player is often of equal importance to the main musician and in some cases more important. In this environment, a poker-faced presentation translates to a poor stage presence. At the other extreme, one finds many young tabla players engaging in wild gyrations and throwing the head this way and that. All of which is accompanied by the most peculiar facial expressions. This too, is bad.

It is important that one's physical mannerisms be natural and conducive to the artistic flow of the performance (Caruso 2016). They should subtly enhance the feel of the performance without ever impinging upon the consciousness of the audience. It is a good idea for young performers to sit and play before a mirror, or video performances, and examine them later for some self-criticism. This can go a long way toward creating a good stage presence.

One of the simplest, yet overlooked means of acquiring good stage presence is the smile. Try it; you will be amazed at how much it helps.

STRUCTURE OF A TYPICAL PROGRAM

Generally, there are five parts to a performance: setup/load-in, preliminary performance, interval, main performance, and the breakdown. This entire process may take anywhere from 4 hours to 14 hours depending on the scale of the performance.

The setup / load-in is an extremely important part of this process. Modern stage performances rely on a lot of high technology. Setting up requires time. The nuts-and-bolts of this process has already been discussed, so we can now move on to the preliminary performance.

The first half of the program we will call the preliminary performance. Its function is one of psychological orientation. Just because people are with you physically, does not mean that they are with you psychologically. By the time they sit in front of you, they have had to fight traffic, get chewed out by the boss, fight with the wife as to why she had to put on three *saris* before deciding upon one, drop the kids off at Aunt Uma's house, and a myriad of other insignificant, yet stressful things. It is your duty to bring them into your psychological space, and create a sense of the shared experience. Fortunately, this is easily accomplished with one thing - time. You cannot rush this. Western concert organisers often have a "warmup act" to accomplish this. A similar situation exists with major Indian performances. When Indian performances have multiple performers, it is usual for artists to fight over who gets to perform last, not first.

These preliminary activities were acknowledged in India from the earliest periods. The *Natya Shastra* (circa 200 BC) spends a considerable amount of time discussing this. In Sanskrit, it is called *"Purvaranga"* (पूर्वरंग). In the Indian tradition of old, this was a series of prayers, offerings, songs, and musical accompaniment, all of which had the desired effect of psychological orientation.

A major issue confronting both organisers and artists alike is when the performance is to start. It is normal for Indian performances to start half-an-hour to one-hour late. This awkward situation is caused by audiences, artists, and organisers. Many artists will refuse to perform until a sufficient number of people have arrived; therefore the artist bears some of the blame. It is also normal for organisers to grossly underestimate the time required for the setup. In the West, most organisers are not program organisers, but members of other professions who happen to be elected by their local Indian organisation. This lack of experience, coupled with a desire to save money by not renting the hall earlier, mean that it is normal for the setup to be going on well after the performance was scheduled to start. Therefore, the organisers must bear a significant portion of the blame. The audiences too, are not blameless. Indian programs naturally attract a primarily Indian crowd. Indians are notorious for coming late to functions.

It is not necessary to go into greater detail as to the reasons why Indian programs are late getting started. It is sufficient to realise that it is an unprofessional way to carry on your craft. If you are a tabla player with aspirations of rising above the mundane string of *desi* programs, it is very important to adopt a professional attitude towards time. Do whatever is within your power to make the performance start on time.

After the preliminary performance comes the interval (intermission). Socialising is what brings a significant percentage of the audience to your program. Don't fight it. With a typical Indian audience you will not be able to make it any shorter then about 30 minutes.

There are artistic advantages and disadvantages to the interval. On the positive side, it is one of the factors which creates a sense of a shared experience. However, there is the added responsibility of getting the audience back to your artistic vision after the interval is over.

Following the interval is the main performance. We can call this the main performance, because this is going to be the first time that people are really willing to sit down and follow your artistic lead. One should generally hold back and save the really good material for this portion of the performance.

The breakdown portion of the program is where one physically packs up the instruments, unplugs the equipment, and everybody goes home. This may seem very simple, but it is not. If you do not pay very close attention now, the little details will come back to haunt you later!

The most important thing to do during the breakdown is take inventory of everything that is there. There will always be people who are willing to help you pack up; but be careful. They may be ever so well-meaning, but if they place the wrong item in the wrong box, it may cause you trouble later. Misplacing a two-dollar item now, may cost you dearly in lost time in a future program!

PERSONNEL MANAGEMENT

Management of people is important for a successful program. It is highly unlikely that you, as a tabla player, are going to go in, set up the sound by yourself, play a solo by yourself, and then break everything down, and go home. Real-world situations mean that you are going to have to deal with many people.

<u>Overview of Personnel Management</u> - This whole discussion of personnel management can be broken down into three simple rules. Let everyone do their work; don't be a prima donna; and be sensitive to cultural differences.

Let everyone do their job without interference. It is physically impossible for you to do everything. Just as you would not try and play every instrument onstage, don't try and do every job backstage either. You must designate jobs to your people, and let them do it. Pay just enough tension to see that things are going as planned; but don't look over their shoulder every second.

Don't be a prima donna. This is best summed up in the injunction "*nakkara mat karo!*" Examples of *nakkara* are strutting about, giving unnecessary orders to people, putting down other people, generally posturing, and trying to show your importance. This simple rule may sound obvious, but it is amazing how many musicians have created such a bad impression by ignoring it.

The previous tips help you avoid most problems; but there are specific issues involved with dealing with the various people involved in a program. These other people may be promoters, artists, stage personnel, or any number of other people.

Promoters and Producers - These are the people who deal with the financial side of a program. This generally involves raising the capital, booking hotels, arranging for food, tickets, and other aspects of the program. When you deal with these people, you have to be sensitive to their situation. For instance, if a performance starts late, or goes beyond the estimated time, these things are adding to the cost of the program. They are not going to be that concerned with what you do onstage, as long as they turn a healthy profit. If they are happy, then they will call you back.

Remember to accommodate them with your time as well. You will have to allocate time before the program for promotion. Time that you spend before the program talking on the radio or to the press, helps everybody. Although dealing with the promoters is professionally important, it is not really on the topic of stagecraft. Therefore, we shall not go into greater detail here.

Stage Personnel - We also need to deal with technical personnel, more commonly referred to as the stage crew. They are vitally important to a successful program. For a large program, the crew usually consists of your own people combined with the theatre's staff. Each group has their own advantages and disadvantages.

The theatre's staff are permanently attached to a particular hall. Do not forget that they know the stage and auditorium better than you ever will. When dealing with the theatre's own crew, you should be sensitive to whether you are dealing with union or non-union staff.

The advantages to working a union stage are simple; you are dealing with professionals who know what they are doing. You do not have to waste a lot of time giving directions, merely a few words to describe the setup is sufficient; for they will take it and give you what you need. Union stages are also safer. A stage is only safe as long as there are professionals who can properly maintain it. I have never seen a union stage that was not up to par.

But the union stage also has disadvantages. They are often inflexible. This is not due to any weakness in their personality, but simply a function of the contracts by which the unions and management are bound. Fortunately, it is easy to work within the limitations; but it will come with experience.

Many times you will be working a stage which is non-union; this too has advantages and disadvantages. The non-union stage is usually smaller, so, you will seldom have many of the luxuries that you find in the larger auditoriums. Usually the venues are flexible, and much more willing to share your artistic vision. The staff of such stages are often musicians themselves who just need another source of income. This flexibility and artistic exuberance, can make the smaller non-union stages a pleasure to work.

The stage crew is good, but having your own people is also good. The biggest advantage is that they know your artistic requirements. If they are working with you for several cities in a row, then they become very fast at breaking down and setting up a show.

The sound man (or woman) deserves special consideration. I have seen artists come and give constant instructions to the sound person during a performance. A constant chatter of "raise this level", "lower this level", "more bass", does no good. It actually makes things worse, because it distracts from the artistic flow of the performance. It is also very bad for another important reason. The way modern auditoriums are constructed, it is impossible to sit on stage and judge what the audience is hearing. All you are hearing is the monitors, which may have little relationship to what is actually going out into the house. Therefore giving commands, without the possibility of knowing what the audience is hearing, is a sure-fire recipe for bad sound. If the sound person is permanently attached the auditorium, then it is better to have one of your people sit with them and politely give suggestions. From then on, you have to simply trust them.

There is another reason why sitting on stage and barking commands at the technical personnel is unprofessional. After all, where was the artist during the sound check? If there was no sound check, and the artist simply arrives and walks on stage ten minutes after the program was to begin, then that artist rightly deserves to have everything go wrong in front of them!

Other Artists - So far we have discussed technical personnel and the promoters; but we also have to deal with other artists. At a minimum, you will have to deal with the "main artist". The term "main artist" is basically obsolete because today, the tabla player is considered on equal footing to the vocalist or the instrumentalist. Either way, you will be have to deal with any number of other artists in a stage setting. It is imperative that one member of the group function as the group leader. This is a matter of simple practicality. Whenever there is no clearly defined leader, tensions and arguments will inevitably arise.

Sometimes you will be part of a large production that may have fifty to a hundred people. In such situations, the leader is the director. The director's artistic vision is the one that you must follow. Spend time to understand what the director's objective is, and do what you can to accommodate.

I remember one situation well. I was working with a dance troupe under a well noted choreographer. This program was a very large, high-budget affair. Unfortunately, the choreographer was taking her usual *desi* (Indian) approach to the whole affair. She would come late to rehearsals rattling off a litany of implausible excuses. She stayed to get our section done with much unnecessary talk and commotion. When our section was finished, she rattled off another string of woes and reasons for her early departure. A day or two later when the program was being finalised, she was upset to find that the majority of her numbers were cut.

The root cause of the problem was cultural. By coming late and doing a lot of *nakkara* (acting like a prima donna), she was under the mistaken view that she was maintaining her prestige. She was actually accomplishing the opposite. In the West, such actions are considered unprofessional. She had manoeuvred herself into a situation were she was not being sensitive to the director's requirements. Since her pieces did not meet the artistic requirements, they were the first to be cut.

The point of this last example is simple; any production is going to have a well established social structure. One should be sensitive to the total artistic process when dealing with others, not your perceived social status. If you get distracted by these matters, you will be cast out!

Managers - The final class of people that we have to deal with is the manager. The various types of managers and their roles in your profession are complex. The manager's role is primarily one of business, so we do not really need to go into it here.

Etiquette - Whenever we are dealing with the myriad of artists and technical personnel, there will be no room for discord. Discord backstage will be reflected in what happens onstage. Since your encounter with many of these people will be for the first time, there is not going to be any chance of getting to know them to establish a deep working relationship. Therefore, it is important that we fall back upon etiquette in order to make the show flow as smoothly as possible.

Unfortunately, maintaining proper etiquette is especially difficult in the real world, because we find ourself straddling two different cultures. It is a fact that Indian etiquette is very different from Western etiquette. This is further complicated by the fact that Western stage etiquette is different from day-to-day etiquette. Let us look into some of these points.

Ch. 17. Stagecraft

Working with the stage involves some special considerations. The stage is going to be your home for the next several hours. I never walk around my house with shoes on, so I am certainly not going to walk all over the stage with them. This will cause no problem with American stage personnel, and will definitely send the correct messages to the Indians in your entourage.

Another further show of respect is the *pranam* (प्रनाम). When you walk onstage for the first time, it is customary to reach down with your right hand and lightly touch the stage, then bring the hand to the forehead.

Remember to greet people. Setup for a program can be a tense affair, and such courtesies can diffuse tensions before they get out of hand.

Do not wish anyone good luck! This is a well-known custom among artists and stage personnel in the West, but is largely unknown to Indians in your group. The superstition is that wishing someone good luck before they go out on stage will actually bring them bad luck. The theatrical expression "break a leg" is a reflection of this. Since you will be dealing with people who may not be aware of this, it is safest to simply say nothing.

Say good things about how people performed. When the job is done, it is always good to complement the people that you worked with. However, do not be insincere! Highlight the good things that happened in a program, but don't mention the things that went amiss. A few kind words at this point will have good results in future programs.

We have covered many of the issues involved in dealing with the various personnel. However, there is one group of people that absolutely must be dealt with. Your very survival is going to depend on how you deal with these people. This of course, is the audience.

AUDIENCE CONTROL

Your effectiveness as an artist is going to be gauged in part by the degree of control you have over the audience. This concept of "control" is not to be interpreted in any Machiavellian way. It is common sense. Just as a driver must have complete control over the vehicle if they are to be an effective driver, so too, you must be in complete control over the performance if you are going to be an effective entertainer. We will now look at several issues involved.

Keep the audience's attention. This may sound obvious, but audiences may become inattentive for a number of reasons. The first section of the performance (before the interval / intermission) is especially vulnerable. This is prone to people coming in late and hunting for their seats. There are the inevitable greetings that members of the audience speak, or shout, oblivious to the fact that a concert is going on. Indian women are especially distracted as they look around and see what kind of *saris* and jewellery their friends are wearing. There are also circumstances such as crying babies and cellular telephones.

The first thing that we must do is identify the problem areas. The most delicate areas are the periods between pieces. It is during this section that the artists are forced to retune the instruments, search for lyrics, or a host of other necessary chores. Unfortunately, this is the time when people begin to strike up conversations with their neighbours and lose attention.

The best way to keep the audience's attention is to keep the program moving. Let us look further into tricks that will do this.

A good master of ceremonies is one of the best ways to keep the program moving. The master of ceremonies, simply referred to as the MC or emcee, is one of the most unappreciated jobs of the whole performance. While the artists are retuning, the master of ceremonies is going to be talking. While the MC is talking, their attention should be focused on what is happening backstage and onstage. They will talk as long as the preparations are going on, and will stop soon as the preparations are finished. Timing and delivery is as important for the master of ceremonies, as it is for any other artist.

The master of ceremonies also performs another important function; he (or she) also sets up the next piece. This setting up may be as simple as stating the name of the piece, or it may be as complicated as relating an entire story. A master of ceremonies is an integral part of the whole function, and a good one greatly enhances a performance.

Unfortunately, an inexperienced master of ceremonies will make the performer's job much more difficult. The majority of master of ceremonies are not artists. They are usually members of the community chosen for some local political reason. Due to a lack of experience, they are blithely oblivious as to what their artistic responsibilities are. Therefore, it will often be up to you to compensate for any weakness.

I believe that the best way to keep the audience's attention during the crucial periods between pieces is to talk to them. If you look directly at people and talk to them, you will immediately get their attention and hold it. Tell them stories, tell them jokes, explain some of the intricacies of the music, anything will do the job. When you return to the task of playing, things will go much better.

The technique of talking to the audience is certainly important; but one must also minimise outside distractions. Let us look at this from a psychological and psychophysical standpoint.

The basic psychophysical process is called masking. It is a phenomenon whereby one form of stimulus can reduce the perception of another. In a performance situation, we will use both optical masking as well as acoustical masking to maintain control of the audience.

Acoustical masking is easily illustrated. Imagine that two people are carrying on a conversation in the back of a crowded auditorium. With the exception of these two individuals, everybody else is quiet and there is nothing going on stage. Under these circumstances, this quiet conversation will be heard by virtually everybody in the auditorium. Now imagine that the performance is going full swing. Even though the people may be talking at the same volume, it is highly unlikely that anyone except the nearest people will even be aware that a conversation is going on. Remember, the presence of sound from the stage did not cause the conversation to become suddenly softer! What is happening is that the volume of the sound system is masking the sound of the conversation. You are using the sound system to help maintain the attention of the audience by masking out potential disruptions. So keep the music reasonably loud.

Optical masking is also important. Imagine that you are riding down the highway in the middle of the night. You have no trouble seeing the road. All of a sudden, a car comes from the other side with high beams on. At this point you are blinded, and may have difficulty seeing the road. Your headlights did not diminish by the approach of another car; but your ability to see was hampered by the oncoming lights. Now imagine an auditorium where the lights on the stage are very bright, but the house lights are very dim. This large difference in lighting is going to make it much less noticeable when people are wandering around and hunting for their seats. It puts a stop to a large number of distractions which plague a performance. If the audience is unable to see who is coming in, then they will not be able to wave their hands in the air shouting "Khem cho" to everyone who comes in.

There is one major obstacle to maintaining control of the audience, that is the *farmaish*

The word *"farmaish"* defies translation. It is often translated as "challenge" or "encore", but both English words miss the meaning by a wide berth. Towards the end of a performance, it was once common for members of the audience to request certain material. The artist would do so, and then from then on, it would be nothing but one request or *"farmaish"* after another. This was acceptable given the cultural climate (i.e., India in the late 19th or early 20th century.) It is still appropriate in the context of a small *baitak* (intimate house program). Unfortunately, it does not work today in a large concert situation. Once the *farmaishs* start, there is a predictable chain of events which will lead the quality of the program into a downward spiral. From that point on, it is one *farmaish* after another. There becomes no end in sight.

The first victim of the *farmaish* is the program organiser. As performances go overtime, the costs start to skyrocket. Remember, the organisers are not going to get any more money from these endless *farmaishs*. You are alienating the most important person in the operation.

The next victim of the *farmaish* is the audience. You start getting *farmaishs* concerning peculiar *rags*, *tals*, or compositional forms. Usually these *farmaishs* come from individuals who merely wish to show off how smart they are. This is a no-win situation. There is usually a good reason why these forms are obscure; they are either unappealing or esoteric. If you give in to the *farmaish*, you will find yourself performing to only a handful of listeners, while the majority of the audience is just wishing that this would end.

As we review this last section, we have shown that maintaining the control over the audience is of prime importance in creating an effective artistic event. The methods by which one holds the audience's attention are both technical and artistic. Proper attention to these techniques is important to giving a good performance.

CONCLUSION

This chapter has gone over many of the details of a stagecraft. The reason is simple; it is pointless to perform tabla exquisitely if the overall program fails to grab the audience's attention. It is very easy for a musician to become preoccupied with details of playing. But the audience is going to be reacting to the program in its entirety. Knowledge of stagecraft is just as important as knowledge of the technique of the tabla.

WORKS CITED

Bharata Muni (translated by a board of scholars)
200 BC (circa) *Natyashastra Shastra* Sri Satguru Publications, Delhi.

Caruso Glusy
2016 *"Gestures as an Interface of Cultural Identity in Musical Performance: Western Embodiment of Karnatic Music"*, Proceedings of the International Conference "Musical Gestures as Creative Interface" (2016), Universidade Católica Portuguesa, Porto, Portugal. (pp. 91–92). Porto: CITAR.

DiBenedetto, Stephen
2012 *An Introduction to Theatre Design*. London, Routledge.

Lord, William H.
1991 *Stagecraft 1; A Complete guide to Backstage Work*, 2nd Edition. Meriwether Publishing Ltd. Colorado Springs, CO.

Oxford University Press.
1937 *Oxford Universal English Dictionary on Historical Principals. Volume 4 Sol - Tol*, Doubleday, Doran and Co, 1937.

Taylor, JW
1890   *Auditorium Building, Chicago. Auditorium interior from balcony*. Library of Congress, Prints & Photographs Division, ILL,16-CHIG,39-89.

CHAPTER 18

CONCLUSION

This chapter really should not be here. There is no conclusion to the theoretical approach to tabla. The subject is extremely vast and we have only touched upon it. I have done my best to present the field in a clear fashion, but I am only human. I apologise for any errors and omissions. Any comments will be welcome (at the time of writing my e-mail is david@chandrakantha.com).

This chapter should instead be called a "Continuation". It is with this chapter that I must pass on the duty of codifying and elucidating the system to you, the reader. I have no doubt that there is someone out there who will be able to build upon this modest foundation. I extend to you my heartfelt support, and best wishes

Good luck!

APPENDICES

APPENDIX 1
LAHARA

The ease with which *laharas* are created makes it impossible to create a truly complete list. New *laharas* are being made all the time and old *laharas* are falling out of use. Here is an extensive collection. This list is in Western notation; therefore, there are a few caveats which must be observed.

The first caveat is that all the notation is fixed from a key of C. This is purely a matter of notational convenience. Indian music may be played from any key.

The second caveat revolves around the conspicuous absence of the time signature. Western concepts of "Four/Four" or "Three/Four" are totally irrelevant. For notational convenience the quarter note has been used to define the beat while the measures will follow the Indian concept of *tal*. Therefore, while a *lahara* in *Tintal* will have all measures of four beats; *Jhaptal* will alternate between two and three beats. One need only refer back to the chapters governing *theka* and *tal* in volume one for details.

The third caveat revolves around the drone. We did not bother to write in the drone, because we felt it was self evident.

One will also notice that on occasion there are superfluous sharps and flat signs. Once an accidental is noted, it will hold true for the entire measure. But many readers are unfamiliar with this convention. Therefore, I have gone ahead and noted them multiple times.

One will notice that the placement of the octaves is inconsistent. This is not an oversight. These *laharas* are noty tied to any particular octave. When they were transliterated into staff notation, I chose which ever octave seemed simplest to understand.

DADRA (6 beats)

Bhairavi (Gopal, et al. undated-b: phonorecording)

Bhairavi (Sharma 1973:233)

Kafi (Misra 1966) One cannot help but notice that this *lahara* is derived from the well known piece "Greensleeves". The use of a well known Western theme underscores the extreme flexibility of the entire *lahara* style.

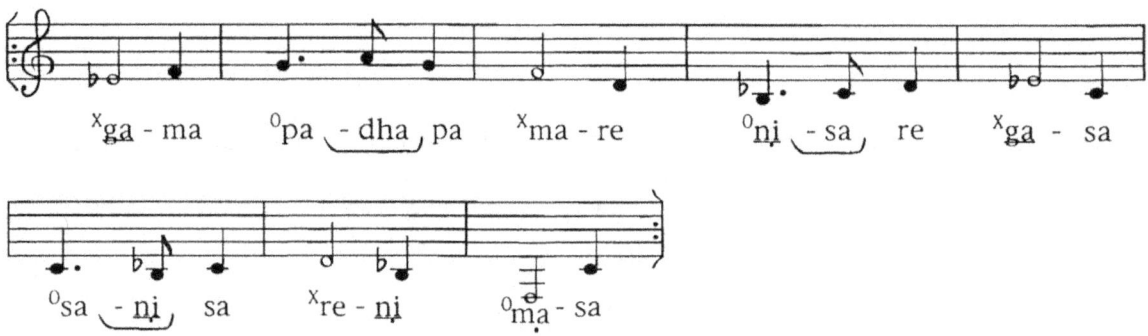

Kedar (Sharma 1973:233)

Mand (Rakha, et.al. ????: phonorecording) This is the longest *lahara* which I have ever encountered. However this *lahara* very clearly indicates the folk origins of *dadra tal*.

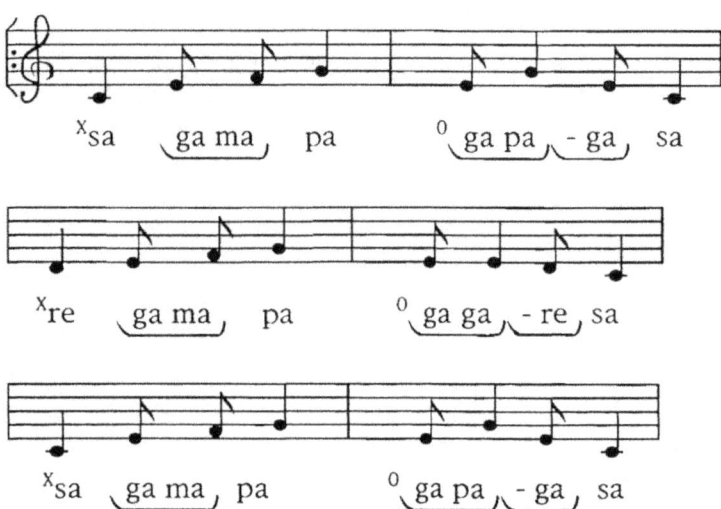

Appendix 1. Lahara

Tilak Kamod (Sharma 1973:233)

FARODAST (7 beat)

Malkauns (Gopal, et.al. ???? a: phonorecording)

RUPAK TAL (7 beats)

Bhairav (Sharma 1973:232)

Bilawal (Misra 1966: phonorecording)

Chandrakauns (Bhattacharya 1968: phonorecording)

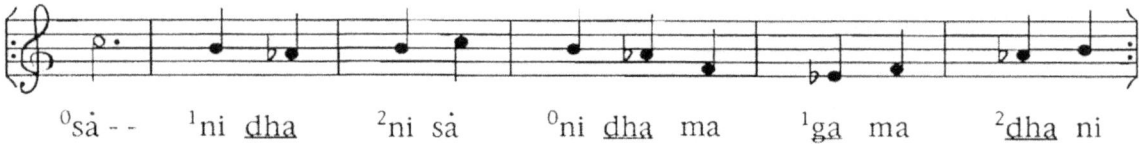

Chandrakauns (Shepherd 1976: 123)

Deshkar (Sharma 1973:232)

Yaman Kalyan (Sharma 1973:232)

Appendix 1. Lahara

KAHERAVA TAL (8 beats)

Bilawal (Gopal, et.al. ????b: Phonorecording)

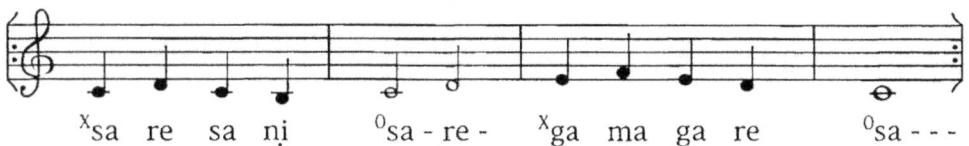

Bilawal (Misra 1966: phonorecording) This is the same theme as the traditional piece *"Au Clair de la Lune"*. The use of this theme underscores the extreme flexibility of the lahara.

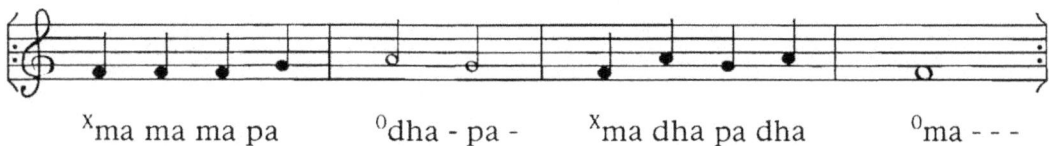

Khamaj (K. Khan 1975: phonorecording)

JHAPTAL (10 beats)

Chandrakauns (Shepherd 1973: 123)

Desh (Sharma 1973:228)

Hamsadhwani (Sharma 1973:229)

Jog (Sharma 1973:228)

Lalitagauri (Sharma 1973:229)

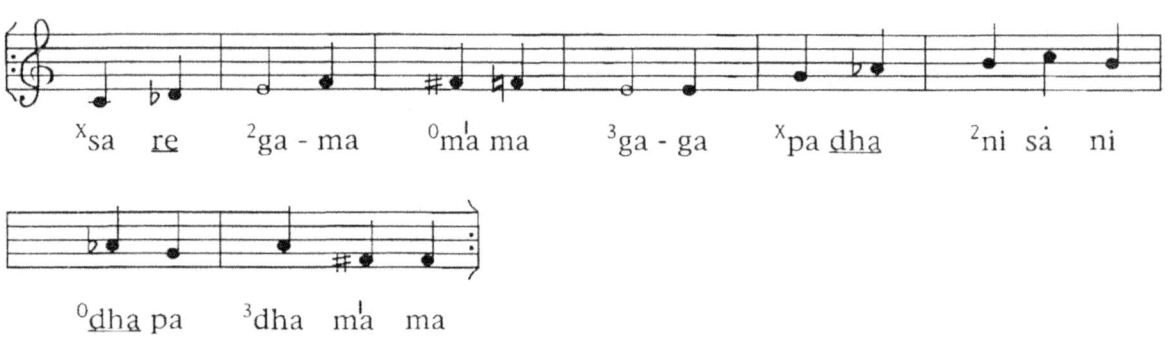

Malavi (Sharma 1973:228)

Appendix 1. Lahara

Puriyadhanashri (Narayan 1975: phonorecording)

Reva (Sharma 1973:229)

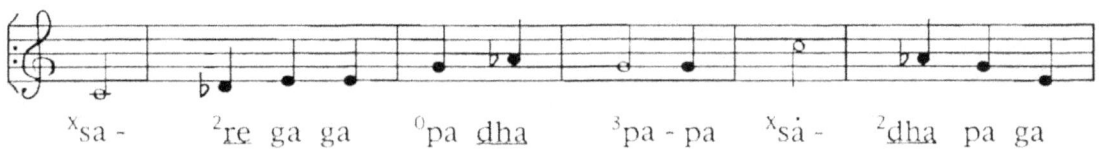

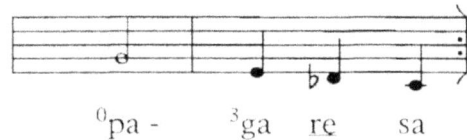

Tilak Kamod (Sharma 1973:229)

Todi (Misra 1966: phonorecording)

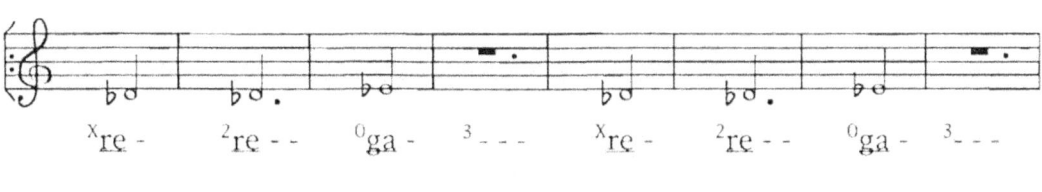

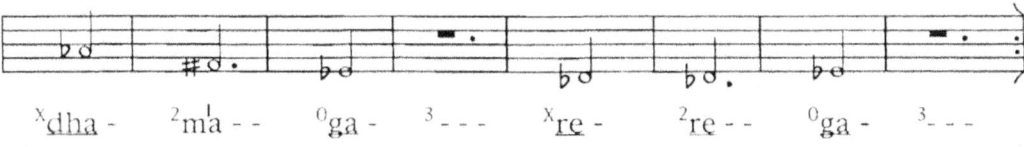

SOOLTAL (10 beats)

Bilawal (Rakha et.al.:phonorecording)

Durga (Sharma 1973:229)

Malkauns (Sharma 1973:229)

Multani (Sharma 1973:229)

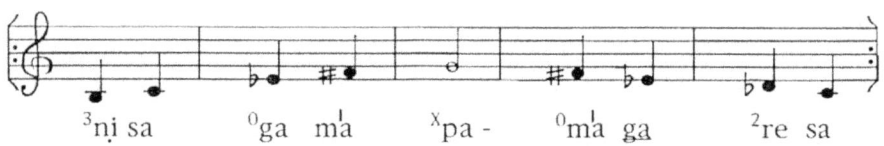

Paraj (Sharma 1973:229)

Sarang (Sharma 1973:230)

Appendix 1. Lahara

CHAR TAL KI SAVARI (or any 11 matra tal)

Desh (Sharma 1973:233)

Desh (Rakha et.al. 1972:phonorecording)

Gaursarang (Sharma 1973:233)

Malkauns (Sharma 1973:233)

Yaman Kalyan (Gopal, et.al. ????a:phonorecording)

CHAUTAL (12 beats)

Bhageshri (Dagar, et.al. 1974: phonorecording)

Yaman Kalyan (Jha 1983:182)

EKTAL (12 beats)

Chandrakauns (Shepherd 1976:123)

Bageshri (Sharma 1973:230)

Jaunpuri (Rakha et. al. 1972:phonorecording)

Malkauns (Sharma 1973:230)

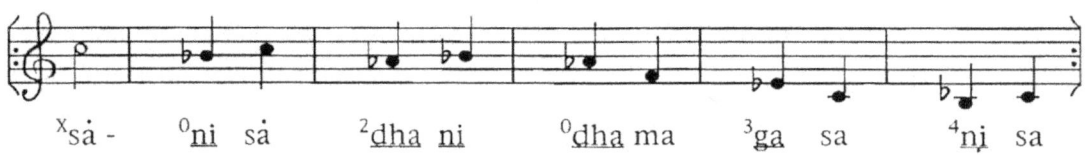

Rageshri (Sharma 1973:230)

Appendix 1. Lahara

Tilang (Sharma 1973:230)

Triveni (Sharma 1973:230)

CHANDRACHAUTAL (or any 13 matra tal)

Chayanat (Sharma 1973:233)

Lalith (Sharma 1973:233)

Sohani (Sharma 1973:233)

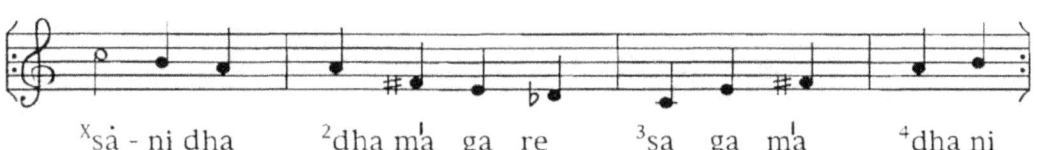

ADA CHAUTAL (14 beats)

Chandrakauns (Sharma 1973:230)

Desh (Sharma 1973:230)

Puriyadhanashri (Sharma 1973:231)

Rageshri (Sharma 1973:230)

Sarang (Sharma 1973:231)

DEEPCHANDI (14 beats)

Durbari (Sharma 1973:231)

Appendix 1. Lahara

Jaitshree (Sharma 1973:231)

DHAMMAR (14 beats)

Adana (Sharma 1973:232)

Bageshri (Sharma 1973:231)

Chandrakauns (Shepherd 1976:123)

Kalyan (K. Khan 1975:phonorecording)

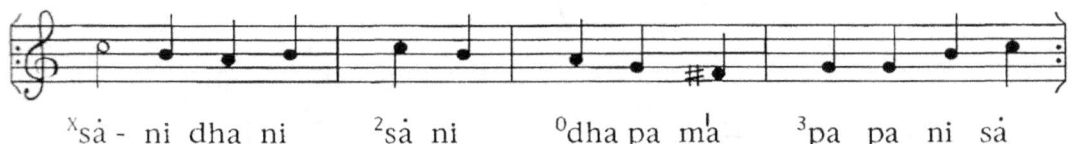

Malkauns (Sharma 1973:231)

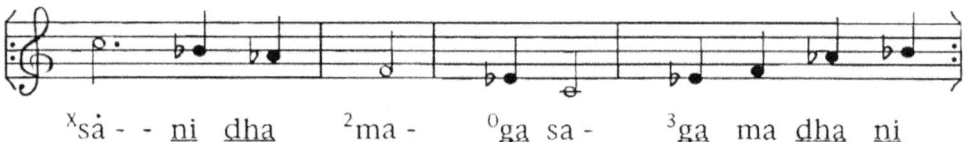

Puriyadhanashri (M. Datta, reputed to be from Birju Maharaj)

Sarang (Sharma 1973:231)

JHOOMRA (14 beats)

Durga (Sharma 1973:232)

Gunakali (Sharma 1973:232)

Hindol (Sharma 1973:232)

Shankara (Sharma 1973:232)

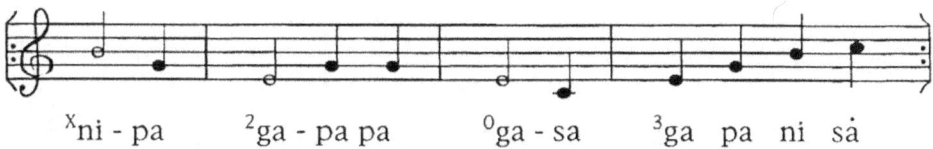

PANCHAM SAVARI (or other 15 matra tal)

Jog (Rakha et. al. ????: phonorecording)

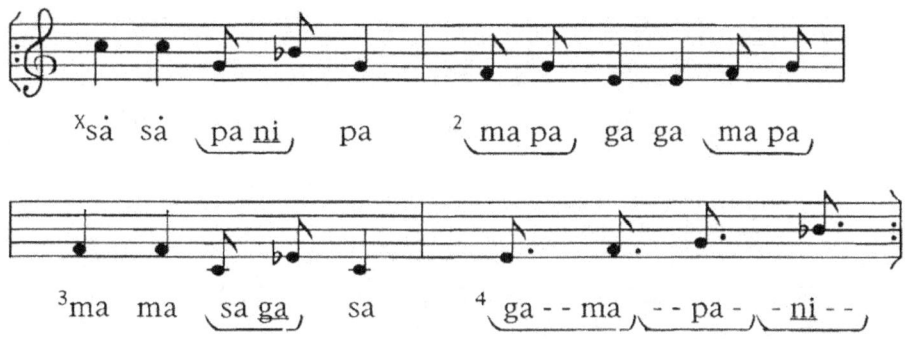

Multani (Sharma 1973:234)

Narayani (Sharma 1973:234)

Shritank (Sharma 1973:234)

TINTAL (16 beats)

Alhaiyabilawal (Sharma 1973:228)

Bhairavi (Gopal, et.al. ????b: phonorecording)

Bhinnashadaj (M. Datta, reputed to be from Birju Maharaj)

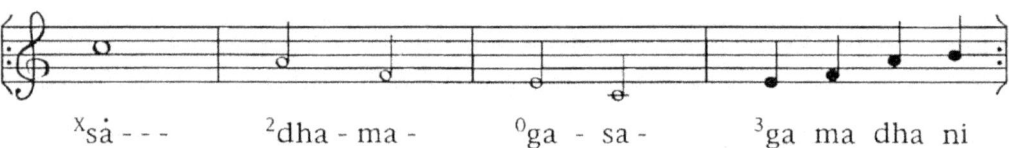

Bhupali (Gopal, et.al. ????b: phonorecording)

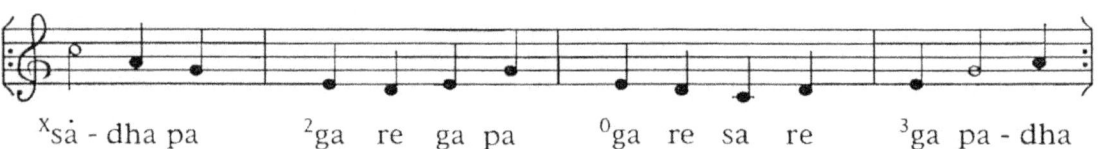

Bhupali (Gopal, et.al. ????b: phonorecording)

Appendix 1. Lahara

Bihagada (Sharma 1973:228)

Chandrakalyan (Sharma 1973:228)

Chandrakauns

This is perhaps the most famous *lahara* in India. Perhaps it may be considered a victim of its own popularity. This is because in recent years there is a tendency to eschew this *lahara* for newer and fresher ones.

Chandrakauns (Gottlieb 1977:40) (Transposed to key of C) This *lahara* is also mentioned in "Tabla and the Benares Gharana" (Shepherd 1976:122)

Chandrakauns (Gottlieb 1977:8) (Transposed to key of C)

Chandrakauns (Gottlieb 1977:116) (Transposed to key of C)

Charukesi (Rakha, et al 1972: phonorecording)

Desh (Gopal. et.al. ????a: phonorecording)

Desh (Gopal, et.al. ????a: phonorecording)

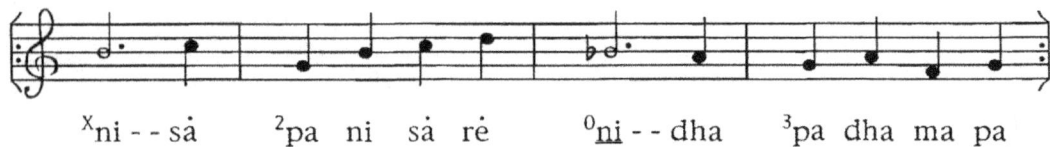

Appendix 1. Lahara

Gorakhkaliyan (Shepherd 1976: 122)

Janasamodhani (M. Datta, reputed to be from Chitresh Das)

Jhinjhoti (M. Datta, reputed to be from Birju Maharaj)

Jhinjhoti (M. Datta, reputed to be from Birju Maharaj)

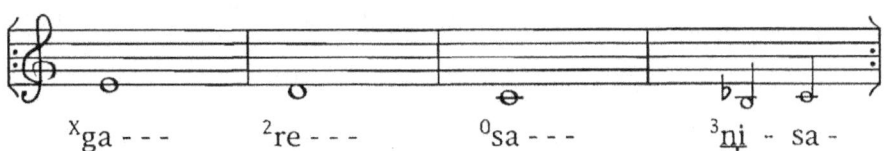

Khamaj (Shepherd 1976: 122)

Khambavati (Sharma 1973:227)

Kirvani (traditional)

Marwa (M. Datta, personal interview, reputed to be from Birju Maharaj)

Nat Bhairav (K. Khan 1975: phonorecording)

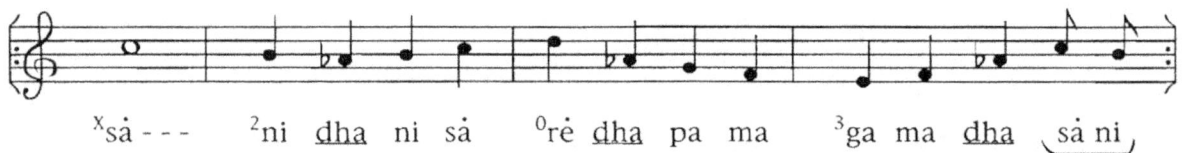

Natkuranjika (Sharma 1973:228)

Natkuranjika (M. Datta, reputed to be from Birju Maharaj)

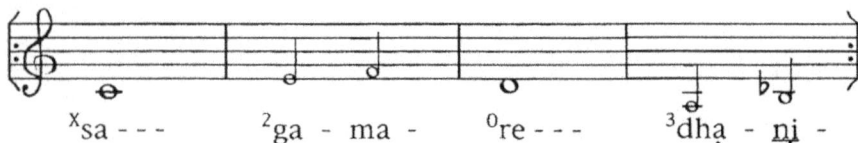

Appendix 1. Lahara

Pilu (Amrohi, et.al. 1972:phonorecording)

Puriadhanashri (M. Datta, reputed to be from Birju Maharaj)

Todi (Misra 1966:phonorecording)

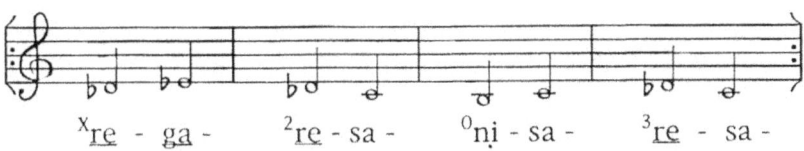

VISHNU TAL (or other 17 matra tals)

Bhageshri (Sharma 1973:234)

Bhinnashadaj (Sharma 1973:234)

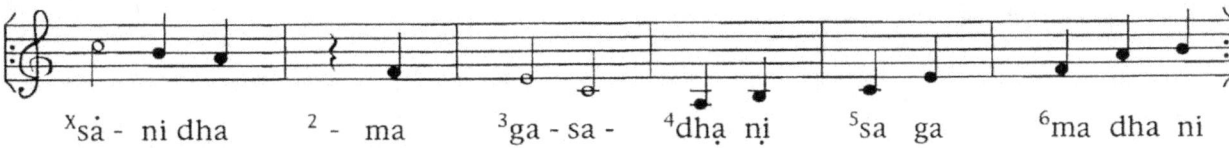

Shri (Sharma 1973:234)

BASANT TAL (Or other 18 matra tals)

Basant (Sharma 1973:234)

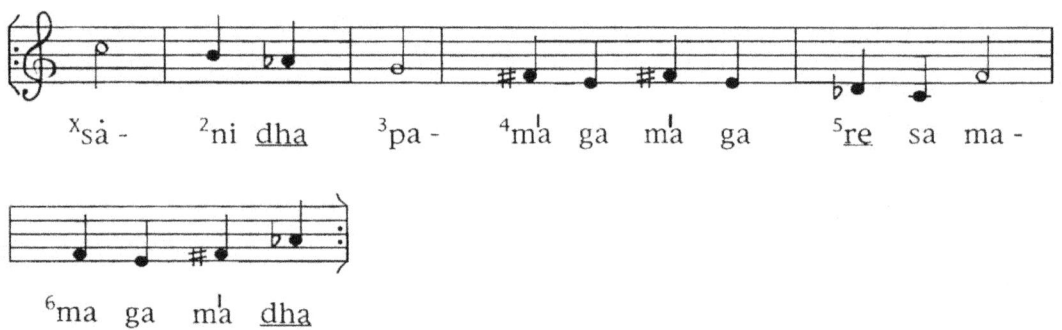

CHANDRA TAL (or other 18 beat tal)

Chandrakalyan (Sharma 1973:234)

MATTA TAL (or other 18 matra tal)

Champakali (Sharma 1973:235)

Appendix 1. Lahara

Malkauns (Sharma 1973:235)

PURNA TAL (Or other 19 matra tal)

Bageshri (Sharma 1973:235)

Malkauns (Sharma 1973:235)

MANSIJ TAL (or other 21 beat tal)

Bhupali (Sharma 1973:235)

Bhimpilasi (Sharma 1973:235)

Sohani (Sharma 1973:235)

WORKS CITED

Amrohi, Kamal, et.al.
1972   Pakeezah. Dum Dum, India: EMI/Odeon. (phonorecording).

Bhattacharya, Deben
1968   Hours of the Night: Ragas from Benares. London: Argo Record Company Ltd. (phonorecording)

Dagar, Zia Mohiuddin, Ram Shankar (Pagal) Das, Iqbal Ahmed
1974   Glimpses of Ancient India . Dum Dum, India: EMI, Gramophone Company of India, Ltd. (phonorecording).

Appendix 1. Lahara

Datta, Mukhund
1995   Personal Interview.

Gopal, Ram, R. Choudhury Devi, T. R. Azad, Durga Lal, Tirith Ajamani, et.al.
undated   When a God Dances: Classical Music and Dance of India, Vol 1. Chicago, Philips (Mercury Record Corporation) (phonorecording).
undated   When a God Dances: Classical Music and Dance of India, Vol 2. Chicago, Philips (Mercury Record Corporation) (phonorecording)

Gottlieb, R. S.
1973   Forty-two Lessons for Tabla. New York: Folkways Records (Phonorecording)
1977a   The Major Traditions of North Indian Tabla Drumming. Munchen, Germany: Musikverlag Emil Katzbichler.
1977b   The Major Traditions of North Indian Tabla Drumming. Transcriptions :Munchen, Germany: Musikverlag Emil Katzbichler.

Jha, Narayan
1983   "Tal Prabhand: Panch Talon Men Yaman-Kalyan", Sangeet (Tal Ank). Hathras, India Sangeet Karyalaya.Vol. 14: Edited by Prabhulal Garg

Khan, Keramatulla
1975   Tabla Recital: Ustad Keramatulla Khan.. Dum Dum, India: EMI/Gramophone Company of India, Ltd. (phonorecording).

Misra, Mahapurush
1966   Indian Drums. New York: Connoisseur Society, (phonorecording).

Narayan, Ram
1975   Master of the Sarangi: Classical Music of India. New York: Nonsuch Records. (phonorecording)

Rakha, Alla, Shamim Ahmed, Taranath Ramrao, and N.C.Mullick
????   Alla Rakha Tabla!. Los Angeles: World Pacific Records. (phonorecording)

Rakha, Alla and Zakir Hussain
1972   Ustad Alla Rakha and Zakir Hussain. Dum Dum India: The Gramophone Company of India. (phonorecording)

Sharma, Bhagavat Sharan
1973   Tal Prakash. Hathras, India: Sangeet Karyalaya.
1977   Tal Shastra. Alighar, India: B. A. Electric Press.

Shepherd, F. A.
1976   Tabla and the Benares Gharana. Ann Arbor: University Microfilms International. (Ph.D. Dissertation).

APPENDIX 2
THE STROKES

This appendix is a key that functions as a common reference. This appendix lays out the various strokes and figure numbers which were used in previous references. Only the common *bols* are shown in the captions. A more detailed description of the *bols* and their technique is found in volume one of this series.

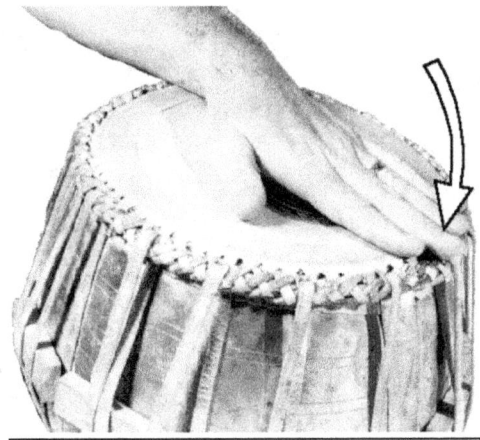

Figure AP2.1. Ka क

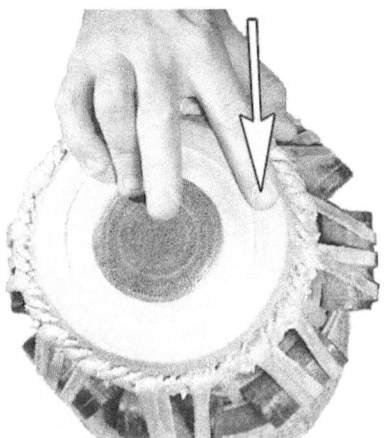

Figure AP2.2. Naa ना, Taa ता

Figure AP2.3. Ga ग

Figure AP2.4. Dhaa धा

Figure AP2.5. Tin तिं, Taa ता

Figure AP2.6. Dhin धिं

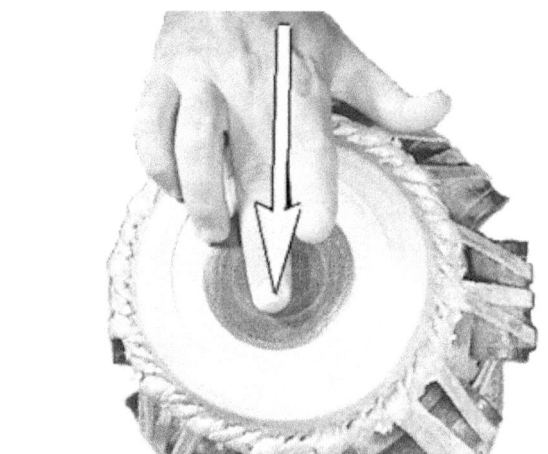

Figure AP2.7. Tee ती, Ti ति

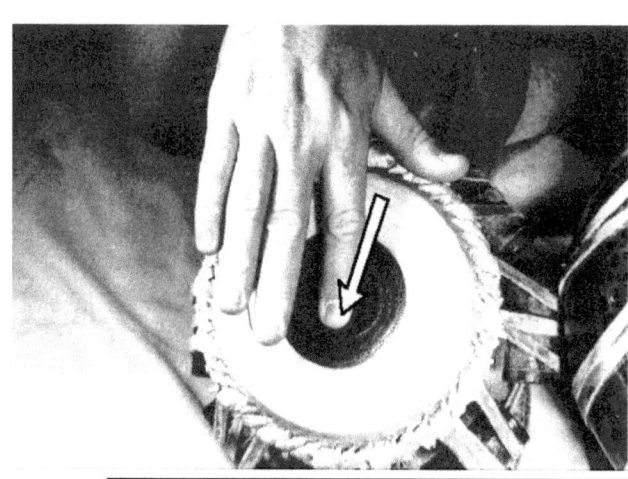

Figure AP2.8. Ta ट, Ra र

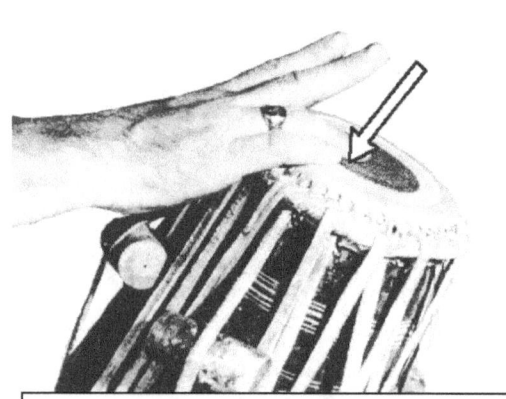

Figure AP2.9. Ta ट, Da ड

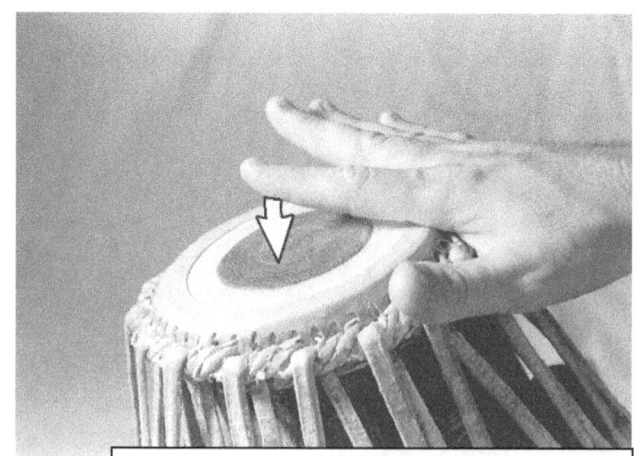

Figure AP2.10. Too तु or Toon तुं

Appendix 2. The Strokes

Figure AP2.11. Tak तक्

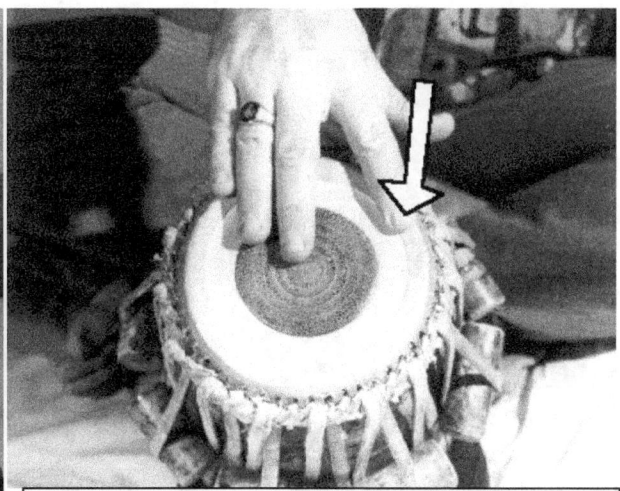

Figure AP2.12. Tet तेत्, tak तक्, or Naa ना (notice position of middle finger)

Figure AP2.13. Tet तेत्, Naa ना (notice position of ring finger)

Figure AP2.14. Ga ग

Figure AP2.15. Ga ग, Ka क

Figure AP2.16. Ga ग

Figure AP2.17. Ga ग (pakhawaj style)

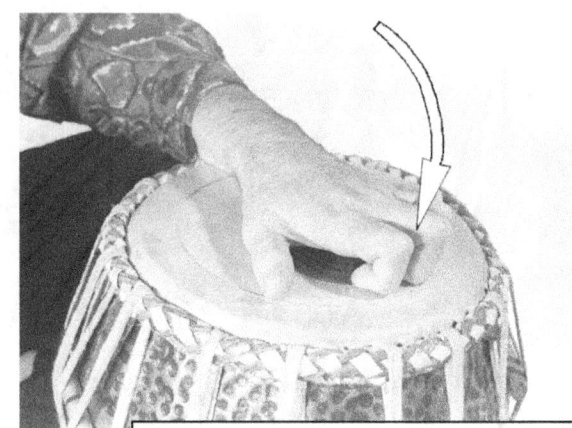

Figure AP2.18. Ka क

Figure AP2.19. Ka क

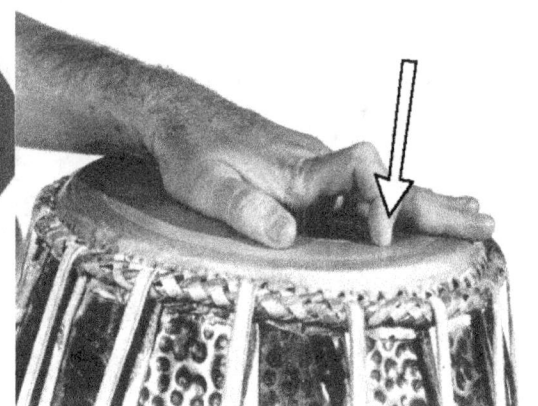

Figure AP2.20. Ka क

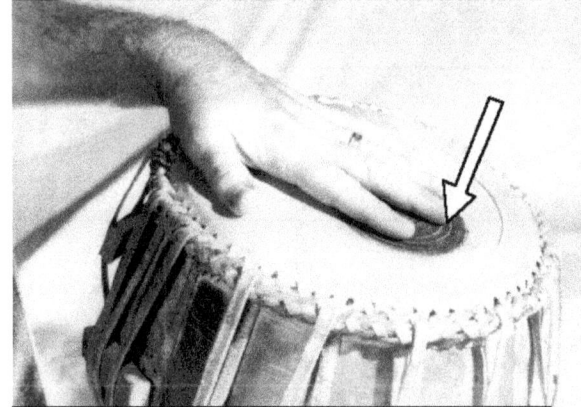

Figure AP2.21. Ka क, Kat कत् (hand back)

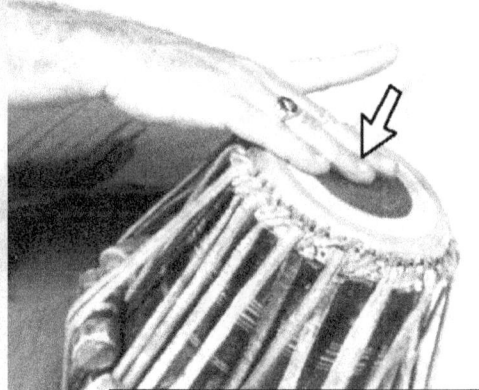

Figure AP2.22. Ti ति (flat sound)

Appendix 2. The Strokes

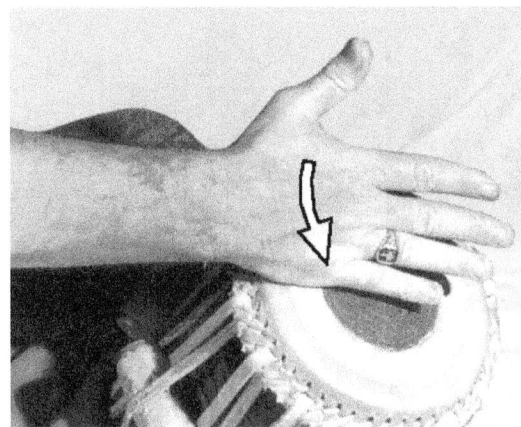

Figure AP2.23. Taa ता (pakhawaj style)

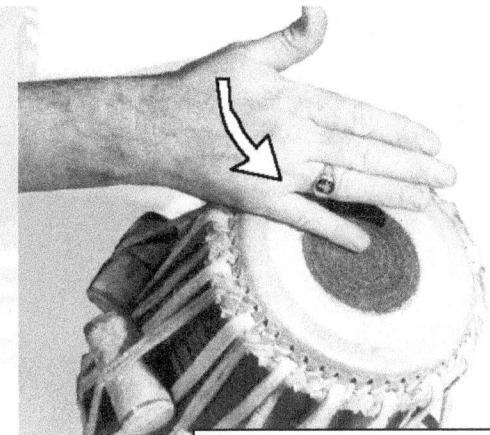

Figure AP2.24. Taa ता (pakhawaj style)

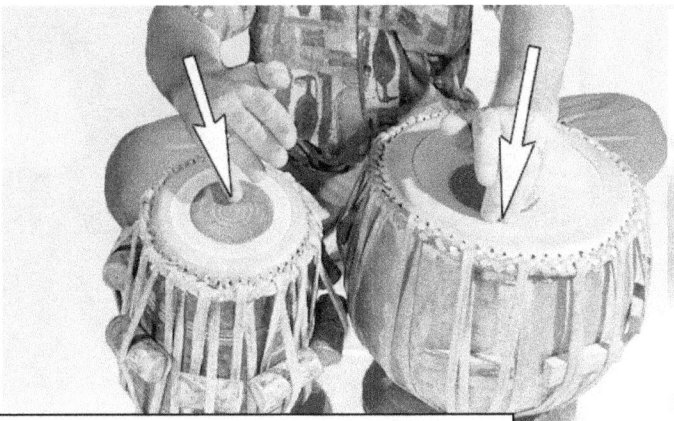

Figure AP2.25. Dhaa धा (pakhawaj style)

Figure AP2.26. Dee दी.

Figure AP2.27. Deen दीं (pakhawaj style).

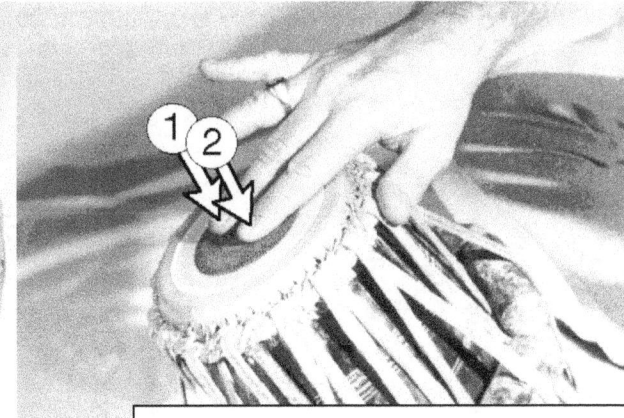

Figure AP2.28. Tra त्र, Tre त्रे

Figure AP2.29. Kra कृ, Kre के

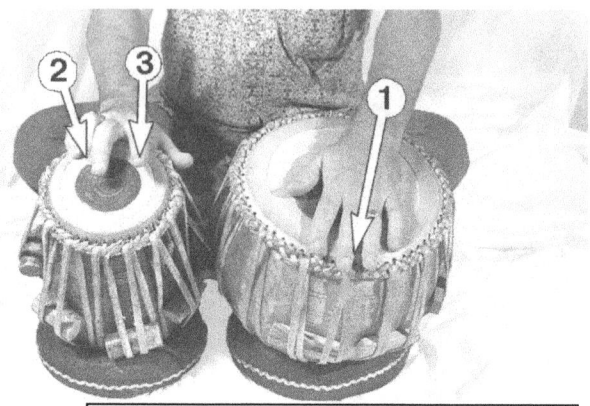

Figure AP2.30. Kdaan क्डां

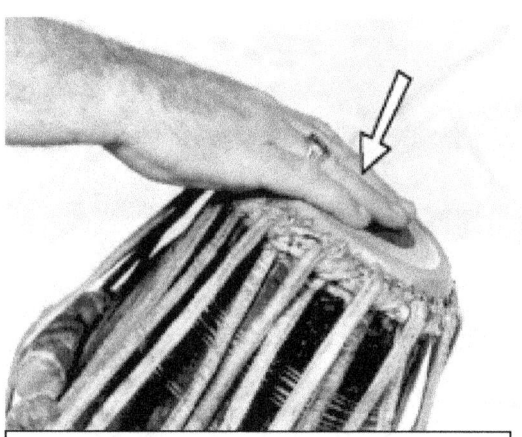

Figure AP2.31. Tet तेत्

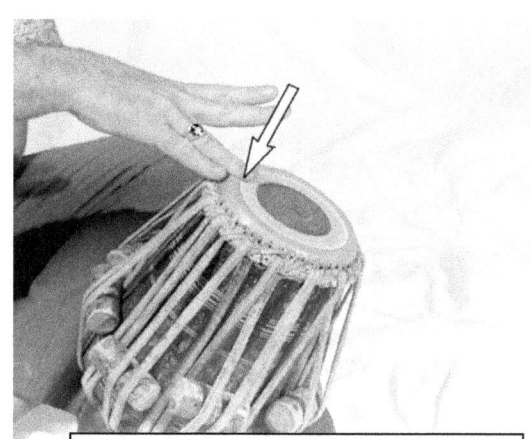

Figure AP2.32. Taa ता

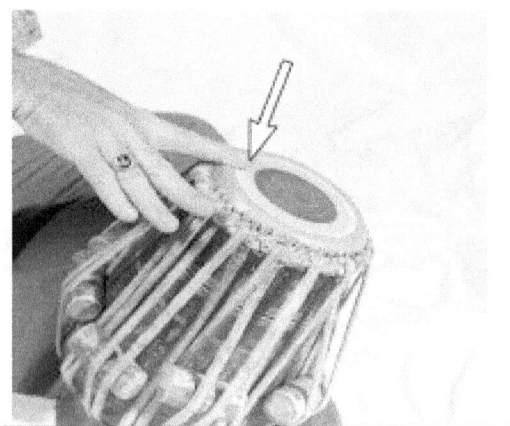

Figure AP2.33. Raa रा

Figure AP2.34. Ti ति

Appendix 2. The Strokes

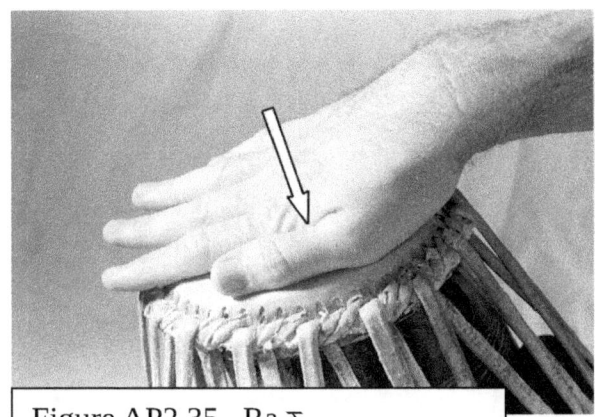

Figure AP2.35. Ra र

Figure AP2.36. Dhi धि

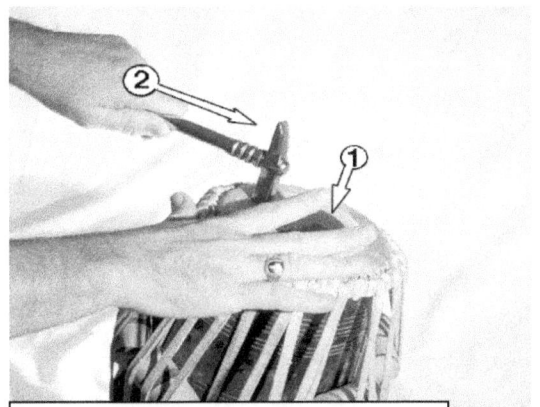

Figure AP2.37. Hammer

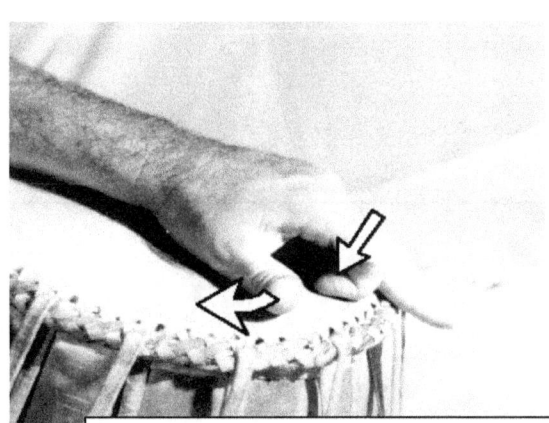

Figure AP2.38. Snap (Ka क)

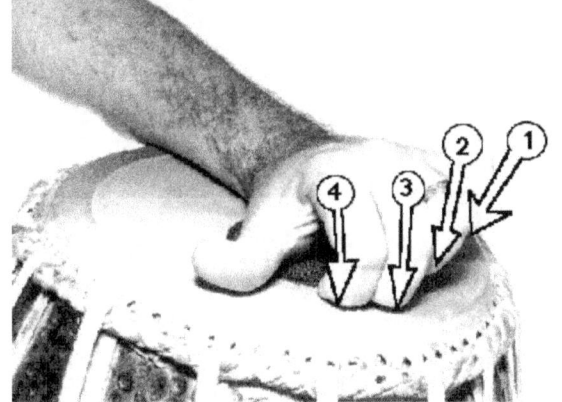

Figure AP2.39. Four finger snap

APPENDIX 3
MITRA'S LAHARA PETI

It was in 1977, I stumbled across an ingenious approach to *lahara* generation. To the best of my knowledge it was the first electronic approach to *lahara* generation. Because if its historical importance, I think that it should be discussed here.

The man behind this device lived in Bangalore. I never met him, but I am told that his name was P. Mitra. He made a small electronic box, similar to an electronic *surpeti*, which generated a *lahara* automatically. It was able to generate a *Tintal lahara* in any key or any tempo. Although it was limited to *Tintal*, its flexibility of tempo and key was outstanding.

The first thing I did was to disassemble it and see how it was put together. All of the parts had their part-numbers painted over. This is a common practice in India used to discourage reverse engineering. However, the simple elegance of the circuit was clearly apparent. Figure AP3.1 shows a diagram of the device.

The heart of the machine was a free running multivibrator. This is nothing more than a low frequency square wave oscillator. It is this circuit that determines the *lay*, or tempo. If the oscillator has a frequency of 50 cycles per minute, then the *lahara* operates at 50 beats per minute. Any number of configurations are imaginable; however a simple oscillator built around the venerable 555 would probably offer the maximum economy and ease of design (Mims 1996).

The pulses from the multivibrator are then fed to a 4-bit binary counter. This reflects curious coincidence; the most common *tal* in north Indian music is *Tintal*. Additionally there are a large number of less common *tals* which also revolve around 16 beats. Remember that $16 = 2^4$, therefore a 4-bit binary counter will assign a discrete four bit code to 16 pulses from the multivibrator before resetting. At that point, the cycle will start over. Counters such as the 74193 perform quite admirably (Fairchild 1986).

It is the responsibility of the demultiplexer to take the 4-bit codes and translate them into 16 independent lines. It is at this point that the circuit's operation becomes a little complicated. Most 16-channel demultiplexers (such as the 74154) keep the output lines high when deselected (National Semiconductor 1989). This is to keep the current dissipation low so that the chip may run cooler. The selected output then toggles high or low depending upon the input conditions. If a 74154 is used and the inputs are tied to ground, then the output lines will sequentially go low on every increment from the binary counter.

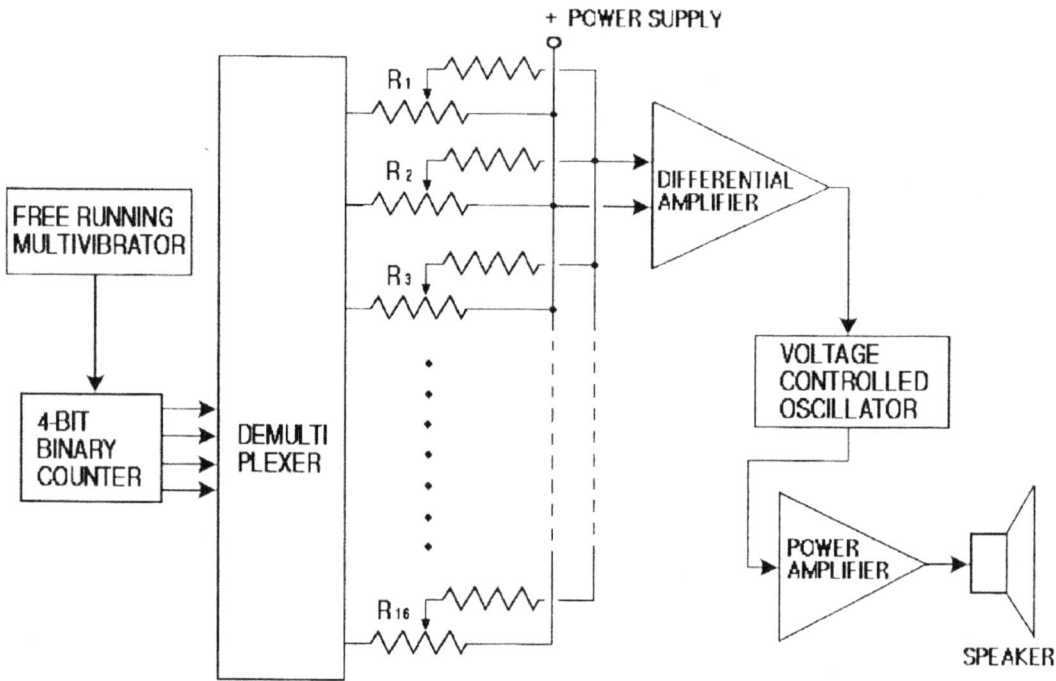

BLOCK DIAGRAM OF LAHARA PETI

Figure AP3.1. Mitra's system (circa 1977)

These voltages may then be varied with the bank of potentiometers specified as R1 - R16. It is these potentiometers which determine the pitches of the 16 notes of our *lahara*.

We must remember that the current flowing through the potentiometer banks are running backwards. That is, when the output of the demultiplexer is high (i.e, deselected) then little current flows. However, when the output is selected, the voltage goes low and initiates a high current flow through the potentiometer.

It is the responsibility of the differential amplifier to correctly interpret this situation. A normal single-ended amplifier will automatically refer everything to ground; but a differential amplifier can refer to the positive power rail. The differential amplifier also serves to isolate the subsequent circuitry from the bank of potentiometers. The output of the amplifier now corresponds to voltage levels set by the potentiometer bank.

This differential amplifier is easily made from common operational amplifiers. There are so many operational amplifiers on the market that it would be pointless to give any part numbers (Jung 1974).

The signal from the differential amplifier is then fed into a voltage controlled oscillator. A 566 works nicely (National Semiconductor 1995). Even the VCO section of the 4046 phase-locked loop works well. It is this section of the circuit that converts the steady voltages into the musical tones. However, these signals are not yet able to drive a speaker.

It is a small power amplifier which raises the signal strength to a point where the speaker may be driven. The original prototype that I saw many years ago used discrete components. Yet today we would not need to go to such efforts, because we have integrated circuits to perform the same function. The LM386, LM383, TDA2002, ECG740, or the ECG1034 are but a few possible ICs which might be considered (Self 2013).

The power level signal is then fed to an eight-ohm speaker. This completes the circuit.

The previously described circuit is a nice project for a hobbyist. However, we must not forget that it is based upon an old technology. Purely digital approaches have been the norm for a very long time.

WORKS CITED

Fairchild Semiconductor
1986   *74193 Datasheet*. Fairchild Semiconductor Corporation.

Jung, Walter G.
1974   *IC Op-Amp Cookbook*. Howard W. Sams & Co.

Mims, Forrest
1996   *Forrest Mims Engineer's Mini-Notebook: 555 Timer Circuits*. USA Siliconcepts Books.

National Semiconductor
1989   *54154/DM54154/DM74154 - 4-Line to 16-Line Decoders/Demultiplexers (Datasheet)*. National Semiconductor.
1995   *LM566C Voltage Controlled Oscillator (Datasheet)*. National Semiconductor.

Self, Douglas.
2013   *Audio Power Amplifier Design*. London: Focal Press.

APPENDIX 4
THE COURTNEY SYSTEM

The first software approach to *lahara* generation appeared in the mid 1980s. Because of the historical significance a brief discussion is in order (Hunkins 1989). The first major effort was the "Courtney System" based upon the old C=64 computer (Indian Express 1987). This was the first all digital approach to *lahara* generation, and is the forerunner of all modern systems.

The C=64 was very small by modern standards. It was built by several loosely connected companies. In the US it was built by Commodore Business Machines (USA) and in India it was built by Commander India Ltd. It was able to squeeze 80 kilobytes of functions squeezed into a 64 kilobyte (16-bit) address bus (Yes - I know, but they really did have a way to do this.) It was based upon the 6510 microprocessor. The C=64 had a 1 MHz clock and produced a standard video output (NTSC or PAL depending upon the model) (Andrews 1985). By today's standards this machine was laughable in its performance; but it was a respectable machine in its day.

This was a general purpose *rag* processor. Yet one of its strongest applications was automatic *lahara* generation. It was able to handle both Indian music notation (Figure AP4.2) as well as provide an audio output (United News of India 1989).

The basic approach to this system was simple. A single audio video (A/V) driver drove the entire section (Figure AP4.3)(Courtney 1989). The function of this driver was to maintain correct timing while appropriate data was gleaned from tables and routed to the appropriate hardware. The object of the A/V driver was to accept a few simple arguments and have it perform the complex hardware oriented processes to create the output. This was the most time critical section of the entire program; therefore the functions of data retrieval, audio, and video generation, were handled by a single integrated routine written in assembly code. This routine relied very heavily on table-lookup approaches to facilitate processing speed.

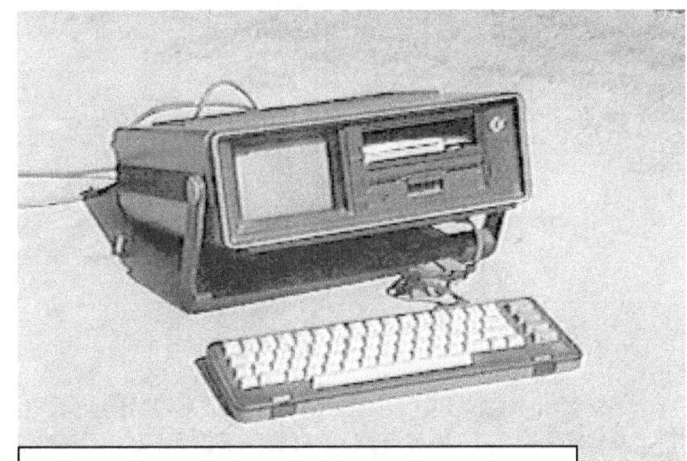

Figure AP4.1. C=64 based Courtney system on SX64 (circa 1986)

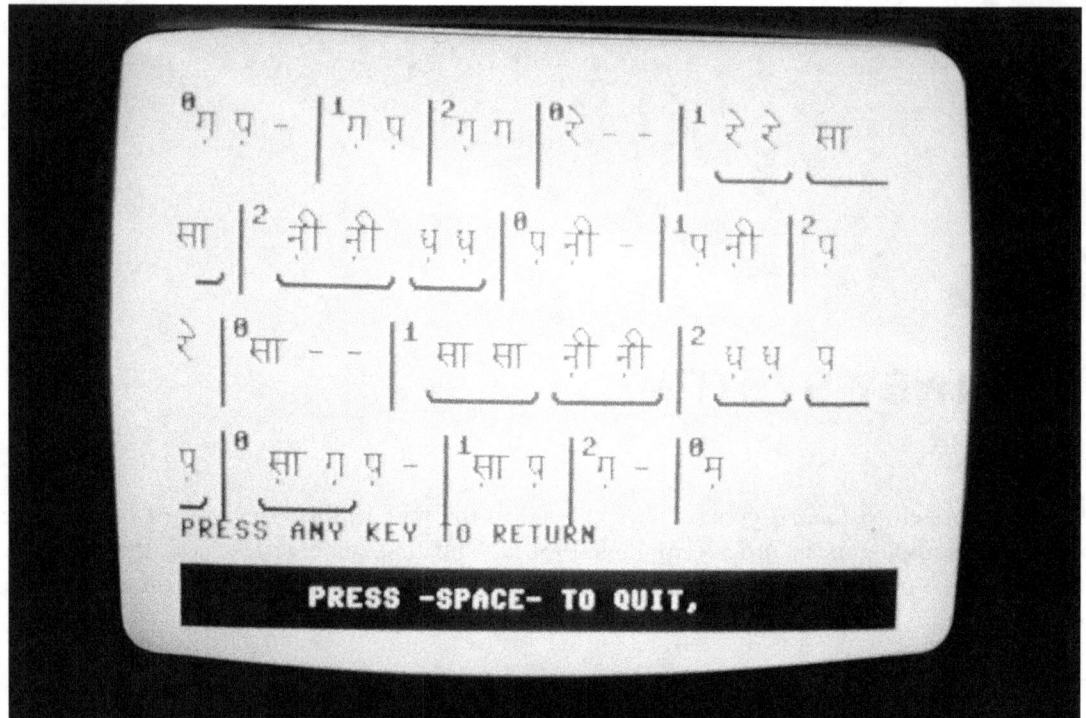

Figure AP4.2. Screen shot

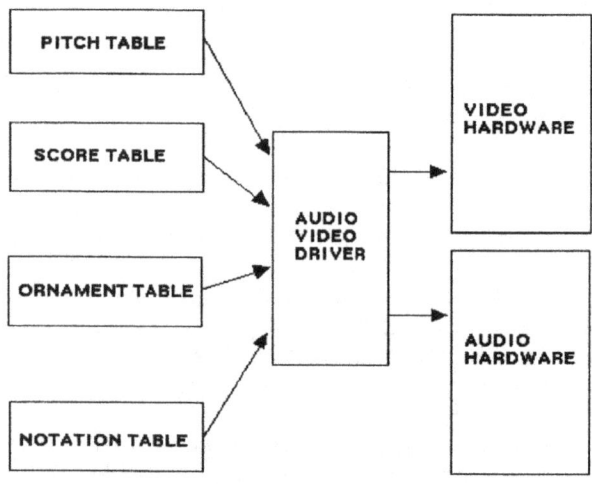

SIMPLE BLOCK DIAGRAM OF COMPUTERIZED LAHARA GENERATOR (COURTNEY SYSTEM)

Figure AP4.3. Indian music A/V driver

The A/V driver was driven by four tables; a pitch table, a score table, an ornament table, and a notation table (Figure AP4.3).

The pitch table contained parameters for a 48-note octave. Twelve of these 48 notes correspond to the values for the 12 pure-tones of an octave. The remainder of the notes were intermediate values which could be used for ornamentation.

The score table contained a list of three-byte words. Each three-byte word corresponded to a musical note or musical operation.

The ornament table contained a list of ornaments which would embellish the notes.

Appendix 4. Courtney System

The notation table contained a collection of bit-maps and cursor movements used to output the musical notation to the screen. Of the above table, only the score table was accessible to the user. The other tables were for internal operation only.

WORKS CITED

Andrews, Mark
1985   *Commodore 64/128 Assembly Language Programming*. Indianapolis, Ind. U.S.A: H.W. Sams.

Courtney, David R.
1989   "An Indian Music Specific Audio Driver", *Journal of the Acoustical Society of India*. Calcutta, Acoustical Society of India.

Hunkins, Art
1989   "East Meets West: Hindu Music from Texas -64 Style", *COMPUTE!'s Gazette for Commodore 64/128 Users*. New York, NY: ABC Consumer Magazines Inc.

Indian Express
1987   "Raga Recording on Computer", *Indian Express*. India November 18, 1987.

United News of India
1987   'American Develops "Raga" Processor', Newstime. Monday November 16, 1987.

(unnamed author)
1989   "Hindustani Sangeet Main Jugalbandi ke Amerikan Yugal Kotni Prashan Kammpyutar Dwara", *Dainak Hindi Milaap Haidrabad*, Dec. 22, 1989.

INDEX

0,1 mode, 165, 168-169, 181
0,2 mode, 165, 168-169
1,1 mode, 165-169, 181-182
1/4" connectors, 195
16 - channel demultiplexer, 285
2,1 mode, 169
2d spectrograms (how to read), 18-21
555 timer, 285
60hz wall current, 15-16
74154 demultiplexer, 285
74193 binary counter, 285
aax (plugin), 220
absolute time, 80
accompaniment, 154-156
acoustic fields (introduction), 178-179
ada chautal (bol paran), 143
ada chautal (lahara), 261-262
adana, 263
addition of sine waves, 14-15
adi (layakari),67
adsr, 12-13
age of tabla, 1
ajrada gharana, 3-4
aksharkal, 78, 80
alhaiyabilawal, 266
amad, 85, 149
amplifier, 204
anagat, 78
anagat tihai, 134-135
analogue (mixer), 198-202
analogue effects track, 219
analogue equipment, 218-219
ang, 77-78,
antinode (of dayan), 173
antinode (string), 163
antiquity (and validity), 71-73
anudrut, 80
arena (stage), 235
arrangement (of speakers), 206
art pro mpa2, 215
art pro vla2, 217
artistic license (in kaida), 104
ati drut, 50
ati vilambit, 50
ati-graha, 78
attack time, 12-15, 32
attack/decay/sustain/release - see "adsr"
attit tihai, 134
au (plugin), 220
audience control, 243
audio cd format, 220
audio mixer, 198-203
audio spectrum, 209-210
auditorium, 233
av driver, 289-290
avartan, 6-7
baaj - see baj
backdrop, 234-235
backstage, 234
baddhi, 2

bageshri, 260, 263, 273
baj, 4-5
balanced connection, 195
banarjee, nikhil, 51
bandh strokes (closed strokes), 5
barabar, 66
barn doors (lighting), 227
basant tal (lahara), 272
basant, 272
batten, 234-235
bayan (dynamics), 61
bayan (physics), 173
bayan (spectrograms) 28-31
bayan, definition, 1
beats-per-min, 49-51
bedam tihai (math of), 132-133
bedam tihai, 132
bell laboratories, 10
benares gharana (and gat), 104
benares gharana, 3-4
bengali (numbers), 40
bessel functions, 167-168
bhageshri, 259, 271
bhairav, 254
bhairavi, 251, 252, 266
bharan (filler), 96, 134-135, 159
bharata, 73, 231
bhari (kaida), 103
bharti, 171-172
bhatkhande, v.n., 72
bhimpilasi, 274
bhinnashadaj, 266, 271
bhupali, 266, 274
biadi, 67
bidirectional mic, 194
bihagada, 267
bilawal, 254, 255, 258
binary counter, 285
bit depth, 219
black body radiator, 229
black box (stage), 235-238
bluebird (microphone), 218
board, 198
bol, 5-6, 39
bol (accenting), 100
bol (in nomenclature), 82
bol (pronunciation), 92, 100
bol density and dynamics, 59-60
bol paran in chautal, 143
bol paran, 142
bolna ("to speak") 5
bols of rela, 111
bols of theka, 89-91
brain and pattern recognition, 28
bus, 199
c=64 computer, 288
cadential form, 83
cadential / cyclic relationship, 85
cadential form (math of), 129
can - see "par can"

cassettes (for timekeeping), 44
chakradar, 137-140, 158
chakradar (definition), 84
chakradar (etymology), 137
chakradar (farmaishi), 141
chakradar paran, 141
chakrakriti paran, 144
chalan, 125
chamada, 2
champakali, 272
chandra tal (lahara), 272
chandrachautal (lahara), 261
chandrakalyan, 267, 272
chandrakauns, 254-255, 260, 261, 263,
    267-268
channel controls, 201
char tal ki savari (lahara), 259
charukesi, 268
chat, 2, 171-172
chati, 2
chaturbhag, 75
chaugun, 69
chauhai, 130
chaupalli, 105, 148
chautal (lahara), 259-260
chautal, 90
chayanat, 261
chimpta, 42
chladni, ernst, 166
chladni pattern, 166-167
clapping (timekeeping), 36
clipping - see "saturation"
closed strokes - see "bandh" or
    "nonresonant strokes"
colour temperature, 229
coloured illumination, 224
commander india, ltd, 289
commodore business machines, 289
complex cadential material, 135
compositional forms, 84-85
compressor, 216-217
computer, 220
condenser mic, 192-193
considerations for improvising, 155-156
console, 198
contemporary practice vs. shastra, 81
controller (lighting), 224-225
copy protection, 221
courtney system, 44, 289
criteria for nomenclature, 81-82
curtains, 234-235,
curtain line, 235
cycle - see "avartan"
cycle-per-second - see "hertz"
cyclic form, 83, 87
cyclic form (math of), 87-89
cymbals 41-42
da (spectrogram), 25
da (technique), 278
dadra (lahara), 251-253

dadra tal, 7, 54, 69
dais, 235,
dam (pause), 132-133
damdar tihai, 132-134
dampening, 171-172
dance forms, 149-151
dance tukada, 146
dasa pran, 35
dasa pran, 75-80
daw - see "digital audio workstation"
dayan (envelope), 12
dayan (spectrograms), 21-28
dayan, definition, 1
dayan, perception of pitch. 27-28
de forrest, lee, 211
dealing with other artists, 242
decay half times, 123, 32
decay time - see "decay half-time"
dedh (layakari), 67
dee (technique), 281
deen (technique), 281
deepchandi (lahara), 262-263
degrees kelvin, 229
delhi baj - see "dilli baj"
desh, 255, 259, 262, 268
deshi tal, 76
deshkar, 254
dhaa, 6, 277, 281
dhagetita, 104
dhammar (lahara), 263-264
dhammar tal, 90
dhi (technique), 282
dhin, 6
dhin (technique), 278
dhumakitataka, 142
dhun (definition), 51
dhun (vocal), 51, 53
differential amplifier, 286
differential connection - see "balanced connection"
difficulty in perceiving pitch, 27-28
diffuse field, 180, 189
digital audio (introduction), 219-220
digital audio workstation, 46
digital hardware, 220
digital mixer, 202-203
digitising, 219
dilli baj, 4
dilli gharana, 3-4
dimmer, 224-225
directional mic - see "cardioid mic" or "shotgun mic"
dohatthu, 121, 145
dohatthu (definition), 105
domukhi (definition), 105
domukhi, 122
dori, 2
dotar, 42
downstage, 234
dropping the sam from a cadential form, 128
drums (for timekeeping), 42-43
drut (dasa pran), 75
drut, 50
dual mic adapter, 185
duct tape, 228
dugun, 66
dupalli, 105, 147

durga, 258, 264
dynamic mic, 192
dynamics (definition), 57
dynamics (effect on timbre), 58
eastern (style of playing) - see "purbi baj"
effects send, 201
effects, 203-204
ekgun, 66
ekhatthu in tintal, 145
ekhatthu paran, 142
ekhatthu, 120, 145
ekhattu (definition), 105
ektal (theka), 7
ektal (lahara), 260-261
ektar, 42
electromagnetic interference, 195
electronic media and dynamics, 61
electronic time keepers, 43
ellipsoidal - see "spotlight"
emcee - see "master of ceremonies"
envelope, 12-15
eq, - see "equalization"
equalization, 201, 204
equalizer, 216
etiquette, 242-243
even harmonics, 213-214
extension cord, 228
external effects - see "effects"
far field, 179-180
fard, 105, 149
farmaish (problems), 245
farmaishi chakradar, 141
farodast, (lahara), 253
farukhabad gharana (and gat), 104
farukhabad gharana, 3-4
fifth harmonic, 170
filler - see "bharan"
filling the dam, 133-134
fingers (snapping), 39-40
fingers, (in timekeeping), 37-39
fire hazards (stage), 236
fletcher - munson equal loudness curves, 10-11
fletcher and munson, 10
fly space, 234
folk pickup, 131
format (audio cd), 220
formula (bedam tihai), 132-133
formula (cadential form), 129
formula (damdar), 133
found space (stage), 235, 238
fourier transform,16-17, 19
fourth harmonic, 170
free field (mic placement), 186-188
free field, 180
frequency (of modes of strings), 163
frequency domain, 15-18
frequency response, 209-210
frequency, 9, 16-22
function (in nomenclature), 82
fundamental (of harmonic series), 169
fundamental (of harmonic series) (definition), 17
ga, 5
ga (spectrogram), 28-29
ga (technique), 277, 279-280
gab, 2

gat (definition), 84
gat-kaida (definition), 105
gat, 51, 104-105
gaursarang, 259
gharana, 3-5
gharanas (and kaida), 91
gharanas (map), 3
gharanas, 81
ghungharu, 42
ginti (counting- for timekeeping), 39
ginti paran, 39
ginti tihai, 39
ginti tukada, 39, 150-151
gobo - 226
gorakhkalyan, 269
got, 2
graha, 78
groove, 57, 64
gujarati (numbers), 40
gunakali, 264
guru (dasa pran), 75
guru shishya parampara, 3
gurumukhavidya, 3
haas effect, 11
haji sahib, 105
hammer (technique), 282
hamsadhwani, 256
hands, (for timekeeping), 35-39
hard saturation. 213
harmonic content and spectrum analysis, 14-19
harmonic distortion - see "signal transfer function"
harmonic spectrum (definition), 17
harmonics (and spectrum analysis), 14-17
harmonics (effect on perceived loudness), 11
harmonics of dayan, 168-170
helmholtz, hermann von, 10
hemiola, 67
hereditary musicians, 72-74
hermann von helmholtz, 10
hermeneutics (musical theory), 71-74
hertz, 9
high speed electronic switch, 225
high voltage (stage), 236
higher order vibrational modes and microphone placement, 183
hinch, 69
hindi (numbers), 40
hindol, 264
hindu concepts of time, 72
house curtain, 235
how to improvise, 157-159
ilok, 221
impromptu material in improvisation, 154
improvisation (compared to speech), 152
improvisation (how to), 157-159
improvisation (overview), 153
improvisation with building blocks, 158
incandescent bulb, 223-224
incredible string band, 49
inharmonic spectrum (definition), 17
inharmonic spectrum, 27-28
instruction, 3

Index

interval (time), 49
inverse domains (and spectra), 15-18
inverse domains, 15-19
inverse square law, 177-178
islam (and music), 72
islamic concept of time, 73
jaitshree, 263
janasamohani, 269
jati (rhythmic class), 78-79
jaunpuri, 260
jhala, 51
jhaptal (bols), 90
jhaptal (paran), 142
jhaptal (rela) 112-114
jhaptal (theka), 7
jhaptal (lahara), 255-257
jhaptal (mukhada), 127-128
jhinjhoti, 269
jhoomra (lahara), 264-265
jog, 265-256
ka, 5
ka (spectrogram), 30
ka (technique), 277, 280
kaal - see "kal"
kafi, 252
kaherava, 54, 64, 131
kaherava (laggi), 116
kaherava (theka), 7
kaherava tal (lahara), 255
kaida, 82
kaida (and gharanas), 91
kaida (artistic license), 104
kaida (definition), 84
kaida (etymology), 91
kaida (manipulation of patterns), 100-103
kaida (mixing other forms), 104
kaida (of nattu khan), 92-100
kaida (procedure), 92-100
kaida (repetition of structures), 103-104
kaida (rules of), 92
kaida and peshkar (comparison), 108
kaida in tintal, 92-100
kaida-peshkar, 104
kaida-rela, 104
kakapad, 75
kal, 75, 79
kali-yuga, 72
kalyan, 263
kamali chakradar, 141
kartal, 42
kasht, 75
kath, 2
kathak, 39
kathakali, 232
kdaan (technique), 282
kedar, 252
kelvin, 229
khabavati, 270
khali (kaida), 103
khamaj, 255
khamaj, 269
khula (open strokes), 5
killer sharks with lasers attached to their heads (sorry, but you have the wrong book.)
kilo-samples-per-second, 219

kilohertz, 9
kilohertz, 209, 219
kinar, 2
kinara baj - see "dilli baj"
kirvani, 270
kitataaka, 104
kra (technique), 282
kriya, 76-77
kshan, 75-76
kuadi, 67
kundal, 2
lab, 2
laggi, 59
laggi (definition), 84, 116
laggi, 154-155
laghu, 75, 79
lahara, 41, 44
lalitagauri, 256
lalith, 261
lalkila paran, 142
laser
lasya, 75
lav, 75
lay, 49-56
laya - see "lay"
layakari, 65-69
layakari (terminology, 66-68
learning to improvise, 154
led, 224, 227-228
leg drops, 234-235
lens, 224
levelling amplifier - see "compressor"
lighting tree, 228
limelight, 223
linearity (frequency response), 209-210
linearity (general discussion), 209
linearity (signal transfer function), 210-211
linguistic diversity, 2
live performance, 231
loading, 168, 170-171
loft, 234
lom-vilom (definition), 105
lord chesterfield, 1
lucknow gharana, 3-4
lucknow gharana (and gat), 104
macro-time, 75
madhya lay, 50
mahabiadi, 68
mahakuadi, 67
maidan, 2
malavi, 256
malayalam (numbers), 40
malkauns, 253, 258-260, 264, 273
managers, 242
mand, 252-253
manipulation of patterns in kaida, 100-103
mannerisms, 239
mansij tal (lahara), 274
map of gharanas, 3
marathi (numbers), 40
marg (definition), 76
margi sangeet, 76-77
margi tal, 76
marwa, 270
masitkhani gat, 51

masking effect, 11, 244
master faders, 200
master of ceremonies, 244
math of bedam tihai 132
math of cadential form, 129
mathematics of cyclic form, 87-89
matra, 6-7, 78, 80
matta tal (lahara), 272-273
mayur paran, 144
mc - see "master of ceremonies"
mechanical timekeepers, 43
melda production
melodic instruments (in timekeeping), 40-41
metronome, 43
micro-time, 75
microphone, 192-197
microphone placement, 183-188
microphone stands, 197-198
mitra, p, 285
mitra's lahara peti (schematic), 286
mitra's system, 44
mixer - see "audio mixer"
mixing of bajs, 5
mnemonic syllables, 5
modes, see "resonance mode"
modes of dayan, 168-170
modulation (spectrogram), 29-30
moghal period, 72-73
mohara, 84, 136
movement of air in near field, 181-182
moving coil mic, 192
mukhada, 130-131, 135, 154-155, 157
mukhada (definition), 84
mukhada (jhaptal), 127-128
multani, 258, 265
multivibrator, 285
mundi, 103
munson, see - "fletcher / munson"
musical sounds (as opposed to nonmusical sounds), 9-10
muslim musicians, 72-74
mxl v67q (microphone), 218
na, 6
na (spectrogram), 25
naa, 6
naa (spectrogram), 23
naa (technique), 277
nagma, 47
nakkara, 240
nalikayantra paran, 144
namaskari paran, 144
narayani, 265
nat bharav, 270
natkuranjika, 270
nattu khan (kaida), 92
natya shastra, 71, 73, 191, 231-232, 239
natya sutras, 231
near field, 179-180
near field and the tabla 181-186
near field speakers, 179
neumann u87, 217-218
nimish, 75
nishabd, 77
nodal circle, 164-165
nodal diameter, 165-170, 184
nodal points, 166

node (string), 163
nohhaka, 141
nomenclature (criteria for compositions), 81-82
nomenclature (parts of tabla), 2
non-union stage, 241
nonlinear signal transfer function, 213
nonmusical sounds (as opposed to musical sounds), 9
nonresonant strokes, 5
normal vibrational modes of a drumskin, 167-168
numbers (in different languages), 40
occidental concepts of time, 72
odd harmonics, 213
off axis rejection, 193, 217
omnidirectional mic, 187, 193
open strokes - see "khula"
operational amplifier, 286
oriya (numbers), 40
overtones - see "harmonics"
overview of improvisation, 153
pakhawaj, 1, 144
pakhawaj technique, 4
pakhawaj thekas, 90
palla, 132
paluskar, v.d., 72
pancham savari (lahara), 265
par can, 226-227
paraj, 258
paran, 130, 141-144, 154-155
paran (definition), 84
paran (etymology), 142
paran (ginti), 39
paran (namaskari), 144
paran (salami), 144
paran (tar paran), 144
paran in jhaptal, 142
parar, 124
paris opera house, 223
pars - see "par can"
parts of tabla, 1-2
pattern manipulation in kaida, 100-103
paunedugun, 67
pause in tihai - see "dam"
pedagogy, 3
period, 10, 16
periodicity - see "period"
permutations in kaida, 100-103
personnel management, 240-243
peshkar, 105-110
peshkar (definition), 84
peshkar-kaida, 104
phase (physics), 161
phrase of tihai - see "palla"
physics and technique (dayan), 172-17
picket fence (math of), 83
pickup pattern (mic), 193-194
piezoelectric mic, 192
pilu, 271
pink noise 209
pirmal, 146
pital, 2 gatta, 2
pitch (psychoacoustics of), 10-11
pitch of dayan, 27-28
pitch, difficulty in perceiving, 27
plugins (for daw), 220

plut, 75
polyrhythm, 65-69
portable sound systems, 206
potentiometer, 286
practice vs. shastra, 81
prakar, 8, 90-91, 154-155
prakar (definition), 84
prakar (formed by addition of strokes), 91
prastar, 79
preamplifier, 215
prima dona, 240
problems with inverse square law, 178
producers, 241
professional relationship with main artist, 156
progression of tempo, 50-53
promoters, 241
pronunciation (of bol), 100
proscenium, 233
proximity effect, 187-188
psychoacoustics (definition), 9
psychoacoustics (fundamentals of), 9-12
pudi, 2
punjab gharana, 3-4
punjabi (numbers), 40
purbi approach to kaida, 91
purbi baj, 4-5
puriyadhanashri, 257, 262, 264, 271
purna tal (lahara), 273
purvaranga, 239
ra (spectrogram), 26
ra (technique), 282
raa (spectrogram), 25
raa (technique), 282
rageshri, 260, 262
raman, c.v., 21, 27-28
range (of human hearing), 9
rao, 124
rawhide, 2
razakhani gat, 51
reciprocal relationships, 16
reflectors, 224
rela, 111-116, 154-155
rela (definition), 84, 111
rela (in rupak), 115
rela-kaida, 104
relative time, 80
repetition of structures in kaida, 103-104
resolution (upon sam), 85, 130
resolution upon sam (chakradar), 137
resonance mode, 162-170
reva, 257
reverb - see "reverberator"
reverberant field, 180
reverberator, 201, 203, 218
ribbon mic 192,
rubato, 54
rules of kaida, 92
rupak tal (chakradar), 139
rupak tal (theka), 7
rupak tal (lahara), 254
rupak tal (rela), 115
safety (stages), 236
salami paran, 144

sam, 78, 139 sam (and the cadential form), 126
sam (dropping in cadential form), 128
samagraha, 78
samay, 74
sampling rate, 219
sampurna tihai, 135
sandbag, 228
sankirna tihai, 135
sarang, 258, 262, 264
sashabd, 77
sath, 149-150
saturation (signal), 213
savai, 67
second harmonic, 169
secretiveness (of gharanas), 4
shankara, 265
shepherd, frances, 83
shiva, 75
shotgun mic, 188
shri, 272
shritank, 265
shure beta 56, 197
shure sm57, 196, 217
shure sm58, 196, 217
sine wave, 10
sine waves (addition of), 14-15
single ended connection - see "unbalanced connection"
sm57 (microphone), 196, 217
sm58 (microphone), 196, 217
snap (technique), 282
soft saturation, 213-214
software, 220-221
sohani, 261, 274
sooltal (lahara), 258
sound (man/woman/person), 241
speakers, 205-206
spectrograms of dayan, 21-28
spectrograms of bayan, 28-31
spectrum analysis (introduction), 14-21
speed - see "tempo"
spoilage (aesthetics of), 211
spot - see "spotlight"
spotlight, 225-226
st67 (microphone), 218
stage, 234
stage etiquette, 242-243
stage left, 234
stage lighting (history), 223-224
stage mannerisms, 239
stage personnel, 241
stage right, 234
stages of learning to improvise, 154-155
standing wave, 162
starting note, 78
stereo mic, 185
sterling st69, 218
stewart, rebecca marie, 83
sthul kal, 75
structure (in nomenclature), 82
structure of rela, 111-112
structure of typical performance, 239-240
styles of gharana - see "baj"
sub-theme (kaida), 102
submaster faders, 200

Index

sukshma kal, 75
sunadamala plus, 47
sur sangat professional, 46
sur, 2
surpeti, 285
swan, joseph, 223
swar systems, 46
swarangini, 47
swatantra-rela (definition), 112
swatantra-rela in dipchandi, 115
syahi, 2
syncopation, 62-65
ta (technique), 278
taa (purbi technique), 278
taa (technique), 277, 281-282
taa, 6
taalmala, 45-46
tabla solos, 155
tak (spectrogram), 24
tak (technique), 279
tal (definition), 7
tal, (etymology). 75
tala - see "tal"
tamasha, 232
tamil (numbers), 40
tandava, 75
tar paran, 124, 144
tasma, 2
teasers, 235,
technique (in nomenclature), 82
techniques of gharanas - see "baj"
tee (technique), 278
teleology, 72-73
telugu (numbers), 40
tempo (as a factor in prakar), 91
tempo, 49-56
tension (musical), 139
terminology (layakari), 66-68
tet (technique), 279, 282
tetekatagadeegena - see "titakatagadeegena"
thay, 66
theka (automatic generation), 45-46
theka (benares), 125
theka (bols), 89-91
theka (criteria), 89
theka (dadra), 7
theka (definition), 84
theka (ektal), 7
theka (jhaptal), 7
theka (kaherava), 7
theka (of pakhawaj), 90
theka (proper dynamics), 58
theka (rupak), 7
theka (tintal), 7
theka, 154-155
theka, 7-8
theoretical problems, 71
theory (obsolete), 71-80
theory (vs. practice), 1
thermionic valve - see "vacuum tube"
third harmonic, 169
thoo ("tun", "toon", "tu", "too", "thoo", "thoon", "thu", or "thun", are all equivalent) - see "thoon"
thoon, (spectrogram), 6, 24
thrust stage, 235, 236, 238

thu ("tun", "toon", "tu", "too", "thoo", "thoon", "thu", or "thun", are all equivalent) - see "thoon"
thumb, 4
thun ("tun", "toon", "tu", "too", "thoo", "thoon", "thu", or "thun", are all equivalent) - see "thoon"
ti (spectrogram), 25
ti (technique), 278, 280, 282
tigun, 66
tihai (damdar), 133-134
tihai (definition), 84
tihai (ginti), 39
tihai (jhaptal), 133
tihai, 82, 130-136
tilak kamod, 253, 257
tilang, 261
timbre, 10, 12
timbre (effects of dynamics upon), 58
timbre (psychoacoustics of), 12
time domain, 15-18
timekeeping, 35-48
timekeeping (with fingers), 37-39
timekeeping (definition), 35
timekeeping (with drums), 42-43
tin, 6, 24
tin (technique), 278
tin, harmonic content. 32
tinmukhi, 122-123
tinmukhi (definition), 105
tintal, 58-59, 77
tintal (amad), 149
tintal (bedam tihai), 132
tintal (bedam tihai), 132-133
tintal (cadential forms), 83
tintal (chakradar), 138, 140
tintal (chaupalli), 148
tintal (dance tukada), 146
tintal (dohatthu), 121
tintal (domukhi), 122
tintal (dupalli), 147
tintal (ekhatthu), 145
tintal (ginti tukada), 151
tintal (kaida), 92-100
tintal (laggi), 116-120
tintal (lahara), 285, 266-271
tintal (nohhaka), 141
tintal (peshkar) 106-110
tintal (theka), 7
tintal (tinmukhi), 123
tintal (tipalli), 148
tintal (tukada), 146
tintal (uthan), 147
tintal, (sath), 150
tipalli, 85, 105 148
tirakita (dynamics), 59
tirakita, 6
tita, 6
titakatagadeegena, 132
titakatagadeegena, 6
toda - see "tihai"
toda, 131, 257
todi, 271
too ("tun", "toon", "tu", "too", "thoo", "thoon", "thu", or "thun", are all equivalent) - see "thoon"

toon ("tun", "toon", "tu", "too", "thoo", "thoon", "thu", or "thun", are all equivalent) - see "thoon"
top (spectrogram), 30-31
topology (of bus), 199
topology (of signal chain), 201
tormentors, 235
tra (technique), 281
trim (mixer), 201
triveni, 261
tu ("tun", "toon", "tu", "too", "thoo", "thoon", "thu", or "thun", are all equivalent) - see "thoon"
tukada (definition), 85
tukada (ginti), 39
tukada, 145-146, 154-155, 158-159
tun ("tun", "toon", "tu", "too", "thoo", "thoon", "thu", or "thun", are all equivalent) - see "thoon"
tun, see - "thoon"
turkish military drum, 1
two-field approach to acoustic fields, 179
typical performance, 239-240
u87 (microphone),
unbalanced connection, 194-195
under utilisation of performance space, 237-238
underpowered filament, 215
union stage, 241
upstage, 234
uthan, 146-147
uthan (definition), 84
utilisation of the performance space, 237-238
vacuum tube, 210-211, 212-215
vadi, 2
variations in rela, 112
vco - see "voltage controlled oscillator"
vedic period, 72-73
vedic tradition of stagecraft, 232
vibhag, 6-7, 78
vibrational modes of string, 163
vibrations (of sound), 9
video lighting, 227-228
vidya, 3
vilambit, 50
visham, 78
vishnu tal (lahara), 271-272
voice (for timekeeping), 39-40
voltage controlled oscillator, 257
volume (psychoacoustics of), 10-11
vst (plugin), 220
warmth (signal), 215
wave (of hands), 36
wave length, 179
when to improvise, 155-156
white noise, 209
wings, 234
xlr connection, 195
yaman kalyan, 254, 259-260
yati, 79

OTHER BOOKS

Fundamentals of Tabla - This is a book about the South Asian pair of hand drums known as tabla. This is the first volume of the series, "The Complete Reference for Tabla". It covers basic technique, exercises, and notation. There is a special emphasis on the compositional forms known as Theka and Prakar.

Manufacture and Repair of Tabla - This is the third volume of this series.

This book has several functions. The primary function is to document the traditional approaches to the manufacture and repair of tabla. This will also deal with the materials science involved. This book covers such additional topics as metal, rawhide, and wood. There is also a discussion of the physics behind the instrument. There is also a special emphasis on issues that effect non-Indian repair personnel. These including labor saving techniques and health concerns.

Focus on the Kaidas of Tabla - This is the fourth volume of this series and the most detailed discussion of the kaida anywhere. It contains over 75 examples from numerous sources, with an extensive discussion.

Learning the Sitar - This is an audio / book instruction set for the Indian sitar. It was originally with a CD, but this has been replaced by an audio download. It may be used by schools and private teachers as course materials to aid in their instruction. It may also be used as a self instruction set.

Learning the Tabla - 1 - This was the first audio CD / book instruction set for the tabla in the US. Today, the CD has been replaced by an audio download. It is the first of a two volume set, the second of which is"Learning the Tabla -2". These may be used by schools and private teachers as course materials to aid in their instruction. They may also be used as a self instruction sets.

Learning the Tabla - 2 - This is a follow-up for the very successful "Learning the Tabla". This was originally a book / CD set. However, the CD has been replaced with an online download (instructions for downloading are in the beginning of the book). This continues where the first volume left off. It may be used by schools and private teachers as course materials to aid in their instruction. It may also be used as a self instruction set.

Other Books

Elementary North Indian Vocal Vol 1 - The 6th edition has swelled to 2 volumes. (A third is in the works.) This is the first volume. There are free links to the supplemental audio material for all of the material in this book.

Elementary North Indian Vocal Vol 2 - The 6th edition has swelled to 2 volumes. (A third is in the works.) This book continues where Volume 1 left off. As with the first volume, there are free links to supplemental audio tracks for all of the material in this book.

An American in Hyderabad: Life in India in the 1970s - What was India like before globalisation, call centres, and Bollywood? The author moved to India in 1976 and lived there for a number of years. This book describes what it was like to live, study, and marry there.

The Music of South Asia - This is an edited version of Elementary North Indian Vocal. Hindustani Sangeet is the name of the classical system of music which covers the majority of South Asia. It covers a region which includes North India, Pakistan, Nepal, Bangladesh, and well into Afghanistan. This book is for teachers in public schools who wish to introduce this music into the curriculum, but run across obstacles. Sometimes the religious nature of the musical texts conflict with the mandate for a secular curriculum. Sometimes long standing geopolitical frictions are stirred up. This book is tailored to help you introduce the subject, but avoid these pitfalls.

History of Valhalla - Being a Study of the Rice Graduate Student Lounge From its Humblest Beginnings in the Year of our Lord One-Thousand-Nine-Hundred-and Seventy to the Present and all the Other Wah-Dah-Doo-Dah - The Rice Graduate student lounge, known as Valhalla, has been in existence for more than half a century. Through its doors have passed individuals who have risen to great heights in industry, politics, academia, aerospace, and number of fields. The clientele is known, not just for intellectual or academic abilities, but also for being extremely quirky and colourful. This book goes into great detail concerning Valalla's history in a humorous, yet fact-filled fashion.

www.ingramcontent.com/pod-product-compliance
Lightning Source LLC
Chambersburg PA
CBHW081416230426
43668CB00016B/2257